D0646122

PERSECUTION & TOLERATION

The Long Road to Religious Freedom

Religious freedom has become an emblematic value in the West. Embedded in constitutions and championed by politicians and thinkers across the political spectrum, it is to many an absolute value, something beyond question. Yet how it emerged, and why, remains widely misunderstood. Tracing the history of religious persecution from the Fall of Rome to the present-day, Noel Johnson and Mark Koyama provide a novel explanation of the birth of religious liberty. This book treats the subject in an integrative way by combining economic reasoning with historical evidence from medieval and early modern Europe. The authors elucidate the economic and political incentives that shaped the actions of political leaders during periods of state building and economic growth.

Noel D. Johnson is Associate Professor of Economics at George Mason University and a Senior Research Fellow at the Mercatus Center.

Mark Koyama is Associate Professor of Economics at George Mason University and a Senior Scholar at the Mercatus Center. He was a 2017–2018 National Fellow at Stanford University's Hoover Institution.

CAMBRIDGE STUDIES IN ECONOMICS, CHOICE, AND SOCIETY

Founding Editors
Timur Kuran, Duke University
Peter J. Boettke, George Mason University

This interdisciplinary series promotes original theoretical and empirical research as well as integrative syntheses involving links between individual choice, institutions, and social outcomes. Contributions are welcome from across the social sciences, particularly in the areas where economic analysis is joined with other disciplines such as comparative political economy, new institutional economics, and behavioral economics.

Books in the Series:

TERRY L. ANDERSON and GARY D. LIBECAP
Environmental Markets: A Property Rights Approach

MORRIS B. HOFFMAN
The Punisher's Brain: The Evolution of Judge and Jury

PETER T. LEESON
Anarchy Unbound: Why Self-Governance Works Better Than You Think

BENJAMIN POWELL
Out of Poverty: Sweatshops in the Global Economy

CASS R. SUNSTEIN
The Ethics of Influence: Government in the Age of Behavioral Science

JARED RUBIN
Rulers, Religion, and Riches: Why the West Got Rich and the Middle East Did Not

JEAN-PHILIPPE PLATTEAU
Islam Instrumentalized: Religion and Politics in Historical Perspective

TAIZU ZHANG
The Laws and Economics of Confucianism: Kinship and Property in Preindustrial China and England

ROGER KOPPL
Expert Failure

MICHAEL C. MUNGER
Tomorrow 3.0: Transaction Costs and the Sharing Economy

CAROLYN M. WARNER, RAMAZAN KILINÇ, CHRISTOPHER W. HALE and ADAM B. COHEN
Generating Generosity in Catholicism and Islam: Beliefs, Institutions, and Public Goods Provision

RANDALL G. HOLCOMBE
Political Capitalism: How Political Influence is Made and Maintained

VERNON L. SMITH AND BART J. WILSON
Humanomics: Moral Sentiments and the Wealth of Nations for the Twenty-First Century

PAUL DRAGOS ALIGICA
Public Entrepreneurship, Citizenship, and Self-Governance

Persecution & Toleration

The Long Road to Religious Freedom

NOEL D. JOHNSON
George Mason University, Virginia

MARK KOYAMA
George Mason University, Virginia

 CAMBRIDGE
UNIVERSITY PRESS

CAMBRIDGE
UNIVERSITY PRESS

University Printing House, Cambridge CB2 8BS, United Kingdom

One Liberty Plaza, 20th Floor, New York, NY 10006, USA

477 Williamstown Road, Port Melbourne, VIC 3207, Australia

314–321, 3rd Floor, Plot 3, Splendor Forum, Jasola District Centre,
New Delhi – 110025, India

79 Anson Road, #06–04/06, Singapore 079906

Cambridge University Press is part of the University of Cambridge.

It furthers the University's mission by disseminating knowledge in the pursuit of
education, learning, and research at the highest international levels of excellence.

www.cambridge.org
Information on this title: www.cambridge.org/9781108425025
DOI: 10.1017/9781108348102

© Noel D. Johnson and Mark Koyama 2019

This publication is in copyright. Subject to statutory exception
and to the provisions of relevant collective licensing agreements,
no reproduction of any part may take place without the written
permission of Cambridge University Press.

First published 2019

Printed in the United Kingdom by TJ International Ltd. Padstow Cornwall

A catalogue record for this publication is available from the British Library.

Library of Congress Cataloging-in-Publication Data
Names: Johnson, Noel D., author.
Title: Persecution & toleration : the long road to religious freedom / Noel
D. Johnson, George Mason University, Virginia, Mark Koyama, George Mason
University, Virginia.
Other titles: Persecution and toleration
Description: New York : Cambridge University Press, 2018.
Identifiers: LCCN 2018038012 | ISBN 9781108425025
Subjects: LCSH: Religion and state. | Freedom of religion. | Religious
tolerance.
Classification: LCC BL65.S8 J64 2018 | DDC 323.44/2–dc23
LC record available at https://lccn.loc.gov/2018038012

ISBN 978-1-108-42502-5 Hardback
ISBN 978-1-108-44116-2 Paperback

Cambridge University Press has no responsibility for the persistence or accuracy of
URLs for external or third-party internet websites referred to in this publication
and does not guarantee that any content on such websites is, or will remain,
accurate or appropriate.

Contents

Figures

Tables

Preface

Today many liberal values are under pressure as a result of tensions arising from a complex combination of economic stress, populism, and large-scale immigration. Religious freedom is a crucial component of liberalism. Yet both ordinary language and judicial interpretations of what this freedom entails and what it means to be "tolerant" are increasingly contested.

In this environment, it is ever more important to understand the origins and development of liberal values such as religious freedom. This is the aim of our book. We seek to understand the rise of religious freedom in Western Europe from the Middle Ages to the modern age.

In so doing we provide a history of the rise of liberalism and of modern states. The Canadian philosopher Charles Taylor describes the present as *A Secular Age* (2007). Church attendance is falling, not only in Western Europe where the decline has been evident for decades, but also more recently in North America. But this should not obscure the importance of religion for understanding either past societies or the present. Not least, the freedom of individuals to choose their own religious faith is crucial to the more general principles of freedom of thought and freedom of conscience. To put it bluntly, to understand the rise of liberalism, one has to study the history of religious freedom. And to understand religious freedom, one needs to study the historical relationship between religion and the state.

Religious freedom did not exist in the premodern world. Because of the role religion played in upholding political order by offering legitimacy to rulers, political elites sought control over religious practice. In the absence of genuine religious freedom, there was at best what we call *conditional toleration*.

We document how these concerns helped shape a self-reinforcing equilibrium that governed most premodern societies and how a series of developments in Western Europe after 1500 undermined it. Our argument focuses on changes at the level of institutions that gave rise to the rule of law and to religious and other freedoms.

This book is a work of social scientific history. It is *history*, as we are primarily interested in explaining how religious liberty arose, rather than in drawing direct policy lessons for today or in making moral or philosophical arguments. It is *social science*, as we use concepts from economics and political science to structure our argument. In particular, we use empirical techniques from economics to provide evidence for our claims. As social science, our arguments should have relevance beyond our specific historical setting.

Though our subject matter is the rise of religious freedom, we are only indirectly interested in the content of religious doctrine or belief. Other scholars know much more about theology than we do. Similarly, our debt to the secondary literature on subjects such as the Albigensian Crusade, the Reformation, and Jewish emancipation is clearly laid out in the endnotes. We write this book as economists who are interested first and foremost in the evolution of political and economic institutions and we hope it will be of general interest to scholars, students, and others interested in economics, history, politics, and religion.

Acknowledgments

There are many people we would like to thank for supporting this project over the past five years. In particular, we thank Claire Morgan, who provided invaluable support in her role at the Mercatus Center, not least in urging us to make progress. We also thank Timur Kuran and Pete Boettke in their capacity as series editors as well as Karen Maloney and Stephen Acerra at Cambridge University Press.

This book builds on a host of papers and collaborative projects that were undertaken with coauthors, and as such special thanks should go to Warren Anderson, Jean-Paul Carvalho, Theresa Finley, Remi Jebwab, Tuan-Hwee Sng, and Melanie Meng Xue. Warren Anderson helped us collect the data employed in Chapter 5. Theresa Finley generated the data used in Chapter 6.

The Mercatus Center organized a fantastic book conference in April 2016. We are especially grateful to Claire Morgan for organizing this and for the comments we received from Metin Coşgel, Jenny Guardado, Philip Hoffman, Ralf Meisenzahl, John Nye, Gary Richardson, Jared Rubin, and John Wallis.

We also greatly appreciate the opportunities we have had to present material from the book, including at Brown University's Political Theory Project, where we are particularly grateful for comments from Dan D'Amico, Steven G. Calabresi, Gianna Englert, Julian Müller, and Thomas A. Lewis. We also presented material from this book at the Fenwick Fellow Lecture at George Mason University; the International Economic Association Roundtable on The Economics of Religion at St. Catherine's College, Cambridge; the University of Pennsylvania; and the University of Colorado, Colorado Springs. Mark used materials from the book to present the Epstein Lecture at the London School of Economics in 2018. Conversations with Ran Abramitzky, Sascha Becker, Dan Bogart, Eric Chaney, Kerice Doten, Saumitra Jha, Andrea Matranga, Nathan Nunn, Yannay Spitzer, and Alex Teytelboym over the years have helped us improve our arguments. Sam Haselby provided us with excellent feedback on an Aeon article summarizing the arguments in this book. Jesus Fernandez-Villaverde provided us with extremely detailed and insightful feedback that helped us write Chapter 8. Timur Kuran read the final manuscript with great care and gave us invaluable comments on both style and substance.

Over the years we have benefited from conversations with our colleagues at George Mason and in Carow Hall, including but not limited to, Paul Dragos Aligica, Pete Boettke, Bryan Caplan, Tyler Cowen, Daniel Klein, Garett Jones, David Levy, Pete Leeson, John Nye, and Alex Tabarrok.

We are both grateful for research support from the Mercatus Center. Stefanie Haefelle, Ginny Choi, Lane Conway, and others at Mercatus have provided great assistance on this project. Mark thanks the Fenwick Fellowship for providing research support in 2013–2014, the Hoover Institution at Stanford University for providing a fellowship in 2017–2018, and the University of Pennsylvania for hosting him for a short visit in November 2017. Throughout we have benefited from excellent research support from Anna Faria, Zhilong Ge, Megan Teague, Jessi Troyan, Michael Watson and from excellent administrative support from Jane Perry, Lisa Hill-Corley, and Kashiff Thompson.

We have benefited from teaching material from this book to numerous classes at George Mason University.

Mark thanks his parents Ninette and Noboru for their boundless support over the years.

Noel would like to thank his children, Elliott and Eleanor, for putting up with an often distracted daddy. He also thanks his wife, Alexandra Mislin, for the support she has shown during the writing of this book. Alex read chapters, exchanged ideas, corrected poor reasoning, and, not least, put up with a lot of complaining.

1

Toleration, Persecution, and State Capacity

1.1 Introduction

1.1.1 Three Myths about Religious Persecution

The relationship between religion and the state remains contentious. Religious differences continue to be a major source of tension and sometimes violence across the world. Even in liberal democracies there are frequent disagreements about the scope of religious freedom. Do states have the right to regulate religious clothing? Can the state prohibit religious organizations from discriminating against individuals who do not share their beliefs? Should states fund religious schools? How stable are institutions that support religious liberty?

We do not provide direct answers to all of these questions. Rather, we argue that to tackle issues such as these we first need to know where our modern notions of religious freedom come from. This requires an understanding of the processes that governed the emergence of religious liberty. It requires not just a knowledge and understanding of history, but also an appreciation of the political and economic challenges that confronted premodern states. This is what we provide in this book.

Doing so requires confronting several popular myths that have grown up around the subject of religious toleration. The first myth is that religious violence was ubiquitous in medieval and early modern Europe. This claim is repeated in popular histories and is sometimes accompanied by the claim that other parts of the world such as Islamic Spain, the Middle East, or the Mongol Empire were comparatively tolerant. Books and films have shaped a widely held view of the Middle Ages and early modern period in which we are led to believe that the execution of heretics and witches was an everyday occurrence. This reflects the influence of novels like Umberto Ecco's *The Name of the Rose* and less edifying forms of entertainment such as the 2010 film *Black Death* starring Sean Bean. These popular depictions of medieval

Europe suggest that religious persecution was an ever present feature of life in the past. In many respects, this is a reassuring image. At least in the West it allows us to view religious violence as the product of intolerant and superstitious individuals.

But were people in medieval Europe, in fact, more prone to persecute religious minorities? An alternative view is that medieval Europeans, like all people, responded to the incentives generated by the institutions that surrounded them. Religious persecutions did not reflect fanatical or irrational beliefs. Rather, they reflected the political economy of the premodern world, in which rulers depended on religious authorities for legitimacy.

Most of the time, religious violence was largely contained. The popular characterizations of the premodern period are, in many respects, misleading. They reflect nineteenth- and twentieth-century concerns as much as they do historical realities. A body of work by historians writing from the 1970s onward has established that witches were, in general, not persecuted in medieval Europe and that the persecution of heretics was rare before 1200, and with some well-known exceptions, sporadic until the Reformation. Even that most reviled institution – the Spanish Inquisition – executed only a tiny proportion of the individuals whom it investigated. Moreover, its fury was largely directed not against Protestants but against converted Jews. Nonetheless, though religious violence was far from ubiquitous in premodern Europe, there was also no religious freedom. Conditional toleration worked by compartmentalizing religious communities into their own separate legal and often physical spheres. In what follows we highlight the costs – both in lives and coin – of organizing society in this manner.

A common view attributes the rise of religious freedom to a changing intellectual climate and to arguments made by thinkers such as John Locke, Baruch Spinoza, and Pierre Bayle for religious toleration. Our approach is different. We ask: "If these thinkers were responsible for the rise of religious liberty in Europe, then why did they come to prominence when they did, at the end of the seventeenth century?" If ideas are all that mattered, then why didn't religious liberty take hold in Europe before the seventeenth century? There were, after all, thinkers writing about toleration during earlier periods.

As early as the fourth century, Quintus Aurelius Symmachus (345–402 CE) put forward a credible case for intellectual pluralism: "We gaze up at the same stars; the sky covers us all; the same universe encompasses us. Does it matter what practical system we adopt in our search for the Truth? The heart of so great a mystery cannot be reached by following one road only" (Symmachus, 1896). Paulus Vladimiri delivered a treatise at the Council of Constance (1414) arguing that Christian and pagan nations could coexist in peace. Why were these arguments unconvincing to their contemporaries?

We propose that ideas played a less crucial role than did the changing incentives facing European rulers in the early modern period. The transformation of early modern economies and states led to the gradual recognition of the importance of religious freedom.

A final misguided feature of our popular image of the past is that the main source of religious violence was the state. Political authorities are often portrayed as having encouraged or used religious persecution for their own ends. The state was rapacious (e.g., *Robin Hood* [1938]) and aspired to absolute power (e.g., *A Man for All Seasons* [1966]). It stoked religious persecution (e.g., *The Devils* [1971]), and above all, it is portrayed as arbitrary and willing to use power uniquely in the interest of the elite against society as a whole (e.g., *The Three Musketeers* [1973]).

But this focus on the oppression of the individual by the all-mighty state largely reflects modern concerns. The state – as we understand it today – was largely absent from the lives and experiences of ordinary people in the premodern world. Authority, as encountered by villagers and townspeople in the medieval and early modern world, was almost always local. While medieval and early modern states did use religious persecution to shore up secular power, religious leaders and local elites were also frequent instigators of religious coercion. In many instances, the elites at the center of government were more liberal than were local elites.

This book seeks to replace these popular images of the rise of religious freedom with a novel account. We do this by studying the institutions that governed the premodern world; in particular we focus on the importance of identity rules. These are rules for which either the form of the rule or its enforcement depends on the social identity of the parties involved (e.g., religion, race, or language). In contrast, impersonal rules are rules for which both the form of the rule and its enforcement are independent of the identity or status of individuals.[1]

Reliance on identity rules both precluded genuine religious freedom and was incompatible with liberalism or the liberal rule of law. We argue that the rise of modern states – states capable of enforcing general rules – provided the precondition for religious peace and for the eventual rise of religious and other liberal freedoms.

A consequence of the fact that religion and political power have been bound together since prehistory was an absence of religious freedom throughout most of history. Even when religious dissidents were not being burned alive for their beliefs, individuals were typically not free to change religion or practice their faith. We investigate the reasons that led some states to persecute individuals for their religious beliefs and other states to refrain from persecution. Doing so allows us to explain why religious persecutions eventually declined in Western Europe, leading to the rise of both religious and other liberal freedoms.

In exploring the connections between state development and religious tolerance, we shed light on a larger story – that of how the rule of law first emerged in Europe. States can govern by devolving power to local elites and allowing them to set rules. The rules that typically result are identity rules.[2] Rules based on religious identity played a vital role in maintaining order in Europe for many centuries. But they also imposed costs: treating individuals differently, and placing them into separate legal categories, on the basis of their identity, prevented individuals from reaping the benefits that come from trading and sharing ideas across religious boundaries and opened the way for religious persecution.

The Victorian sociologist Henry Sumner Maine called the transition from identity rules to general rules the move from status to contract (Maine, 1861). Maine described the development of societies from legal systems in which individuals were bound by compulsory obligations that derived from their status to societies organized on the basis of obligations individuals enter into by volition. Reliance on contracts and on general rules is conducive to individual liberty while status and identity rules are inimical to it. This is also an important part of the emergence of what North, Wallis, and Weingast (2009) call open access orders and what Acemoglu and Robinson (2012) call inclusive economic and political institutions.

As states built their own apparatus for tax collection and the enforcement of laws, they were forced to abandon identity rules and to employ more general rules of behavior. These general rules increased the legibility of society, to use James C. Scott's evocative term; they made it easier for governments to govern (Scott, 1999). Building on the work of Thelda Skocpol and Michael Mann, scholars have adopted the term state capacity to describe this increase in the taxing and rule enforcing powers of the state (Evans et al., 1985; Mann, 1986).

The growth in state power that we document is one of the key facts of the last few centuries. The process of state building was often brutal and we view its results with a degree of ambiguity. On the one hand, it made possible the totalitarian nightmares of Nazi Germany and Soviet Russia. On the other hand, modern states bring many benefits, especially when viewed in comparison to their premodern predecessors.

Our argument is based on three claims. First, throughout history rulers have used religion to legitimize their power (Chapter 2). In medieval Europe, a partnership between a comparatively strong religious authority and a weak state emerged that resulted in reliance on religious legitimation and the enforcement of identity rules to govern (Chapters 3–6).

Second, as rulers tried to raise more tax revenue, tensions grew between the existing identity rules based on religion and the ability of states to govern. These tensions were exacerbated by shocks such as the Black Death and the Reformation. The latter led to intense religious persecution (Chapters 7–9).

Finally, unable to restore the old partnership between religion and the state, many policymakers chose to resolve the tension between religious identity rules and state power by abandoning identity rules altogether. Instead, they developed systems of governance that ignored individual differences and subjected all to common sets of laws and regulations (Chapters 10 and 11). This last step, which reinforced (and was, in turn, reinforced by) developments in the intellectual sphere, laid the foundations for modern liberal states governed by rule of law.

The final part of the book focuses on the consequences of this transformation. In Chapter 12 we consider the relationship between Jewish communities and city growth. Chapter 13 studies how national identity came to replace religious identity in enforcing social order. Chapter 14 applies the argument to other parts of the world including the Middle East, China and Japan, and North America. Chapter 15 studies the rise of nationalism and the totalitarian interlude of the twentieth century. Chapter 16 concludes.

To establish these claims, we bring together new data on the persecution of minority groups throughout European history. This wealth of evidence allows us to systematically analyze the relationship between persecution and political development and to uncover underlying causal relationships.

Addressing the issue of causality requires counterfactual reasoning. Historians are often skeptical of such reasoning. For E. H. Carr, "a historian should never deal in speculation about what did not happen" (Carr, 1961, 127). Michael Oakeshott described it as "a monstrous incursion of science into the world of history" (quoted in Ferguson, 1999).[3] But understanding what causes what *requires* counterfactual reasoning. David Hume described as follows the meaning of cause: "an object, followed by another, ... where, if the first object had not been, the second would had never existed" (Hume, 1748, Part II). Hume's reasoning can best be understood in the context of a controlled experiment. Suppose a group of randomly selected patients are treated with a new drug while those in another randomly selected group are assigned a placebo. If the treatment and control groups were ex ante indistinguishable, then the difference between the outcomes for these two groups *is* the causal effect of the drug. The outcome for the control group provides the relevant counterfactual with which to assess the drug's effect.

Scholars interested in long-run development and history can rarely run experiments; by and large, we are limited to observational rather than experimental data. Nevertheless, economists have developed tools that allow us to construct counterfactuals and thus to estimate the causal impact of, say, bad harvests or higher taxes. For example, in Chapter 5 we estimate the impact of economic stress on the probability that a Jewish community will be persecuted. To overcome the lack of accurate data on local economic conditions in premodern Europe, we use estimates of temperature constructed by climate scientists. Because this proxy for economic stress is exogenous – unconnected with other factors that might cause an economic downturn and increase the probability of a pogrom, such as war or political crises – we can use it to credibly identify the effects we are interested in. In so doing, we make a counterfactual argument: the chances of a persecution in the absence of a decline in average temperatures would have been 50 percent lower.

Similarly, in Chapter 12, we assess whether cities that tolerated Jewish communities experienced more rapid economic growth. We find a correlation between the presence of a Jewish community and subsequent city growth. But this correlation could be biased if, for instance, Jews either chose to settle in faster growing cities or if they were forced to settle in stagnating ones. We disentangle these arguments and provide evidence that tolerating a Jewish community did indeed increase city growth, at least from 1600 onward. Of course, the statistical tools we use have their limitations. For this reason, we supplement them with qualitative evidence about what contemporaries thought and said.[4]

To begin with, let us see how identity rules worked for one particular group and how they were eventually removed. We focus on the experience of one of the most important, and visible, religious groups in early modern Europe: Jewish communities.

1.1.2 Identity Rules and Their Removal: Jewish Communities in Central Europe

The experience of a member of the Jewish community of the Imperial Free City of Frankfurt-am-Main around 1600 is illustrative. From 1462 onward, Jews had been confined to the *Judengasse* – a single street, a quarter of a mile long and only twelve feet wide. They faced countless regulations that restricted their ability to leave the *Judengasse* (not during the night, on Sundays, or on Christian holidays). They were not allowed to bear arms, and their status was explicitly inferior to that of Christian members of the city. They were obliged to wear a yellow ring as a sign of their inferior status and required to doff their hats every time a Christian called to them: "Your manners, Jew!" (Magnus, 1997, 19).

By the same token, Frankfurt's Jews had a measure self-governance. The community had its own laws concerning fraud, debasement of the coinage, and religious practice. They elected religious and secular leaders to represent them (the Hochmeister and Baumeister).

During the Renaissance, the Jewish community in Frankfurt flourished. Between 1543 and 1613 the official population of the ghetto increased from 260 to 2,700 persons.[5] The Frankfurt community also became a cultural and religious center. When a Rabbinical Synod brought together Jewish leaders from Mainz, Fulda, Cologne, and Koblenz in 1603, it was in Frankfurt that they met. Students went to Frankfurt to study under famous rabbis such as Akiva b. Jacob Frankfurter (c. 1530–1596). All of this reflected on the degree of religious toleration that was granted to the Frankfurt Jews within the confining walls of the *Judengasse*. Like hundreds of other Jewish communities across Europe, the Frankfurt community was able to live in relative peace, but at the cost of being a separate and inferior class of citizenry.

The cluster of identity rules that governed Frankfurt's Jews are an example of conditional toleration. Similar rules guided the treatment of other religious minorities in premodern Europe. The uneasy peace between Protestants and Catholics prior to the Thirty Years' War was another instance of conditional toleration. So was the treatment of Catholics in Stuart England, where the queen (Henrietta Maria, wife of Charles I) was a Catholic and permitted her retinue of priests and a chapel, but Catholics were officially prohibited from inheriting property and Jesuits liable to being hanged, drawn, quartered for entering the country.

Conditional toleration was ubiquitous because it reflected the political economy of late medieval and early modern Europe. Political authorities maintained social order by keeping groups with different beliefs legally, and often physically, separated. The maintenance of civil order through legislated separation and discrimination was part of the institutional structure of all European states, ingrained in law, politics, and the economy.

This equilibrium based on conditional toleration had more or less disappeared throughout Europe by the late nineteenth century. To see how this transformation took place, consider the policies of a ruler like Joseph II, Habsburg emperor between 1780 and 1790.[6] Joseph II sought to centralize the Habsburg realms, refusing to submit to separate coronations in Hungary and Bohemia. He attempted to "Austrianize" the Hungarian nobility by bringing them to Vienna; halved the number of religious holidays and abolished 700 monasteries, pensioning off half of the monks and nuns; abolished torture and capital punishment; expanded public eduction; and divided the disparate Habsburg territories into standardized administrative units (Evans, 1991).

One of Joseph II's most important reforms was the Edict of Toleration or *Toleranzpatent* of 1782. This act granted civic rights to Jews on the proviso that they be integrated with the rest of the population as active citizens.[7] Distinctive dress codes for Jewish communities, such as the wearing of yellow bands or the ban on carrying swords, were eliminated. The tax on Jews known as the body tax was suppressed. In return Jews had to attend secular schools and learn German. Joseph's reforms restricted the use of Yiddish and Hebrew to purely religious contexts. Jews were discouraged from engaging in their "characteristic and deceitful trade" of usury and, instead, pushed toward work in manufacturing, transportation, and agriculture. These reforms dismantled the institutions of conditional toleration.

The *Toleranzpatent* was not popular among the Christian majority, and within the Jewish community there was far from universal support for it. The usual interpretation is that these reforms represented greater toleration toward Jews. Above all, however, the reforms were aimed at eliminating the *differential treatment* of religious groups by the state. As such, they represented a serious invasion into the lives of Jews. Less than welcome changes included a general Justice Patent restricting the authority of rabbinical courts; a Marriage Patent in 1786 that intervened in traditional Jewish family law; and a law requiring a two-day waiting period before burial that hindered traditional funeral rites. In 1787 Jews were even forced to change their naming practices by adopting family names. Perhaps most striking was a series of regulations enacted between 1784 and 1787 that forbade the centuries-old practice of leasing monopolies (on lending money, trade, etc) to Jews. As we will see in Chapter 4, this last reform marked a fundamental shift in how the state dealt with Jewish communities. Though Joseph II's successors tried to partially reverse this policy, further acts of toleration took place across Europe following the French Revolution and the old system of separation and conditional toleration was brought to a close.

Joseph II sought to make the Jews the same as everyone else, rather than permit a distinct society within society. Furthermore, it was not just regulations concerning Jews that were altered. Across almost every dimension of society, reforms were introduced that standardized rules with the consequence that it gradually became more difficult to discriminate against individuals on religious grounds.

Jewish emancipation, for example, though initially pursued by autocratic rulers such as Joseph II, came to be a signature liberal policy in the nineteenth century. Religious freedom laid the groundwork for freedom of conscience and freedom of thought more generally and is therefore properly seen as a cornerstone of liberal freedom.

1.1.3 Conditional Toleration versus Religious Liberty

The rights possessed by Jews in Frankfurt were fragile, limited, and contested. Everyone at the time recognized that the Jews of Frankfurt could be expelled (as they temporarily were in 1614). Employing the word toleration to describe the treatment of Jews in the city of Frankfurt-am-Main is, therefore, fraught with difficulties.

Today, the word toleration is used in a fundamentally different way.[8] It has come to embody both a commitment to individual freedom or autonomy to choose one's own beliefs and lifestyles and a commitment to equality of treatment regardless of beliefs: "The modern idea of tolerance is essentially permissive, allowing those with different beliefs and lifestyles to live together without any civil or economic disadvantage" (Scribner, 1996, 34).

But this was *not* the meaning of tolerance in the past. Its Latin root is *to bear*. To tolerate religious diversity was to accept the existence of something unpleasant. It was a practical, rather than a moral principle, and as such it was recognized as contingent and subject to revision. Episodes of de facto toleration often came about because the costs of enforcing religious conformity were too great. Thus toleration today did not preclude religious persecution in the future. Furthermore, as we have seen in the preceding examples, governments often maintained tolerance between the peoples they ruled simply by erecting barriers to limit interactions among groups with different beliefs. Toleration – or conditional toleration, as we refer to it – was based on group, rather than individual rights. As a group, Jews in Frankfurt were allowed to practice their religion. But as individuals, they did not have freedom of expression or freedom of worship. Any individual Jew could be sanctioned by his own community if he expressed unorthodox beliefs. He thus lacked religious freedom. A Christian who tried to convert to Judaism would be persecuted as a heretic.

In contrast to the conditional toleration of the premodern period, modern liberal states are committed to toleration as part of a wider commitment to individual freedom. We call this form of toleration "religious liberty."[9] We use a broad definition of liberalism – one that is consistent with its use by thinkers such as Adam Smith and John Stuart Mill.[10] The political philosopher Chandran Kukathas provides a suitably encompassing statement that can stand in lieu of a definition: "Liberalism does not care who has power; nor does it care how it is acquired. All that matters is that the members of society are free to pursue their various ends, and that the polity is able to accommodate all peacefully" (Kukathas, 2003, 253).[11] Liberal societies are justified by the principle first articulated by John Stuart Mill that individuals should be free to do whatever they choose so long as this does not cause harm to others (Mill, 1859, 1989). The conditional toleration of the early modern period was incompatible with these goals of a liberal society since recognition of the authority of religious groups can clash with commitment to individual autonomy.[12]

Of course real-world societies fall short of this liberal ideal. And in practice many aspects of their commitment to religious liberty remain disputed – for example, in the discussions of religious schools in the United Kingdom, the separation of church and state in the United States, or the wearing of the hijab in France – but freedom of religion remains an ideal to which liberal democracies aspire (Rawls, 1971, 1993). It is a feature of liberal societies that these questions are continuously revisited.

This commitment to religious freedom is based on a form of egalitarianism that insists on equality of treatment. As T. M. Scanlon has observed, modern notions of toleration go beyond bearing the existence of other religions and lifestyles. It requires an acceptance of those other religions and lifestyles as deserving of equal treatment. Modern notions of toleration involve "accepting as equals those who differ from us" (Scanlon, 1996, 228). Intolerance denies this and insists that one particular religion or way of life should be predominant and receive favored treatment. In contrast, the system of conditional toleration was based on discrimination and systematic inequality.

This system of maintaining conditional toleration through the erection of formal barriers between groups was pervasive. Religious peace was maintained in a similar fashion in the Islamic Middle East.[13] For example, a major institution in the Ottoman Empire was the millet system that assigned non-Muslims *dhimmi* status: they were free to practice their religion and had a degree of self-governance including the right to maintain their own legal system, but they were not allowed to proselytize to Muslims, had to pay additional taxes, and sometimes had to wear special, distinctive, clothing.[14] Other celebrated instances of supposed religious toleration such as Islamic Spain operated on a similar basis.[15] Legacies of this system survive in the Middle East today: in Lebanon and Iraq, for example, positions of authority are reserved for members of specific religious groups. Such forms of governance are inimical to liberalism.

Legal codes in premodern Europe were based on group as opposed to individual rights. In the kingdom of Aragon in the thirteenth and fourteenth centuries, for example, the Jewish community was governed by an assembly called the *aljama*, which had complete legal autonomy over each community within the kingdom. This enabled Jews to follow their own laws and customs. But it also meant that the *aljama* had the authority to punish those who violated Jewish law. In Barcelona in 1280, a Jewish youth who was accused of criticizing the Jewish religion was tried and sentenced to death by the *aljama*. As the community lacked the capacity to enforce these laws, they were carried out by the Christian state (Pérez, 2007, 21).[16] Religious order was important, not only for the Christian majority, but also for the Jewish minority. Rabbinical leaders wanted to preserve Judaism. To that end, they limited interfaith social interactions while maintaining the benefits of economic exchange with gentiles; the system of conditional toleration enabled them to do this.[17]

The discriminatory laws that characterized conditional toleration for religious groups in early modern Europe were mirrored in many other the institutions, such as those regulating inheritance or marriage. Europe was a society of orders whose legal systems treated individuals differently based on the class to which they belonged. In France, Germany, and Spain, the nobility either did not pay many taxes or were assessed at a lower rate of taxation than were commoners. Sumptuary laws determined what clothes could and could not be worn. Commoners and aristocrats were subject to different legal treatment and different punishment.[18] Indeed, in many parts of Europe the nobility ran the legal system through seigniorial courts.

This was rule by law, but not rule of law. Equality before the law is a defining characteristic of modern liberal regimes. In medieval and early modern Europe, a common law did not apply to all; Jews, Protestants, and Catholics faced different treatment.[19] General rules applicable to all were largely absent. And it is precisely the existence of general rules that is an important feature of rule of law as it is understood in modern liberal societies – rules that are stable, consistent, and applicable to all.[20] General rules are at the heart of the liberal ideal of a state that maximizes the scope of individual freedom and social cooperation because they provide the necessary stability and space for individuals to create such private spheres of activity.[21]

The system of identity rules restricted individuals' economic as well as their religious freedom. It directly prohibited certain types of contracts: Jews were not allowed to hire Christians, for example; lending at interest was prohibited as usury prior to the Reformation; and partnerships between individuals of different faiths could not be enforced in court. And it indirectly restricted trade by limiting social contact between different groups. The identity rules required by the conditional toleration equilibrium constrained the scale and the scope of the division of labor, which economists since Adam Smith have understood to be the font of increases in specialization, productivity, innovation, and ultimately economic growth.[22]

A vital question, then, is how was the system of differential rules and restrictions that existed in the late Middle Ages transformed by 1850?

Furthermore, why did this transformation result in the shift in the ways in which religious minorities were treated?

1.2 The Rise of Modern States and the Birth of Religious Liberty

A modern state is a political entity that collects taxes and imposes general rules on its population within a fixed territorial space.[23] Two characteristics of modern states are fiscal capacity and administrative capacity.

Fiscal capacity refers to the state's ability to raise tax revenues. In particular, the ability of a state to directly collect taxes matters. A ruler faces a decision of whether to "make or buy" tax revenues. For a ruler to "make" or collect his own tax revenues requires investment in the organizational capability to obtain information on whom to tax and the enforcement capacity to collect it. For most of history, rulers overcame these costs, not by sending out their own well-informed collectors, but by relying on private individuals to do the job. Medieval states had relatively low fiscal capacity. They collected little in taxation and what taxes they did collect were often farmed out to private individuals. One of the main French taxes, the *Taille*, was collected in some regions by agents of the regional courts or *parlements*. The king would tell a region how much it owed (known as the *repartition*) and then local authorities in the region itself had a great deal of discretion on who would pay and how the payments would be collected. The crown was not, in this case, "making" the revenues in the sense of investing in the capacity to collect them on its own. Rather, it was, in a very literal sense, "buying" the revenues by offering each region independent control over fiscal policy in exchange for a cut of the proceeds.

The other critical feature of the modern state is administrative capacity. This refers to a state's ability to enforce rules in a consistent way. Premodern European states often relied on local elites to administer their territories and this resulted in a complex web of unequal rules and laws. In contrast, when we say a state possesses administrative capacity, we mean that the ruling coalition could impose a common set of rules on the entire population.[24]

Political authority rests on legitimacy. Absent legitimacy a ruler only has resort to the threat of violence. The direct threat of violence alone cannot enforce obedience in a large-scale society. Today states largely rely on secular ideologies such as democracy and nationalism in order to legitimate their claims to authority. In contrast, in the medieval era, the social order was legitimated almost solely through religion. The allocation of worldly power was seen to reflect the ordering of heaven. Preservation of this order was the basis for political authority.[25]

Reliance on religion in order to provide political legitimacy reflected both the tremendous influence of the sacred in premodern societies and the absence of alternative sources of political legitimacy. But it was also a function of the weakness of medieval and early modern states.[26] In the absence of a quid pro quo in which the populace paid taxes and the government provided valuable public goods, religion could be used to legitimatize rule by making subjects more willing to comply with the taxes and laws of the government.[27] In turn, religious authorities benefited from this partnership with the state. They obtained wealth, power, and prestige but especially the backing of the secular authority in enforcing religious conformity. Secular rulers received in return the blessings of the church, including honorifics such as "Holy Roman Emperor," "Most Christian King," "the Catholic," and "Defender of the Catholic Faith."[28]

1.2.1 The Rise of the Modern State

In the period after 1500, the size, scope, and capacity of European polities grew. In countries such as France, Spain, and later, Austria and Prussia, previously loosely governed feudal appendages were gradually fused into single, territorially contiguous, entities. These new states attempted, under an ideology that became known as absolutism, to subordinate their respective nobilities and centralized authority in the hands of administrators directly responsible to the ruler. In many respects, their claims to absolute authority should be viewed as corresponding to their ambitions and not the reality of their rule. The actual power of rulers such as Louis XIV was overestimated by earlier generations of historians and more recent scholarship points to the limitations that he faced.[29] But the increase in capacity was real and, by the eighteenth century, these states differed from their medieval predecessors across a range of dimensions.[30]

Figure 1.1 traces the evolution of the tax-raising capacity of many European states. Civilian bureaucracies and military establishments grew, as did the ability of the state to extract tax revenues from the populace.[31] Taxes were higher in Western Europe than in any other part of the world at that time. Taxes generally increased faster and were higher in economic success stories such as England and the Netherlands, which in the eighteenth century had both the highest tax burden per capita in Europe and the highest level of market integration. Other parts of Europe, such as Spain and Italy, did not experience such dramatic increases in per capita tax revenue.[32] Furthermore, this increase in fiscal capacity came as part of a package that included legal and administrative standardization and greater market integration.

As the vast bulk of this additional tax revenue was used to fund wasteful wars, shouldn't it have retarded economic growth? Certainly, a case can be

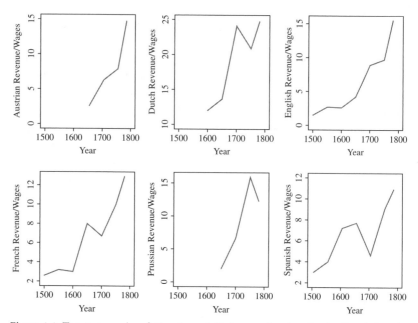

Figure 1.1 Tax revenues in relation to unskilled wages for Austria, the Dutch Republic, England, France, Prussia, and Spain between 1500 and 1800. Source: Karaman and Pamuk (2013).

made that the burden of high taxes and massive debts did slow growth.[33] However, in general, modern historical research indicates that the taxes that the new high-capacity states imposed, though often regressive, such as the excise tax in Britain, distorted the incentives facing private individuals *less* than had previous means of raising revenue. Therefore, as tax revenues rose, the deadweight loss per unit of tax revenue fell. Thus, though increased fiscal extraction did place burdens on European economies and credit markets, it did not prevent the expansion of markets and trade that occurred in the century before the Industrial Revolution.[34]

Along with the rise in fiscal capacity, the early modern period saw states acquire the ability to enforce more general rules of behavior. For instance, in 1539 the French king, François I, issued the Edict of Villers Cotterêts. This proclamation mandated that official documents be written in the vernacular – French, rather than Latin – that Roman Canon Law be adopted for high crimes across the land, and that marriages be recorded in a consistent way across all jurisdictions. This was just one small step in the process of creating modern France, but it exemplifies the ways in which rulers sought to increase their administrative capacity.

The move away from conditional toleration and toward religious freedom required the development of modern states. We study how European states changed from being narrow, particularistic, and patrimonial to being broad based and more or less committed to liberal principles by the second part of the nineteenth century.

1.3 A Conceptual Framework

Economists are pretty good at modeling market behavior. How the price of grain changes in the face of a drought – and who benefits or loses from this – is the type of question any undergraduate economics major can tackle. Once we move away from traditional markets, however, things become more difficult. Political and cultural interactions rarely create prices that we observe. Yet, politics and culture are important. We want to know how religion and the state interacted through history and what this implied for religious freedom. To address this, we need a framework for thinking about how these two sets of institutions – political and religious – interacted.

Following the work of Douglass North (1990), economists often think of institutions as rules: "the humanly devised constraints that shape human interaction" (North, 1990, 3). Viewing institutions as rules, however, suggests that the sources of institutional change are exogenous and does not leave room to consider the process of endogenous institutional change. Greif and Laitin (2004), by contrast, provide a way of thinking about endogenous institutional change. In their framework, a self-reinforcing equilibrium induces changes in underlying parameters that makes the equilibrium even more stable over time. A self-undermining equilibrium, by contrast, induces changes in underlying parameters that make the equilibrium less stable.

Conditional toleration is an outcome generated by an equilibrium in which weak states rely on identity-based rules to govern. The reason that it is self-reinforcing is that as states become more reliant on identity rules to collect taxes and administer justice, they also face lower incentives to invest in the fiscal and legal institutions that would increase state capacity. This, in turn, makes them more likely to rely on identity rules and less able to enforce general rules of behavior. Thus, low state capacity and identity rules are self-reinforcing. As shorthand, we call this equilibrium the conditional toleration equilibrium (Figure 1.2).

Consider the Jews in Frankfurt-am-Main during the sixteenth century. Formal governmental institutions were weak. The Holy Roman Empire was legally and fiscally divided and the Imperial Free City of Frankfurt-am-Main had a great deal of discretion over how to raise revenues or what rules to impose. The city, therefore, like the rest of the empire, used identity rules because they cost little to implement and generated revenue for

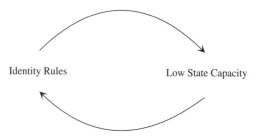

Figure 1.2 The conditional toleration equilibrium that prevailed in Europe prior to 1500.

the city through the creation of rents. The Jews possessed monopoly rights over certain activities such as lending money. The city also granted the Jews the autonomy to govern many aspects of their lives. In return, the Jews both provided revenues to the city (which were higher because they had monopoly rights) and social stability was maintained because contact was minimized between Jews and Christians. In this case, low state capacity and identity rules reinforced each other, and the result was conditional toleration for the Jewish community of the city.

In the case of Frankfurt, this equilibrium gave the Jews limited protection but also led to violence and persecution. In particular, two mechanisms were responsible for channeling economic or political shocks into outbreaks of religious violence. The first mechanism was the state's use of religious legitimacy to maintain legal and fiscal capacity. States that rely on religion as their main source of political legitimacy have an incentive to demonize religious outsiders. In Chapter 2, we explain how this relationship emerged in many societies as a result of a bargain struck between church and state. We show how periods of state building could give rise to intense religious persecution.

A second mechanism responsible for episodes of religious persecution was the dependence of political authorities on economic rents as a source of tax revenue. In economics, a "rent" refers to the returns over and above the normal return needed to keep a resource in its current use.

For example, Chapter 4 considers the example of how rulers granted Jews monopoly rights over lending money. The resulting monopoly profits were rents. Rulers extracted most of these rents in exchange for the promise of protection; for if necessary they could always resort to the threat of violence backed up by the antisemitic sentiment of the population. This equilibrium could easily break down when either the need for short-run revenue led rulers to expropriate the Jews outright or if the governing elites could not control the antisemitism of the population. When the government traded "protection" of religious minorities in exchange for tax revenues, there was always a chance that religiously motivated violence could break out.

Both the use of religious legitimization and the use of rent-seeking to raise revenues were important constituent elements of the equilibrium described by Figure 1.2. As states obtained greater taxing and administrative capacity, however, the self-reinforcing relationship in Figure 1.2 began to give way, and along with it, the prominence of both mechanisms diminished. As a byproduct, the persecution of religious minorities declined.

Beginning in the sixteenth and seventeenth centuries, two processes began to undermine the reliance on identity. First, as rulers found themselves searching for greater sources of revenue to finance ever more costly warfare, they also started to invest in fiscal and legal capacity.[35] Technological changes made warfare more capital intensive and economies of scale involved in running a state increased. This meant states that could invest in fiscal and legal infrastructure outcompeted and eventually replaced those that did not. Investing in fiscal and legal infrastructure meant standardizing taxes and regularizing the laws and regulations that governed economic activity. During the period between 1500 and 1800, the old regime, along with its baroque maze of obligations and rules, began to be reordered along centralizing principles.

The second development that undermined identity rules after 1500 was that, as rulers began to extend and solidify the territorial boundaries of their states, they were also confronted with more heterogeneous populations. This fact, combined with the pressures to homogenize fiscal and administrative institutions, made it more costly to rely on religion to legitimate rule.

As we discuss in Chapters 7–9, the costs of relying on religious legitimacy increased once the Reformation spread new ideas and religious beliefs across Europe. In France, François I and his successor Henri II (r. 1547–1559) initially attempted to repress religious heterodoxy. As Calvinism spread across France during the 1540s and 1550s, Henri II instigated a full-scale nationwide persecution of Protestants that resulted in thousands of executions. However, as we detail in Chapter 7, this proved too costly. And, after Henri's death, France passed the first laws that allowed for two religions to be practiced in the kingdom. Bloody civil war followed, but these principles would eventually be encapsulated in the Edict of Nantes of 1598. Similarly, in England the intense religious persecutions of Mary I's (r. 1553–1558) reign ended with the coming to power of Elizabeth I (r. 1558–1603), who pursued more moderate policies than her predecessors, required only superficial conformity to the new Anglican church, and did not mandate large-scale executions for the many who remained Catholic. These developments, modest as they were, represent the first stage that European states took on the road to religious freedom.

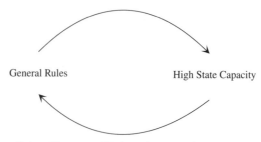

General Rules   High State Capacity

Figure 1.3 The religious liberty equilibrium that arose in many parts of Europe after 1800.

State building involved the expansion and standardization of fiscal and legal apparatus over a wider geographic expanse and more heterogeneous populations. This tended to weaken the reliance on identity rules for revenue collection and on religious legitimacy. We depict this institutional equilibrium in Figure 1.3.

There were important exceptions where religious liberty did not take hold (as in Spain and Portugal), or was faced with a serious setback. It was not the case that state building led inexorably to religious freedom. Rather, almost all movements toward greater religious liberty in the absence of states capable of enforcing general rules were unstable. Temporary episodes of toleration in Muslim Spain or early medieval Francia were just that, episodes that proved fragile in the face of changing economic and political circumstances. To explain why the move from identity rules and conditional toleration toward general rules and religious liberty in the West was permanent and stable we have to understand the changing nature of the state in the period between 1500 and 1800.

Massacres, religious violence, and large-scale expulsions were frequent outcomes of the state-building process. Spain expelled its Jewish population in 1492 in the aftermath of the conquest of Granada. Louis XIV (r. 1643–1715) expelled Protestants from France in 1685. Other less notorious events include the campaign against Anabaptists in the Tyrol and Switzerland, the expulsion of converted Muslims from Spain in 1609, and the War of Cévennes waged against Protestants in south-central France.

After 1700, however, the development of modern states capable of enforcing general rules in conjunction with the rise of markets and civil society became a self-reinforcing process. This process helped bring about the political institutions that we recognize all around us today.

As a consequence of this transformation in political institutions, the cultural environment became more sympathetic to religious freedom. The arguments of Spinoza, Bayle, Locke, and others found more fertile soil after 1700 than their predecessors had in prior centuries. An important reason that the Enlightenment arguments in support of religious toleration found favor among rulers and elites in the latter part of the eighteenth century was that the political environment in which they wrote had changed decisively. The rise of more centralized states intent on governing through standardized rules, applicable to all, meant that the old system based on differential treatment was seen as cumbersome and inefficient.

Notes

1. Our use of the concept of identity rules draws on North, Wallis, and Weingast (2009) and Wallis (2018).
2. Building on North, Wallis, and Weingast (2009), ongoing work by John Wallis analyzes the significance of the transition from identity rules to a world in which contracts and relationships are enforced by general rules. Wallis stresses the ability of the state to recognize corporations and other impersonal organizations outside of the state as a crucial point in the transition from a closed to an open access order. He argues that this transition took place once it was evident to elites that they stood to benefit more from the economic opportunities created as a result of the shift to open access than they did from maintaining the old system of restricted access.
3. More recently, Eric Foner, for instance, is said to have found "counterfactuals absurd. A historian's job is not to speculate about alternative universes ... It's to figure out what happened and why" (cited in Parry, 2016). Others have embraced counterfactual arguments. Ferguson (1999) notes that the rejection of counterfactual history by Carr and also by E. P. Thompson was rooted in a Marxian notion of historical inevitability but it is not confined to Marxist historians.
4. For accessible treatments of these methods and how they have helped to bring about a credibility revolution in many areas of applied microeconomic see Athey and Imbens (2017) and Angrist and Pischke (2010). For skepticism about reliance on these econometric approaches in economic history see Morck and Yeung (2011).
5. By the early eighteenth century, the population was 3,000. This resulted in crowding as the community remained confined to a single street. As a result, fires were frequent, and in the 1780s the mortality rate was 58 percent higher among the Jewish population than it was for non-Jews (Ferguson, 1998, 27–38). Their residency rights were always conditional. Although Frankfurt hosted the largest Ashkenazi Jewish community in Germany, when a group of Portuguese Jews asked to settle there, they were refused permission by the city (Israel, 1985, 54).
6. See Blanning (1970), Beales (1990), and Scott (1990). The Hapsburg crown lands were not the same as the lands of the Holy Roman Empire to which Joseph's reforms did not extend, for reasons that will become apparent later on in the book.
7. The Edict did not grant Jews legal equality with Christians. Jewish settlement, in Vienna, for example, remained restricted and no public synagogues were allowed to be built (Katz, 1974, 163–164). These reforms nevertheless "clearly went far beyond what public opinion in his lands would have demanded" (Beales, 1990, 46) and Joseph's detractors called him the "Emperor of the Jews" (Blanning, 1970, 171). Numerous new restrictions were placed on the Jews during the reign of Francis II (1792–1835). See Katz (1974, 163–164) and Mahler (1985, 3–10).
8. See the discussion in Scribner (1996, 34–39), Walzer (1997), and Laursen (1999, 1–8).

9. This distinction between toleration and religious liberty goes back to the work of Francesco Ruffini (1912).

10. This usage is more in keeping with its meaning in contemporary Europe than with its politicized usage in the United States.

11. This definition of liberalism is compatible with, but does not require, a specifically liberal theory of justice such as Rawls argues for in his *Theory of Justice* (Rawls, 1971, 523) (see, for a detailed discussion, Gaus, 1983). As Ryan (2012, 23–26) observes, there are many "liberalisms" encompassing both the classical liberalism of Smith (1776) and Hayek (1960) and the social democratic liberalism of Rawls. Or, as Tomasi (2012) notes, both classical liberal and high liberalism belong to the same intellectual family. Dan Klein has traced the evolution of the words liberal and liberalism in Western political discourse as part of his *Lost Language, Lost Liberalism* project (Klein, 2014).

12. For extensive discussion see Kymlicka (1996) and Kukathas (2003).

13. See Kuran (2004, 2006, 2010). Saleh (2018) discusses the case of Copts in Egypt.

14. See Braude and Lewis (1982). As Kuran (2010) has shown, this system had important implications for long-run economic development in the Middle East. It was also incompatible with the rule of law because it meant that different groups faced different laws depending on their religious status.

15. See, for example, Menocal (2002). The idea was made famous in the work of Américo Castro (see Wolf, 2009). Smith (2014) developed an economic analysis of religious toleration in medieval Spain. But the evidence demonstrates that the medieval *convivencia* celebrated by these historians was in fact a form of conditional toleration. It enabled Muslims, Christians, and Jews to coexist for centuries. But it should not be celebrated as an instance of religious freedom, for as Joseph Pérez notes, it is "wrong to refer to this era as a time when Jews, Moslems, and Christians lived side-by-side in mutual tolerance and respect"; rather, the situation of minority groups was governed by the self-interest of the ruling elite – Muslim and Christian rulers were willing to protect Jews when they saw them as useful (for instance, as doctors, moneylenders, or tax collectors), and willing to dispense with them once they were seen to be political burden (Pérez, 2007, 12). This perspective reflects a shift in the historiography away from the celebration of the medieval *convivencia* evident in the work of Américo Castro toward more nuanced views (see Ray, 2005, 2011 and Soifer, 2009). Fernández-Morera (2016) provides a polemical demolition of the notion that Islamic Spain was especially tolerant. We return to this topic in Chapter 8.

16. This practice continued until 1380, when Juan I removed the *aljama*'s right to pass death sentences on Jews who violated Jewish law. Further details on the structure of the *aljama* are provided by Assis (1997).

17. See the discussion in Ray (2005), who notes that the expansion of Christian society in thirteenth-century Spain made it harder for Jewish religious leaders to ensure that their communities remained religious and socially separated.

18. For more on the society of orders see Blum (1978) and Mousnier (1979). In England, for example, aristocrats found guilty of high treason were beheaded while commoners were hanged, drawn, and quartered.

19. In particular, see Blum (1978, 11–28 and 80–94) for a description of seigneurial privileges in early modern Europe. For the ways in which the old regime limited women's labor market opportunities see Ogilvie (2003).

20. See Dicey (1908, 198–199), Hayek (1960), Fuller (1969), and Hadfield and Weingast (2012).

21. See Hayek (1960, 1973, 1976, 1982), Buchanan (1975), and Tomasi (2012).
22. For a recent discussion see Boettke and Candela (2017).
23. The modernity of this form of state is contested. Fukuyama (2011) argues that the first modern state emerged in China in the third century BCE. Nevertheless, in a European context demonstrably modern states first emerged in the eighteenth and nineteenth centuries. The word "state" was not used in the medieval period. It first acquired its modern political meaning in the sixteenth century. As Michael Oakeshott put it "[t]he political experience of modern Europe began with an important addition to the European political vocabulary: the word 'state', *l'etat*, *stato* etc. It is a word for a new political experience" (Oakeshott, 2006, 361). Many scholars would add to our definition of a state a monopoly on legitimate violence and a well-developed bureaucracy (Weber, 1968).
24. See Greif (2007) and de Lara, Greif, and Jha (2008) for a related analysis of administrative power.
25. For a recent analysis see Greif and Rubin (2018).
26. These polities did not in general provide any public goods apart from defense. Tax revenues were spent almost exclusively on patronage and on warfare. See Brewer (1988), Félix and Tallett (2009), and Wilson (2009). As warfare was often seen as the "sport of kings," the public goods component of much of this spending is highly questionable (see Hoffman and Rosenthal, 1997 and Hoffman, 2012).
27. A model of this is developed by Coşgel and Miceli (2009).
28. Respectively, the titles granted to Charlemagne (r. 768–814), Charles VI of France (r. 1380–1422), Ferdinand of Aragon (r. 1479–1516), and Henry VII of England (r. 1509–1548) and, in some cases, their successors.
29. France, Spain, and the Austrian Habsburg lands remained "composite states" in John Elliott's words (1992). We discuss the extent of legal fragmentation in France in Chapter 11. The limits faced by the French monarchy are discussed in a large literature (see Moote, 1971; Beik, 1985; and Collins, 1988).
30. Conceptually, one indication that a transformation had taken place is that it became accepted that states had "interests" and that their purpose was to pursue policies and to make laws in order to further these interests. See Oakeshott (2006, 365–372) and Skinner (2009).
31. See Brewer (1988), Bonney (1999, 1995), and Dincecco (2009).
32. For British taxes in comparison to France see Mathias and O'Brien (1976) and more generally O'Brien (2011). Grafe (2012) discusses how fiscal fragmentation accounts for Spain's inability to raise tax revenues. We discuss this in Chapter 8. For levels of market integration in England compared to continental Europe see Shiue and Keller (2007). For discussions of comparative levels of taxation in Europe and China see Ma (2013), Vries (2015), Ko et al. (2018), and Ma and Rubin (2017).
33. Economic historians have long thought that government spending on war and debt repayment crowded out private investment and impeded growth during the British industrial revolution. See discussions in Hartwell (1981), Williamson (1984), and Temin and Voth (2005). For the argument that British debt accelerated the switch out of agriculture and into industry, see Ventura and Voth (2015).
34. See Nye (2007) for a discussion of how the British state developed excise taxes to raise revenue on an inelastically demanded product, alcohol.
35. Historians describe these changes as part of the military revolution of the sixteenth and seventeenth centuries (see Parker, 1976). Also see Hoffman (2012), Voigtländer and Voth (2013b), and Gennaioli and Voth (2015). We discuss this in Chapter 7.

PART I

CONDITIONAL TOLERATION

Religion and the State in the Premodern World

2.1 Religious Legitimacy and the State

By what right does a government collect taxes? What distinguishes such taxation from robbery at the point of the sword? These are abiding questions in political philosophy. In his great apologia for Christianity, *The City of God*, Augustine of Hippo tells the apocryphal story of a pirate captured and brought before Alexander the Great. When the Macedonian ruler asked him how dare he keep hostile possession of the sea, the pirate replied, "How do you dare to seize the whole earth? Because I do it with a petty ship, I am called a robber, while you who does it with a great fleet are styled emperor?"[1]

This is a profound and difficult question. Answering requires the concept of political legitimacy. Principles of legitimation vary widely across societies. The president of a modern democracy might respond to the pirate's question by saying: "Because I was elected by the people in a democratic election." An Egyptian pharaoh might answer by saying he was the embodiment of Horus and the son of Ra. A legitimate government is one that is *perceived* to be so. That is, the legitimation principle has to cohere with the belief systems of the population.[2] An American presidential candidate who claimed to be the embodiment of Horus would not get very far. This is because today the most important source of legitimacy is democratic. Prior to 1800, however, the most important sources of legitimacy were religious.

The significance of religion as a source of political legitimacy was a key feature of medieval societies in both Europe and the Middle East.[3] Modern anthropological research shows that rulers of the earliest known states all based their authority on the claims of religion. In the Egyptian case, scholars have documented that "the Egyptian conception of kingship was that the king was a god – not merely godlike, but the very god" (Fairman, 1958, 75). This emphasis on the religious origins of political authority was common in antiquity, the sociologist of religion Robert Bellah notes:

Some form of divine kingship can be found in Old Kingdom Egypt, the Aztecs, Mayas, Incas and Yorubas, and in Zhou China the king was the "Son of Heaven", though he was not himself considered divine. In Mesopotamia, the earliest periods of what was probably priest-kingship is obscure, but there were sporadic claims to divine status by the kings in the Akkadian and Ur III dynasties in the third millennium BCE, and perhaps, even in the Old Babylonian dynasty in the first half of the second millennium. (Bellah, 2011, 212–213)

"Above all," Bellah notes, "the gods were kings and queens, and the temples were their courts" (Bellah, 2011, 219). Scholars of early religion argue that the gods of tribal peoples typically denote powerful forces or beings. Therefore, it was natural to gradually associate worldly power, embodied in kings and chiefs, with them. Individuals were more willing to obey the commands of a Pharaoh who was the son of Horus or a high priest of Re who would ensure that the Nile would flood on time than they were any old strongman who could command several thousand spearmen.

This entered the Western tradition via Hellenistic rulers from Alexander the Great onward who claimed to be divine themselves – a practice that evolved into the ex post deification of Roman emperors and then greatly shaped the development of Christianity in the Roman Empire after the conversion of Constantine the Great (r. 306–337) in 312 CE. It continued in the medieval period with the close relationship between the papacy and secular monarchs. In the early Islamic empires it was reflected in the title *khalīfat Allāh*, or deputy of God.

What is it that gives religion the ability to confer legitimacy on political authority? To answer this question we need to delve further into the nature of religious belief and religious organizations. To do this we draw on work by sociologists of religion such as Rodney Stark and economists of religion such as Laurence Iannaccone.[4]

According to Stark, religion provides intangible rewards as a substitute for more tangible, but scarce, incentives. "To the degree that rewards are scarce, or are not directly available at all, humans will tend to formulate and accept explanations for obtaining the reward in the distant future or in some other nonverifiable context" (Stark, 1999, 268). And religions comprise "general explanations that justify and specify the terms of exchange with a god or gods" (Stark, 1999, 270).

Religions are successful when they have the ability to offer powerful and convincing explanations to people. Moreover, there is a reason supernatural religions have proven the most successful. In particular, central to the appeal of religion is that it can provide indirect compensation for the inevitability of death: "No one, rich or poor, can gain eternal life by direct methods in the here and now. The only plausible source of such a reward is through religion" (Stark, 1996, 36). As Stark (1999) elaborates, religions are based on exchange relationships between individuals and supernatural beings. And given the inescapable importance of our own mortality, most successful religions have offered the reward of possible life after death in return for membership.

Of course, supernatural religions do not only offer the promise of life after death. Membership in the religion is bundled together with other goods and services, notably insurance in this life; religions in practice vary considerably in the extent to which they emphasize the importance of rewards in the next life. Nevertheless, it is the supernatural element of religion that makes it a particularly credible provider of these secular services. Consider mutual insurance: systems of mutual insurance are subject to well-known free rider problems as individuals have an incentive to take out from these systems when they are in need, such as when their crops fail or they fall ill, but less of an incentive to pay into the insurance system when times are good. Religious institutions leverage supernatural beliefs to inculcate prosocial preferences – so that the would-be defector takes into account the welfare of other group members and not just his own – and to threaten additional supernatural punishments on those who still choose to defect.

What supernatural rewards and punishments can a religious organization make use of? Credence goods are goods, the quality of which cannot be discerned prior to purchase. No one in this world can verify the claims of religion. Hence Robert Ekelund and Robert Tollison (2011) describe the promise of an afterlife a "metacredence good": a good "whose qualities – despite warranties of investments in quality assurance claims – cannot be discerned over the short or (lifetime) long-run. No church or religion ...can offer a money-back guarantee to a soul dissatisfied with his or her afterlife experience" (Ekelund and Tollison, 2011, 34). To attract followers, therefore, a religion has to give a convincing explanation about the relationship between an individual's contribution to the religious organization and the benefits she can expect in terms of worldly or other worldly rewards. Religions are narratives about humankind's relationship with the divine or supernatural.

Because they provide metacredence goods, successful religions have to be social. As individuals cannot test and validate the promise of supernatural rewards, the rewards assured by religion are inherently uncertain. But if an individual observes that others appear to believe in the promises offered by religion, this will increase the probability that she assigns to such promises being valid. Religions wither and die unless they are able to organize groups of individuals to worship in a social setting (Iannaccone, 1992).[5]

Plenty of evidence indicates that religion plays a crucial role in supporting social cooperation and rule-following behavior. In particular, this research suggests that religion played a key role in expanding the scope of cooperation between small human groups. According to these studies, religion is a cultural adaptation: a cognitive by-product of evolution that has both shaped, and been shaped by, cultural development.

In particular, anthropologists and psychologists such as Joseph Henrich and Ara Norenzayan, and their coauthors find that so-called "big gods" play a crucial role in expanding the scope of human cooperation.[6] Big gods are supernatural observers who can punish behavior that is held to be immoral. The existence of moralizing high gods is associated with more cooperative behavior across a range of experimental settings. Shariff and Norenzayan (2007) study the dictator game, in which individuals are randomly assigned to distribute $10 between themselves and a receiver. The prediction of economic theory is that a purely self-interested individual will assign $10 to himself and 0 to the other player. Shariff and Norenzayan contrast the case where players are anonymous, in which 38 percent of players keep all the money to themselves, with the situation where they prime the participants with god concepts. In this case, only 14 percent of givers keep the money for themselves while the number giving away half of the money increases from 20 percent to almost half.

Successful religions tell persuasive narratives that capture the imaginations of listeners and readers. In the terminology of Ekelund and Tollison, such religions build up cultural capital in the provision of meta-credence goods. They invest in a complex ecology of stories that together provide powerful explanations about how the world works, the nature of the heavens, and divine justice. In the preindustrial world, prior to the rise of universities or scientific institutions, religion had no comparable rival for its role in deciphering human experience.

Religion can also play an important functionalist role in enforcing cooperation. From this perspective, religions with moralizing big gods can be viewed as a cultural innovation that enabled some societies to scale up their level of cooperation. The religions of hunter-gatherer societies often lack big gods. Hunter-gatherers are religious, but they do not ascribe great powers to the deities that they worship. Big gods were likely an innovation that different human societies stumbled into, more by accident than by design, which then spread because they generated important social benefits. The "invention" of big gods in turn accelerated the process of cultural innovation and evolution. The worship of big gods is associated with supernatural punishment, with strict laws prohibiting violations of group norms and with more organized rituals and practices of religious observance.

The research summarized by Norenzayan (2013) points to the different ways religious belief – and in particular belief in big gods – could have helped support social cooperation. Moreover, we know from the early history of monotheism that the scale of the claims made on behalf of big gods coevolved as human societies grew and became more complex.

The increase in trade between strangers is a good example of behavior supported by belief in big gods. Long-distance trade in the absence of third-party enforcement can be viewed through the lens of what economists call the prisoner's dilemma. If a seller wishes to exchange valuable silks for silver with a buyer, a spot transaction may be feasible even without an elaborate or developed legal system or institutional infrastructure. But suppose the buyer's silver has not yet arrived because he is himself waiting on a valuable shipment of spices. In this case the trade won't take place unless the seller is willing to accept the buyer's *credit*. But should he do so? If he hands over the silks now, it will be in the buyer's best interest to disappear without ever paying him his silver. In this case, no trade will take place, even though such exchange would be mutually beneficial for both buyer and seller. This has been called the fundamental problem of exchange: the problem of making a credible commitment to make a payment at some future date (Greif, 2006a).

One solution is repeated play. If the buyer and seller repeatedly engage in trade then there may be no incentive for either to cheat the other, even if they have the opportunity to do so because the value of their future interactions is such that it outweighs the incentive to cheat. Such direct reciprocity works well in small-scale societies. In a simple version of this theory, players reciprocate trustworthy behavior by trusting their partner again in their next interaction, while punishing cheating partners by refraining from trade with them in all subsequent interactions.[7] Direct reciprocity can explain trust and cooperation in long-run relationships formed in small communities, but it does not apply to large-scale societies in which the preponderance of exchanges occurs between individuals who have not met before and will probably never meet again.

Religious beliefs, however, can help overcome some of these problems. In the absence of third-party punishment, belief in the presence of higher gods who are capable of viewing one's actions can enable some degree of social cooperation. Individuals who are true believers, and thus believe that the gods are watching them, are more likely to honor agreements (at least when the stakes are not too high). Trade can also occur in the absence of institutions capable of enforcing contracts if other individuals are willing to punish cheaters. Research suggests that believers in big gods may also be willing to engage in costly punishment of individuals who do cheat. Such costly punishment of defectors can enforce peace agreements and alliances. This accounts for the origin of widespread distrust of those who do not practice religion. Experimental studies reveal that even today believers distrust atheists. Free thinkers are seen as free riders (Norenzayan, 2013, 77).

Religion thus has the power to increase within group cooperation and even to moderate violence between coreligionists (Iyigun, 2015). In this spirit, Michalopoulos et al. (2016, 2017) provide a functionalist explanation for the spread of Islam. According to this view, the geographic characteristics of the Arabian Peninsula can explain why a religion like Islam, which limited capital accumulation, controlled inequality, and mandated charity, was a particularly attractive religious innovation. In regions where land inequality was high and highly unequal returns to land, the pre-Islamic equilibrium was characterized by high levels of raiding and violence. Fertile regions benefited from trade because it allowed them to sell their output at higher prices, but poorly endowed regions did not benefit. Individuals in the poor regions could threaten the trade activities of the former, rendering any type of trade risky and uncertain. Islam offered a set of redistributive principles as part of the religious ideology in order to mitigate geographically driven inequality and social tensions, allowing sedentary people to safely enter the mobile networks of the desert and gain from trade. Such a functionalist explanation is, of course, subject to criticism; for one, it does not explain all of the features of a religion or take into account the specific geopolitical conditions that also help to explain the rise of Islam. But it does help us understand that the power religion possessed in premodern societies not only stemmed from otherworldly concerns, but also reflected the importance of preserving social order.

The rise of monotheistic religions such as Christianity and Islam had important consequences. One mechanism through which religion creates powerful cooperative forces within in-groups is by defining outsiders as members of the out-group. This had important benefits for members of the in-group.[8] The proselytizing Abrahamic monotheisms, for instance, condemned the enslavement of one's fellow Christians or Muslims. This prohibition was often violated and "observed only in the breech" – but did come to carry moral weight. Fynn-Paul (2009) documents that the advent of monotheism led to the creation of "no-slaving zones" that had not existed in antiquity as Christians sought to enslave only non-Christians and Muslims only non-Muslims.[9]

But the other side of religious solidarity is the need for religious enemies who can be demonized.[10] With the rise of monotheism, outsiders who belonged to other religions came to be seen as cut off from the source of divine order and hence irredeemable. The ability to label outsiders as enemies is an effective strategy for building within-group trust and cooperation. But it comes at the cost of permanent conflict with those deemed outsiders.

Religion is thus a powerful force in human society. The role religious organizations played in interpreting the world placed them in a unique position to confer legitimacy on political authorities.

Religion's role in validating secular authority is evident throughout history. Consider the celebration of the "rain miracle" that saved the armies of Marcus Aurelius (r. 161–180 CE) from being destroyed by the Marcomanni and Quadi in 172 CE. The Roman army, isolated deep in enemy territory, surrounded, and without access to water, faced annihilation when the heavens suddenly opened saving his army and inspiring the troops to victory. Cassius Dio described this victory as "vouchsafed him by heaven" while reporting that an Harnuphis, an Egyptian magician, had called on Mercury (the Egyptian god Thoth) to call forth the rain (Heather, 2009).[11]

This example illustrates the importance of exchange in Roman religion. Prayer and piety brought material rewards. But a similar quid pro quo is evident in the manner that Constantine the Great propagated the notion of divine favor following his victory at the Milvian Bridge in 312 CE. The emperor was said to have told the historian Eusebius that he saw a cross of light in the sky before the battle against his pagan rival. Inspired, he used the Chi Rho sign on his battle standard and won a decisive victory.[12] In a similar fashion, the Frankish war leader Clovis (r. 481–581 CE), who would later be seen as the founder of the kingdom of France, attributed his victory at the Battle of Tolbiac in 496 to his prayer to Jesus Christ and his promise to convert to Catholicism if God brought him victory. Thus the link between religion and political power was ubiquitous in antiquity and the early Middle Ages.

The temptation for religious leaders in Europe to enter into partnership with the state was overwhelming. After the conversion of Constantine, Christian bishops quickly abandoned their scruples and set to work making the best of this opportunity to attract revenue and followers and strengthen the position of their religion – in the words of one historian they became "players in the game of empire" (Drake, 2002, 73). Throughout history, religious leaders have acted in an alike manner. Nevertheless, to go beyond merely observing this correlation and to better understand the mechanisms driving it, we now need some concepts from economics and political economy.

2.2 A Simple Model of Church and State

We consider a simple model to explain the incentives facing secular and religious authorities. This will provide the skeleton of our argument throughout the book.

Just as economic models can be used to study the macroeconomy or a single market, so too they can be applied to the study of the interaction of politics with economics. An economic model is best thought of as a map. Like maps, all models are false; but good models contain some truth. They are simplifications of reality that economists use to shed light on the causal mechanisms at work.[13]

Economists distinguish between variables which are chosen by actors in the model – often called endogenous variables – and parameters that are determined outside the model and are labelled exogenous. The endogenous choice variables we wish to explain are the decisions of secular rulers and the religious authorities. There are other factors that we will discuss but which we will treat as exogenous. These include the Commercial Revolution, the Black Death, the Reformation, and the Military Revolution. These developments were, of course, part of the development of the European economy and hence not entirely exogenous. Keeping them fixed here, however, maintains conceptual clarity. Simplifying further, we focus on just two actors: a ruler and a religious authority or "church."[14]

There are two important components to model. The first is the legitimation problem facing the secular ruler and the role religion can play in helping to resolve this problem. The second is the decision to employ identity rules or general rules to govern.

2.2.1 Legitimation by the Religious Authority

Suppose the ruler wants to pass a law. The religious authority can choose to legitimate this law or to oppose it. If the religious authority opposes it, the law will be seen as illegitimate, and the ruler will face unrest or opposition in attempting to enforce it. If the religious authority legitimates the law, then compliance with the law will be greater and the law will be enforced at a much lower cost for the ruler. Rulers therefore have a good reason to want legitimacy. Because religious authorities were the most powerful source of legitimacy in the premodern period, it was natural for rulers to rely on religious legitimacy.

In return, religious authorities could charge a price for such services. Even if religious leaders are purely altruistic, they will desire power and revenue in order to serve their congregation.[15] Therefore, religious authorities may enter into partnership with political authorities in order to obtain revenue and to gain and maintain adherents. In return for allying with religious leaders, secular rulers received legitimacy. And, while it is certainly true that many secular rulers truly believed in the religions they endorsed, it didn't hurt that this legitimacy also lowered the cost of taxing and governing.

Monotheistic proselytizing religions such as Christianity and Islam have traditionally sought converts and to limit apostasy.[16] One common bargain, therefore, was for a sufficiently strong secular ruler to promise to enforce religious conformity in return for legitimacy. But this was not only the bargain that could be struck. A weaker ruler, unable to enforce conformity, could obtain legitimacy from the religious authority by granting the religious authority land or resources.

Religious authorities could also provide important administrative services. For instance, the medieval Catholic church provided welfare, healthcare, and education. Churchmen were literate and could thus serve as administrators and bureaucrats. Religious organizations excel at the provision of public goods because they have evolved institutional practices such as strict rituals and rules that enable them weed out free-riders (Iannaccone, 1992).

What ensured that this bargain was stable? Borrowing from the language of game theory, the concept of equilibrium helps us to understand the stability of bargains of this sort in medieval Europe. In an equilibrium, neither party has an incentive to deviate.[17] In our context, for the bargain between church and state to hold, it has to be in the individual interests of both the secular ruler and the religious authority to maintain it, given the actions of the other. The laws and rules that the ruler enacted had to be broadly consonant with the interests of the religious authority.

To illustrate, Figure 2.1 depicts the coronation of Charlemagne in 800 CE by Pope Leo III. The coronation was not uncontroversial. The biographer Einhard later reported that Charlemagne had told him he would not have entered Rome had he known that the pope would crown him. Regardless of whether this was true, the act itself was highly significant. It reinforced the sacral claims of the papacy. Subsequent Holy Roman emperors would seek to be crowned in Rome by the pope. The Church came to play a crucial role in endowing secular rulers with the right to rule in the name of God. Whereas among the Germanic tribes that conquered the Roman empire, kings were typically acclaimed in a proto-democratic fashion on the shields of their soldiers, now it became the role of the church to endow the ruler with the authority to govern.

The importance of the church grew in the centuries after Charlemagne, reaching a peak in the thirteenth century. Thereafter, however, the pope's power waned. The Reformation struck a decisive blow to papal authority. By 1800, the pope's ability to convey legitimacy even on rulers of Catholic countries was much weaker. This is illustrated by Napoleon's coronation as emperor in 1804. In France, Church land had been taken over by the state and redistributed as a result of the French Revolution. Pope Pius VII signed the Concordat of 1801 with Napoleon, which accepted this

Figure 2.1 Coronation of Charlemagne in 800 CE. Raphael. Stanze di Raffaello, Vatican Palace, Vatican State. Photo credit: Scala/ Art Resource, NY.

Figure 2.2 Coronation of Napoleon in 1804. Jacques-Louis David (1807). Musée du Louvre. Photo credit: Scala/ Art Resource, NY.

as a fait accompli. So when Napoleon was crowned emperor, he deliberately emphasized the diminished power of the papacy to convey legitimacy by crowning himself. This is shown in Jacques-Louis David's celebrated depiction (Figure 2.2).

2.2.2 Identity Rules or General Rules?

As societies evolved from small tribal units into larger groupings with the development of settled agriculture and cities, systems of law also emerged. These legal systems were largely based on identity rules. The Code of Hammurabi, for example, prescribes punishment based on the relative status of perpetrator and the victim. As urbanization and the complexity of the social order increased, there were significant movements toward more general systems of rules in classical Athens and later in the Roman empire.[18] However, the collapse of Rome led to a severe economic and demographic contraction in Europe and the emergence of legal systems based predominantly on identity rules. The system of landholding and bonded labor that evolved over the course of subsequent centuries that historians have traditionally labeled feudalism similarly relied on identity rules.

Medieval society was divided into three orders: those who worked – the peasantry, those who fought – the aristocracy, and those who prayed – the clergy. This division was both an ideological construct and a legal reality. It was the Catholic Church that validated this social order as just and divinely ordained. As George Duby observed: "[i]n this ideological model constructed by intellectuals, all members of the Church in those days, the specialists in prayer were obviously to be placed at the apex of the hierarchy of orders" (Duby, 1973, 165).

Identity rules were so prevalent for a reason. As North, Wallis, and Weingast (2009) argue, identity rules are a ubiquitous way of ordering basic human societies because they have several advantages. They are an easy way to generate economic rents. Monopoly rights can be issued to favored elites. Landowners can be restricted in their ability to alienate land. Aristocrats can be prohibited from engaging in commerce. Entry to trades can be restricted by guilds who in turn pay fees to secular and religious authorities. The resulting economic rents can be distributed to members of the ruling coalition to ensure that there is political order. They are low cost to enforce because they can leverage private enforcement mechanisms. The individuals who benefit from the existing system based on identity rules have the resources to defend them.

In contrast, general rules are more costly to enforce. They cannot rely on personal or family based enforcement but require institutions capable of impersonal enforcement such as law courts and impartial enforcement agents. These institutions are costly to maintain and became commonplace in European societies only fairly recently – there was no professional police force in much of England until the second part of the nineteenth century, for example (Koyama, 2014). Semiprofessional bureaucracies emerged in central Europe in the eighteenth century, but were established in countries like England and France only in nineteenth century (Kiser and Schneider, 1994; Kiser and Kane, 2001).

General rules cannot easily be used to generate rents. They allow for open competition, which undermines the position of incumbents and thus weakens systems of political order based on the existing distribution of rents. Even the partial introduction of general rules into a society governed by identity rules causes disturbance and disruption. General rules, however, are of crucial importance for economic development because, by ensuring legal equality, they provide the basis for competition and innovation. They make it possible for new entrants to compete in industries via innovation and lower prices.[19] For this reason, the transition from reliance on identity rules to general rules was crucial to the onset of sustained economic growth in the Western world after 1700.

2.2.3 Identity Rules and Religious Legitimacy

Thus far we have argued that rulers can be legitimated on the basis of religion and cooperation with the religious authorities or through some other source of legitimacy. We have also reviewed the two forms of legal order that rulers could choose to implement and enforce: identity rules or general rules.

Now let us put 2 two parts of the argument. Identity rules and a reliance on religious legitimacy *complemented* one another. Together, they formed part of a self-reinforcing equilibrium. States that were not strong enough to enforce more general rules, governed through identity rules and had a need to rely on religious legitimation. These states gave religious leaders secular power in return, reinforcing their use of identity rules.

More powerful secular rules have less need for religious legitimacy and are better able to enforce more general rules. As rulers pushed toward reliance on more general rules, this reduces the ability of the secular ruler to offer privileges to the religious authorities. General rules entail legal equality and are incompatible with privileges for one religion over another. Therefore, a movement toward more general rules is likely to diminish the ability of the state to bargain with the religious authority for legitimacy. As states adopt general rules, they have to find alternative sources of political legitimacy. This argument has several implications.

In a world where religion is the primary source of legitimacy, the ruling coalition in any society will comprise both secular and religious authorities. Their relative position within this coalition will depend on their relative strengths. First we consider environments where the religious authority is "strong" in the sense that it has the power to bestow and take away political legitimacy.

Assumption 1: Religious Conformity and Religious Legitimacy. Monotheistic religious authorities desire the enforcement of religious conformity. Secular authorities desire religious legitimation.

This claim is the foundation for the partnership we describe between religious and secular authorities.

Implication 1 *If a weak ruler is unable to enforce religious conformity, such a ruler is more likely to "purchase" religious legitimacy by transferring land and resources to the religious authority.*

In this equilibrium, there will be little religious persecution. But an absence of religious persecution is not the same as religious freedom. This describes the situation in much of early medieval Europe where rulers alienated royal land to the church in return for religious legitimacy.

A stronger secular ruler, however, has the ability to strike a different bargain.

Implication 2 *If a strong ruler is capable of enforcing religious conformity, then this ruler can "purchase" religious legitimacy by enforcing religious conformity.*

Until modern times, religious conformity was viewed as an essential characteristic of a well-functioning society. Two principle arguments were advanced in favor of it. The first was epistemic: If there was a single true religion, then surely everyone in society should belong to it. The second argument was pragmatic: as the role of religion in society was to reinforce the social order, a single religion could produce social harmony, while a multiplicity of different religions would produce social discord.

According to this second argument, small-scale societies could each have their own gods. But large-scale societies could function only if they could be bound together by a common religious faith. It was not that the social order was impossible without everyone believing in the same god. This was refuted by Roman paganism, which was syncretic, as were the religions of ancient Persia and India. So long as different people prayed to different gods for the same ends, i.e., the success of the empire and of the emperor, this was acceptable. This is why the Roman state could tolerate a variety of competing and overlapping pagan cults, but was deeply troubled by both Judaism and Christianity, as these religions denounced other faiths as literally demonic. Once monotheism had been introduced into the Roman empire, the tradition of syncretic religious toleration became increasingly less viable precisely because the Christians sought to openly undermine and subvert pagan religion.

Thus the advent of monotheism as a concept (itself likely the product of the rise of larger scale societies) made the idea of unifying a people under a single religion increasingly attractive to rulers and the existence of different and hostile faiths within a single polity came to be seen as a potential threat to social order.

In monotheistic societies, therefore, religious freedom poses a twin danger. First, it leads to a multiplicity of competing religious sects. Second, a multiplicity of competing religious sects is a guarantee for disorder, as it is expected that each religion will seek to gain control of the state in order to better perpetuate their faith and to persecute its opponents.[20] Religious division was a source of civil disorder.

Conversely, atheism was denounced because it eroded the bonds that held society together. Atheists, it was felt, had no reason to hold with covenants because they did not believe in supernatural punishment. Subverting popular religious beliefs, atheism, or even deism, undermines the oaths of allegiance subjects swore to rulers and the contracts merchants signed with one another. In this case, we will observe the persecution of religious dissent by the secular authorities.

Assumption 2: Costs and Benefits of Persecution. Political authorities will persecute religious dissent unless the costs of doing so exceed the benefits. They will cease to persecute when the perceived costs become too high. Large or more established minorities or groups that provide important economic services will be less likely to face persecution. Groups such as the Jews were also more costly to persecute, partly because their protection was mandated by Church Fathers such as St Augustine in the West and the Koranic tradition in the Islamic Middle East, and partly because of their economic significance. In contrast, heretical groups that challenged both the political authority of the state as well as the religious authority of the church were less costly to persecute.

Implication 3 *(Heterogeneity)*

    a. A bargain whereby the secular authority persecutes religious dissent in return for legitimation from the religious authority may be enforceable in a world where religious beliefs are fairly homogeneous. But it may become unenforceable if religious beliefs become more heterogeneous.

    b. Both highly heterogeneous and highly homogeneous societies will see little religious persecution. Religious persecutions are more likely in societies with intermediate levels of religious diversity or where the distribution of religious beliefs has recently changed or are in flux.

Now we can consider the case where the secular authority is able to draw on alternative sources of political legitimacy.

Assumption 3: Declining Need for Religious Legitimacy. As secular authorities become stronger relative to religious authorities, the need for religious legitimacy falls.

This proposition stems from Greif and Rubin (2018), who document the declining importance of religious legitimation in early modern England as Parliament became an increasingly important source of legitimacy.

This proposition has the following implication.

Implication 4 *As states need less religious legitimation, they have less incentive to enforce religious conformity. State building will be associated with first an increase and then a decrease in religious persecutions.*

Finally, we can connect the need to rely on religion for political legitimacy to the importance of identity rules in governing society.

Assumption 4: Identity Rules. Weak secular authorities will rely on identity rules to govern as they are unable to enforce general rules.

Implication 5

   a. *A society that predominantly relies on religion for political legitimacy will also rely on identity rules.*
   b. *As secular authorities become less reliant on religious legitimacy, they will also become less reliant on identity rules.*

By stating our argument in the form of testable predictions, we can use it to shed light on the history of Europe between the end of antiquity and the Late Middle Ages. Many of the details will follow in subsequent chapters. This review is necessarily concise but it will serve as a useful road map for where we are going.

2.3 Applying the Model: The Medieval Equilibrium

In the pagan Roman Empire, religious authorities were weak and subordinated to the cult of the Emperor. Different religious faiths and practices were viewed benignly and interchangeably by the Roman state so long as they were not subversive. For most of the history of the Roman Empire, religious legitimation played a relatively small role in enabling the imperial authorities to rule. The imperial authorities enjoined the practice of *religio* – the correct ways of worshiping the gods – but they did not actively direct religious activity. Over time, religion did take on more importance. Emperors like Decius (249–251) and then Diocletian (284–305) elevated the importance of sacrificing to the emperor; the imperial office became a sacral monarchy, and as a consequence embarked on much more extensive persecutions of the Christians than had hitherto been the case. The Christianization of the empire, under the fourth-century emperors, strengthened this reliance on religion.[21] This model of government continued under the Byzantine Empire in Eastern Europe. But it did not survive the fall of the Roman Empire in the West.

In Western Europe, the Germanic kings and chiefs who founded successor states to Rome initially relied on success in battle and descent from pagan gods such as Thor and Odin for legitimation. But the latter was a fairly week source of legitimacy, and the authority of early medieval kings hinged critically on their ability to win battles and acquire plunder for their followers.

What we call the medieval equilibrium – a situation characterized by the dependency of the secular authorities on the church for legitimacy only emerged gradually in the centuries that followed the fall of the Western Empire.[22] Let us briefly outline some of the key features of this equilibrium.

2.3.1 The Fall of Rome and the Decline of the State

The Roman Empire was a strong and highly capable state by premodern standards. It possessed a bureaucracy and a large professional army. As it encompassed an immense amount of territory, it was naturally decentralized, but as numerous examples attest, the emperor could and did intervene in distant parts of the empire in order to limit local rent-seeking and corruption.[23] The Roman state governed an extensively commercialized and heavily urbanized economy. Most importantly the Roman Empire had a system of centralized and highly organized tax collection based on a land survey; this enabled the state to support both its army and its bureaucracy.

The Roman Empire supported widespread trade and market exchange across a fairly unified economic area that spanned Europe and the Near East. In Rome, Constantinople, Alexandria, Carthage, and Antioch, it possessed cities with many hundreds of thousands of inhabitants, something which would not be seen in Europe until after 1700. It supported high population densities, not only in the core region of Italy, but also in other parts of the empire, such as the Rhineland (Jongman, 2015, 79). Moreover, archeological evidence suggests that the demographic expansion of the first two centuries CE was not associated with greater immiseration. The number of amphoras, iron tools, animal bones, and fine pottery suggests increasing material prosperity (Jongman, 2015, 81–87). This rise in prosperity was driven by trade and specialization. The city of Rome was a hub of consumption importing wheat, wine, olive oil, and manufactured goods. The financial and banking system was highly sophisticated.[24] The economy probably peaked in the second century CE, but it remained able to support high levels of urbanization, specialization, and a complex division of labor until around 400.[25]

The fall of the Roman Empire saw a decline in trade, specialization, and urbanization. Ward-Perkins describes "a remarkable qualitative change, with the disappearance of entire industries and commercial networks. The economy of the post-Roman West is not that of the fourth century reduced in scale, but a very different and far less sophisticated entity" (Ward-Perkins, 2005, 117). Economic complexity declined. Farmers returned to "a more mixed, and hence less productive agriculture" (Ward-Perkins, 2005, 144).

As the size of the average farm declined, agriculture became less capital intensive and productive; the division of labor contracted, and a village-based society replaced the old urban network of the Roman West (see Heather, 2009, 333–376). The economic changes caused by the decline of Rome had far ranging consequences.

The decline of agricultural productivity and the collapse of the old commercial networks reduced the amounts of tax revenue that could be extracted. The Germanic successor kingdoms initially attempted to maintain the Roman tax system – collecting taxes much as the Roman state had, but solely to distribute the proceeds to groups of Germanic warriors rather than to the legions of old. But eventually, the old tax system ceased to be worth the bother of maintaining. The inflow of migrants from the east disrupted the old agrarian system that was based on large estates and capital intensive agriculture. After the initial booty-laden period of conquest was over, the Germanic rulers responded to the problem of keeping their supporters content by distributing land to them, a process that required the breaking up of the established estates and an extensive reorganization of property rights (Wickham, 2005). As the main purpose of taxation was to pay for the army, Western European rulers found it easier to simply require that their noblemen provide solders when needed in lieu of collecting costly taxation.[26]

2.3.2 Identity Rules and European Feudalism

As we have noted, under Roman rule there was a gradual move toward more general legal rules.[27] The movement was already in the process of being reversed in the late empire. One indication is the growing importance of distinctions such as those between the *honestiores*, who were deserving of respect, and the *humiliores*, who were not. Another is in the treatment of the Jews who lost many of their rights as Roman citizens – in 428 they were debarred from practicing law and in 438 they were banned from any imperial office.[28] The collapse of the Western Empire brought a decisive end to the old imperial goal of a common law governing all peoples within the empire.

Roman authority was replaced by that of successor kingdoms that maintained order on the basis of identity rules. Authority was personal. In the territories ruled by Merovingians – the dynasty of Frankish kings who followed Clovis – separate legal codes applied to Franks, Romans, Burgundians, and Visigoths. The same was true in Anglo-Saxon England and in northern Italy, where first the Goths and then the Lombards imposed an extractive military elite on top of the old Roman landowning class. The clergy carved out a separate legal sphere for themselves and bishops came to play an increasingly important role in providing basic public order in the cities. To rule was to enforce existing and inherited norms of justice. Legislation was not seen to be a prerogative of a secular ruler. As Bertrand de Jouvenel remarked, law was "tied down, not only in theory but in practice, by the *Lex Terrae* (the customs of the country), which was thought of as a thing immutable" (de Jouvenel, 1948).[29]

Two things stand out in contrast to the Roman period. First, there was no single overarching legal system in early medieval Europe. Second, many legal issues were handled locally and in a manner dictated by custom.[30] Individuals of different status had recourse to different legal systems. In sixth- and seventh-century Francia, those of "Roman" descent were tried by different legal codes than those of Frankish or Germanic origins. As Marc Bloch observed:

Each human group, great or small, whether or not it occupied a clearly defined area, tended to develop its own legal tradition. Thus, according to the different departments of their activity, men passed successively from one to the other of these zones of law. The family law of the peasants normally followed much the same rules in the whole of the surrounding region. Their agrarian law, on the other hand, conformed to usages, peculiar to their community. Among the obligations with which they were burdened, some, which they incurred as tenants, were fixed by the custom of the manor whose limits did not always coincide with those of the village's agricultural lands. Others, if the peasants were of servile status, touched their persons and were regulated by the law of the group, usually a more restricted entity, consisting of the serfs of the same master living in the same place. (Bloch, 1961, 112)

Justice was accusatory – charges were brought by victims against perpetrators, and individuals who levied false accusations could be severely punished.[31] Evidence was oral rather than written.

The Carolingian Empire created by Charlemagne (r. 768–814) saw a recovery in political power and an attempt to recreate a western empire but it was unable to rebuild the Roman tax state. The collapse of the Carolingian Empire led to a further period of political decentralization in Western Europe. This breakdown in political authority was so dramatic it is frequently noted that "states" did not exist in many parts of Western Europe between 900 and 1100.[32] Political authority remained but rulers were no longer able to raise taxes, legislate, or claim a monopoly of violence within their territories.

To describe the new political and economic order that eventually emerged in the Middle Ages, historians often employ the concept of feudalism. We follow Joseph Strayer in defining feudalism in minimal terms as a form of government into which political authority was dispersed: "As a result, no leader rules a very wide territory, nor does he have complete authority even within a limited territory – he must share power with his equals and grant power to his subordinates. A fiction of unity – a theory of subordination or cooperation among feudal lords – exists, but government is actually effective only at the local level of the county or the lordship. It is the lords who maintain order, if they can, who hold courts and determine what is the law. The king, at best, can merely keep peace among the lords and usually is unable even to do this" (Strayer, 1965, 16–17).[33]

What provided order in the absence of the state? The Church was a crucial source of intellectual and political leadership. The authority of local bishops provided legal and administrative continuity with the Roman past. Moreover, intellectually and culturally, Christianity was all pervasive. There is little evidence that the Middle Ages was an "age of faith" in the sense that ordinary people were particularly religious.[34] But it was an age of faith in the sense that "any conception of the world from which the supernatural was excluded was profoundly alien to the minds of that age" (Bloch, 1961, 81).

It was natural that religion was the predominant source of legitimacy. Writing of the Late Middle Ages, but in words that could easily be applied to earlier centuries, Carlos Eire writes: "all we need to keep in mind is the inescapable fact that religion was symbiotically linked to politics, social structures, culture, the economy, and even climate as all these other factors were to another. It was a symbiosis as intense and complex as that found among components of an ecosystem" (Eire, 2016, 22).

At the same time, the institutional power of the Church remained dispersed. Pagan customs continued and were often incorporated into local Christian festivals. Early medieval Europe was characterized by a variety of what Peter Brown terms "micro-Christendoms" (Brown, 2013, 13). Fragmentation in political authority was accompanied by a fragmentation in religiosity as cults of local saints took center stage in the imaginations of believers. Indeed it was entirely natural that in the absence of widespread literacy, local beliefs naturally differed from place to place.

2.3.3 The Absence of Heresy Trials

Contrary to popular imagination, there were no formal heresy trials in this period. What can explain the *absence* of formal heresy trials for a period of 600 years in Western Europe? In part as a consequence of the reliance on accusatory justice, heretical belief was not defined as a crime in early medieval legal codes, and could not be pursued in secular courts. Local bishops pursued ad hoc methods against religious dissent but with little effect. Secular authorities were, moreover, weak and largely unconcerned with enforcing norms of belief or with the proliferation of local christianities.[35]

Priscillian of Avila was sentenced as a heretic, or witch, in 383.[36] No one was again tried and executed for heresy in western Europe until 1022 and then no heresy trials resulted in executions between 1022 and 1143.[37] Until the middle of the twelfth century, the Church was officially opposed to the death penalty for heretics. Scattered outbreaks of heresy occurred during these centuries but these "were treated mildly by the authorities" (Lambert, 1977, 25).

There was both a decline in religious discord, and a diminution of the ability of secular or religious authorities to police religious dissent. The factors responsible include the collapse of the empire and with it the disappearance of a "cultivated laity" (Lambert, 1977, 25), and a fall in literacy and urbanization. Richard Southern observed that there was something about urban life that bred dissent (Southern, 1970, 46). But perhaps the most fundamental reason for the disappearance of heresy in the Early Middle Ages is that for there to be a heretic there had to be an authority willing and able to recognize and condemn her heresy. A heretic did not merely possess heterodox beliefs. Individuals who were ignorant of the Church's teaching or held mistaken views about religious matters were not heretics if they acknowledged their error and recognized the authority of the Church.

Heresy is, to employ the terminology of the philosopher John Searle, an observer dependent phenomenon – "a person became a heretic only by refusing to accept a bishop's pronouncement that his express views were heretical, and by refusing to undertake not to preach without the bishop's permission." Precisely because heretics were "self-defined and indeed self-proclaimed," they could exist only to the extent that they were in contact with a church that had the capacity to recognize, proscribe, and condemn their views (Moore, 1987, 64). An absence of heresy trials does not imply an absence of religious heterogeneity or religious dissent so much as it signals the absence of an authority capable of enforcing conformity.

2.4 The Absence of Persecution Does Not Imply Religious Freedom

Early Christianity provides an instructive case, as Christian leaders did not always believe that it was the role of the Church or the state to enforce religious conformity. The persecution of early Christians by the Roman state indicated to the faithful that persecution strengthened rather than weakened the faith.[38]

However, by the end of the fourth century, the Church had become willing to sanction force to punish those who adopted alternative forms of Christianity. St. Augustine wrestled with this issue in dealing with the Donatist Church in North Africa. The issue at the core of the Donatist Controversy was whether a group of believers who compromised their faith under persecution could ever be allowed to return to the church with full status.[39] He came to the conclusion that the price of saving an individual's soul from damnation was sufficiently great that force could be used against obdurate heretics. Augustine described this as "good will" spending "itself in merciful efforts to guide another's evil will" (Letter 173 to Donatus (411/414), 153), a position he buttressed with the Parable of the Wedding Feast (Luke: 14:16–23) in which strangers are compelled to "come in" to attend the wedding.

This theological debate reveals that even in Christianity – a religion predisposed against persecution – other forces were strong enough to produce a political equilibrium in which dissenters faced persecution. Systemic factors were at work that made it likely that whatever monotheism was adopted by Europe in the late Roman Empire, it would have desired state enforcement of religious conformity.

As Rome declined, the absence of state capacity generated a shift in the attitudes of the Church. While Augustine lived in a world in which the power of the Roman Empire and its magistrates to coerce dissidents like the Donatists remained very real, Church leaders in the aftermath of the fall of Rome, and particularly by the seventh and eighth centuries, had to rely on persuasion rather than coercion to convert disbelievers and to confront religious deviants. This was not due to an intellectual commitment to toleration, as no one openly advocated freedom of worship; rather, it was part of the established "facts on the ground" that they did not challenge.

Ronald Hutton (1996) describes the struggles of the early medieval Church to discourage celebration of pagan New Year festivals as follows:

Among those who attacked them were some of the most renowned fathers of the early medieval Church, including Jerome, Ambrose, Augustine, and John Chrysostom. Especially concerned, and voluble, were Maximus of Turin, Chrysologus of Ravenna, Caesarius of Arles, and Pacian of Barcelona ... [In the eleventh century] they were still being issued in England. At some point between the years 1004 and 1008 Archbishop Wulfstan of York, facing a province recently given a fresh infusion of paganism by heavy Viking settlement, condemned "the nonsense which is performed on New Year's Day in various kinds of sorcery." At the other end of the realm, Bartholomew Iscanus, bishop of Exeter, prescribed a penance for "those who keep the New Year with heathen rites." (Hutton, 1996, 7)

Dissenting practices were condemned, but there is no evidence of action taken against them. This lackadaisical attitude also applied to witchcraft. Laws against witchcraft and sorcery had existed in Roman times and continued to exist thereafter. But there is little evidence that they were enforced. Belief in witchcraft was seen as a relic of paganism. St. Boniface considered belief in witchcraft unchristian. John of Salisbury's discussion of witches and magicians was highly skeptical: "The evil spirit with God's permission uses his power to make some people believe that things really happen to their bodies which they imagine (through their own error) to occur" (quoted in Moore, 1987, 274). Burchard of Worms prescribed penance for those who repeated such tales.

In the ninth century Agobard, bishop of Lyon, wrote a tract entitled *On Hail and Thunder* in which he railed against those who attributed hail and thunder to the acts of magicians on the grounds that this was a form of unbelief that took away power from God. He blamed this on the ignorance of the rural population, noting that "[s]o much stupidity has already oppressed the wretched world that Christians now believe things so absurd that no one ever before could persuade the pagans to believe them, even though these pagans were ignorant of the Creator of all things" (Agobard of Lyons, 2001, p. 15). Agobard was no rationalist nor was he "enlightened" by modern standards – in fact he wrote extensively against the Jews – but he believed that the correct response to belief in magic and witchcraft was to educate peasants that such things did not exist. Persecuting individuals for such widely held beliefs would have appeared impossible and fantastical to him.

To account for the absence of persecution in a world of intolerance, we turn to our analytical framework. When political authority is weak, there can be little effective official persecution of religious dissidents. States that struggle to provide basic public goods such as defense or law and order will also be unable to enforce religious conformity. Heresy requires a legal apparatus capable of recognizing and prosecuting deviant beliefs.

Rulers of such weak states, however, still desired religious legitimacy. In fact, their need for religious legitimation often exceeded that of rulers of stronger states. Unable to exchange their services as enforcers of religious conformity for the support of the church and lacking the resources to buy the church's support, they faced a problem.

Weak rulers resolved this quandary by simply giving away land and granting special privileges to the Church. Such transfers were common in the Early Middle Ages. By 900, as much as 30 percent of the land in continental Western Europe was owned by the Church. Though this proportion declined overall in the tenth century, ecclesiastical authorities still held 32 percent of cultivated land in northern France in the twelfth century (Herlihy, 1961, 86).[40]

2.5 Chapter Summary

This absence of persecution did not imply a commitment to religious freedom. There was little religious persecution in the Early Middle Ages because (1) in the absence of powerful states, religious authorities were unable to enforce religious conformity; (2) in a largely illiterate population beliefs were fluid and ill-defined, making it difficult to define heretical beliefs; and (3) in the absence of trade there was little commerce between regions so individuals and communities could develop their own folk beliefs and practices.

At a more decentralized level, that is, at a strata below that of the state, communities no doubt employed a variety of informal methods to enforce conformity. But individuals with different beliefs seldom came into direct contact with one another.

This conditional toleration equilibrium was stable because no ineluctable forces were working to undermine it. However, in Western Europe, two historically contingent developments began to unfold in the twelfth and thirteenth centuries that would eventually lead to European societies transitioning from this conditional toleration equilibrium, through a period of religious persecution, to a political equilibrium based on religious liberty. These developments were the rise of stronger political units – nascent territorial states – with higher fiscal and administrative capacity and their increased reliance on religious legitimacy.

Notes

1. The story appears in Book IV, Chapter 4 of Augustine (2003).
2. Political scientists discuss legitimacy as a systems-level characteristic: the legitimacy of a state "involves the capacity of the system to engender and maintain the belief that the existing political institutions are the most appropriate ones for the society" (Lipset, 1963, 61).
3. This is similar to the argument developed in detail by Greif and Rubin (2018). Coşgel and Miceli (2009), Coşgel et al. (2012), and Rubin (2017) make the point

that religious legitimacy is valuable to rulers because it reduces the costs citizens face in complying with the state; it makes it easier to collect taxes, to provide public goods like defense, and it reduces the likelihood of revolt. Also see Eric Chaney's (2013) analysis of how variation in the flooding of the Nile increased the power of the Islamic religious authority during the Middle Ages and early modern period.

4. In particular, see Iannaccone (1992, 1995, 1998) and Iannaccone et al. (1997) and Stark (1999, 2001, 2004). For a survey of the economics of religion see Iyer (2016).

5. The key insight of the club goods theory of religious organizations is that religion is a collectively produced commodity and, as such, subject to a potential free-rider problem. Successful religious organizations surmount this free-rider problem. Evidence for this proposition is provided by Sosis and Ruffle (2003), who found that religious kibbutzim are more successful at eliciting cooperative behavior than secular kibbutzim. See also the discussion of how kibbutzim dealt with free riding in Abramitzky (2018).

6. See Shariff and Norenzayan (2007), Shariff et al. (2009), Atran and Henrich (2010), Laurin et al. (2012), Slingerland et al. (2013), Norenzayan (2013), Purzycki et al. (2016), and Norenzayan et al. (2016).

7. This punishment strategy is known as *grim trigger*. Other more forgiving punishment strategies can also enforce cooperation so long as the interaction has no definite end point. There is evidence that human beings have specialized cheater-detection cognitive programs for this purpose (Cosmides and Tooby, 1992; Stone et al., 2002).

8. Ruffle and Sosis (2006), for example, find that kibbutz members are more cooperative toward anonymous kibbutz members than they are toward anonymous city residents. The ways in which monotheism cultivates traits that can help societies expand is the subject of Iyigun (2015).

9. Fynn-Paul observes that "Prior to the spread of the Christian world view, ancient society felt no overriding moral reason why one citizen might not become the slave or the master of a fellow citizen" (Fynn-Paul, 2009, 14). Christianity in practice was compatible with ancient slavery. But following the fall of the Roman empire, a norm emerged whereby Christians ceased to seek to enslave other Christians. Fynn-Paul notes that this "is remarkable in so far as it was the first time in history that a philosophical system, rather than political force maintained the integrity of a large-scale no-slaving zone" (Fynn-Paul, 2009, 15–18).

10. In *The Song of Roland*, for example, written some time at the end of the eleventh or beginning of the twelfth century, the Saracens are depicted as worshiping an unholy Trinity of Mohammed, Termagant, and Apollo (Anonymous, 1957).

11. See Cassius Dio as summarized by Xiphilinus (Cassius Dio, 235, 1927, Book 72, Chapter 9). Xiphilinus contradicts Cassius Dio and reports an alternative tradition mentioned by Justin the Martyr that attributes the rain miracle to a Christian legion from Melitene that prayed to God for the rain.

12. Many versions of this story survive, and there is some evidence that Constantine first interpreted this as a sign that he was favored by the sun god Sol Invictus. Numerous historians, going back to Edward Gibbon, have debated the sincerity of Constantine's conversion (see discussions in Barnes, 1981 and Drake, 2002). Stephenson (2009) convincingly argues that Constantine's conversion was a gradual but sincere process.

13. For an excellent summary and defense of the economic approach see Rodrik (2015).

14. We can relax this assumption and consider cases in which a government is ruled by a coalition of ruling elites rather than a single ruler and where there are multiple religious authorities. This framework shares some elements with the theory of when religious organizations will be coopted by autocracy developed by Auriol and Platteau (2017). See also Platteau (2017). An examination of why state religions are adopted is provided by Vaubel (2017).

15. If they are not sufficiently worldly, then they will not remain religious leaders for long, or their religions will not prove successful over time.

16. This bargain between the church and the state was particularly attractive to the proselytizing monotheistic religions of Europe and the Near East that desired the enforcement of religious conformity. This desire was present but weaker in most other world religions and in the polytheism of classical antiquity (see Stark, 2001; Iyigun, 2015).

17. This definition of equilibrium refers to the concept of Nash equilibrium. A Nash equilibrium is a best response to a best response.

18. For discussions of the sophistication of Roman law see Arruóada (2016). For an analysis of the Athenian legal system see Carugati et al. (2015).

19. As discussed by North, Wallis, and Weingast (2009), they enable the creative destruction that Joseph Schumpeter associated with capitalist economies (Schumpeter, 1942).

20. For thinkers like Machiavelli, Hobbes, and Rousseau the concern was that Christianity did not provide the best basis for social stability. Machiavelli felt that it undermined bellicosity and independence and made states weak. Hobbes wanted a civil religion that was subordinated to secular authority. Rousseau's position was more ambiguous, but he declared himself in favor of a civic religion that could make possible a strong republican citizenry (Beiner, 1993).

21. For more on this transition from *religiones* to religion see Brown (2013). Our argument is consistent with recent accounts that Constantine "chose" Christianity in part because of its potential to provide religious unity and thereby strengthen the imperial monarchy (van Dam, 2007).

22. Moore (2011) documents the rising importance of religious legitimation in the Frankish kingdoms from the end of the Roman empire to the Carolingian period.

23. See for analysis Heather (2006) and Kelly (2004).

24. See Harris (2006).

25. This view is contrary to the impression given by many late twentieth century historians who argued for a gradual transition and emphasize the continuities between the Roman and post-Roman world (Goffart, 1989, for example). A good short account of the traditionalist position is Walbank (1978). This traditionalist position is most consistent with both archeological evidence, economics, and what we know about both the classical Roman economy and the medieval economy. An up-to-date general discussion is provided by Harper (2017).

26. For details on the collapse and reorientation of trade networks see McCormick (2001); for more on the fiscal transformation see Wickham (2009). The most obvious explanation for the decline of the Roman economy is the tremendous increase in transaction costs caused by the disruptions of civil war and external invasion that affected the Western empire after 400 CE.

27. This movement was never complete and historians such as Bang (2008, 183–190) point to the existence of overlapping legal systems in many of the provinces.

Nevertheless, even Bang concedes that Roman law did increase legal unity in the empire.

28. See the account in Netanyahu (1995, 18–27).

29. Berman, for example, notes that "the basic law of the peoples of Europe from the sixth to the tenth century was not a body of rules imposed from on high but was rather an integral part of the common consciousness, the 'common consciousness' of the community. The people themselves, in their public assemblies, legislated and judged; and when kings asserted their authority over law it was chiefly to guide the custom and the legal consciousness of the people, not to remake it" (Berman, 1983, 77).

30. See Cam (1962).

31. See Lea (1973, 44).

32. For example, Strayer observes: "It is not surprising that the *regnum* had little resemblance to a state, for, in the early Middle Ages, it is doubtful that anyone had a concept of a state. Some memory of the state lingered among the better-educated members of the clergy, but even they were not able to express the idea very clearly" (Strayer, 1963, 1971*b*, 342). For a somewhat different view see Wickham (2016). For an assertion of the relevance of the concept of the state to medieval history see Davies (2003).

33. The traditional definition of feudalism hinged on the prominence of the legal concept of vassalage (Ganshof, 1951; Bloch, 1964). This has been critiqued by Reynonds (1994). The usage we have in mind is closer to the classical Marxian definition as employed by Anderson (1974*b*) and Anderson (1974*a*). The appropriate timing of the transition to feudalism is also a subject of debate. Some scholars have argued that feudalism proper emerged only in the tenth century, after the failure of the attempt to recreate imperial political authority in Western Europe by Charlemagne and his successors (Heather, 2014).

34. The idea that the medieval mind was particularly credulous and irrational is a trope dismissed by all serious historians. As we will see in subsequent chapters, it was not, and knowledge of Christianity was often sparse and contradictory.

35. See Kieckhefer (1979), Religious controversies continued to be prominent in the East Roman Empire, but ceased to be of central importance in Western Europe after the widespread adoption of Catholicism by Rome's successor states in the sixth century.

36. Moreover, the most recent in depth analysis of this case by Brown (2012) indicates that the motives for this persecution were political rather than religious. "Priscillian was not executed as a heretic" is his conclusion (Brown, 2012, 212).

37. See Moore (1987, 13–23). Note, however, that heretics were "burnt by the people" in Cambrai in 1077, Soissons in 1114, and Liège in 1135 (Moore, 2012, 7).

38. In the words of Tertullian, martyrs were the seedcorn of the Church. Tertullian had in fact argued that true religion and compulsion were incompatible (see Lecler, 1955, 35). Critics of Christianity typically caricature it as inherently intolerant but, as Drake notes, "there are many tenets of Christianity which favor tolerance and pacifism as there are those that would justify a more militant and aggressive posture. The real challenge, then, is to identify conditions that allow the views of those individuals who favor coercion . . . to prevail" (Drake, 2002, 75). The rise of "sacred violence" in late antiquity is the subject of Shaw (2011).

39. The Donatist religious sect came about as a result of Diocletian's persecution of Berber Christians in the fourth century. Those believers who compromised their faith in order to avoid the worst of the violence were later shunned by "pure" Christians and came to be called Donatists.

40. Similarly, in southern England between one fifth and one third of all land was held by the Church according to the Doomsday book (Fleming, 1985, 249).

3

Why Do States Persecute?

> Heresy, having questioned the Church and her teachings, was initially the business of the clergy and believers. It could have stayed that way. But heresy often happened to overlap with politics, whether by virtue of its internal logic or in response to initiatives made by the State itself . . . as Church and state were closely interlinked and each supported the other, religious protest could very easily provide a cloak for social protest: a challenge to the Church might feed on social discontent and end by undermining the fabric of the State.
>
> Guenée (1985, 195)

In early Spring 1401 at Smithfield market, on the edge of London, a crowd gathered to watch the execution of a heretic for the first time in England. At the behest of King Henry IV (r. 1399–1413), Parliament had passed *De heretico comburendo* – the first legislation in English history to prescribe death for heretics – and the multitude at Smithfield had assembled to see its first victim: a priest named William Sawtrey.

Sawtrey was a Lollard – the pejorative name given to followers of John Wycliff (1330–1384), a radical Oxford theologian and critic of the Church, who had translated the Bible into English. Sawtry had been caught preaching against the Roman Catholic religion and accused of rejecting its central doctrines. He denied the existence of the saints, free will, and doubted that sacraments were the blood of Christ. And, as this was the second time that he had been arrested for preaching these beliefs, he now stood condemned as a relapsed heretic.

The crowd watched as he was degraded from the priesthood and excommunicated. According to one chronicler, on being stripped of his priestly vestments, Sawtrey retorted "now your anger is spent" in the belief that this was the end of his punishment (Strohm, 1998, 43). During the fourteenth century, priests convicted of heresy in England faced merely clerical sanctions: they were degraded of the priesthood and subject to excommunication. However, *De heretico comburendo* prescribed a different and new sentence for relapsed heretics. Following John 15:6 which states that "If a

Table 3.1 *Brief chronology of medieval heresy*

Year	
1028	First heresy executions in western Europe since fall of Rome.
1166	Assize of Oxford. First edict of a secular monarch against heresy.
1184	Papal Bull *Ad abolendam.*
	Introduction of inquisitorial procedure against heresy.
1184	Waldensians condemned as heretics.
1209	Beginning of the Albigensian Crusade.
1215	Fourth Lateran Council.
1229	Treaty of Meaux-Paris ends Albigensian Crusade.
	Languedoc incorporated into France.
1231	The Holy Roman Emperor Frederick II imposes death sentence for heresy.
1233	Appointment of Inquisitors in Toulouse.
1244	Capture of Montségur. Over 200 heretics burnt.
1244–45	Inquisition of Bernard de Caux in the diocese of Toulouse.
1307–14	Trial of the Templars.
1401	*De heretico comburendo* passed in England.
	William Sawtrey executed.

man abide not in me, he is cast forth as a branch, and is withered; and men gather them, and cast them into the fire, and they are burned," Sawtrey was burnt alive.

Why was Sawtrey burned? In this chapter we study how an alliance developed between church and state. Table 3.1 outlines some of the major developments in the history of the repression of heresy in medieval Europe. This alliance had two important implications for the evolution of religious freedom. First, the state became involved in enforcing conformity of belief and persecuting religious deviants. This is exemplified by the execution of Sawtrey. Second, when the state did not find it in its interest to repress heretics or other religious groups, it instead maintained its legitimizing link to the church by placing groups with unorthodox beliefs in a separate social and economic sphere.

3.1 The Commercial Revolution, Religion, and Identity Rules

Between 1000 and 1300, the European economy expanded: population grew, the volume of trade and per capita income increased. As temperatures warmed, conditions for agriculture improved. North of the Alps, the growing season lengthened. New settlements expanded across Germany and Eastern Europe. Total population rose from perhaps 30 or 35 million in 1000 to 80 million in the 1340s, on the eve of the Black Death. More

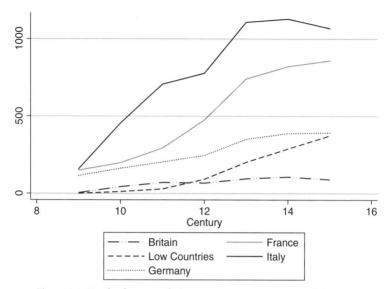

Figure 3.1 Total urban population 800–1500. Source: Bairoch (1988).

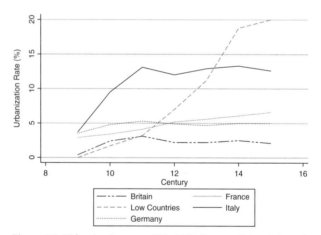

Figure 3.2 Urbanization rates 800–1500. Source: Bairoch (1988).

striking of all is the increase in urbanization: the "human landscape was transformed in the two centuries after 1100 by the foundation of thousands of new 'towns', and even more by the physical expansion of existing settlements" (Nicholas, 2003, 11).

Some historians date the rise of the Western world to this period of expansion.[1] Figure 3.1 documents the increasing numbers of people who lived in towns with 10,000 inhabitants or more in the regions that later became Italy, France, Germany, Britain, and the Low Countries.[2] Figure 3.2 plots urbanization rates. Together these figures show that urbanization increased dramatically during the high medieval period – particularly in Italy and in the Low Countries. This development was partly made possible by the weakness of territorial states. The revival of urban life was not driven by cities that were political or ecclesiastical capitals (the population of Rome in fact continued to shrink until the fourteenth century) but by the rise of new commercial centers: Florence, Pisa, Bruges, Venice, Genoa, and many others.

These new cities were manufacturing centers and trade entrepôts. Genoa and Pisa came to dominate trade in the western Mediterranean; Venice became the leading trading power of the eastern Mediterranean; Florence, a center of textile production, and later a hub for banking and international finance. Many cities benefited from the opening up of Mediterranean trade achieved by the Crusades (Blaydes and Paik, 2016). Cities like Bruges became major manufacturing and commercial centers linking together the British Isles, the Rhineland, and Northern Italy.[3] This was what Goldstone (2002) calls a "growth efflorescence."

3.1.1 The Role of Religion in Enforcing Identity Norms

Economic growth set in motion changes in the political and religious institutions of Europe.[4] Urbanization and economic growth generated a demand for new types of religious goods and experiences. Literary rates increased and educated individuals came together to discuss religious ideas. The religious economy of medieval Europe flourished. As Swanson (1999, 60–61) notes "the Church [w]as a provider of services that people wanted to pay for." People were deeply interested in religion and concerned with the afterlife. This provided the demand for the rise of the indulgence industry. At the same time, the expanding economy created new sources of rents that could be captured by religious and secular rulers. Together these factors produced tensions that would give rise to both religious dissent and to religious persecution.

Secular authorities could rely on the Church validating the social order. In return, secular rulers granted the Church tremendous wealth and power. Despite the radical positions inherent in the teachings of Jesus, the medieval Church also had an interest in supporting the existing order. If it was to survive and flourish, it had to do so in the world as it *was* rather than attempting to radically change it and to build a heaven on earth. Such attitudes came naturally to the majority of the higher clergy, who were drawn from noble families and hence shared a common aristocratic sensibility with secular elites.

The Church could also provide administrative services. As medieval rulers started to rebuild fiscal systems in the late twelfth and thirteenth centuries, they also frequently taxed the clergy or used the Church to collect taxes. This was because the Church possessed organizational and administrative capacity that the medieval state lacked. The Saladin tithe raised in 1188 was specifically collected by priests and the clergy on their revenue and moveable property, exempting those who joined the crusade in person.[5] In Spain, as land was reconquered from the Muslims, Drelichman and Voth (2014, 80) note that the churches were employed to collect taxes on behalf of the king. The reasoning was similar: "Priests were likely to know in detail the resources of their parishioners and, holding moral sway over them, also had a better chance than royal collectors in ensuring that they paid their due."

3.1.2 Guilds and Identity Rules

One example of the role of religion and identity rules in medieval Europe are guilds. Guilds were ubiquitous in medieval society. They formed a layer of self-government between the individual and the state. Merchant guilds played an important role in enforcing contracts and regulating long-distance and overseas trade. Craft guilds controlled who could be employed as a skilled worker in industries such as brewing, baking, tanning, smithing, construction, glasswork, and many other specialized occupations.

Guilds provided charity and organized the celebrations of feast days and other religious festivals. They acted as drinking and dining societies for members and provided local bridges, roads, and schools. Guilds provided services that are usually left to government today. In England, guilds collected the tax on wool and cloth and lent money to the king. Their chief expense was often burials and prayers for the departed (Hanawalt, 1984). Indeed a shared religious identity was crucial to their functioning. They were usually based around the worship of a saint, often the patron saint of a particular industry – as St. Anne was for mining for example – or the saint of a local area (Richardson, 2005, 149–151). Religion thus helped to reinforce guild's economic role. Guilds, in turn, supported the existing religious order. They mandated church attendance, regulated the behavior of their members and supplemented the Church in instructing members on how to conduct themselves: imposing "strict moral rules on their members" such as warning brothers "not to fornicate or commit adultery, not to swear and not to sin any other way" (Madigan, 2015, 313).[6]

Individuals who missed religious services were fined by their guild (Richardson, 2005, 158). Guilds did provide charity to the poor and to nonmembers. But their core services were for members only and membership was conditional on social identity. Guilds excluded Jews and other religious minorities, migrants, the illegitimate, and other outsiders as well as those who could not afford the membership fees (Ogilvie, 2014).[7] Such was the importance of religious identity to how guilds functioned that converted Jews in Spain and Portugal established their own separate guilds. And lepers, otherwise excluded from mainstream Christian society, set up "associations that were regarded, by their contemporaries, as fraternities, or 'leprosaries'" (Madigan, 2015, 313–314).

Expulsion from a guild meant social as well as economic exclusion.[8] Guilds and fraternities were a crucial part of the system of identity rules governing medieval Europe.

In an economy dependent on identity rules, guilds helped to enforce contracts. Thus they increased the volume of trade relative to a world of no general rules and no guilds. But guilds enforced contracts via exclusion and the creation of monopoly rents. They offered a very different system of governance from that which has characterized the modern world.

3.2 Rise of the Medieval State and the Persecuting Society

The fragmented political environment described in Chapter 2 began to change after 1100. A lessening in the frequency and intensity of Viking, Magyar, and Arab raids in combination with warmer temperatures allowed population growth to pick up. Greater population density and economic activity was accompanied by the emergence of new, comparatively more organized, states, in England and then in France and later in Castile and Aragon.[9] Kingship came to be associated with a fixed territory instead of ruling distinct peoples and tribes. Gradually, these new states established fiscal systems. For the first time since the fall of the Roman Empire, there arose states capable of policing the beliefs of their subjects. These states were increasingly equipped with organized bureaucracies and powerful armies that enabled them to confront the power of local lords.

Of course, medieval polities were hardly impressive in comparison with those of other periods in history or other parts of the world. Twelfth-century bureaucracies were small compared to later standards. Nevertheless, these developments represented a dramatic increase in state power in comparison with the disorder and localized lordship characteristic of preceding centuries.[10]

Our framework predicts that this state building would lead to greater demand for religious legitimation from secular rulers seeking to strike bargains with the Catholic Church in order to gain its support at the pulpit. Rather than paying for this support in land and money, which the rulers of these new territorial states needed to wage war and suppress internal opposition, they bought the Church's support by promising to enforce religious conformity through the threat of violence. They also gained religious legitimacy by going on crusade. Stronger states had the capacity to investigate the religious practices and beliefs of their subjects and, in return, they could secure legitimation from the religious authorities. Thus a new political equilibrium emerged, one that saw the religious sanctification of secular government and religious persecutions carried out by the state.

To see how this framework explains the history, we consider three medieval polities: France, the Holy Roman Empire, and England. France provides a paradigmatic case of a monarchy building a state through increased reliance on religion for political legitimacy. The Holy Roman Empire, in contrast, provides an illustration of abortive state-building. The break between the Pope and the Emperor, which began with the Investiture Controversy, impeded the Emperor's ability to build a strong monarchy in partnership with the Church. Instead, Holy Roman Emperors frequently found themselves excommunicated, with Popes' sponsoring rival claimants to the imperial throne.

Finally, the English case demonstrates how the strong Norman monarchy established by William the Conqueror and his successors initially had little need of religious legitimation. As it did not require religious legitimacy, the English monarchy did not engage in large-scale religious persecution. However, this changed after 1400 as England experienced prolonged periods of disorder following the usurpation of Henry IV; from then on, rulers forged a closer relationship with the Church and began to persecute those deemed to be heretics such as William Sawtrey.

3.2.1 France and the Rise of Theocratic Monarchy

France in 1000 was not a kingdom but a geographic entity.[11] In the eleventh century, the kings of what would become France controlled only a fraction of the country around Paris and the Île-de France, and even in this territory, they struggled to enforce justice and collect revenue.[12] When Philip Augustus was crowned king of France in 1179, he was far from being the greatest lord within his own kingdom (Baldwin, 1986, 13). Philip was much weaker than Henry II, king of England, lord of Ireland, the Count of Anjou, and Duke of Normandy whose Angevian empire stretched from the north of England to the Pyrenees. Figure 3.3 shows the lands inherited by Philip in 1179. Over the course of the next thirty years, however, through warfare and diplomacy, Philip reduced the holdings of his rivals dramatically; Figure 3.4 shows the French kingdom at his death.

The kings of France used religion to support their claim to rule all of the regions originally ruled by Clovis in the fifth century. Their coronations emphasized the sacred aspect of their rule: each swore an oath to defend the church from his enemies.[13] Jacques Le Goff describes Philip August's legacy

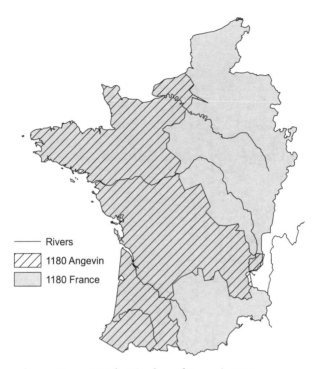

Figure 3.3 The Kingdom of France in 1180.

as the development of a royal religion. He inaugurated rituals such as the depositing of the royal regalia at the Cathedral of Saint-Denis as a way of sacralizing the monarchy. Close to death, Philip advised his successor Louis VIII to "honor God and the Holy Church, as I have done. I have drawn great usefulness from this, and you will obtain just as much" (quoted in Goff, 2009, 552). The religious character of the French king was strengthened under his successors, particularly Louis IX – canonized as St Louis in 1297 – the first French ruler to ritually attempt to heal the sick through his touch, who cemented the role of the French monarch as the *rex Christianissimus* – most Christian king.

According to this distinctive political theology, the king and the Church both "represented God in its own way. The king held his function from birth and directly from God. He was God's lieutenant in his own kingdom. He was God's 'image', but he only assumed possession of this grace through the intermediary of the Church represented by the prelate who anointed and crowned him. The Church definitely made him a king, and he committed himself to protecting it. He benefited from its sanctifying power and was its secular arm" (Goff, 2009, 553).[14] This political theology buttressed the authority of the king and gave strength to the idea that the lands that

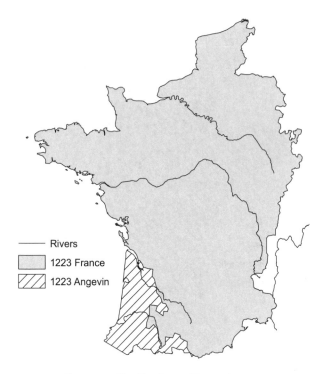

Figure 3.4 The Kingdom of France in 1223.

comprised France were part of a single territorial kingdom protected by God: to injure France or the French king was to injure Christ and the church (Strayer, 1969, 1971a, 309). The development of this alliance of the altar and the throne was accompanied by religious persecution. This is most evident in the religious war launched against "heretics" in the south of France, known as the Albigensian Crusade.

3.2.2 The Crusade against the Heretics

As Philip Augustus and his successors began incorporating independent dukedoms and principalities into the political agglomeration that would become France, they encountered different customs, different languages, and different religious traditions. This was particularly so in Languedoc.[15]

Two differences between northern and southern France stand out. First, lordship was weaker in the south. Languedoc was highly urbanized and had a rich local nobility but was not unified under a single aristocratic family. The weakness of central authority provided conditions in which many dissonant religious beliefs could flourish. The Count of Toulouse was simply not strong enough to enforce religious conformity even had he wished to.[16]

Second, the Church was much weaker in Languedoc. The north of France was the center of the eleventh-century religious reform movement. It had seen the building of new grand cathedrals and a resurgent monarchy champion Catholicism.[17] This was not the case in the south of France, where religious practices evolved along an alternative path. Christianity in Languedoc was localized and focused on the holiness of specific individuals and preachers.[18] Local saints and customs were celebrated. But doctrine was poorly understood, and expressions of religiosity varied greatly from place to place (Moore, 2012, 120). Filling the gap left by the Church, pious groups championed apostolic poverty. Some of these groups opposed clerical abuses and became hostile to the Church. These dissenting critiques were openly discussed and preached in Languedoc and they gave rise to heresy.

The extent to which the heretical beliefs held by many in southern France constituted a distinct dualistic faith is debated. Nevertheless, it is common to refer to the dissenting beliefs in Languedoc during the twelfth century as the Cathar heresy. Catharism, as described by Church chroniclers and inquisitors, was influenced by Eastern heresies and by older Gnostic and Manichean ideas that the god who created the material world was not the god of the New Testament but the demiurge or the devil. Cathars are also said to have believed that since the material world is irredeemably tainted, Christ could not therefore have been born in human flesh and have suffered on the cross. Following the writings of contemporary Cistercian chroniclers, traditional historians argue that the Cathars had developed a church-like organization in opposition to the Catholic Church.[19]

Modern historians question the extent to which a distinctive and well-organized dualistic religion actually existed in Languedoc before the crusade waged against them (see Pegg, 2001).[20] Certainly, heterodox beliefs flourished. But it is less clear how well formed these beliefs were. For example, adherence to some "heretical" doctrines was not incompatible with a positive view of the Church. This is evident in Le Roy Ladurie's study of the village of Montaillou. Examining the period after the Albigensian crusade, Ladurie noted that:

On several occasions the shepherds Pierre and Jean Maury and Guillaume Maurs remarked on their annual confession of sins; and yet these men were never more than lukewarm towards orthodox Catholicism, and two of them at least were heretics for long periods … While first communion and marriage acted as rites of passage, other sacraments seem to have been almost unknown in the upland villages. For example, there are no instances of confirmation. There is good reason for this: the Bishop, who would have performed the ceremony, rarely left Pamiers and his inquisitorial tasks, and in any case was not eager to travel among the mountainous areas of his diocese. (Ladurie, 1978, 311–313)

The peasants of the region were often ignorant about the details of the Christian faith: they failed to fast and had only a vague notion of the holy days.

At the turn of the twelfth century, Pope Innocent III began to deal seriously with reported heresy in Languedoc. He commissioned preachers to convert those holding dualist beliefs and when this policy encountered local resistance from lords hostile to outside interference, in 1209, he called for a crusade.

In response, men-at-arms from northern France moved into the lands of the Count of Toulouse who was accused of protecting heretics. The cities of Béziers and Carcassonne were sacked. Everywhere they burnt alive those they called heretics. One of the main sources for this invasion – known today as the Albigensian Crusade – is Peter of les Vaux-de-Cernay, a young monk who accompanied the Crusading armies. For Peter of Cernay, this was a just war in which diabolical heretics were opposed by virtuous crusaders whose victorious invasion was accompanied by numerous events he hails as "miracles." He reports one case in which a man survives a crossbow bolt at short range and another in which an old man who predicted the doom of the heretics is able to escape unscathed. Similarly, he ascribes the survival of prisoners and the low price of bread at the siege of Carcassonne to such miracles.[21]

It is often observed that medieval people were used to cruelty. But we do not need to assume that medieval mentalities were different from ours to know that people, who in normal times would never commit murder, are capable of extraordinary cruelty in certain circumstances. Morality is situational: our actions and moral assessments are strongly influenced by framing.[22] Mass killings are much more likely during periods of war during which ordinary rules and laws are set aside and are usually preceded by rhetorical demonization or dehumanization.[23]

The rhetoric of heresy served this purpose in southern France. Those who opposed the crusading army were labeled heretics even though none of the lords who did so are known to have held dualist beliefs themselves (see Graham-Leigh, 2005). Béziers was, according to Peter, "entirely infected with the poison of heresy … Its citizens were not only heretics, they were robbers, lawbreakers, adulterers and thieves of the worst sort, brimful of every kind of sin" so that it deserved the fate it received when the crusaders "killed almost all the inhabitants from the youngest to the oldest, and set fire to the city" (Peter of les Vaux-de Cernay, 1998, 48–50). Heretics were sufficiently demonized that their execution by the flames was hardly worth noting. This is evident in the writings of Peter who describes heresy as "poison of superstitious unbelief … ancient filth" that infected the people of Toulouse, "a dreadful plague" and he castigated those who sought to defend or protect those accused of heresy as heretics themselves (Peter of les Vaux-de Cernay, 1998, 8–10).

What followed was a brutal war of conquest. The sack of Béziers was followed by a massacre of the civilian population, which included the burning of declared heretics. One hundred and forty who refused to renege their heretical beliefs were burnt alive at Minerve in 1210 and numerous other mass burnings are reported. Ultimately, the crusade led to the defeat of the nobility of Languedoc. Leadership of the crusade devolved to the French king, and the war against heresy became a war of conquest – adding Languedoc to the French monarchy. The inquisition was created to police beliefs in the conquered territories.[24]

The fate of Languedoc is consistent with the framework in Chapter 2. Political weakness allowed religious diversity to flourish in Languedoc for longer than elsewhere. Heresy provided a justification for the intervention of the French monarchy. The Albigensian Crusade that resulted burnished the orthodox credentials of the kings of France, who in the thirteenth century established an increasingly theocratic kingship.[25]

Other religious radicals who emerged from the turbulent atmosphere of twelfth-century Europe were either incorporated into the Church or repressed. Francis of Assisi (1181/1182 – 1226) was not a priest but a lay preacher whose commitment to apostolic poverty posed a challenge to the Church. Pope Innocent III recognized Francis, endowed the Franciscan order, and beatified Francis in 1228. The Franciscans drew their popularity from championing poverty in a society that was increasingly commercialized. They railed against moneylending and often opposed Jewish settlement. The incorporation of the Franciscans into the Church deflected popular anger away from the wealth and corruption of the clergy. But a branch known as the Spiritual Franciscans remained committed to vows of poverty and they were duly suppressed by the Pope, with those who refused to recant being burnt alive.[26]

The power of medieval polities faced tight geographical limits. James C. Scott has discussed how geography often set the limits of state power in the preindustrial world, constraining the ability of rulers to impose their own belief structures on those they sought to control. In his accounts of the uplands of Southeast Asia, Scott noted that "it merits emphasis that the hills are associated as much with religious heterodoxy vis-à-vis the lowlands as they are with rebellion and political dissent." He went on to argue that "[t]he religious 'frontier' beyond which orthodoxy could not easily be imposed was therefore not so much a place or defined border as it was a relation to power – that varying margin at which state power faded appreciably" (Scott, 2009, 155).

One area where religious dissidents were not successfully repressed was in the Alpine passes of southeastern France and northern Italy, where another heretic group – the Waldensians – continued to flourish, despite military campaigns launched against them. Several attempts were made throughout the fifteenth century but these were unsuccessful, partly because the Alpine mountain passes enabled local communities to resist the encroaching power of the state and fostered a "spirit of resistance to interferences" (Cameron, 1986, 12).[27]

The process of state construction was a ceaseless process. From a modern perspective, the efforts of medieval rulers appears Sisyphean: successful rulers established powerful polities only for these proto-states to collapse into disorder in subsequent decades. Moreover, this process was inherently coercive and violent. Yet, as the example we turn to next, that of the Holy Roman Empire, demonstrates, the absence of a powerful, centralized, state in central Europe was also "no utopia" (Volckart, 2002).

3.2.3 The Holy Roman Empire and the Investiture Crisis

To understand the importance of religious legitimacy in medieval Europe, we consider a case where the partnership between the papacy and the secular rulers went awry. Figure 3.5 shows the major European political boundaries in 1300. It is clear that in German speaking territories of the Holy Roman Empire something interrupted the state-building process. This level of fragmentation was persistent – by 1500 there were more than 1,200 independent political entities within the Holy Roman Empire (Whaley, 2012). These entities included the comparatively large electorates and dukedoms of Brandenburg, Saxony, and Bavaria as well as much smaller statelets such as free imperial cities and independent knights. There was no territorial monopoly on violence within the empire as a whole.[28] What generated the centripetal forces that pulled the state building project apart in Germany?

Part of the answer lies in the Investiture Controversy (1075–1122), which saw the breakdown in the relationship between secular and religious authority and impeded the development of state capacity.

Celibacy, simony, and election were the three major issues of contention in eleventh-century Germany. All three related to the power that the papacy had over its priests and bishops. The papacy desired celibate priests to break the power that the noble families had over Church lands and offices. The incentive of clergy to pass on their benefices to their families or otherwise manage property in a manner inconsistent with the goals of Rome undermined both the power and the legitimacy of Church. Simony, the practice of buying and selling clerical positions, was also frowned on by

Figure 3.5 Political boundaries of Western Europe in 1000. Based on Nussli (2011).

the popes since this reduced their control over who held office. Similarly, the demand for popular election of priests and bishops undermined their ability to wield power from Rome.

Simony inevitably brought the Church into conflict with secular rulers. The distribution of offices (and their corresponding revenues) was a means through which rulers cemented power.[29] When this involved a religious position, such as a bishopric, then the beneficiary of the office was expected to directly or indirectly support the policies of the ruler: "[i]f a king invested him, a bishop was the king's man, exercising the authority of his office on the behalf of the monarch" (Miller, 2005, 3).

The actions of the aggressive reforming pope, Leo IX (r. 1049–1054), shows how serious the Church was. In 1049 Leo IX held a major meeting of bishops and archbishops to clarify issues of doctrine known as the Lateran Synod. There Leo condemned simony and clerical marriage. Celibacy for members of the clergy at or above the level of a subdeacon became official policy. Furthermore, Leo took the unprecedented step of openly accusing powerful churchmen present of violating doctrine. According to contemporary accounts, he publicly accused the Bishop of Sutri for paying for his office and the accusation was so disturbing that the bishop dropped dead where he stood.

The confrontation between an activist papacy and princely authority came to a head when Pope Gregory VII came to power in 1073 and grasped the chance to make permanent gains for the Church at the expense of a weak Holy Roman Emperor, Henry IV.

Henry IV became emperor at the age of six. At his coronation in the cathedral at Aachen, the hymns sung heralded him as the "vicar of the Creator," "the image of God," the king appointed by God "to rule the world" (Miller, 2005, 17). But as often happened in the middle ages, the reign of a young monarch was accompanied by instability. As he came to adulthood he gained control over the empire but faced continuous rebellions in Saxony.

Without a stable source of tax revenues, one of the main sources of power that Henry had was his ability to appoint Church offices. By 1073, the bishops that Henry had been investing for the past decade or so were the core of his power base.

While Henry IV needed the right of investiture to rule, Pope Gregory VII was set on expanding the authority of the Holy See. Gregory began by attempting to persuade secular rulers to relax their control over religious appointments. Once this failed, he became more aggressive. In 1075 he sent an open letter to courts across Europe in which he asserted that, "I find hardly any bishops who conform to the law either in their appointment or in their way of life and who rule the Christian people in the love of Christ and not for worldly ambition. Among all the secular princes I know of none who place the honor of God before their own and righteousness before gain …Since there is no prince who troubles about such things, we must protect the lives of religious men." This last line was directly aimed at Henry IV (Heather, 2014, 389).

Soon Gregory resorted to more open confrontation. He called on the people of Milan to boycott church services offered by simoniac or married clergy. Henry, for his part, saw this as a challenge to his authority and began to work behind the scenes to force Gregory to abdicate. In 1073 he also attempted to reclaim lands in Saxony that had previously belonged to his family and this resulted in Saxony openly rebelling.

After winning a victory over the Saxons, Henry IV openly flouted the pope by investing several bishops personally. Gregory VII saw this as a direct challenge to Rome's authority and excommunicated Henry. The excommunication of Henry by the pope illustrates what could happen to a secular ruler when the religious authority abandons him. The act released all of Henry's vassals from their obligations to him. Saxony again rebelled and Henry was forced to travel to the Alpine town of Canossa, where the Pope was staying, and beg him in the snow outside the walls to be reinstated in the Church – which Gregory eventually granted.

The conflict between church and state did not end at Canossa, however. As soon as the Saxon rebellion was suppressed, Henry again started appointing bishops. He advanced a new pope and Gregory was forced out of Rome and would die in exile.

Over the next forty years instability reigned in the Holy Roman Empire as a consequence of the inability of secular and religious authorities to cooperate. The Investiture Controversy was only resolved with the Concordat of Worms in 1122. The pope and emperor agreed on the outward ceremonial forms to be followed in investing bishops. The practical work of actually choosing the bishops, however, largely defaulted to the secular authorities.

In subsequent years, Emperors attempted to rebuild imperial authority. This again brought them into conflict with the papacy. As a result, the empire declined into insignificance in the fourteenth and fifteenth centuries. By the Late Middle Ages, the most important rivals of the Emperor were other German princes.

This legacy of divided and weak rule generated perhaps the "worst of all possible worlds" in terms of treatment of religious minorities as we document in subsequent chapters. While England and France conducted large-scale expulsions of their Jewish populations in the later middle ages, it was in the Holy Roman Empire that the worst pogroms and massacres of Jews occurred. It was also in Germany that the schism between Catholics and Protestants would lead to the horrors of the Thirty Years' War. And, it was in Germany that the most intensive witch hunts occurred largely as a result of weak government and political and legal fragmentation.

3.2.4 England and the Repression of Lollards

As a final case study we consider England. At first glance, England might appear to be an exception to our argument because as noted in the introduction to this chapter, it saw no heresy persecutions until the fifteenth century. In fact, the English example supports the mechanisms highlighted in the preceding pages.

Medieval England after 1066 was a conquest state in which royal power was more centralized than elsewhere in Europe. English kings had a degree of independence from Rome and, compared to their French counterparts, they relied less on religious legitimation. In the early fourteenth century when the Knights Templars were arrested all across Europe on trumped up charges at the behest of the French king and the pope, the English refused to comply with the pope's demands that they be arrested and put to torture.[30] The English disbanded the Templars, but unlike elsewhere in Europe they were allowed to return to lay life and not executed.[31]

Sawtry's fate, however, would be grimmer. He would be burned alive. What explains the change in attitudes to religious dissent in fourteenth-century England? The transformation in attitudes to heresy we observe at the end of the fourteenth century came about because the position of the English crown also changed dramatically. The legitimate Plantagenet king Richard II (r. 1377–1399), grandson of Edward III (r. 1327–1377), was over-thrown by his cousin Henry IV (r. 1399–1414). Henry IV – Shakespeare's Bollingbroke, also known as Henry of Lancaster – was descended from a young son of Edward III. As such, he was in need of legitimacy.[32]

Henry was backed by "the orthodox party in the Church" in his attempt to seize the crown from his cousin Richard II (Davies, 1935, 204). In return, Henry owed the Church and "must have known that would be required to pay for that support" (Davies, 1935, 204). Prior to this usurpation, Lol-lardy had not been persecuted seriously in England despite the wishes of the Church, led by the Archbishop of Canterbury. Lollardy was a home-grown heresy. Unlike the heresies we considered earlier, it was not a response to urbanization or economic growth, but rather a specifically English critique of an overpowerful and distant Church. Wycliff's arguments found an audi-ence among elite circles because many resented the outflow of money to a Papacy that was seen as corrupt and in the pocket of the French king. Wycliff argued that the secular powers could tax the clergy and cast doubt on the Church as a vehicle of salvation (because only God knew who was in a state of grace).

Wycliff's teaching came to be seen as destabilizing after the Peasant's Revolt of 1381. What had previously been an intellectual position held by scholars within the Church acquired the name of Lollardy and was deemed heretical.[33] Papal backing was crucial in winning support for Henry's inva-sion of England and the deposing of a reigning monarch. Reversing his father's policy, he formed a close alliance with the Archbishop of Canter-bury, Thomas Arnold, a fervent opponent of Lollardy. The orthodox party within the Church backed Henry's rebellion: "Holy Church gave him her blessing" (Davies, 1935, 204).

Henry's new regime was fragile from the start. After he colluded in the killing of Richard II, his position was questioned from all sides and he faced a series of rebellions. Richard II had been a supporter of the Franciscans and Dominicans, and both orders were said to support the restoration of the old king whom they did not believe was dead. Following a series of plots involving members of religious orders, the king engaged a Franciscan from the Priory at Leicester, Roger Frisby, who stated that if Richard II was dead "then is dead by you, and if that be so, you have lost all right and title that you might have had to the crown." Frisby and his eight fellow Friars were executed shortly thereafter and Frisby's head was taken to Oxford, where he had been a Master of Divinity, and put on stake. This was not a heresy trial, but the Franciscans were singled out because as churchmen they were influential figures in society and their execution demonstrated the new regime's lack of compunction about eliminating all threats to the new political order.

It was in this more unstable political context that William Sawtrey's execution should be understood: "A usurper king needed all the help he could get from clergy, and he may have thought that the measures intended to deal with unauthorized preachers could also be useful in checking the growth of political conspiracies and conventicles" (Lambert, 1977, 261–262). Under the new, and fragile, regime, heretics began to be burnt.

3.3　Chapter Summary: Persecutions and the Rise of States in Medieval Europe

Medieval rulers persecuted heretics because it enhanced their political legitimacy. They sought to portray themselves as defenders of religion. There could be no acknowledged religious dissent. In practice, however, there was plenty of religious diversity. Most early medieval states lacked the capacity to enforce religious conformity and the Church consequently did not attempt to legislate against heretics or belief in witchcraft. As a result, few individuals died for their religious beliefs.

After 1100 this began to change. A combination of factors – economic growth, urbanization, and the consolidation of larger sovereign political entities – made it possible for increasingly powerful secular rulers to strike a different deal with the Church. They became champions of orthodoxy and enemies of heresy. Persecution of heretical or deviant belief became more common. Nascent states were more willing and more able to persecute these individuals in exchange for religious legitimation and increasingly the subordination of religious authority to political authority. This was the rise of a "persecuting society."

There were always important limits to this process. More often than not, secular rulers did not just wipe out any population that deviated from orthodox belief. Not only would this have often been unfeasible, it also would have been throwing away valuable fiscal resources. Thus, in practice, the late medieval state's position toward religious deviancy became that of the enforcer of conditional toleration. In the next chapter, we will see how this could both perpetuate religious differences and distinctions while at the same time serve both the fiscal and legal needs of the state.

Notes

1. Economic historian Carlo Cipolla described the "rise of the cities in Europe in the tenth and twelfth centuries" as one of the "turning points in the history of the West – and, for that matter, of the whole world" (Cipolla, 1976, 139). Greif argues that the "Rise of the West" was "a process that began in the late medieval period with the growth of European commerce" (Greif, 2006*b*, 24). Greif goes on to argue that "the West developed distinct institutions as early as the late medieval period" (Greif, 2006*b*, 25). Similarly, the main argument of Jan Luiten Van Zanden is that the root causes of the Industrial Revolution lie in the Middle Ages. He concludes "that in many respects the medieval period was more dynamic than the three centuries from 1500 to 1800" (van Zanden, 2009, 5).

2. We use the Bairoch data, as these are the most widely accepted and comprehensive figures on urbanization. Note that they are conservative estimates of the urban population, as they miss those individuals who lived in smaller towns. The true urbanization rate of medieval Holland, for instance, may have approached 40 percent (see Epstein, 2001).

3. This market-based trading network emerged in the absence of a central authority. The "kingdom of Italy" was nominally subject to the German Holy Roman Emperor, but in reality the emperor had little authority past the Alps. Before 1000, the Italian towns and cities were ruled either by feudal lords or by bishops. In the period 1000–1300, numerous Italian cities were able to overthrow these feudal rulers and organize as self-governing communes (see Abulafia, 2011, 271–303).

4. Belloc et al. (2016) studied this transition from feudal rule to self-governing communes in Italy during this period. They provide evidence that religion played a crucial role in upholding the old feudal arrangements and that the transition toward self-government was retarded by positive shocks to religious belief generated by natural disasters such as earthquakes. Earthquakes were interpreted as "acts of God." Public religiosity increased in their wake and this strengthened the power of local bishops. Thus in the cities where the religious rulers were also secular rulers, the transition from feudal to communal, self-governing, institutions was retarded.

5. For an analysis of the economic impact of the Crusades, see Blaydes and Paik (2016, 559–560).

6. How likely it was that these rules were enforced at the numerous dinners and feasts organized by the fraternities is, of course, open to question!

7. There were, it should be noted, charitable fraternities for women, and many of the parish guilds studied by Hanawalt (1984) were mixed.

8. Richardson notes that "Expellees lost the business benefits of membership, what those were, and much more. Expellees lost their church, pastor, and the network of individuals who promised them a proper burial, a respectable funeral, and prayers for their soul into perpetuity. Expellees also lost friends, colleagues, and access to their guild's social services. Expellees no longer had feasts to attend, friendly neighbors working in the same industry, or someone to talk to about the state of trade" (Richardson, 2005, 162).

9. Various accounts of this process are provided in Strayer (1969, 1971*a*, 1970), Bisson (2009), and Wickham (2016). For an analysis of why Europe remained persistently fragmented after the fall of the Carolingian empire (see Ko, Koyama, and Sng, 2018).

10. Thus while the number of state officials was very small in comparison with that in later periods of European history, this was not the perception at the time. "The multiplication of the number of lay officials is one of the most striking phenomena of the thirteenth century. In every country the conservatives protested again and again that there were too many officials, and in every country the number of officials went on increasing in spite of the protests" (Strayer, 1940, 1971c, 256).

11. The kings of France traced their claim back to Hugh Capet, who had been crowned "king of the Gauls, the Bretons, the Normans, the Aquitanians, the Goths, the Spanish, and the Gascons … there was no one West Frankish people, let alone one country to which all these different people belonged" (Dunbabin, 1985, 4).

12. See Dunbabin (1985, 163). Similarly, in mid-eleventh century England, the earls of Wessex and Northumberland possessed their own armies and had the authority and power to defy the king.

13. See Baldwin (1986, 13) and Ullman (1961, 201), who notes that "[e]ach succeeding recension of the *ordo* improved its predecessors by symbolic details and expansion of individual features."

14. Intriguingly, the historical literature notes that the French kings' reliance on religious legitimation was partially a product of their comparative weakness: "The Emperor Frederick Barbarossa, the kings, Henry I and Henry II of England, had abandoned theocracy to develop the secular potential inherent in their offices. The French king, with fewer resources, was reluctant to go so far." Instead, in partnership with the church they accepted a place "below the saints and martyrs of the church, with his vassals the princes on the rung below, and other lesser men in their serried ranks below again" (Dunbabin, 1985, 250).

15. The language of its inhabitants was *langue d'oc* rather than *langue d'oil* and in many ways it was culturally and economically more connected to Catalonia and northern Italy than it was to the region north of the Loire (Given, 1990; Pegg, 2008). Given notes that "the French monarchy, however, had little to do with Languedoc since the break-up of the Carolingian empire. In the middle of the twelfth century the Capetians began to show a renewed interest in the affairs of the south. But when the wars to end Languedocian autonomy began in 1209, the French monarchy and the various southern lordships had behind them only a relatively brief history of important political contacts" (Given, 1990, 39). The remainder of this analysis draws on Johnson and Koyama (2013).

16. See Given (1989, 20) and Deane (2011, 37).

17. A common elite-level Catholic culture emerged that spread across northwestern Europe, as exemplified by the wearing of the cross as a mark of belonging to the church, an uncommon practice before the late eleventh century (Moore, 1999).

18. The wealth of the church was also greater in northern France compared to Languedoc. See Goldsmith (2003, 238).

19. See Oldenbourg (1961, 28–81), Lambert (1998), Hamilton (1999), and Barber (2000). This view sees the Cathars as decisively influenced by the Bogomil heresy which arose in Macedonia in the tenth century. For a study of the role urbanization and economic growth played along with political decentralization in fueling the growth of Cathar beliefs see Lansing (1998).

20. While historians still believe that there were genuine dualists in Languedoc, they see the boundaries between these beliefs and those of more orthodox Christians as fluid and ill-defined. They reject the term Cathar in favor of "Good Men" or

"Good Christians," as this was the label in common usage in the period before the crusade was launched against them.

21. For the "miracle" of the abundance of bread see paragraph 97 of Peter of les Vaux-de Cernay (1998, 53). The old man who asks the defenders of Toulouse how they will defend themselves from God is mentioned in paragraph 87 on page 49. The man surviving a crossbow bolt is reported in paragraph 144 on page 79. The survival of prisoners in a ditch for three days is described in paragraph 126 on page 70.

22. This was revealed in the famous Milgram experiment and the Stanford Prison Experiment (Milgram, 1963). Also, see Pinker (2011, 320–344) on genocide and the discussion in Snyder (2015). As Pinker points out, though mass killings were not particularly well studied, "[a]s soon as one realizes that the sacking, razings, and massacres of past centuries are what we would call genocide today, it becomes utterly clear that genocide is not a phenomena of the 20th century" (332).

23. See Yanagizawa-Drott (2014). This is attested to in countless studies of the Holocaust such as Friedländer (1997, 2008). Psychological research suggests that individuals who take part in genocides often adopt an ideological position that demonizes their victims in order to reduce cognitive dissonance. They hate their victims because they have to kill them, rather than they kill them because they hate them (see Hayes, 2017).

24. The medieval inquisition was a personal office and not a permanent institution, unlike the later Spanish and Roman Inquisitions (see Kelly, 1989; Kieckhefer, 1995; and Arnold, 2001). In this respect, it set the precedent of the persecution of heresy for the subsequent centuries.

25. Ullman (1961, 195). Also see Lerner (1965, 189).

26. See Deane (2011, 144–147).

27. Harsh attempts at repression were eventually abandoned because French king Louis XII "was not convinced that small groups of Waldensians in *remote* Alpine valleys really constituted a threat to French society" (Cohn, 1975, 61).

28. See Volckart (2000*a*, *b*, 2004).

29. As outlined in North, Wallis, and Weingast (2009).

30. This was largely because of "the resistance of royal officers and the reluctance of those familiar with English common law to engage in it or support those who did" (Peters, 1985, 70).

31. Of course, other factors help to explain the absence of heresy trials in England. England's comparative isolation from trends on the continent also meant that heretical movements like the Cathars had limited opportunities to spread to England. In addition, England's comparative economic backwardness in the twelfth and thirteenth centuries, when it remained a primary commodity exporter, spared it from the development of urban-based heretical movements.

32. For details on Henry IV's life and reign see McFarlane (1972) and Mortimer (2008). An older biography is Davies (1935).

33. In fact, Henry's father, the rich and powerful John of Gaunt, had been a patron and protector of Wycliffe. John of Gaunt had been de facto ruler of England during much of Richard II's early reign, and, as a younger son of Edward III, could have himself claimed the throne. He was attracted to Wycliffe's teachings as a means of strengthening the position of the English crown vis-à-vis the Church.

4

Jewish Communities, Conditional Toleration, and Rent-Seeking

the prohibition of usury thus became ...the keystone of the political economy of the Middle Ages.

Holdsworth (1903, 101)

On the morning of July 22, 1306 every Jewish home in France was surrounded by soldiers and bailiffs on the order of the king. The timing was inauspicious: the Jews had concluded the ninth day of the fast of Tisha B'Av, which commemorated the destruction of the First and Second Temples in Jerusalem in the seventh century BCE and the first century CE respectively. As fate would have it, this date would mark a similar catastrophe for the Jews of France. They were arrested, their possessions seized, and given just one month to leave the realm on pain of death.

The writer Ishori Haparchi (1280–1355) was training to be a doctor at the time. He recalled the event as the great tragedy of his age:

I was torn from the house of study, forced naked in my youth to leave my father's home, and wandered from land to land, from one nation to another, whose languages were strange to me ...I now give the date of destruction of the "small sanctuary," that is the destruction of the schools and synagogues in France and part of Provence, when I took flight from the battle. Through our sins, it took place in the year 5066, in the month of retribution. (quoted in Golb, 1998, 538)

In this chapter we describe how the 1306 expulsion of French Jews was related to the new political equilibrium between church and state that emerged in Europe after 1100.

The 1306 French expulsion, and the many other incidents like it, reflect the nature of the conditional toleration equilibrium that emerged in medieval Europe. The alliance between political and religious authorities had two consequences. First, rulers began to persecute religious minorities when this could buttress their sacred credentials. Second, when it was too costly to eliminate the religious minority, states would instead attempt to separate them from the rest of society. In other words, the state would conditionally tolerate the religiously deviant groups.

In this chapter, we describe how this conditional toleration equilibrium applied to Europe's Jewish communities, focusing on why it was self-enforcing, how it also reinforced antisemitism, and how it could break down, resulting in tragedies such as the expulsions of 1306.

4.1 Rent-Seeking and Conditional Toleration

4.1.1 "Privileged" Outsiders in Early Medieval Europe

In the ancient world Jews were mostly farmers whose religious activities centered on the Temple in Jerusalem. They were not more educated than their neighbors (Botticini and Eckstein, 2005, 2012). According to an influential argument introduced by Botticini and Eckstein, this changed in late antiquity, and the Jews came to specialize in trade and commerce, because of a shift in religious doctrine following the destruction of the Temple in 70 CE. This saw the rise of Rabbinical Judaism with its emphasis on mandatory male literacy. As a result of this change in religious doctrine, individuals for whom the opportunity cost of acquiring literacy was high had a strong incentive to move away from Judaism over time and to convert to either Christianity or Islam.

The economic decline caused by the fall of the Roman Empire in Western Europe reduced the returns to literacy. As a result, Jewish communities dwindled, as many found it too costly to invest in literacy, and converted. Judaism became the religion of a small, selected, educated, and disproportionately urban population. This minority specialized in long-distance trade, in the wine industry, in medicine, and in providing financial services and moneylending (Botticini and Eckstein, 2012, 194).

Rulers encouraged Jewish settlement. Charlemagne gave Jews legal protection and the freedom to travel in the Carolingian Empire (Bachrach, 1977, 66–83). Jews regained the status that they had enjoyed in the Roman empire as citizens protected by the emperor (Iogna-Prat, 2002, 282–283). Jews "were largely free to build synagogues and practiced their faith in the vernacular so that gentiles could understand their sermons" (Collins, 2013, 119).[1] An indication of the level of respect Jews experienced among elites in the tenth century is that Christian nobles sometimes took Jewish names.[2]

Others followed Charlemagne's example. The Bishop of Speyer in 1084 wrote: "When I wished to make a city out of the village of Speyer, I Rudiger, surnamed Huozmann, bishop of Speyer, thought that the glory of our town would be augmented a thousandfold if I were to bring Jews" (quoted in Chazan, 2010, 101). Duke William of Normandy brought a small number of French Jews with him to England during the conquest. As a result of migration, Jewish settlements sprung up across Western and Central Europe in the years between 800 and 1100. Though they were undoubtedly perceived as aliens, there appears to have been little or no opposition to Jewish settlement. No major expulsions or persecutions are recorded during this period.

This acceptance of Jewish communities was consistent with the writings of St. Augustine, who taught that the Jews were to be protected because they were "witnesses" to the errors of their ancestors who had turned away the Savior Jesus Christ. This theological position was complex and nuanced. It insisted that the conversion of the Jews was not to be forced because this could be achieved only with the coming of the anti-Christ and the end of the days. Yet it contained seeds that would develop into medieval antisemitism, as it emphasized the intransigence of a people among whom the messiah was born, but who nonetheless stubbornly rejected his message.

Over time, the position of the Church toward the Jews became harsher. Theologians debated the appropriate status of the Jews in the thirteenth century and the consensus was that they should be protected "in life and limb" because of their role as witnesses to the faith (Baron, 1965, 7–8). But, at the same time, Jewish suffering was crucial to the Christian self-image: Jews had rejected Christ and as witnesses to this mistake, they were not to enjoy a higher status than Christians. Pope Innocent III's letter to Philip Augustus in 1205 held that the Jews should be allowed to practice their religion but that they should not be in a position to lord over Christians:

> It does not displease God, but is even acceptable to him that the Jewish dispersion should live and serve under Catholic kings and Christian princes until such time as their remnant should be saved, in those days when "Judah will be saved and Israel will dwell securely." Nevertheless, such [kings and princes] are exceedingly offensive in the sight of the divine majesty when they prefer the sons of the crucifiers – against whom the blood cries to the Father's ears' – to the heirs of the crucified Christ and when they prefer the Jewish slavery to the freedom of those whom the Son freed, as though the son of a servant could and should be an heir along with the son of the free woman. (quoted in Chazan, 2010, 138)

Jews were not to be allowed Christian servants or to be advisors to kings. The toleration that Jews could enjoy in Christendom was conditional – "general sufferance with severe qualifications" (Baron, 1965, 5).

As we saw in Chapter 3, secular rulers came to increasingly rely on religious legitimacy as a source of political authority during the medieval period. Thirteenth-century monarchs like Henry III in England – builder of Westminster Abbey – and Louis IX, in France, openly identified themselves as pious Christians and this was increasingly at odds with favoring nonbelievers.[3] There was a new desire to stigmatize and separate out Jews from Christians.[4]

4.1.2 The Development of Medieval Antisemitism

The origins of popular and elite antagonism toward Jews are complex. Elements can be found in ancient Egyptian sources.[5] It was present in Greek and Roman sources and was an important theme in the writings of Early Church Fathers, who were keen to distinguish Christianity from its parent religion (see Nirenberg, 2013). But there is little evidence of widespread virulent popular antisemitism in the Early Middle Ages. Arguments from an absence of evidence are always problematic, but it is clear that many of the long-lasting tropes of antisemitism only emerged gradually in the medieval period.

We use the term antisemitism to describe hatred of Jews even though the term emerged only in the nineteenth century. We follow historians such as Langmuir (1990) who use it to describe the rise of virulent anti-Jewish hatred and violence after 1100.[6] This is because, although medieval antisemitism was generally religious rather than racial in origin, like modern antisemitism it was based on a common set of tropes that sought to blame Jews for personal misfortunes and tragedies (e.g., in the case of ritual murder accusations) or for general social ills (e.g., in charges of host desecration, well poisoning, coin-clipping, or diabolism) that largely survive to this day.[7]

One source of hatred toward Jews was that they were outsiders in an otherwise homogeneous religious environment; "the very model of an outsider: a paradigm of the excluded" (Iogna-Prat, 2002, 266). Over time hatred of the Jews became more developed and more persistent than the hatred directed toward any other group of outsiders in the West. The view that the Jews were the enemies of Christ, "the central and cruelest threat of European antisemitism," grew and spread during the twelfth century and spanned the myths of the blood libel and of widespread accusations that the Jews murdered children for ritual purposes (Moore, 1987, 32).[8]

The latent antisemitism that pervaded medieval society should not overshadow the fact that for centuries Jews and Christians coexisted. Plenty of evidence suggests that their relationships could be neighborly.[9] Jews lived side-by-side with Christians and were not confined to ghettos until the early modern period. It was only in England that the Jews spoke a different language than the rest of the population.[10]

Antagonism toward Jews, though partly religious in origin, was aggravated over time by the relationship that developed between the state and the

Jews. To understand this relationship, we need to study a key feature of the political economy of the Middle Ages: the prohibition on lending money at interest. This ban on interest played an important role in governing the conditional toleration of Jews.

As attitudes hardened, the situation of Jews in Western Europe became more precarious. Jews were in a different position to heretics. Unlike Waldensians or Spiritual Franciscans, who initially wanted to radically reform the Church, or the Cathars or Lollards, who were its declared enemies, Jews were members of a recognized religion that had the official protection of the Church. Nevertheless, many of the same forces that led to the campaign against heresy were important in explaining the intensification of anti-Jewish sentiment after 1100.[11]

Important factors include the heightened religious tensions of the period after the First Crusade, which saw greater religious intolerance and the rise of both popular and intellectual antisemitism. We have already described the religious reform movement initiated by the Popes of the late eleventh century. The success of the reform movement made individuals cognizant of their identity as Christians. In addition, the romance of the Crusades made them increasingly see this Christian identity as in opposition to "enemies of the faith" such as Muslims or the nearer infidel, the Jews.[12]

Why did attitudes toward Jews became more hostile at the same time that church and state entered into a mutually beneficial alliance? One answer to this question lies in the way secular rulers used Jews as a source of tax revenue. By restricting "sinful" activities such as moneylending, secular rulers pleased Church authorities and bolstered their legitimacy. However, these prohibitions also enabled them to raise large amounts of revenue by granting Jewish communities special privileges to lend, then taxing the resulting monopoly profit away. This political arrangement was self-reinforcing and a key part of the conditional toleration equilibrium.

Of particular importance was the fact that the Jews provided an indirect way of taxing the growing commercial economy. As we saw in Chapter 3, this was a period of economic and demographic expansion. The problem for medieval rulers was that the feudal system of government had evolved in an era of sparse population and low levels of trade in which land was the sole source of income. Feudal rulers rarely collected money in the form of cash; rather they demanded feudal service from their lords and vassals and payments in kind.[13] The commercial revolution, and the new urban economy it called into being, undermined the manorial economy and the conditions that made feudal monarchy a self-supporting political and economic equilibrium. Feudal rulers lacked the capacity to regularly tax their populations. Exploiting Jewish moneylending provided access to an alternative source of revenue: the growing economy.

Chapter 1 introduced the term identity rules to describe laws that discriminated on the basis on an individual's social, religious, or ethnic identity. Jews had higher levels of human capital and highly developed credit and trading networks, giving them a comparative advantage in moneylending to begin with. But medieval monarchs used identity rules to create barriers to entry into the market for loans. These barriers to entry, in turn, allowed those Jews whom the ruler allowed to make loans to reap monopoly profits. The ruler then taxed these profits away. In this way, the state could support itself without investing a great deal in either fiscal or legal capacity. Taxes could be raised without the need for investment in monitoring or enforcement, as the Jews were relatively easy to extort. The simple threat to cease protecting the Jews from the antisemitic society that surrounded them was ample leverage to extort tax revenues from them. It was, in effect, easier to tax vulnerable Jews than to impose more uniform taxes.

Unfortunately, as we will lay out below this conditional toleration equilibrium also reinforced antisemitic attitudes because people came to resent the part played by Jews in the exploitive fiscal system established to tax the new commercial economy. In this sense, the equilibrium was self-reinforcing – monopoly rights led to antisemitism and antisemitism lowered the cost of exploiting the monopoly of Jewish moneylending.

4.1.3 The Usury Prohibition and the Creation of Monopoly Rents

On its face, the prohibition of Christians from engaging in usurious lending can be explained in religious terms.[14] In this section, however, we will see how usury restrictions were exploited for political reasons. They were also part-and-parcel of the state's relationship with Jewish communities. In fact, the usury restriction and the conditional toleration of Jews came to constitute elements in a self-reinforcing political and economic equilibrium.

The Church prohibited all interest above the principal as usury. Charging payment for a loan was usury according to Aristotle and the Church Fathers because it meant taking back more than one originally lent out and hence, according to Peter Lombard (1100–1160), "the illicit usurpation of another's thing" (quoted in Nelson, 1969, 1949, 9).[15] Interest payments were seen as unjust regardless of the purpose of the loan or the circumstances of the borrower or the lender.[16]

Usury was forbidden both *in foro conscientiae* – before the tribunal of conscience – and in the courts. Social penalties complemented and reinforced legal sanctions. The centrality of usury is evident in medieval art and culture. Boccaccio's *The Decameron* gives us insight into the public perception of usurers. As a notary Ser Ciapperello da Prato lies dying in a house in Burgundy, his two hosts, both Florentine usurers, fear what will happen to them if attention is drawn to them.

the folk of these parts, who reprobate our trade as iniquitous and revile it all day long, and would fain rob us, will seize their opportunity, and raise a tumult, and make a raid upon our houses, crying: "a way with these Lombard dogs, whom the Church excludes from her pale;" and will certainly strip us of our goods, and perhaps take our lives also. (Boccaccio, 2005, 1371)

The frescos of Giotto that decorate the Arena Chapel in Padua depict the punishment fated for usurers. Figure 4.1 reproduces a fresco depicting the punishments of hell shows a man handing "a bag of money to a woman, presumably in exchange for sexual favors; the transaction suggests prostitution, which (like sodomy) was specifically associated with usury" (Derbes and Sandona, 2004, 208).[17]

This prohibition raised the cost of capital.[18] Of course the prohibition could be evaded. It applied only to loan contracts and not to partnerships so contractual devices could be used to get around it. There were always Christians, like the two Florentines Boccaccio described, who were willing to violate the prohibition. Nevertheless, the net effect of the prohibition

Figure 4.1 Details showing the punishment of usurers from Giotto's Arena Chapel. Photo Credit: Alinari/ Art Resource, NY.

was to reduce the supply of loans and acted as a tax on liquidity. The usury prohibition created what economists call monopoly "rents."[19]

4.2 Jewish Moneylending

Jews shared the general distaste for lending money at interest. Indeed, Judaism was perhaps the first religion to condemn the practice. But, despite Old Testament disapproval of interest, by the Middle Ages, the words of Deuteronomy 21 that "Unto a foreigner thou mayest lend upon interest; but unto thy brother thou shalt not lend upon interest," were interpreted so as to allow Jews to lend money at interest to Christians and for Christians to lend at interest to Jews while forbidding usury within religious communities.

In the eleventh and twelfth centuries both Christians and Jews worked as moneylenders and Jews worked in a variety of occupations aside from moneylending. But the usury prohibition became enforced more strictly after 1200.[20] The sanctions for manifest usury increased so that after the Third Lateran Council of 1179, usurers could be threatened with excommunication, and the numerous methods previously used to evade the usury ban were themselves prohibited. These included the outlawing of loan instruments such as sea loans and mortgages.

After 1207, the Church could prosecute usurers in the absence of a plaintiff. This innovation introduced an element of uncertainty into all relationships involving credit, as these were all potentially usurious. Previously, usury became a matter for the courts only if a displeased borrower sought to gain restitution from a lender. This enabled borrowers and lenders to collude using devices that disguised the interest. After 1207, it became possible for third parties to initiate proceedings against lenders suspected of charging interest.[21]

The Church's campaign against usury culminated in 1311–12 at the Council of Vienne, when usury was equated with heresy and sexual perversion. Rulers who tolerated, or profited from the practice were threatened with excommunication and the inquisition was given the authority to investigate usury. Those who associated with usurers, including their wives and children, their business associates, lawyers, and notaries, were also implicated.[22] As a consequence of the intensification of the usury prohibition, Christian moneylending decreased and Jewish moneylending grew in prominence.[23] And with the growth of the commercial economy, all members of society came into contact with and became increasingly reliant on credit and Jewish moneylenders.[24]

The Church's attitude toward Jewish moneylending was complex. Usury was condemned universally but canon law applied only to Christians and not to Jews.[25] The debate was between the "certain purists among the prelates demanded that reality confirm strictly to this theory" and the practice of many popes who condoned Jewish lending so long as the interest charged was not immoderate (Stow, 1981, 161).[26] But regardless of the Church's position, secular rulers protected and supported Jewish moneylending. This relationship was the foundation of the precarious conditional tolerance that characterized the experience of Jews throughout the Middle Ages.

4.2.1 The Fiscal Compact

Medieval rulers lacked the ability to raise substantial tax revenues. They were supposed to live on the returns from their private estates. Taxes could be raised only with the consent of the nobility. Usually they were imposed to meet immediate crises. In England, for example, taxes were raised to pay off Viking invaders, to meet the expense of a crusade, or to ransom a king. If they wished to obtain more money they had to tax resident aliens such as the Jews.

Given the lack of fiscal and legal capacity in medieval Europe, Jews offered an important source of revenues for the ruler. The taxation of Jews was justified by the theory that they were serfs of the king because they submitted themselves to him in return for his protection.[27] In France, this implicit agreement was first stated in 1198, when the Jews were readmitted into the Royal Domain by Philip Augustus (Moore, 2008, 41). In Germany, Rudolph I in 1286 stated that Jews who left the Reich were to have their possessions confiscated because they were his serfs and the property that they acquired through moneylending belonged to him.

Such intellectual justification accorded with political and economic realities. Over time, the Jews were becoming an important source of taxation for medieval rulers as they enabled the government to indirectly tax the growing trade-based commercial economy – a factor of growing importance as the traditional revenue streams that they enjoyed from their crown lands and exercising their feudal rights declined.

Medieval kings came to see Jews as belonging to their private estate: their income was regarded as the king's own private income and this doctrine increasingly became a self-fulfilling prophecy. The rulers of Christian Europe set the Jews to work for them as moneylenders, employing them as "fiscal sponges" to use a contemporary metaphor: "No sooner did they suck up the money [from the population through their usury], than the overlords proceeded to squeeze it out of them into their own pockets" (Baron, 1967, 199).

This fiscal compact between Jews and rulers also reinforced the latent antisemitism that was already present in medieval Europe. Among borrowers, the stereotype of the usurious Jewish lender emerged.[28] This contained a kernel of truth as the rates of interest charged by Jewish lenders typically reflected the market power they often possessed because of the restrictions placed on moneylending. But it missed the fact that these monopoly profits typically found their way into the coffers of kings and city authorities. If anything, the growth of antisemitism served the interests of rulers. As both popular and elite antisemitic sentiment rose, Jews became more and more dependent on the protection offered by rulers, and this made extracting the monopoly rents easier. All a ruler had to do was threaten to release antisemitic agitation upon the unprotected Jewish community in order to extort more funds. At the same time, as Jews became more specialized as moneylenders, rulers became more interested in extracting as much as possible from their Jewish subjects. This was a vicious circle, as it intensified popular antagonism toward the Jews. As we will see in the next chapter, however, rulers often did not follow through with their promises to protect "their" Jews.

We now focus on how this ill-fated political bargain developed in England to illustrate the fiscal compact. Conditional toleration meant that the Jews were protected when it suited the ruler to protect them but left them exposed when a ruler needed money quickly or was too weak to protect the Jewish community from the animosity of debtors or religious bigots.

4.3 The Path to Expulsion in England

The first Jewish communities in medieval England, established following the Norman Conquest, were small and retained close ties to communities in Rouen and Flanders. Over time Jewish traders and merchants spread out across the country.[29] In the 1160s, Henry II dismissed moneylenders from regional mints as part of a policy of centralizing the coinage and he expropriated the leading Christian moneylender, William Cade.[30] Thereafter England's Jews became increasing involved in the trade (Streit, 1993). Table 4.1 documents this fateful chronology.

Reliance on Jewish moneylending was widespread. Evidence from the Norwich court rolls indicates that all members of society borrowed from Jews (Lipman, 1967). The most prominent borrowers were the lesser nobility.[31] The only major group in society that did not rely on Jewish moneylenders were the peasantry, who had informal systems of credit (see Briggs and Koyama, 2014).

Jewish moneylenders in England became very rich. Aaron of Lincoln, the wealthiest of all of them, left approximately £100, 000 on his death in 1186

Table 4.1 *Brief chronology of England's Jewish community*

Year	Events
1066	Jews begin to settle in England following Norman conquest.
1186	Death of Aaron of Lincoln. His estate is expropriated by Henry II.
1190	Massacre of the Jewish community in York.
1194	Establishment of the Exchequer of the Jewry by Richard I.
1211	King John assesses a tallage of £44,000.
1215	Magna Carta attempts to limit Jewish moneylending.
1240	Henry III begins to exploit Jewish moneylending on a large scale.
1241	Census of the wealth of the entire Jewish community conducted.
1244	A tallage of £40,000 assessed.
1258	Provisions of Oxford attempts to limit Henry III's authority.
1263–67	Second Baron's War. Jews massacred and debt registries destroyed.
1268, 1270, 1274	Parliament petitions for a ban on Jewish lending.
1275	Edward I phases out Jewish moneylending.
1290	Jews expelled from England.

(Jacobs, 1898).[32] But the position of Jewish lenders was highly uncertain. On Aaron's death, Henry II seized his entire estate.[33]

In 1189, the coronation of the new monarch Richard I (1189–1199) was accompanied by a massacre of thirty Jews in London by a mob convinced that Jews were casting the evil eye on the king. Other massacres followed. The Jews of York suffered the most horrifying fate when a group of noble debtors incited townsfolk against their Jewish creditors. Many members of the community took their own lives rather than perish at the hands of the mob.[34] Even in a comparatively well governed kingdom such as England, Jews were always vulnerable.

King Richard reacted angrily to the killings. In the account given by William of Newburgh: "He [Richard] is indignant and in a rage, both for the insult to his royal majesty and for the great loss to the treasury, for to the treasury belonged whatever the Jews, who are known to be the royal usurers, seem to possess in the way of goods" (quoted in Schechter, 1913, 129). The massacre was an affront to royal authority and represented a loss of royal revenue.[35]

4.3.1 The Exchequer of the Jewry

In the wake of these pogroms, the royal government imposed measures intended to prevent another such incident. In 1194 the Ordinance of the Jewry formalized royal authority over all Jewish moneylending. The Exchequer of the Jewry became a repository for all Jewish debts. It was a bridge between the Jewish community and the king. All Jewish moneylenders were protected by officers of the king; their debts were recorded in a system of registries. Jews were required to declare in writing before Christian witnesses all debts owed to them as well as how much property they owned. Unrecorded transactions were illegal, and the chirographs recording each loan, known as the *starrs* from the Hebrew word *shtar*, meaning "contract," were kept in a special chest, the *archae cyrographorum*, whose keys were entrusted to two Christians and two Jews.

The main business of the Exchequer of the Jewry was regulating and reclaiming loans. By limiting the number of lenders and by preventing them from competing with one another (by controlling where Jews could settle) the Exchequer enabled the king to maximize revenue from indirectly taxing credit markets (Brown and McCartney, 2005, 312).[36] Every major town contained a chest of Jewish debts, and Jews were confined to towns in which there were chirograph chests, unless they had special permission to live elsewhere. The chirograph chests meant that the king's officers knew exactly how much debt was owed to Jewish lenders and thus made the task of protecting Jewish lenders from indebted borrowers and enforcing debt contracts easier. Because every debt was recorded, taxing the profits of usury was "dreadfully simple" (Stow, 1992, 218). These measures gave the king control over all Jewish moneylending in the country. The king became "a sleeping partner of Jewish usury" (Cramer, 1940, 327).[37]

The Exchequer of the Jewry was a significant source of Royal revenue during the reigns of four kings of England: Richard I, John (1199–1216), Henry III (1216–1274), and Edward I (1274–1307). The most important tax on the Jews was the tallage – a feudal tax a lord could levy on his dependents at a time of his choosing but that had largely disappeared from England by the thirteenth century except for its imposition on the Jewish community. It was a collective levy imposed on the community as a whole. In practice, the bulk of it was paid by a small group of wealthy moneylenders (Stacey, 1985).[38] The tallage was discretionary: if the king needed a lot of revenue quickly, a tallage could be assessed at punitive rates.[39]

The Exchequer of the Jewry thus enabled the king to indirectly profit from Jewish moneylending. Its shortcoming was that both lenders and borrowers were put at risk if the king imposed "too large" a tax on the Jews. This remained a possibility because, although the Exchequer of the Jewry helped to mitigate the commitment problem facing the sovereign, it did not resolve it. If the king was able to limit his tax demands, he was assured of a steady stream of revenue from the Exchequer. But if he extorted as much as possible from the Jewish community, then this would risk not only bankrupting the Jewish population temporarily, but would also damage their ability to earn money in the future by impeding their effectiveness as lenders.

4.3.2 The Breakdown of Conditional Toleration in England

The establishment of the Exchequer of the Jewry was resented by the lesser nobility, who saw it as an indirect form of taxation. This was evident at Runnymede in 1215, where the barons brought King John to agree to Magna Carta. Magna Carta limited the activities of the Exchequer of the Jewry.[40] However, while some of the provisions limiting Jewish lending were accepted by the advisors of the new king Henry III, there was no move to limit fiscal extractions from Jews because "they were unwilling to impair so useful a financial resource, which has been compared to a sponge which slowly absorbed the wealth of the nation to be quickly squeezed dry again by the king" (McKechnie, 1905, 271). Thus the unpopular institution continued.

The royal exploitation of Jewish moneylending resulted in the creation of a secondary market for debt owed to Jewish lenders. Most debts were secured on land.[41] When the king imposed a large tallage on the Jewish community as in the 1240s and 1250s, Jews were forced to sell debts at a discount to whoever could purchase them. These debts were purchased by powerful aristocrats, including the king's brother, who were thus able to accumulate land. As a result, land became consolidated in the hands of a few great lords.[42]

Extraordinarily high taxes of the kind imposed by Henry III undermined the solvency of the entire community. Stacey notes that the "savage financial exploitation forced Jews into a variety of expedients to raise cash" including calling in loans early (Stacey, 1997, 93). Lenders, who in normal circumstances would have accepted deferred repayment, could not do so because that had to raise money for the king. This short-sighted policy damaged the ability of the Jewish community to meet the financial demands of the king and marked the "start of a catastrophic decline in Jewish wealth" (Mundill, 1998, 77).

The exploitation of the trade in Jewish debts was a major grievance behind the Second Baron's War (1264–1267). This civil war saw a baronial faction, demanding a greater role for parliament in government, oppose the party of the king. Massacres of Jews occurred in London, Worcester, and Canterbury (Maddicott, 1994, 315). The *archae cyrographorum* were destroyed. The rebel leader, Simon de Montfort, cancelled debts owed to Jews.[43]

By this point, the high taxes imposed on the Jewish community had reduced the financial potential of the Exchequer of the Jewry. Henry's successor Edward I decided to appease the barons by promising the abolition of the Exchequer in exchange for a tax on the lucrative wool trade. The newly formed Parliament agreed and Edward shed himself of an asset of uncertain and diminishing value in return for a stable and growing source of income.

He prohibited the Exchequer of the Jewry from issuing new loans and even tried to encourage Jews to enter other trades. This experiment was not successful. The comparative advantage and human capital of England's Jews was concentrated in moneylending, while commerce and trade was controlled by guilds, who denied access to outsiders. Edward expropriated and executed a large number of Jews on the accusation of coin-clipping in 1277 and seized much of what was left of their wealth. In the 1280s it was rumored that the Exchequer of the Jewry would be reinstated to raise new revenues for wars in Scotland and France. But in order to credibly demonstrate to Parliament and the nobility that he would not reinstate the Exchequer of the Jewry and because their financial value to him was greatly diminished, Edward resolved on expelling the entire Jewish community in 1290.[44] In return Parliament granted a new tax on wool exports – the largest tax of the Middle Ages.

4.4 Chapter Summary and the Road to Expulsion in France

So much for the Jews of England. We opened this chapter with the expulsion of the Jews from France. We are now in a better position to understand how the Jews of France came to meet this fate.

The French Jewish community was larger, richer, and more established than the English community. By 1100, Jews had been in France for centuries; they spoke the language and formed an important minority in many French cities.[45] Importantly, the Jews of France were not all under the protection of the king. As we saw in Chapter 3, France in the twelfth century was governed by numerous princes and feudal lords. At least fifty barons had the right to control the settlement of Jews and tax them within what is now France. Jurisdictional fragmentation gave Jewish communities some leeway as they could "play one lord off against another in times of crisis" (Jordan, 1998, 3). Lords offered protection for Jewish communities in return for a payment (a *captio*). But if a single lord imposed too high a *captio* on a community that community could offer its economic services to a nearby lord in return for a lower payment.

However, the process of state building in France described in Chapter 3 saw the monarchy establish control over France's Jews. In keeping with the tradition of earlier rulers, Louis VII (1137–1180) supported the Jewish community because of their economic importance. Notably, he defended the Jews of Blois from blood libel charges in the wake of accusations that resulted in the execution of thirty-one Jews (Chazan, 2010, 92). But royal policy changed with his successor, Philip Augustus, who began a policy of systematic fiscal exploitation of the Jews backed up by the threat of expulsion (he expelled Jews from royal territories in 1182 before readmitting them in 1198).

Philip Augustus's policies were continued by his successors. In 1230, the government of Louis IX asserted the king's jurisdiction over whether or not the Jews had a right to settle in any part of his kingdom.[46] The king now had the ability to regulate and tax Jewish moneylending. As in England, the Jews of France came to dwell in towns and to specialize as moneylenders and a system of fiscal exploitation was established.[47] Philip III (1270–1285) drew up documents registering, and promising to protect, Jewish moneylending.[48]

Philip IV (1285–1314), like Edward I in England, switched from a policy of systematic taxation of the Jews to expropriations and expulsions. He seized all their profits "if it could be shown that excessive usury was involved in the contract" (Golb, 1998, 509). This diminished the long-run value of the Jews as a potential fiscal resource and increased the payoffs associated with a one-off expropriation. This policy was trialled in Normandy, where in 1291 Jews were expelled from many small towns. The promise of short-term gain at the expense of a loss in long-run revenue became more attractive as a financial crisis faced the king in the early fourteenth century.

Wars in Flanders and against England intensified the royal need for revenue and brought him to the point where it made sense to expel the Jews from France for good and to expropriate all of their belongings.[49]

Philip IV planned the expropriation carefully. There had been many smaller expulsions previously.[50] But this was a much larger operation – the Jewish community of France was the largest and richest in Europe outside Spain. At conservative estimates there were 100,000 Jews in France (Chazan, 2010, 96). Philip expelled them all, and not just from his own royal lands, but from the lands of all of his barons and lords (Jordan, 1989, 202). Expelling Jews proved lucrative.[51] Jordan estimates that it may have earned the king one million *livre tournois* – 35,000 livres was taken from the Champagne Jews alone – the bulk of it in outstanding debt contracts. The property of the Jews was auctioned off and, though much of it was sold below its value, it brought the king important support among the lower nobility and townsfolk who acquired it on the cheap.[52]

This chapter has illustrated the mechanics of the conditional toleration equilibrium in which Jews were subject to separate laws than Christians and the resulting rents that this differential treatment created were used by monarchs to support their rule without investing in state capacity. However, this equilibrium also put Jews in a precarious position. It reinforced antisemitism and could break down with disastrous consequences. The fate of the Jews indicates that although minority groups could flourish for short periods of time in medieval Europe, in the absence of the generalized rule of law and states capable of enforcing it, they could not form a permanent part of society. Jews were vulnerable to changes in royal policy and to more general economic downturns.

Notes

1. Charlemagne encouraged Jewish settlement and mercantile activity and pursued "a vigorous pro-Jewish policy" (Bachrach, 1977, 83). Shatzmiller notes "In the first stages of the European revival, Jews were more than welcomed into the revitalized Latin West" (Shatzmiller, 2013, 8).

2. "Cluny's foundation charter included mention of a 'Count Aron' among its signatories. It seems that the Duke of Aquitaine's entourage contained a dignitary whose name was of Old Testament origin: Aaron. Such a choice of patronym at the beginning of the tenth century does not indicate whether the bearer was a Christian or a Jew" (Iogna-Prat, 2002, 277).

3. Stow, for example, points out that thirteenth century monarchs perceived their duties and their roles in religious terms. They could not therefore fail to view the Jews, by the same light, as a "perennial threat to the integrity of the *utility communis*" (Stow, 1992, 285).

4. For more on the "hostility and a strong desire to exclude the infidel Jews from the company of Christians" see Cohen (1994, 40). Also see Chazan (1973–1974).

5. See Netanyahu (1995) for an account that traces the origins of antisemitism to ancient Egyptian sources from which it was propagated in the Hellenistic and Roman world.

6. See Arendt (1951, ix–xvi). Nirenberg (2013) uses anti-Judaism to denote attacks on Judaism as a concept whereas antisemitism refers to speech or action against Jews themselves.

7. See Cohen (1957), Moore (1992, 42–43), Stacey (2000, 163–166), and many others). Peter the Venerable's anti-Jewish polemics had a racial as well as a religious component and, in particular, he excluded Jews from the ranks of humanity (see Iogna-Prat, 2002, 320).

8. See Menache (1985, 357).

9. See Shatzmiller (1990) for evidence of distinctly philo-semitic attitudes among at least some of the citizens of Marseilles. Elukin (2007) calls for historians to place more emphasis on peaceful interactions between Jews and Christians in medieval Europe.

10. Yiddish, the main language of Ashkenazi Jewry in the early modern period, emerged later as a dialect of German spoken by Jews. Therefore, by the early modern period "few Jews in any part of Europe had more than such a limited knowledge of the language of a country, namely the language of their gentile neighbors, as might be necessary to conduct commercial transactions with them. Even this rarely extended to the ability to read and write in the vernacular" (Vital, 1999, 21–22). It is important to note that this was not the case in the Middle Ages.

11. See Cohen (1957), Cohn (1975), and Moore (1987).

12. "The Christian population in early modern Europe associated Jews with heresy, with disbelief, and with the devil. Other groups fell under the same verdict – for example, the Anabaptists and those singled out, labeled, and persecuted as witches. The aggressive potential of the Christian majority could be directed

against Jews, Anabaptists, and against those called witches in a similar manner, and the destruction of those various nonconforming groups served to strengthen the self-definition of the Christian majority in a similar way" (Lehmann, 1995, 308–309).

13. See Hoyt (1950), Ganshof (1951), and Mitchell (1951).

14. See de Roover (1967) for an overview of usury restrictions in Western Europe. See Rubin (2009) for an analysis of how the early Church developed its views on usury once it became the residual provider of social insurance in the late Roman empire.

15. It was seen as a form of theft (see Baldwin, 1970; Maloney, 1973; Langholm, 1992).

16. See Melitz: "the whole thrust of the doctrine was to promote usury as a sin independent of the borrower's circumstances and his allocation of credit" (Melitz, 1971, 476).

17. The frescos also allude to usury in the prominent presentation of Judas for "[u]sury was, of course, one manifestation of the sin of Judas" (Czarnecki, 1978, 216).The Arena Chapel was paid for by the *Cavalieri di Beata Santa Maria*, or the jovial friars. The constitution of the Cavalieri was granted by Urban IV in 1261 "it was stipulated that the members pursue two goals: devotion to the Virgin Mary, and suppression of usury" (Rough, 1980, 25). The Paduan chapter had been formed in 1267. To be a member of this order according to the Bull of Urban IV: "No one is to be received in the order who is or is held to have charged any others exorbitantly, who either has gained any other good through usurious wickedness, or through other illicit or unjust means for himself or for others who succeed him by will or interstate, if he does not first make restitution of everything he holds illicitly or unjustly, or offer to the prior general or his bishop, full and satisfactory security or compensate" (quoted in Schlegel, 1998, 1955, 48). Similarly, the 7th circle of Hell in Dante's inferno was reserved for usurers. Paduans, however, were particularly notorious for committing usury (see Hyde, 1966, 40).

18. See Koyama (2010*a*) for a detailed analysis. Also see Rubin (2010) for an analysis of how the bill of exchange functioned as a way around the usury prohibition. Kuran (2006) details how similar restrictions on lending at interest were evaded in the Islamic Middle East.

19. This analysis draws from the classic discussion of Tullock (1967) as well as Ekelund and Tollison (1981) and Ekelund et al. (1996). Also see the discussion in Volckart (2000*b*).

20. See Goff (1979, 28) and the extensive discussion in Koyama (2010*a*). The "people were to be reminded every Sunday that the penalty for usury was excommunication" (Parkes, 1976, 287). Usury "was dealt with in France in councils at Avignon in 1209, Paris in 1212, Montpellier in 1214, Narbonne in 1227, Château Gontier in 1231, Béziers in 1246, Le Mans in 1247, Albi in 1254, and Sens in 1269. From the British Isles canons survive of a Scottish Council of 1225, and of a council at Worcester in 1240; German prelates dealt with it at Trier in 1227 and 1238, and at Vienna in 1267. Though such a list is in no way complete, it is enough to indicate both the seriousness of the effort put forth by the Church and the extent of the practice which she was attempting to suppress" (Parkes, 1976, 283). A recent discussion is Rist (2016).

21. The auricular confession also became mandatory in 1215. This was a powerful form of social control and it enabled the Church to better monitor the behavior of merchants and moneylenders. In the long run, historians have argued that making the confessions obligatory put pressure on the Church to actually liberalize its

attitude to commerce in the long run. Thus Morris writes: "[l]ike purgatory, it was a facility designed for the no-so-good and forced the church to say what was the minimum of acceptable behavior. The entrepreneurial spirit was legitimized from the confessor's chair" (Morris, 1989, 492–493).

22. Decree 29 explicitly states that "since money-lenders frequently conclude loan-contracts in an occult or fraudulent manner, which makes it difficult to convict them on a charge of usury, we decree that they should be forced by ecclesiastical censure to produce their books on such occasions" (Kirschner and Morrison, 1986, 317).

23. As Baron notes, "In one domain, however, the Church actually promoted Jewish economic endeavors. In its unending struggle against Christian usury, it often encouraged Jews to take over that economic function, the indispensability of which, under the expansive economy of the later Middle Ages, even churchmen could not wholly deny" (Baron, 1965, 50). Noonan observed: "Jews, however, not believing themselves bound by the canon law, felt free to enter business, and did so because few Christians would openly compete with them" (Noonan, 1957, 35). See also Roth (1961, 131).

24. See, for example, Richard Emery's study of Jewish moneylending in Perpignan (Emery, 1959). Jews had a comparative advantage as moneylenders because of their high literacy rates and access to wide-ranging commercial networks that connected them to their co-religionists. Indeed, Botticini and Eckstein argue that the different incentives Jews had to acquire skills and develop networks may provide an alternative explanation for the ethnic distribution of moneylending in the Middle Ages (Botticini and Eckstein, 2012). And their role as traders – particularly in the wine industry – led naturally to the provision of financial services such as credit. But it was the tightening of the usury prohibition that can explain the timing of when moneylending became almost exclusively associated with Jews.

25. As Stein notes "even Innocent III ... accepted *de facto*, if not *de jure*, a differentiation between Jew and Christian before the law. Moreover we have no court decisions against against Christians who took interest from Jews" (Stein, 1956, 144). Jews could face sanctions from canon courts. In particular, they could be excommunicated, i.e., which entailed being denied any contact with Christians. On this see Jordan (1986).

26. Baron also notes that "Wherever popes ruled as sovereigns, they, like the other monarchs, often exploited their Jewish tax payers" (Baron, 1965, 44). This is highly consistent with a self-interested interpretation of Church behavior: "On the one hand, Gregory IX in 1237 pacified Louis IX's conscience by declaring the king's subsidy to the Latin Empire of Constantinople for its struggle against the Muslims a sufficient restitution for deriving revenues from usurer. On the other hand, Innocent IV enjoined King Thibaut II of Navarre in 1247 to force Christian debtors to repay 'honest loans' from Jews despite the French baron's oath not to make such repayments" (Baron, 1965, 47–48). Such a self-interested model of Church behavior is developed by Ekelund et al. (1989, 1996).

27. See Baron (1967). In England, according to Henry of Bracton, a leading thirteenth-century jurist, as summarized from *De Legibus et Consuetudinibus Anglia*: "The Jew can have nothing of his own, for whatever he acquires, he acquires not for himself but for the king; for the Jews live not for themselves but for others and so they acquire not for themselves but for others" (quoted in Pollack and Maitland, 1895, 468). Similarly, according to the contemporary *Leges Edwardi Confessoris*,

"the Jews and all that they have are the king's, and should any one detain them or their chattels, the king may demand them as his own" (quoted in Pollack and Maitland, 1895, 468). This "same legal fiction" held that all Jews "were slaves of the king's chamber, his royal treasure, and therefore not to be harmed by anyone except, of course, the king himself" (Nirenberg, 1996, 21). Later writers speculated that the status of the Jews as serfs of the king was the result of the death of Christ (Iogna-Prat, 2002, 283).

28.   The rates of interest charged by Jews were high by modern standards. However, Jewish lenders charged lower rates than did Christian lenders, in part because they had access to a network of co-religionists, which gave them greater ability to smooth economic shocks. Botticini (1997) finds that peasants, smallholders and merchants used Jewish finance to smooth their consumption decisions, provide dowries, and finance larger scale investments. Jews played an important role in providing local capital markets that were not serviced by larger Italian bankers.

29.   Jews were involved in the plate trade. But they were excluded from the profitable wool trade.

30.   In Anglo-Saxon England local elites could hold the office of moneyer from the king and this gave them the right to manage mints and coin money. These moneyers were prominent moneylenders. They were largely suppressed and expropriated by the early Norman kings (see Fleming, 1993). William Cade was the most prominent twelfth-century moneylender. Cade's estate, which was worth some 5,000 pounds, was seized in 1166 (Jenkinson, 1927). Robert Chazan writes that "The overwhelming impression from this wide-ranging evidence is the significance of Jewish moneylending to the general English economy … moneylending was the mainstay of Jewish economic activity, the means by which the Jewish community as a whole maintained its economic viability and won the political support requisite to its survival" (Chazan, 1997, 26).

31.   For example, many of the landowning benefactors of the Hospital of St John the Evangelist in Cambridge owed money to Jews (Rubin, 1987). In 1240, one landowner "granted the hospital 2 acres in Babraham 'to God and the hospital' … for which he received 23s 'to acquit me of the Jewry'" (Rubin, 1987, 219).

32.   In 2014 pounds this is approximately £80 million. In contemporary terms, it made him the second richest individual in the country after the king.

33.   Unfortunately, for Henry II, Aaron's goods and gold were put on a ship to be transported from Lincoln to London and the ship sank at sea, so the entire fortune was lost (Mundill, 2010, 27).

34.   See Mundill (2010, 79–81). The motives for these massacres are difficult to unravel. Some historians see this as a reaction by the barons to "their own financial exploitation at the hands of the Angevin government" (Dobson, 2003, 147). Stow observes that "the town patriciate disassociated itself from the massacre; the initiators were heavily indebted members of the middle and even upper knightly class, motivated by fears of foreclosure" (Stow, 1992, 111). The leader of the mob was the fittingly named Richard Malebisse or Richard the Evil Beast, who was in debt to Jewish lenders (Mundill, 2010, 81).

35.   See McKechnie (1905), Cramer (1940), Brown and McCartney (2005), and Mundill (2010).

36.   The Exchequer was in principle supposed to prevent lenders from charging extortionate interest. The maximum legal interest rate was set to $2d$ per pound per week. This amounted to an annual [noncompounded] rate of 43 1/3 percent. Even a

commentator, as unsympathetic to Anglo-Jewry as the chronicler Matthew Paris, observed that the terms offered by Jewish moneylenders were fairer than those a borrower could obtain from a Christian usurer, for, he noted, "when you return to a Jew the money he has lent you, he will receive it with a good grace, and with only interest commensurate with the time the money has been lent" (quoted in Menache, 1997, 154). It was not in the long-term interest of either the officers of the Exchequer or professional lenders themselves to bankrupt their clientele.

37. See Brand (2003, 74). McKechnie (1905) observed that "[i]f this cunningly-devised system prevented the Christian debtor from evading his obligations, it also placed the Jewish creditor completely at the mercy of the Crown; for the exact wealth of every Jew could be accurately ascertained from a scrutiny of the contents of the *archae*. The king's officials were enabled to judge to a penny how much it was possible to wring from the coffers of the Jews, whose bonds, moreover, could be conveniently attached until they paid the tallage demanded" (McKechnie, 1905, 268).

38. According to the chronicler Matthew Paris, in 1242 the king obtained "four marks of gold and four thousand marks of silver" from Aaron of York (Paris, 1852, 459). This impression is confirmed by Stacey (1985), who found that half of the total tallage was paid by just three individuals.

39. The proceeds of the Jewry could also be pledged to pay for a number of expenses incurred by the king. For example, it is recorded that on 3rd July 1250, the king promised a "[b]ond to Raymond Makeyn, citizen of Bordeaux, to pay him out of the first issues of the Jewry 792 marks for divers debts, to wit, a moiety next Michalemas, and the other moiety the following Easter" (Calendar of the Patent Rolls, preserved in the Public Record Office, Henry III AD. 1247–1258, 1908, 69).

40. See Koyama (2016). Chapter Ten of Magna Carta stated that "[i]f one who has borrowed from the Jews any sum, great or small, die before that loan be repaid, the debt shall not bear interest while the heir is under age, of whomsoever he may hold; and if the debt fall into our hands, we will not take anything except the principal sum contained in the bond" (McKechnie, 1905, 265).

41. In England, Jews were prohibited from owning land (as they were outside of the feudal system and could not fulfill the military obligations incumbent on landowners). Therefore, they sold their rights to secondary investors.

42. For a formal analysis of the effects of the emergence of a market in land on inequality of land holdings see Bekar and Reed (2013).

43. Simon de Montfont (1208–1265) was the son of the Simon de Montfort, who led the Albigensian Crusade and who we encountered in Chapter 3. Between October 1264 and June 1265, de Montfort pardoned 60 men of debts owed to Jews. As Maddicott comments, the object of the policy "was to gain popularity for Montfort's government, at no cost to himself, but at the expense of the Jews and of the king who was the lord of the Jews" (Maddicott, 1994, 316).

44. See Mundill (1998) and Koyama (2010*b*) for a more detailed analysis.

45. In contrast, the Jews of England spoke French rather than English, the language of the nobility.

46. As Jordan (1998) writes, this occurred parallel to the establishment of royal control over the coinage and over the status of runaway serfs.

47. See Nahon (1975) and Jordan (1989). French Royal policy toward Jewish moneylending alternated between condemning and profiting from it. Louis IX attempted, but failed, to legislate against Jewish usury (perhaps for religious

reasons) but his successors continued to see the Jews as a financial resource to be tapped when necessary.

48. See Golb (1998, 508). The protection offered by Philip was sometimes just a sham for fiscal exploitation. In Troyes in 1288 the burning of thirteen Jews by Dominicans was condemned by the king. Nevertheless, "Whatever the reasons behind the king's subsequent change of mind, he did not hesitate to take possession of the property of the executed Jews, rather than turning it over to the Jewish community – or even Troye's gentile community" (Taitz, 1994, 218).

49. Golb notes that the onset of a new war in 1302 intensified the king's need for revenue and that the "seizure of Jewish goods, the detention of the Jews, and their expulsion from France in the summer of 1306 are events manifestly connected with this situation" (Golb, 1998, 536–537).

50. For example, from Brittany in 1240, Gascony in 1288, Anjou and Maine in 1289, Niort in 1291, and Nevers in 1294 (Jordan, 1998, 2).

51. As to why Philip chose to expel rather than just steal from the Jews, we know he was concerned that local officials might either sell off Jewish goods for their own profit or accept bribes from the Jews themselves. He was also concerned the Jews might get wind of what was happening and try to leave with their possessions before the orders for their arrest and expulsion came through and that "the townspeople could discover that the Jews were being expelled and preempt the confiscation, taking for themselves Jewish property and the records that revealed their own indebtedness" (Taitz, 1994, 220–221).

52. Taitz notes that "Since a full two-thirds of Jewish assets consisted of unpaid loans, obtaining these loan records was a significant accomplishment and more than justified the elaborate secrecy with which Philip approached the maneuver. After the expulsion itself and for many years afterward, large amounts of money from these debts were still outstanding in Champagne" (Taitz, 1994, 222). Jordan observes that "the *captio* was an enormously dramatic and dreadful statement of the administrative capacity of the Capetian monarchy. There would be arrears for decades ...Philip IV ...could only be delighted by the extremely large amount of money that entered the royal coffers" (Jordan, 1989, 208–209).

5

Climatic Shocks and Persecutions

Medieval Europe's rent-seeking equilibrium enabled Jews to settle and often to flourish. However, it also left them highly vulnerable to the whims of rulers and to both local elites and commoners who resented their fiscal role. Antisemitic beliefs were deeply rooted in medieval culture, but they manifested themselves most strongly when economic conditions deteriorated. We now describe how these factors combined to bring about a crisis for Jewish communities after 1300.[1]

Already by the end of the thirteenth century the situation of Europe's Jewish communities had deteriorated, but the fourteenth century – a century of plague, warfare, and famine for the entire continent – was nothing short of catastrophic. First, in 1290 England's small Jewish community was expelled wholesale by Edward I. Then, in 1306 Philip IV of France expelled the Jews of France. Though they were invited to resettle a decade later by his son, the unrest that followed the Great Famine of 1315–1321 saw a series of pogroms across the country. Numerous pogroms also took place in the German lands during this period, but these pale in comparison to the Europe-wide persecutions that commenced with the Black Death (1347–1352), which we discuss in Chapter 6.

In this chapter we seek to explain why the conditional toleration equilibrium was particularly fragile in societies whose economies were close to subsistence and where political authority was weak. We test this argument by identifying the impact of economic shocks on the conditional toleration equilibrium using random fluctuations in growing season temperatures across European cities. We then use these temperature fluctuations to probe under what sorts of geographic and institutional constraints the conditional toleration equilibrium was more or less stable.

5.1 The Vulnerability of the Conditional Toleration Equilibrium

Agricultural output in medieval Europe was highly dependent on weather patterns. Farmers did not have access to chemical fertilizers or scientific agronomy. Storage technologies were underdeveloped and transporting grain over long distance expensive.[2] The risk of harvest failure due to climatic fluctuations was very real. In Bruce Campbell's evocative words, nature was a "historical protagonist."[3]

This vulnerability was heightened by the early fourteenth century, as Europe was densely settled by the standards of a preindustrial economy. During the previous two centuries of economic and demographic expansion, forests had been cut down, marshes drained, and marginal land taken into cultivation. With a population of around 80 million, the continent was close to its Malthusian carrying capacity.

The majority of the population lived close to subsistence. Reflecting the relative scarcity of land compared to population, real wages were low and rents high. Greg Clark estimates that in 1300 a farm laborer's wage was enough to purchase three loaves of bread a day while a craftsman might be able to afford six loaves.[4] Furthermore, the political institutions that governed medieval society often made its economic institutions even more vulnerable. Landlords and princes extracted the economic surplus produced by the peasantry, leaving the poorest with a thin margin between starvation and subsistence even in years when the harvest was abundant. Negative shocks could thus generate a crisis of "surplus extraction."[5]

The events of 1306 demonstrate how a relatively strong medieval ruler could decree the expulsion of an entire Jewish community. This opened an "era of crisis" as many smaller-scale expulsions and persecutions convulsed Jewish communities across Western Europe. While chroniclers suggest that there was popular approval for the action of the king, the poor who depended on Jewish lenders for day-to-day loans were said to been harmed as a result of the expulsions. In the wake of the French expulsions of 1305, the poet Geffroi de Paris recorded the following verse:

> All the poor complain
> For the Jews were much milder
> In the conduct of their business
> Then the Christians are now.[6]

In 1315, the new king of France, Louis X, was desperate for money and a much smaller and poorer Jewish community was invited back into his domain to replenish the royal coffers. The king intended to use the Jews to reclaim unpaid loans that the populace had believed were abrogated by the expulsion of the previous decade (Nirenberg, 1996, 48). Unfortunately for both the Jews and the monarchy, their return coincided with a series of disastrous harvests due to unusually cold and wet summers between 1315 and 1321. The resulting famine was followed by an outbreak of a bovine disease that killed 60 percent of livestock in Europe.[7] These economic shocks produced civil unrest across swathes of northern Europe. France was shaken by an uprising known as the Shepherds' Crusade, or the *Pastoureaux*, that challenged royal authority and specifically targeted the Jews.[8]

The *Pastoureaux* targeted Jews because of millennial fantasies about the End of Days or because they were projecting their anger at the Muslim reconquest of the Holy Land onto the nearer infidel.[9] But the *Pastoureaux* were supported in their attacks on the Jews by townspeople and others because of economic hardship and unrest in conjunction with widespread resentment against royal policy and taxation.

The *Pastoureaux* were incited by debtors of the Jews (Barber, 1981*b*, 146). Following their expulsion in 1306, the conditions under which the Jews had been allowed to return to France in 1315 required them to act as fiscal agents for the crown. This reinforced popular antisemitism: the relationship between the Jews and royal exploitation was evident to the shepherds who "recognized that the heavy taxes placed on Jews were a form of indirect taxation on Christians" (Nirenberg, 1996, 48).

Beginning in Normandy and the Paris region, the shepherds attacked royal castles, then they moved south where they persecuted Jews throughout Languedoc and the south. When the *Pastoureaux* attacked Jews and looted their possessions in face of royal attempts to protect them, "they were both attacking a much-resented aspect of administrative kingship and dramatizing the state's inability to protect its agents, the Jews" (Nirenberg, 1996, 50). The *Pastoureaux* were repressed wherever possible: the official documents that have survived "reflect the concern of the authorities for public order and tell a story of punitive military action, fines and confiscations, stressing that the *Pastoureaux* were mortal enemies of both the king and the public weal" (Barber, 1981*b*, 157).

The *Pastoureaux* episode illustrates the fragility of the conditional toleration equilibrium. Under economic stress, constraints tightened and the desire to scapegoat and expropriate increased, and the result was often antisemitic violence. But how general was this relationship between economic hardship and Jewish persecution?

5.2 Temperature Shocks and Jewish Persecutions across Europe

We can first show that economic shocks in general, as proxied by periods of colder growing season temperatures, made the persecutions of Jewish communities more likely. Then we will demonstrate that this relationship was stronger in areas with poorer geographic endowments or that were located within weaker states.

Consider an economy in which colder than usual temperatures lower agricultural output. Lower agricultural output, in turn, means lower incomes and leads to political unrest. This unrest can be driven by either peasants or elites. One possibility is that low incomes cause peasants to rebel simply because they desire relief from the normal obligations they owe local landowners or moneylenders. However, low agricultural output could also cause a crisis of "surplus extraction" if elites exert pressure on traditional fiscal institutions in order to maintain the flow of rents. Jews were often targets – either because they were held to be directly responsible for the misfortune of the population or because they were vulnerable and perceived to possess large amounts of wealth.

Rulers of stronger states can quell such rebellions. But rulers of weak states will be more vulnerable to unrest stemming from either the masses or the elites. Stronger rulers can credibly commit to protecting their Jewish community regardless of the income shocks that they face. Weaker rulers cannot make such a commitment.

Furthermore, rulers of states with less developed fiscal capacity will be more likely to face a fiscal crisis as a result of successive bad harvests, whereas rulers of states with greater fiscal capacity will have more access to alternative sources of revenue and revenue-smoothing technologies. For states with low fiscal capacity, on the other hand, the easily appropriable wealth of the Jewish community will be a more temping target in periods of fiscal distress. As a result, weaker rulers are more likely to expropriate Jewish communities themselves, in anticipation of antisemitic violence or unrest. Hence, we expect the relationship between colder temperatures and Jewish persecution to be stronger in areas governed by weak states.

Consider the Armleder Massacres that occurred in Alsace and Franconia between 1336 and 1339. Arnold von Uissigheim, a knight turned highway robber, instigated this "economically motivated social uprising" that eventually turned against the Jews (Levenson, 2012, 188). He led a group of peasants with leather patches affixed to their arms and became known as Rex, or King, Armleder. Uissigheim was ultimately arrested and executed by Count Gottfried of Hohenlohe. But other individuals took up the cause and the massacres continued across Bavaria and Alsace, destroying more than 100 Jewish communities (Rubin, 2004, 55–57).

Various explanations are proposed for the massacres. One contemporary explained that Uissigheim's brother had been killed by Jews. Others attributed it to resentment against usury. In some areas, antisemitism had been stirred up by prior allegations of host desecration. All are possible

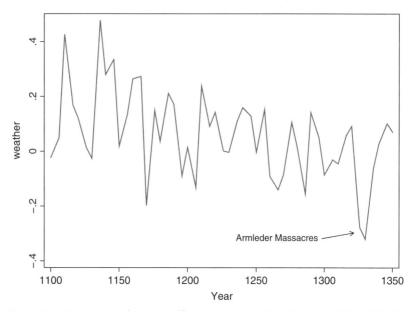

Figure 5.1 Temperature deviations (five-year averages) in Kitzingen 1100–1350. The Armleder pogroms (1336–1338) followed a period of extremely cold temperature in Alsace and Franconia. The *y*-axis measures average temperature deviation from 1961 to 1990 average. Source: Anderson, Johnson, and Koyama (2017).

explanations, however, there is also evidence that economic hardship played a role. Figure 5.1 shows that the Armleder massacres occurred during a particularly cold period. In the town of Kitzingen, which saw its Jewish community massacred during this episode, the average temperature between 1325 and 1335 was more than two standard deviations below the mean for the previous two centuries.

The Armleder Massacres suggest that economic shocks could indeed trigger antisemitic outbursts, especially in areas of weak political authority. To explore this claim, we create a dataset containing yearly average growing season temperatures across Europe.

Identifying causal effects is at the core of modern social science. A claim such as "income shocks cause Jewish persecutions," for example, can be confounded by many other variables. A variable may be correlated, for example, with both income shocks and Jewish persecutions through separate channels. In our case, such variables are easy to come up with. An outbreak of a disease, for example, could easily lower incomes by disturbing trade and agriculture. However, through an entirely different channel, disease epidemics might also lead to the persecution of Jewish communities that were likely to be scapegoated for such disasters. This means that an observed correlation between the income shocks and Jewish persecution may be spurious – it could all be driven by disease.

The point, of course, is not that we are simply worried about disease epidemics biasing our claims. We are worried about *all* the potential confounding third factors, both those that are potentially observable and those that may be *unobservable*. This is where temperature shocks become useful; it is implausible that fluctuations in any potential third factor will be related to temperature fluctuations. Furthermore, while temperatures are definitely not random across geographic locations (it's warmer, on average, in Italy than in Sweden), temperature movements from year to year in a given location have a large random component.[10] Randomness is at the crux of modern empirical social science for precisely the reason outlined earlier – a random variable is unlikely to be correlated with third factors that might lead us astray in making a causal argument. Using temperature shocks as a proxy for income shocks gives us confidence that if we see a relationship between temperature and Jewish persecutions, then this is likely to reflect the causal relationship of economic shocks on the likelihood of a persecution.

Where do we find yearly temperature data for locations across Europe from hundreds of years ago? As accurate thermometers only became widespread in the eighteenth century, we rely on proxies compiled by climate scientists to infer past temperatures. The best proxies are the rings in the wood of very old trees. If you cut a tree down and look at its cross section, there are many concentric rings. There is one ring for every year (or growing season) the tree has lived through. The thicker the ring, the more it grew that year and hence the better was the climate that year for growth. Scientists can calibrate a model using either growing season temperature or rainfall using the rings from modern trees and hence infer temperature or rainfall in the past.

The tree ring data are useful, but one shortcoming is that few trees are old enough to give us information all the way back to the twelfth century. Thus, climatologists complement the tree data with information from pollen. Pollen is everywhere and when it gets trapped in sediment layers, the different kinds of grains can be counted to determine what types of plants were flourishing in different times. Pollen counts are especially useful because they have exhaustive geographic coverage. However, they have a lower time resolution than the information from tree rings.

By combining tree ring data, pollen counts, ice core data, and historical records, climate scientists can estimate temperatures from the past. Our data come from Guiot and Corona (2010), who created a temperature index for Europe going all the way back to 800 AD. They checked the accuracy of their model against events that would have affected world temperature. For example, major volcanic eruptions can significantly lower temperatures across the world due to the particulates they project into the upper atmosphere.

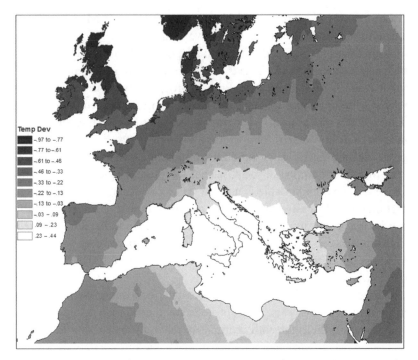

Figure 5.2 Reconstructed growing season temperature deviations in 1300. Darker shading cooler. Source: Anderson, Johnson, and Koyama (2017).

In Figure 5.2 we show what growing season temperatures looked like in 1300. Darker shading represents cooler temperature deviations.[11]

We also collect city-level data on the presence of a Jewish community in Europe between 1100 and 1800 taken from the twenty-six volume *Encyclopedia Judaica* (2007).[12] In Figure 5.3 we map out the number of persecutions in our data for each community to give a sense for where Jews lived and where the most persecutions occurred. A Jewish community was *persecuted* in a given year if either Jews were killed (a pogrom) or they were forced to leave (an expulsion). There are 1,366 such events in our data: 821 expulsions and 545 pogroms.[13]

In addition to being fairly confident that year-on-year fluctuations in city-level temperatures are random, we are also able to control for many other factors using a technique known as difference-in-differences. To illustrate how this works, consider a stylized example. Consider two cities – Frankfurt-am-Main and Bordeaux and assume there are only two time periods, $t - 1$ and t. In the first period, the temperature is normal for both Frankfurt and Bordeaux. However, in the second time period, Frankfurt experiences an extreme cold snap, whereas Bordeaux again enjoys normal temperatures.

Table 5.1 *An example of difference-in-differences*

	Frankfurt-am-Main (%)	Bordeaux (%)	Difference (%)
$t-1$ (normal temp for both cities)	12	5	7
t (cold for Frankfurt, normal for Bordeaux)	25	11	14
Difference	13	6	7

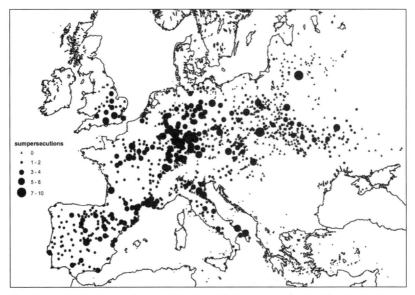

Figure 5.3 Jewish persecutions, 1100–1800. Circles represent a Jewish city that has at least one persecution. Larger circles represent more persecutions. Triangles are Jewish cities in our data that never persecute. Source: Anderson, Johnson, and Koyama (2017).

Table 5.1 gives the probability that a Jewish community is attacked in each city for each period. In Frankfurt in the first period, there is a 12 percent chance that the Jewish population is persecuted. In Bordeaux, there is "only" a 5 percent chance they are persecuted in the first period. In the next period, however, there is colder weather in Frankfurt so the probability of persecution increases to 25 percent in Frankfurt. In Bordeaux, the weather is normal but the probability of persecution also increases to 11 percent.

A naive way to estimate the effect of cold weather on persecution probability would be to compare persecution rates in a place that is cold compared to a place with normal temperatures. In other words, subtract 11 percent from 25 percent, which yields an effect size of 14 percent. However, a little thought makes it clear that this is actually an overestimate. The baseline persecution probabilities given in time t when temperatures were normal for both cities is *already* positive. As such, it would be a mistake to associate all probability of persecution when it's cold just to the temperature.

The true size of the temperature effect in this example is arrived at by taking two sets of differences. First, for each city take the difference in persecution probability between $t - 1$ and t. These values are given in the last row. Second, take the difference in the differences between Frankfurt and Bordeaux by subtracting 6 percent from 13 percent. The result: 7 percent is likely to be closer to the "true" effect of temperature on persecution probability.

Why is it closer to the truth than naive estimates? The reason is because it controls for potentially confounding third factors we discussed earlier. In fact, it controls for both factors we can observe and collect data on and factors that we can never observe directly. To be specific, the difference-in-difference estimate of 7 percent controls for all potential third factors that are either time invariant, or that vary with time in the same way for both cities. Examples of time-invariant factors include local antisemitic culture or proximity to seas, rivers, or Roman roads. Examples of time-varying factors common to each city might be long-term global trends in temperature such as the Little Ice Age.

To see why difference-in-differences controls for time invariant factors, imagine that local culture in Frankfurt is more antisemitic than in Bordeaux. In a period of ordinary temperature, such as period $t - 1$ the Jews of Frankfurt are 7 percent more likely to be persecuted than in Bordeaux. Of course, this culture doesn't go away in the next period. As such, one can think of 7 percentage points of the observed 25 percent persecution probability in Frankfurt in period t as being due to the unique antisemitic culture of the city. However, recall that when we calculated our difference-in-differences estimate we took the difference in persecution probability in Frankfurt between the two periods: 13 percent. This difference drops the unchanging effect of culture from our calculation, so when we compare the two differences for the cities, 13 percent and 6 percent, these numbers only reflect the *change* in persecution probabilities in the two places over time.

Similarly, when we take our second difference ($13\% - 6\% = 7\%$) we drop variation in persecution probability due to factors that change over time, but that affect Frankfurt and Bordeaux similarly. To see this, first note that we can get to our difference-in-differences estimate either by subtracting rows first (as we've been doing so far) or by subtracting the columns first. Imagine that in time period $t - 1$ there are no shared disturbances across cities that affect persecution probabilities. However, in time t imagine there is a disease epidemic which causes both cities to scapegoat their Jewish communities and, thereby, increase persecution probability by 6 percent in both places. When we take the column difference in period *t* (25% − 11%) we are dropping that common 6 percent. Taking the row difference of the two column differences (14% − 7%) then drops the time invariant factors and gives our, by now familiar, difference-in-differences estimate of 7 percent.

Difference-in-differences is a powerful technique to get us closer to causal estimates of effects because it controls for all confounding factors that are either time invariant or that vary over time in a similar way across our units of analysis. We implement this approach in a regression framework. Regression analysis allows us to include other variables such as urban population which might also have affected the probability of a persecution.[14]

5.2.1 The Baseline Relationship between Colder Weather and Persecution Probability

We use difference-in-differences to investigate the effect of temperature shocks on the probability that a Jewish community is persecuted. During colder periods crops failed and this, in turn, put economic pressure on peasants which raised the return they faced to killing or expelling the Jews to whom they either owed money (as loans or taxes) or from whom they wished to expropriate wealth. We focus on five-year average data for temperatures and persecutions so as to minimize measurement errors in the persecutions variable and to focus on extended periods of cold weather.[15] We find that a one degree decrease in average temperature in the five-year period leads to about a 3.2 percentage point increase in persecution probability.

Considering that the baseline probability of a persecution in the data is 2 percent, this effect is substantial. Imagine two Jews living in different cities who both expect to reach an age of 45. If one lives in a time and place with completely average temperature then, according to our results, he or she would have faced a 17 percent chance of being a victim of antisemitic violence in their lifetime.[16] If the other person lived during a colder period of the sample, let's say just one degree colder, then they faced a 38 percent chance of being victimized. The figure of 17 percent is already a high number, and 38 percent is very large, and this is just the estimated effect of an *economic shock* on persecution probability. Many other factors might lead to antisemitic violence.

5.2.2 Persecution Was More Likely in Weak States with Poor Endowments

The conditional toleration equilibrium was vulnerable to negative temperature shocks on average for all the cities between 1100 and 1800. However, our framework makes additional predictions. First, since the theoretical mechanism we outlined earlier works by having the temperature shocks cause crop failures, perhaps it was the case that Jews living in cities with less productive agriculture in the first place would be even more vulnerable to shocks.

One of the great boons to empirical social science research has been the development by the Food and Agricultural Organization of detailed measures of a region's potential for growing various crops. These measures are constructed at a very finely grained level of spatial aggregation.[17] For each of these grids, geologists, meteorologists, and geographers have compiled contemporary data on soil types, drainage patterns, slope characteristics, humidity, rainfall, and other physical geography variables. They then combined these with what agronomists know about what different sorts of crops need. The result is a map, like Figure 5.4, which shows how suitable each grid is for growing a given crop – in this case wheat.[18] These data can provide city-level estimates of how constrained agriculture was in the surrounding countryside.

We extract the data in Figure 5.4 for every city and then run another difference-in-differences regression in which we estimate the coefficient as function of a city's suitability for wheat. Because wheat suitability is scaled so that 1 = most suitable and 7 = least suitable, we expect that the marginal, or incremental, impact of a decrease in temperature should

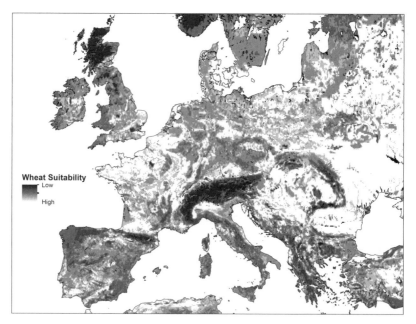

Figure 5.4 Cereal suitability in Europe. Source: Anderson, Johnson, and Koyama (2017).

become more negative as the wheat suitability measure increases (a negative coefficient times a negative temperature shock yields a positive impact on persecution probability). We find that in cities that were well endowed agriculturally (a soil quality measure of about 2) temperature shocks did not lead to pogroms. By contrast, in a city with poor agricultural endowments (a soil quality measure of 6), a one degree decrease in average temperature led to about a 5 percentage point increase in persecution probability, or double the baseline results.[19] This finding, that agricultural constraints exacerbated the impact of supply shocks on the probability of a pogrom, is in keeping with the political economy equilibrium between Jews and rulers we have described. Places that were less able to absorb supply shocks were also more likely to attack their Jewish populations when times were tough.

Another factor that could interact with the temperature shocks was the political environment. As Chazen writes: "governmental weakness or breakdown posed significant danger to the Jews of medieval western Christendom" (Chazan, 2010, 179). Weaker rulers lacked the ability to intercede in order to protect Jews from the violence of either local elites or of the masses. The Armleder massacres, for instance, occurred in a region of weak political authority – the Rhineland.

Measuring the strength of governments in the medieval period is exceedingly difficult. Nonetheless, scholars have generated proxies for historical state capacity. We use one of the best known measures: state antiquity. Bockstette et al. (2002) measure state antiquity by asking how far back can we trace the institutions of present-day countries. For every fifty-year period they assess: (1) was there a government in place above tribal level within the borders of the modern-day country; (2) was the government locally based, foreign based, or in between; and (3) what proportion of the country's modern-day territory was ruled by the historical polity? They create an index number based on these scores for each fifty-year period.[20] While this is nowhere near as subtle a measure of state capacity as we would like, it does capture much of what we associate with high capacity states.

When we perform our difference-in-differences analysis interacting temperature with state antiquity the results are even stronger than when we looked at agricultural constraints. A city located in a weak polity (index between 40 and 50) has a coefficient on temperature between −6.0 and −7.0. High capacity states (index between 0 and 10), on the other hand, have predicted coefficients of around −2.0.

5.3　Chapter Summary: Climate Shocks on the Conditional Toleration Equilibrium

This chapter has examined the effect of negative supply shocks on the vulnerability of Europe's Jewish community to persecution. Periods of colder weather brought with them economic crises during which the risk of persecution was elevated. A one degree decrease in average temperature increased the probability of a Jewish community being persecuted from a baseline of 2 percent every five years to about 5 percent.

Medieval political institutions were simply not robust enough to offer meaningful protection to Jews. The fiscal compact that underlined the condition toleration of Jews in Europe failed at the point at which it was most needed.

Notes

1. This chapter draws on joint work with Robert Warren Anderson (Anderson, Johnson, and Koyama, 2017).
2. Storage technology, or the lack thereof, is discussed by McCloskey and Nash (1984). Estimates of transport costs are provided by Bairoch (1990) and Masschaele (1993). Bairoch (1990) suggests an average cost of transportation by land of between 4 and 5 kg of cereals per km/ton. Water transportation was much cheaper at approximately 0.99 kg per km/ton for river transport.
3. See Campbell (2010). For more on epidemic shocks see McNeil (1974).
4. A farm laborer earned approximately 1.4 pence per day while a craftsman might earn 3 pence per day at a time when a loaf of bread cost $\frac{1}{2}$ a penny. See Clark (2005) for nominal wage estimates. The approximate price of a loaf of bread around 1300 is from Ross (1956).
5. There is a venerable debate about the extent to which the crisis of the fourteenth century was Malthusian as argued by Postan (1966) and Ladurie (1977) or due to a combination of institutional and political factors as argued by Marxist historians such as Brenner (1976) and Bois (1976, 2009).
6. See Benbassa (1999, 21).
7. Campbell describes it as possibly "the single worst subsistence crisis, in terms of relative mortality, in recorded European history" (Campbell, 2010, 7). For details on the so-called Great Bovine Pestilence see Slavin (2012).
8. See Barber (1981a, 12). The French king had promised to go on Crusade and as a result groups of country people known as the *Pastoureaux* began to organize crusading forces. Historians have also argued that the *Pastoureaux* targeted Jews because of millennial fantasies about the End of Days or because they displaced their anger at the Muslim reconquest of the Holy Land onto the nearer infidel. See Cohen (1957) and Shepkaru (2012).
9. See Cohen (1957) and Shepkaru (2012).
10. We say "largely" as there is some evidence of long-run trends, especially during this period, of a Little Ice Age, which reached its minimum during the seventeenth century (Parker, 2013). There is debate regarding the exact timing of this trend and, as we will discuss later, given that the trend is posited to have affected all of Europe, there are things we can do to minimize its impact on our causal interpretation.

11. We use GIS software to create a heat map based on the gridded data provided by Guiot and Corona (2010) based on an inverse distance weighting procedure. We then extract the predicted temperature for the location of each of our Jewish communities, which are represented by the small black circles. We do this for all 700 years between 1100 and 1799.

12. There are 933 cities in our complete dataset. When combined with our temperature data, this results in a dataset that contains an observation for every city in every year between 1100 and 1800. Thus we have 655,200 city×year observations on temperature and Jewish persecutions.

13. We provide further details on our data and empirical specification in Anderson, Johnson, and Koyama (2017).

14. Note that difference-in-differences does not control for third factors that vary with time, but that are unique to the city. For example, if disease epidemics were more likely in colder years and if antisemitism increased during epidemics as well, then disease would be a troublesome, unaccounted for, third factor in our analysis that would lead to bias in our estimates.

15. In Anderson et al. (2017), we also conduct the analysis using yearly data.

16. The calculation is $0.98^9 = 0.83$, where 98% is the probability in any given period there is no persecution and there are nine periods.

17. The data are actually calculated for 0.5 by 0.5 degree grids, the area of which changes slightly with latitude (we provide it for 40 degrees latitude – about the latitude of central France) where it corresponds to 40 km × 40 km grids.

18. The data we use assumes minimal irrigation or fertilizer technology.

19. These estimates are based on the difference-in-differences specification in Anderson et al. (2017, Column 2 of Table 2).

20. We interpolate the value of the index for the years in between each fifty-year observation and then extract these modern-day country-level variables at the city level. We end up with a state antiquity measure that goes from 0 (highest antiquity) to 50 (lowest antiquity).

6

The Shock of the Black Death

On the night of April 12th (Palm Sunday) 1348, townsmen stormed the street where Toulon's Jewish community predominantly resided. They killed forty Jews and pillaged their houses. In this way a long-standing Jewish community was destroyed. This pogrom coincided with the arrival of the Black Death, the most devastating epidemic in European history. It was one of the first pogroms in a wave of violence against Jews between 1348 and 1350. Why were the Jews blamed for the plague? And how was the scapegoating of Jews mediated by political and economic considerations?

The Black Death was an unprecedented demographic and economic shock. Between 1348 and 1353, it killed between 30 and 40 percent of Europe's population.[1] Moreover, it was a catastrophe with huge consequences. Many distinguished scholars view it as a turning point in European history. In the short run, commerce and trade dried up, agricultural land went untilled, prices soared, and disorder spread. In the long run, wages rose, rents fell and, more importantly, the plague brought about an institutional transformation across much of Western Europe.[2]

The plague spread first from Kaffa, a trading port on the Black Sea run by Genoese merchants, to Messina in Sicily. But the story that it was spread by Mongol besiegers catapulting infected bodies into Kaffa is almost certainly false. The disease vector was black rats that likely entered the city through simpler means. These black rats bore fleas infected with bubonic plague.[3]

From Sicily the plague spread to Marseilles and from there it spread to much of Western Europe in 1348. When it arrived in a country, it moved quickly. For instance, it arrived in southern England in June 1348. It reached London by November and northern England in summer 1349. By late 1349, it had also spread across Central and Northern Europe, including the Low Countries, Scandinavia, and Germany.

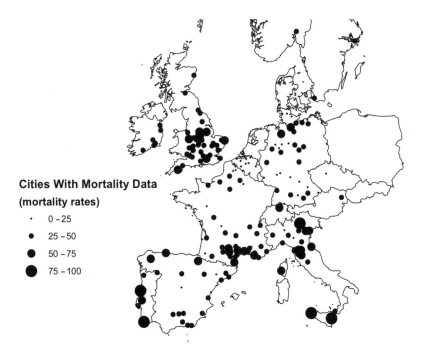

Figure 6.1 Black Death mortality rates (%) in 1347–1352. This map plots the location of all 140 existing cities in 1300 for which we also know the Black Death mortality rate (%) in 1347–1352. The main source for the mortality data is Christakos et al. (2005). See Jebwab et al. (2016) for more details on data sources.

The demographic and economic impact of the plague was tremendous. Rural and urban populations died at similar rates. Medical knowledge was rudimentary and ineffective. And there was no effective policy response to the new disease. Figure 6.1 from Jebwab, Johnson, and Koyama (2016) depicts estimates of Black Death mortality. Cities like Florence saw their populations fall by around 60 percent. But other cities escaped with mortality rates of 15–20 percent. The plague hit the Mediterranean economy hard but it also had a huge impact in England, where average mortality rates may have exceeded 50 percent.[4]

This demographic shock resulted in a scarcity of labor relative to land and capital. Attempts to fix wages by law proved unsuccessful. In the following century, real wages doubled across Europe.[5] As incomes increased, richer peasants demanded manufactured goods that were produced in cities. This raised the rate of urbanization. And new centers of economic activity emerged in the wake of the plague.[6]

The Black Death had important consequences for the religious economies of medieval Europe. The plague itself was widely considered to be an act of God. Religious leaders organized processions to beg forgiveness from God; but they proved unable to prevent or limit the disease. In September 1348, the Bishop of London issued the following letter:

Our most excellent prince and lord, Edward by the grace of God the illustrious King of England and France, after giving serious consideration to these things, accordingly sent letters requesting John Stratford, formerly Archbishop of Canterbury, to have prayers said throughout the province of Canterbury for the peace of the church and of the realm of England, and so that Almighty God, of his ineffable mercy, might save and protect the king's realm of England from these plagues and mortality. But death stopped the archbishop putting the royal requests into practice. We, therefore, wishing, insofar as it pertains to us, to make good what he left unfinished, command and order you, on our authority as metropolitan of the church of Canterbury, to give strict instructions in all haste to every suffragan of our church of Canterbury that they, on our authority, urge and encourage those subject to them (or see that they are urged and encouraged) to intercede with the most high by devout prayers for these things. Bishops and others in priests orders should celebrate masses and should organise, or have organised, sermons at suitable times and places, along with processions every Wednesday and Friday; and should perform other offices of pious propitiation humbly and devoutly, so that God, pacified by their prayers, might snatch the people of England from these tribulations, of his grace show help to them and, of his ineffable pity, preserve human frailty from these plagues and mortality (quoted in Horrox, 1994, 114).

In many quarters the plague was blamed on the sinfulness of mankind. It was seen as heralding the final judgement. In some cases, the shock of the plague inspired renewed religiosity. The year 1350 was declared a Jubilee Year, a year in which pilgrims received a full remission of their sins for going to Rome (Horrox, 1994, 96). But the fact that the plague killed indiscriminately also caused problems for those who sought a religious explanation for the disaster.

In Avignon, the pope saw his moral authority weaken. The clergy died at an even higher rate than the normal population, perhaps because in their pastoral role they tended to the sick or because they shared living quarters. One consequence was that in subsequent years, there was a shortage of trained priests and monks.

As the established Church offered little to those looking for consolation, many sought answers outside the Church. The most dramatic response were the flagellants who marched through towns publicly mortifying themselves in an attempt to ward off the disease. The flagellants began in Austria and Hungary in the autumn of 1348 and spread into Germany, then France and England by the summer of 1349. The principle attraction of this movement was "the redemptive power of their penance viz-à-viz the plague" in a world where the established religious authorities appeared helpless (Aberth, 2010, 2000, 140). The flagellants evoked the suffering of Christ and the mercy of Mary. They cultivated their own saints such as Saint Sebastian and claimed that those who performed the penance could not die from the plague. Fearful of these public and uncontrolled outbursts of religious piety, the authorities clamped down on the flagellants, though the Pope shied away from labeling them heretics.[7]

The plague returned in subsequent decades. That of 1361 was particularly fierce, killing children and adolescents who had no immunity to bubonic plague. Again the clergy were heavily hit; a Canterbury chronicle, noted that many churches were "left unserved and empty through lack of priests" (quoted in Horrox, 1994, 86). In some cases confessions had to be made to lay people or even to women. The disease returned again in 1369, 1374–1379, and 1390–1393. For the next three centuries, bubonic plague was endemic in Europe, though subsequent outbreaks tended to be localized and none had the impact of the Black Death.

The economic collapse that followed the Black Death is even visible in ice cores.[8] In France, these decades coincided with the worst ravages of the Hundred Years' War. After the capture of the French king at the battle of Poitiers in 1356, France descended into anarchy and civil war. The defeat of the royal armies and English raids left the country vulnerable to ravages by mercenary companies who occupied castles, kidnapped notables, raided villages, and choked off trade. Even where local towns were able to fend off bandits and mercenaries, the cost of doing so was often considerable. Towns spent heavily on fortifications and local defenses. Suburbs where traditionally many economic activities had taken place had to be destroyed or abandoned. Grain mills were dismantled and taken within city walls. All of this had the effect of repressing economic recovery (e.g., Sumpton, 1999, 396–400). In affected areas the population continued to decline and economic activity plummeted. In Normandy, population fell by more than 50 percent between 1347 and 1374. Much of this was caused by the plague, but at least 20 percent of the fall occurred after 1357 and was partly driven by the effects of war and political disorder (Bois, 1976, 2009).

In the immediate wake of the plague came social disorder. In Florence, Boccaccio wrote about the sexual excess and immorality that accompanied the plague, as people rejected existing norms about sexual propriety during the initial plague years (Boccaccio, 2005, 1371). Contemporaries decried laborers who demanded higher wages or refused to provide servile dues to their lords. The Black Death disrupted trade. Institutions such as guilds, which required the discipline of repeated dealings to sustain cooperation, ceased to function properly.

Nevertheless, society gradually rebuilt itself. Trade recovered; the survivors had more land and capital per person and thus enjoyed higher incomes; urbanization actually increased; and the revival of commerce was accompanied by changes in the religious economies of Europe. Richardson and McBride (2009) document how traditional craft guilds were replaced by chantries and new guilds that combined religious services with their traditional functions. By incorporating religious services, including prayers for individuals while they were in purgatory, craft guilds were able to sustain cooperation in the face of a massive mortality shock and a world in which death rates from disease were permanently higher.

6.1 The Black Death Pogroms

The Black Death was accompanied by a wave of antisemitic violence (Cohn, 2007; Voigtländer and Voth, 2012). These pogroms were the worst in premodern European history. A recent account describes these massacres as "precursor(s) of the Holocaust" (Goldhagen, 2013, 38). While this may be an overstatement, research has shown that they left a legacy of antisemitism that was associated with twentieth century violence against Jews, support for Nazism, deportations, and modern indicators of antisemitism (Voigtländer and Voth, 2012, 2013a).

Almost all Jewish communities in Germany suffered some form of violence between 1348 and 1350. Pogroms also broke out in France, Spain, Switzerland, and Italy. The most horrifying episode was in Strasbourg, where chroniclers claimed about 2,000 Jewish men, women, and children were burnt alive.

Given the role Jews had come to play in medieval society by the fourteenth century, this violence was horrific but not surprising. Previous outbreaks of disease had been blamed on Jews. Well-poisoning accusations had been made in Germany in the 1330s. As we have seen, Jews were convenient scapegoats for social ills. The well poisoning accusations were not unnatural ones. The water supply of many medieval cities often left much to be desired. Contaminated water was a source of many diseases including typhus, though this was not understood until the nineteenth century. And it is likely that Jews often had their own wells separate from those used by Christians.

So the ground was prepared for accusations against the Jews that began to spread in Switzerland and Germany even before the arrival of the plague itself (Ziegler, 1969, 103). Jews were first killed in Toulon in 1348. In Switzerland in early 1349 Jews were put on trial for well poising, beginning in Geneva. They were tortured into confessing and copies of these confessions soon spread across the Holy Roman Empire despite the pope denouncing the rumors as a lie (Nohl, 1924). Massacres of Jews followed. These massacres were often orchestrated by local elites who were either in debt to Jewish lenders, wished to seize Jewish wealth, or saw this as an opportunity to drive out an economically prosperous but unpopular minority (Cohn, 2007).

6.1.1 State Weakness in the Holy Roman Empire

To understand why Jews were particularly vulnerable in the lands of the Holy Roman Empire, we have to revisit the reasons why centralized political authority was so weak in that part of Europe. As we saw in Chapter 3, in the aftermath of the Investiture crisis, the Holy Roman Emperor failed to impose centralized control over his territories. Emperors were repeatedly excommunicated throughout the late eleventh century and twelfth century. And in the thirteenth century, this conflict between the papacy and the emperor intensified. Frederick II (r. 1212–1250) challenged papal power in Italy; but from a German perspective he was an absentee ruler for most of his reign who conceded power and authority to the electors while he focused on maintaining imperial authority in Italy (Abulafia, 1998; Arnold, 2000). The resulting "jurisdictional autarky of the princes" that characterized the Holy Roman Empire was thus a response to the needs of a weakened emperor to maintain some semblance of peace and order, but it had "the inevitable result" of the "territorial particularism of churchmen, lay princes, and interstitial cities which persisted until modern times" (Arnold, 2000, 244).[9]

The legacy of these developments was "the nadir of the medieval *Reich*, viewed as a system of power" by the fourteenth century (Scales, 2005, 177). Despite the nominal overlordship of the emperor, the secular princes, archbishops, and bishops effectively functioned as independent political authorities (Arnold, 1991). Many cities were also able to assert their autonomy. The Hansa cities in the north of Germany particularly flourished, establishing a league of city-states.

The emperor in the period leading up the Black Death, Louis IV of Bavaria (r. 1328–1347) was embroiled in a civil war with rivals backed by the pope. As a result of this breakdown in civil order, the power of the ecclesiastical princes, archbishops, and bishops was at its height.[10] Civil war was ended only by the sudden death of Louis IV, which saw Charles of Luxembourg become Holy Roman Emperor as Charles IV (1347–1378). As the first emperor from a new dynasty and having his power stem in a large part from papal backing, his position was fragile.

The politically fragmented nature of medieval Germany made Germany's Jewish communities particularly vulnerable. Thus, Baron (1965) describes the Jews of Germany as "victims of feudal anarchy." Finley and Koyama (2018) test this claim using data on the persecution of Jews in the Holy Roman Empire between 1348 and 1351. Information on pogrom intensity from the *Germania Judaica* allows them to distinguish between persecutions that resulted in communal expulsion from those involving violence, which could range from a few killings or executions to the extermination of an entire community.[11]

Local rulers in some places tried to protect the Jews, partly because of their financial value. However, in most parts of the Holy Roman Empire these attempts were unsuccessful. In Erfurt, the town council offered the Jews protection, but openly admitted that they could not guarantee it in the event of popular rioting (Ziegler, 1969, 107). Elsewhere, as Cohn (2007) emphasizes, it was city elites who exploited the situation in order to expropriate their Jewish communities. In Brandenburg, where Louis I faced a rebellion, initial attempts to protect Jews from accusations of well-poisoning "broke down under the frenzy of the populace, whose good will the embattled margrave could not afford to lose" and in 1351 Louis allowed Jews to be burnt in Königsberg (Baron, 1965, 211).

6.1.2 Political Fragmentation and Antisemitic Violence

State weakness made the Jews vulnerable during the Black Death. Yet it was not merely the weakness of the Holy Roman Emperor; it was the fact that political authority was fragmented and contested within the empire. The emperor claimed ownership of the empire's Jewish population. But in practice, unlike the kings of England or France, he was unable to make good on his claim and instead the right to tax Jewish moneylending was held by a variety of local princes, independent cities, bishops, and archbishops.

Finley and Koyama (2018) ask: What incentive did a ruler have to protect a Jewish community in the face of such antisemitic violence? A single ruler could internalize the fiscal value of the Jewish community when deciding whether to protect it from violence. Where ownership of the Jews was contested, however, no single authority had an incentive to invest resources in protecting them.

This suggests that in areas with multiple political authorities, Jewish communities were more likely to face intense persecutions. In particular we expect persecutions to be more intense in areas where the authority of the emperor was challenged by that of bishops, archbishops, and the imperial free cities. While the pope denounced the well poisoning libel, many bishops and archbishops used it in order to destroy Jewish communities either to seize their wealth, so as to undermine the authority of the emperor nominally responsible for protecting them, or burnish their credentials as opponents of Jewish usury. Independent cities were also more likely to try to persecute their Jewish communities. Magnus (1997, 18) notes that "the expulsions of the pre-Reformation period had a heavily urban character, guilds often taking the lead against the wishes of territorial lords or the emperor. Imperial free cities were especially hostile to Jews."

Finley and Koyama (2018) measure pogrom intensity on a 0 to 5 scale, where 0 means that the community was spared from the persecutions during this time and 5 means that the entire community was eliminated through large-scale violence.[12] Communities for which records indicate that Jews were killed in large numbers (including several martyred or burnt), but not eliminated, received a value of 4. A community that had a few deaths (but no indication of widespread deaths) received a value of 3. Communities that were expelled received values of 1 or 2. If the Jews returned to expelled communities within 25 years, they earned a value of 1. Communities in which Jews returned later or in which there is no record of Jews returning receive a value of 2.[13]

6.1.3 Fragmentation Increases Pogrom Intensity

Avneri (1968) provides information about whether a town was an imperial free city, in imperial lands, or in the territory of one of the other major houses and if the town was the seat of a bishopric or archbishopric. Finley and Koyama use this information to measure political fragmentation. Figure 6.2a compares the mean intensity score of communities located in imperial free cities with those that are not. Figure 6.2b compares the mean intensity score of communities that are located in archbishoprics with those elsewhere. Figure 6.2c compares the mean persecution intensity score of communities that are located in bishoprics with all other communities. Figure 6.2d compares all communities combined in imperial free cities, bishoprics, and archbishoprics with other communities. There is a visible difference in persecution intensity in those communities where the emperor faced a challenge to his direct authority.

Finley and Koyama (2018) conduct a formal regression analysis where they control for a host of geographical and economic factors that might influence the likelihood of a persecution.[14] They find that the presence of an Imperial Free City is associated with a greater pogrom intensity of just less than one fifth of the range of the intensity measure. This is equivalent to moving from a community suffering "few deaths" to suffering "many deaths."

This pattern of political fragmentation and pogroms continued after the Black Death. As the power of the Holy Roman Emperor waned, Jews across Germany suffered persecution. In 1420–1421, 400 Jews in Styria and Carinthia were executed and the rest of the population expelled. Jews were expelled from other territories in Austria in 1453 and 1455. The Jews of

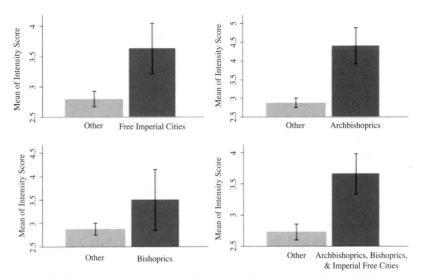

Figure 6.2 Persecution intensity in archbishoprics, bishoprics, and imperial free cities. Top left panel (a) depicts persecution intensity in imperial free cities versus other communities. Top right panel (b) compares persecution intensity in archbishoprics compared to other communities. The bottom left panel (c) compares persecution intensity in bishoprics compared to other communities. The bottom right panel (d) compares communities located in archbishoprics, bishoprics, and imperial free cities in comparison with all other communities. 95% confidence internal. Source: Finley and Koyama (2018).

Augsburg were expelled in 1440, as were those in Saxony in 1498. Over the course of the fifteenth century, Jews were progressively banished from the cities of Bavaria, including Upper Bavaria 1442, Lower Bavaria in 1450, and Eichstädt and Passua in 1477–1478, Nuremberg in 1498, and finally from all Bavaria in 1551. The long-standing Jewish community of Ratisbon (Regensburg) was expelled in 1519, an event that had been preceded by a series of expropriations and fiscal exactions. The Hussite king of Bohemia, George Poděbrad, permitted Jews to settle in Eger in 1462 in return for tax payments. However, within a few years Jews were being forced to pay taxes to the urban authorities and in 1470 the city council decided to expel them against the wishes of the king.[15]

6.2 Black Death Pogroms across Europe

The conditional toleration equilibrium made Jews easy scapegoats. They were more likely to be persecuted during economic downturns as measured by colder temperatures and the biggest shock of the Middle Ages, the Black Death, saw a spike in pogroms and violence against Jews.

However, we also wish to emphasize patterns of antisemitic violence that are not solely explained by the desire to scapegoat. The conventional theory of scapegoating struggles to explain why the Jews (rather than other groups) were such perennial target in premodern Europe. Our analysis can explain this by locating the unique role Jews played within medieval society. In this chapter we have shown that the political fragmentation of the Holy Roman Empire exacerbated the vulnerability of Jewish communities to being scapegoated.

Jedwab, Johnson, and Koyama (2017) looked across Europe to study the impact of the Black Death on the probability of a pogrom. At a macro-level, pogroms were associated with the huge shock of the Black Death. However, looking at a more micro-level, using the city-level data depicted in Figure 6.1, Jedwab et al. (2017) found that the intensity of the Black Death was *inversely* related to the probability of persecution.

Jews were less likely to be persecuted at higher plague mortality rates in cities where they could offer specialized economic services, i.e., where *complementarities* effect was stronger. Conditional on the size of the mortality shock, we find a lower probability of persecution in cities where Jews were offering moneylending services or services to the trading sector.

Jews were more likely to be persecuted where there was a legacy of antisemitism. Conditional on the size of the mortality shock, Jews were more likely to be persecuted in towns where people were antisemitic or inclined to believe antisemitic canards, i.e., where the blood libel was spread or where there was a legacy of past persecutions. Furthermore, they were more likely to be persecuted when the arrival of the plague coincided with the religious festivals of Christmastide and Easter – periods when antisemitism was especially salient.

The finding that Jews were less likely to be persecuted in cities where they could offer specialized economic services sheds light on the other side of the conditional toleration equilibrium. The reliance on identity rules and the absence of the rule of law both made Jews highly vulnerable to persecution while also creating an economic niche for them, which can help explain their resilience in the face of growing antisemitic hostility.

6.3 The Argument Thus Far ... A Summary of Part I

We have outlined a set of relationships between reliance on identity rules, low state capacity, and reliance on religion for political legitimacy. Together, these relationships generated the medieval equilibrium, an equilibrium we have described as one of conditional tolerance.

This equilibrium lasted for many centuries. But changes over time can be detected. Religion became more important in enforcing adherence to the political order with the rise of more powerful states after 1100. This increase in state power and in the religious claims made by the Church helped to produce the "war on heresy," a war that spawned the Albigensian Crusade, the Papal Inquisition, and the establishment of an infrastructure to police religious belief across Europe (Chapter 3).

To understand the nature of this conditional toleration equilibrium we focused on the experience of Europe's Jewish communities. Jews were a tiny minority of Europe's population, but they lived across the continent and played an important role in the medieval economy as traders, merchants, doctors, and moneylenders. Church policy gave them a place in European society, albeit as a maligned remanent subject to discrimination.

Chapters 4 and 5 described how the situation of Europe's Jews became more precarious over time. The tightening of the prohibition on usury played a crucial role in these developments. Rulers used Jewish moneylending as a source of indirect taxation, obliging Jews to act as their fiscal agents in return for physical protection: fiscal faucets who could be turned on when needed. This arrangement was sustainable in normal times but broke down under stress, as we documented.

As urbanization and economic growth produced more complex economic and political organizations, religious change also took place. Tremendous resources were spent on erecting the great Gothic cathedrals of Europe. Mendicant orders proliferated and the Church, for the first time, was able to enforce many of its strictures through the establishment of religious courts. The great works of scholasticism were written in these centuries. Looking back from the late nineteenth and early twentieth centuries, traditional Catholic historians saw the thirteenth century as the high point of European Christian civilization. However, the economic and social equilibrium underling medieval society was always fragile and it was already coming under pressure by the early fourteenth century. It was swept away by the Black Death.

The Black Death pogroms all but destroyed Europe's remaining Jewish communities outside Spain and Italy. The epidemic weakened the Catholic Church and helped spawn heretical movements like the Lollards and Hussites, and which prefigured the Protestant Reformation. Among religious thinkers, the Black Death induced a movement toward inward reflection, evident in the writings of Catherine of Siena (1347–1430) and Nicholas of Cusa (1401–1464). Following the plague, the Church placed even greater emphasis on the importance of purgatory and the possibility of buying indulgences in order to hasten one's way into heaven. The spiritual authority of the papacy sank to a new low. Relocated to Avignon early in the fourteenth century to avoid the turmoil of Rome, the papacy came under the dominion of the French monarchy. An attempt to return the papacy to Rome in 1378 prompted the Great Schism (1378–1417), which saw pope battle anti-pope. The shocks papal authority received helped spur the rise of movements critical of the Church led by intellectuals such as John Wycliffe. In the next chapters we will see how the process of state-building interacted with religious change to put new pressure on the conditional toleration equilibrium.

Notes

1. See Benedictow (2005); Campbell (2016); Jebwab, Johnson, and Koyama (2016). Conventionally the death rate was estimated at one-third of the population. More recent studies suggest that the overall death rate was considerably higher than this. Benedictow (2005) argues for a mortality rate as high as 60 percent. This higher estimate, though controversial, has not been rejected by other scholars. "Benedictow's mortality estimates may eventually come to be regarded as the standard, in spite of readers' doubts that the remarkably similar die-off across regions is due in part to rejecting data indicating lower figures through source criticism. The estimates are internally consistent with his assessments of plague case-fatality (circa 80 percent, p. 350) and prevalence. If plague lethality is over 50 percent in modern populations, then 80 percent is not implausible for medieval times, considering the nutritional stresses of the fourteenth century" (Noymer, 2007, 624). Recent research by Lewis (2016) confirms a high estimate for plague mortality in England.
2. See discussion in Haddock and Kiesling (2002) and Acemoglu and Robinson (2012).
3. Since the late nineteenth century, the consensus view among scholars has been that the Black Death was bubonic plague. Revisionists cast doubt on this assessment. But the traditionalist view has been confirmed by recent research based on extracted DNA from plague pits and the identification of the bacterium *Yersinia pestis*. This is the same bacterium responsible for bubonic plague, a disease studied intensively in the late nineteenth century in China and India. The bubonic plague was spread by fleas that usually lived on black rats. When infected fleas bit humans, death from bubonic plague occurred in 70 percent of cases within 7 to 10 days.
4. See Benedictow (2005) and Theilmann and Cate (2007).
5. In Western Europe, attempts to repress rising real wages led to peasant rebellions and urban revolts. In the long run, however, conditions for laborers improved, and serfdom went into terminal decline. In Eastern Europe serfdom remained in place.
6. See Dyer (2005), Voigtländer and Voth (2013*b*), and Jebwab et al. (2016).
7. See Horrox (1994, 97) and Aberth (2010, 2000, 143).
8. More et al. (2017) find that the lowest levels of lead pollution occurred in the period just after the plague, indicating a major contraction in mining activity.
9. Frederick II established a centralized state administration in Sicily but in Germany he left a legacy of decentralized and contested authority. Arnold discounts the possibility of Frederick reversing this situation and imposing centralized control in Germany because "[t]he German magnates were so well equipped with economic, jurisdictional, and military resources and opportunities, all of which were phenomenally expanded during the twelfth and thirteenth centuries" (Arnold, 2000, 243).

10. "The long arm of the universal Church reached into corners of German society seldom or never touched by the institutions of imperial rule, reminding their denizens that they too were subject to a temporal, as well as a spiritual, head – and that this subjection could have consequences" (Scales, 2005, 178).

11. Finley and Koyama do this rather than measuring the mere existence of a pogrom, as very few Jewish communities were entirely spared during the Black Death period (Toch, 1997, 70).

12. Further details are available in Finley and Koyama (2018). To code these data, Theresa Finely read every entry of the *Germania Judaica*.

13. This coding is ordinal and not cardinal. A level 4 persecution was more intense than a level 2 persecution but it was not necessarily twice as intense. Persecutions can also be coded as either not involving fatalities (1–2) or involving fatal violence (3–5); the results are not sensitive to different ways of coding the data.

14. These include wheat suitability; ruggedness; where a city is on a navigable river; urban density; proximity to a medieval trade route or to major economic centers where grain, linen, and wine were grown and the actual spread of the Black Death itself.

15. See Baron (1965, 198–199, 204, 209, and 233–234).

PART II

THE ORIGINS OF RELIGIOUS FREEDOM

7

State Building and the Reformation

The Reformation was a turning point in history. Many scholars have argued that it played a crucial role stimulating economic growth, liberal ideas, and institutional change.[1] However, assessing these claims is challenging because identifying the effects of the Reformation is extremely difficult.

The schism between Reformed and Catholic Christianity coincided with so many other developments that clear chains of causation are difficult to pick out. Many important events occurred between the invention of the printing press circa 1450 and 1648 when the Thirty Years' War ended. Stronger and more centralized political units emerged in France, Spain, the Netherlands, and England. The New World was discovered, and colonial empires were established.[2]

We describe how, in conjunction with the rise of more powerful and centralized states in Western Europe, the Reformation undermined the equilibrium of conditional toleration that we outlined in Part 1. By significantly increasing religious diversity across Europe, the Reformation placed pressure on existing systems of conditional toleration. Keeping Jewish communities confined to ghettos was something an early modern city could manage, but separating Catholics from Protestants would often prove too much. The larger the polity in question – and the more involved the government was in people's lives – the more severe the problem of heterogeneity became. When the pressure was too great, civil conflict, always a possibility, became a terrible reality. The years following Martin Luther's declaration of independence from Rome saw some of the most savage acts of religious violence Europe had ever experienced. Violence and unrest instigated political reform; however, many rulers decided to abandon the use of identity rules and religion to legitimate rule, relying instead on more secular institutions that were founded on more general rules.

The states that emerged out of the inferno of persecution and violence of the sixteenth century differed fundamentally from their medieval predecessors, and these differences would have important consequences for economic development and the rise of liberalism. In the Dutch Republic, Great Britain, and to a lesser extent, France, the enforcement of strict religious conformity ceased to be viable by the eighteenth century. All three of these polities were relatively powerful and centralized, qualitatively different from their medieval predecessors even if to modern eyes they appear to have been riddled with cronyism and corruption. All of these societies saw fierce religious persecution in the decades after 1517. In the long run, however, they all came to rely less on religion to legitimate rule. Instead, first in the Netherlands and then in England, rulers moved toward greater toleration for Jews and Protestant dissenters. France followed a similar path, though there were setbacks when Protestants were subject to renewed persecution at the end of the seventeenth century.[3] Parallel processes occurred in both Prussia and Austria after 1700. These developments were gradual, but by 1850 the conditional toleration equilibrium had been largely dismantled in northwestern Europe and a new model based on the idea of religious freedom had come to replace it.

7.1 The Reformation

The church–state partnership described in Chapter II involved the persecution of religious dissenters. Secular rulers used coercion to enforce religious conformity in return for religious legitimacy from the Church. This relationship was an equilibrium in the sense that it generated economic and social outcomes that reinforced the existing set of institutions. New heresies and religious movements could, and did, emerge, and depending on their doctrines and stances, some were successful in gaining the recognition of the church. However, most were suppressed by both church and state authorities unless exceptional circumstances gave the dissidents secular protection.[4] But even in these rare cases, local heresies did not seriously destabilize medieval Catholicism. Even the schism between pope and antipope that occurred in the late fourteenth century did not disrupt the doctrinal unity that medieval Europe exhibited.

Unity should not be confused with homogeneity. Uniformity of religious practice was impossible in medieval conditions. Rather, there was a tremendous amount of local variation and diversity.[5] This variety was a reflection of the decentralized nature of all authority in medieval Europe. Despite the wide variety of religious practices at the local level, however, belief in a unitary church was unchallenged. This commitment to doctrinal unity helped to maintain belief in the truth of Church doctrine: a single orthodox Catholicism that alone could convey religious legitimacy on rulers. The Reformation shattered this unity.

Many scholars have viewed the Reformation as a response to the corruption of the Catholic Church (Chadwick, 1990). Humanist scholars who stayed within Catholicism were fierce critics of clerical abuses and corruption and initially sympathized with Luther. Reginald Pole – the last English Cardinal and later a persecutor of Protestants – blamed the behavior of the Church and its bishops for the schism. Quoting Luke's warning in the Bible that "The Lord's Apostles are the salt of Earth" he admonished the clergy for having "lost its savor" (see Parker, 1968, 45). After all, the direct trigger for Luther's 95 Theses was the sale of plenary indulgences by Johann Tetzel to rebuild St. Peter's in Rome.[6]

History is full of chance events. Nevertheless, even in a world full of shocks, we can talk about the balance of probability. One can imagine a world in which the leadership of the Church was less corrupt. Similarly, we can envision a papacy in which the conciliatory views of a Reginald Pole or even an Erasmus held sway. In either case, perhaps the Catholic Church could have held together for several more decades or longer. In this sense, there was nothing inevitable about the Reformation. In the counterfactual novel, *The Alteration*, Kingsley Amis imagined that the Reformation could have been stopped and Catholic unity restored had Martin Luther been made pope. After all, Luther saw himself as a Catholic Reformer rather than a Protestant, a term he never used. Nevertheless, if the precise events that set off the Reformation in the late 1510s and early 1520s were contingent, this does not diminish the chance that a subsequent controversy may have sparked a similar event. Urbanization, economic development, and tensions between secular and religious authorities all made some kind of crisis for the Church highly likely.

When that crisis did occur, the new technology of printing would have enabled religious entrants to challenge the Church. Wherever printing was adopted, it had an important impact in disseminating new ideas and allowed religious dissidents to form new and cohesive religious identities. Previous schisms had occurred within the medieval church and, as we have seen, heretical movements such as the Lollards espoused similar views to Martin Luther, Huldrych Zwingli, and Jean Calvin, but it was the printing press that enabled Luther's critiques of the Church to be disseminated at low cost throughout Germany.[7] Once this occurred, despite the impression of some who still hoped for reconciliation, the unity of the Catholic world was rendered asunder.[8]

By undermining the main source of religious legitimacy, the Reformation posed a challenge to the political economy of early modern states. Since the authority of secular rulers stemmed from their alliance with the church, rooting out heretics was incumbent upon them: "Once church authorities defined dissidents as heretics, the king who failed to proceed against them risked compromising the legitimacy of his rule. He opened himself up to the accusation of willfully permitting a corruption of the social body for which all of his subjects must pay the price" (Dienfendorf, 1998, 2). Political revolution thus threatened to follow religious reformation.[9]

7.2 State Building

There was an important difference between the Magisterial Reformation of Luther and Philipp Melanchthon (1497–1560), which was an alliance between the Protestant reformers and the princes and electors of the empire who sought to throw off the yoke of Rome, and the Radical Reformation.

In Germany, religious reform was initially successful because it was seized upon by secular rulers as an excuse to expropriate the Church. The secular princes protected Luther from the Pope and the Holy Roman Emperor Charles V. After his celebrated confrontation with the representatives of the papacy and the emperor himself at the Diet of Worms in 1521, Luther was spirited off by Frederick III of Saxony and secluded in the Castle of Wartburg for his own protection.

Many of those inspired by Luther, like Thomas Müntzer, were willing to go much further in attempting to return to what they saw as the original message of Christ. To their opponents they were heretical Anabaptists, as they denied the trinity and insisted on adult baptism.[10]

This Radical Reformation soon became linked with the demands of peasants against the fiscal and feudal impositions made by secular rulers. Opposing both Catholicism and the feudal system, the Anabaptists connected reformation of a corrupt Church with reform of a corrupt world. By returning to the apocalyptic message of early Christianity, the Anabaptists threatened the power of religious authorities to legitimate political authority.

The resulting Peasants' War in Germany was a bloodbath. Hundreds of thousands are thought to have died in central and southern Germany alone. The forces of radical reform were soon crushed by the organized militaries of the German states, both Protestant and Catholic. The Peasants' War was a warning to other political leaders considering whether to support the Reformation. Thereafter, rulers in England, Denmark, Sweden, and Germany ensured that the process of church reform was tightly controlled by the political authorities.

As these events make clear, the Reformation was not solely a religious event – it could hardly be limited to the sphere of religion as there was no distinction between secular politics and religion in this period. The Reformation had important ramifications for the political structures of Europe. In particular, it had consequences for the project of state building that was being undertaken concurrently by European rulers.

A particularly important driver of state building was gunpowder. Until the end of the fifteenth century, cannon were difficult to move, with larger pieces often cast at the site of a siege. But in their invasion of Italy in 1494, the French brought a mobile artillery train that enabled them to rapidly move through the country reducing to rubble previously impregnable fortifications. Contemporaries like Machiavelli saw this invasion as a catastrophe for the Italian city-states. It made centuries of investments in protective walls obsolete and necessitated investments in new types of defenses capable of withstanding artillery.[11] The response was a form of fortification known as the *trace italienne* – star shaped fortifications – that were designed to withstand artillery fire. Yet these were extremely expensive to construct and beyond the means of many smaller polities.

Gunpowder weapons had a further effect on early modern armies. Warfare in the middle ages relied on skilled labor. Almost without exception, highly trained, mounted men-at-arms defeated untrained peasants. Trained mounted men lost only when they faced equally highly trained opponents – English longbow men or Swiss pikemen – or fought in extremely adverse terrain or conditions. Skilled labor, however, was costly. The English armies that dominated the battlefields of France in the Hundred Years' War were small because their backbone was comprised of longbow men, who had practiced from childhood to use their weapons effectively. The Swiss pike squares required tremendous discipline, and were the unique product of the egalitarian social cohesion that characterized the Alpine communities of Switzerland.

In contrast, gunpowder weapons could be used with little training. States that could afford to equip large numbers of men with the new weapons could field much larger armies than before. The gunpowder revolution, thus changed warfare, not just because guns were more effective than traditional arms, but because it enabled a transformation in scale (Hoffman, 2011, 2015*b*).[12]

This military revolution placed new fiscal pressures on early modern European states. The European state system that emerged out of the Middle Ages was fiercely competitive – "anarchic" in the sense used by realist scholars of international relations.[13] States that were unable to invest in new military technologies or otherwise mobilize the resources at their disposal in order to field larger and better equipped forces were either destroyed or subordinated by the major European powers.[14]

The states that succeeded in staying at the forefront of European great power competition were those that imposed the most far-reaching fiscal and administrative reforms. They invested in state capacity, developed bureaucracies, and increasingly imposed standardized laws. It was precisely in those parts of Europe that were making these investments in state capacity that the increased religious heterogeneity prompted by the Reformation laid bare the weaknesses of the conditional toleration equilibrium. The effects of the Reformation and Counter-Reformation *differed* between those states that underwent the Military Revolution and the state building process that this entailed, and those states that did not go through this process.

The Reformation and the state building prompted by the Military Revolution *interacted* in such a way so as to initially generate an intensification of religious persecution in those regions where the state was strongest. These persecutory policies were, in general, unsuccessful in reestablishing religious conformity. Following this failure, many states did establish some manner of religious peace, but it was not possible to reconstruct the old conditional toleration equilibrium. The crises that overtook France, England, and Germany in the sixteenth and seventeenth centuries thereby set the stage for the gradual separation of political and religious sources of legitimation. This undercut the original motivation for the enforcement of religious conformity.

7.3 The Reformation and Religious Persecution

We now consider the initial period of intense persecution that followed the Reformation. The examples of Germany, England, France, and the Low Countries emphasize several points. First, while executions for heresy were, in general, rare events in medieval and early modern Europe, the years between 1520 and 1560, when large numbers of Europeans died for their religious beliefs, were an exception to this generalization. Second, this period of intense heresy hunting was profoundly destabilizing. Third, once it was over, early modern states sought to establish a new connection between religion and the state through what historians call confessionalization. But this response was no longer congruent with the broader political equilibrium of European states; there was no returning to the old medieval equilibrium.

7.3.1 The Holy Roman Empire

The Holy Roman Empire was the heartland of the Reformation. Its political fragmentation and the weakness of the mostly absentee Holy Roman Emperor ensured that Luther did not suffer the fate of earlier heretics, despite the wishes of the pope and the emperor. The Protestant princes protected Luther and used the reformed religion to legitimate their own claims to independent authority.

Radical reformers and Anabaptists challenged this alliance. Both Protestants and Catholics persecuted Anabaptists as a threat to the overall

Figure 7.1 (A) Michael Servetus. Theologian, cartographer, physician, humanist. Condemned by Catholics and Protestants alike for his non-trinitarian views, he was burned at the stake by order of Protestant Geneva in 1553 while attempting to escape Catholic Inquisition. (B) Jean Calvin: "Whoever shall maintain that wrong is done to heretics and blasphemer in punishing them makes himself an accomplice in their crime and as guilty as they are" (Calvin, *Defensio orthodoxae fidei* [1554], 46–47). Photo credit: HIP/ Art Resource, NY.

social order. Luther condemned Anabaptism and supported the repressive policies of the secular princes. In Switzerland, Zwingli had an Anabaptist executed in 1527. Most notorious was the siege of Münster in 1535. Anabaptists seized control of the city, introduced adult baptism, redistributed the property of the rich, and imposed bigamy. Social and religious rebellion raised fears of a general social breakdown. As a result, the city was besieged by an alliance of Protestant and Catholic forces, and the leaders of the rebellion were tortured and executed with exemplary cruelty.[15]

Elsewhere in Germany and Switzerland, Anabaptists faced fierce persecution during the 1520s and early 1530s. There were at least 715 and perhaps as many as 1,200 executions during this period. In addition, as many as 400 Anabaptists were executed in the Low Countries between 1534 and 1540. Altogether several thousand Anabaptists may have been executed during the sixteenth century. This included large numbers in Switzerland, Swabia, Franconia, and the Habsburg Tirol (Classen, 1972). The period of most intense persecution was the 1520s and 1530s, before the perceived threat posed by Anabaptism began to recede.

Anabaptism put paid to any notions of religious toleration among most Reformers. Because the role of religion was to safeguard social order, Anabaptists and other non-trinitarian thinkers were seen as posing a threat to society analogous to that posed by witches and the devil. Luther was famous for the statement, "the Word tolerates nothing," and Lutherans fully supported the executions of Anabaptists as heretics. When Calvin conspired to have the doctor and non-trinitarian theologian Michael Servetus condemned to death in Geneva in 1553, Protestant opinion across Europe was generally supportive.[16] The only notable Protestant writer to disapprove of the execution and to argue in favor of religious liberty was Sebastian Castellio, but he was an isolated voice.[17] The execution of Servetus was part of Calvin's establishment of a theocratic state in Geneva where dancing and wearing jewelry was illegal, and failure to attend church or to criticize a preacher made one liable to criminal prosecution. And while Servetus was the only individual explicitly executed for heresy, others such as Jacques Gruet who were suspected of free thinking were also accused of plotting against the Calvinist regime and executed. Calvin's hard stance won him acclaim and "the appeal of the Genevan creed was clear at every social level, and its defenders would not brook equivocation" (Salmon, 1975, 119).[18]

The Protestant repression of Anabaptism and other heresies is hardly surprising. During the 1530s and 1540s the fate of Protestantism rested on the ability of the German princes to resist the Holy Roman Empire. Charles V won victories over them, but he was unable to crush resistance largely due to the threat posed by France and the Ottoman Empire. Even the pope undermined Charles's attempts to reunify the Empire, because he feared being under the thumb of an over mighty emperor.[19] Unable to impose religious conformity on the empire, Charles agreed to the Peace of Augsburg in 1555. "This treaty was 'neither Catholic nor Protestant in inspiration' and consisted of 'neither oppressive persecution nor effective toleration'. Instead, it offered a form of licensed co-existence" (Sutherland, 1984, 159).[20]

The Peace of Augsburg recognized Lutheranism in those parts of Germany ruled by Lutheran princes. However, it did not acknowledge Calvinism, nor did it provide a mechanism for recognizing further religious change. This stored up trouble for the future as both Lutherans and Calvinists anticipated converting the rest of Christendom to their new faith, while after 1560 a revitalized Catholicism began to win back Protestants. The Peace of Augsburg made official the policy that each local jurisdiction could set its own, relatively narrow, standard of orthodoxy: "the license was for the princes rather than the subjects" (Sutherland, 1984, 159). Catholics were expelled from Protestant lands, as were Protestants from Catholic territories. Universities in Lutheran territories were allowed to admit only Lutheran students and vice versa in Catholic lands.[21] People found ways to get along as neighbors despite deep-seated religious tensions that divided denominations during these centuries. From the perspective of our framework, the Peace of Augsburg was a reimposition of the conditional toleration equilibrium, this time between Catholics and Protestants. It initially managed to achieve religious peace. But, as we discuss in Chapter 9, it ultimately failed, precipitating the Thirty Years' War.

7.3.2 The Persecution of Religious Dissent in England

The peace of Augsburg was the first of a number of settlements that brought an end to intense religious violence. But, as the processes by which religious peace was forged in England and France differed from the German experience, we consider each in turn.

While Germany was a decentralized and politically fragmented conglomeration of polities ruled over by an absentee emperor, England and France were, in 1520, relatively unified kingdoms ruled by two strong monarchs – Henry VIII of England (r. 1509–1547) and François I of France (r. 1515–1547). Henry VIII had earned the title "Defender of the Catholic Faith" for his critique of Luther and remained largely conservative in his personal religious beliefs and practices. Nevertheless, he exploited the Reformation to divorce Katherine of Aragon and marry Anne Boleyn.[22] Imposing a religious revolution from above for dynastic and geopolitical reasons, he made himself head of the Church of England. To implement these policies, Henry dispensed with many of his existing advisors, replacing them with able and ambitious new ministers like Thomas Cromwell and Thomas Cranmer who, unlike him, were committed to the new Evangelical religion. As a result, the process of Reformation began to take on a life of its own.[23]

There was widespread agreement in England that clerical abuses needed to be restrained and the monasteries reformed. The break with Rome enabled Henry to seize the monastic and church revenues to vastly engorge the royal domain.[24] As Henry's regime went from persecuting proto-Protestants for Lollardy to espousing Protestantism itself, the definition of religious deviancy became vague; those who refused the oath of royal supremacy that recognized his position as head of the English church died as traitors, while radical Protestants, particularly Anabaptists, continued to be executed as heretics. Often Henry switched the ideological tone of his religious propaganda in response to geopolitical concerns (Hall, 2003, 126). At no point did England under Henry VIII cease to be a persecuting society; all that changed was the religion that Henry used in order to legitimate his authority.

Henry VIII died in 1547 and was succeeded by his infant son Edward VI (r. 1547–1553). During Edward's reign the royal council succeeded in advancing a more radical reform agenda that was influenced by Calvin. The old heresy laws introduced by Henry IV (see Chapter 3) were abolished. Nevertheless, like Calvin's Geneva, Edward VI's government was committed to enforcing religious conformity, burning alive two individuals as Anabaptists. Had Edward lived longer, England may have become a Calvinist state on the model of Geneva.

This was not to be. Edward died at the age of 15 in June 1553. His sister, Mary, was a Catholic who succeeded him only after raising an army to overthrow the Protestant Lady Jane Grey, queen for nine days. Initially on coming to the throne, Mary compromised and allowed Reformed services to continue. However, once secure, she pursued a policy of re-Catholicization. In 1555, the heresy laws of Henry IV were reenacted, and instructions given for their enforcement.

Mary's desire to return to Rome made the resumption of heresy trials inevitable. Resurrecting the heresy legislation of her predecessors in an environment in which religious preferences had dramatically changed meant criminalizing a significant segment of the population. Most victims came from the southeast – a third, more than 100, came from the greater London area.[25] In total, during the reign of Mary I, 280 people were executed for heresy, four times the number burned in the reign of Henry VIII, and three times the total figure executed between 1401 and 1529 (Solt, 1990, 60).

So while Germany, the Low Countries and Switzerland saw intense persecutions and religious violence in the 1520s and 1530s, in England it was the 1550s that saw mass trials and executions. Mary's policies were counterproductive. Her two main advisers, Gardiner and Pole, "seem to have regarded heretical depravity as an acute, but small-scale problem, to be solved by determined action against the leaders of Protestantism. Their followers, once separated from this corrosion, would then be reconciled to Catholicism" (Hall, 2003, 175). In fact, the opposite occurred. The scale of the executions shocked many. The victims were commemorated in John Foxe's *Book of Martyrs*. This reign of terror destabilized a political regime that had enjoyed considerable popular support at the onset of her reign. After 1558, England saw no more large-scale executions of heretics.

7.3.3 The Persecution of Protestants in France

From the 1520s onwards, the Reformation filtered into France from Germany and Switzerland. Luther's writings were burnt at the Sorbonne in 1523. Heretics were increasingly identified as "Lutherans"; the first heretic executed as such, a weaver from Meaux, was burned to death in 1524.[26] The Parlement of Paris tried a number of individuals for adhering to the

Lutheran heresy in the 1520s and early 1530s.[27] But the numbers involved were small.

The Reformation, however, coincided with attempts to centralize the patchwork of territories and principalities that made up the medieval kingdom of France.[28] A Renaissance monarch and patron of Leonardo de Vinci, François I was initially a reluctant prosecutor. He attempted to protect notable religious dissidents from the Parlement of Paris.[29] This comparatively liberal attitude, however, proved a thin veneer. It disappeared once the "Lutheran" heresy spread and threatened his authority.

In 1534 placards were posted around Paris denying the validity of the Catholic sacrament. This Affair of the Placards was seen to herald social disorder and even to threaten the king himself.[30] After this, individuals had to choose, as Calvin put it, between idolatry and the "true faith" (Cottret, 2003, 113). Protestantism became associated with rebellion in the eyes of the Catholic authorities. A wave of persecution followed across France.

Edicts against heresy were effective only when local authorities could enforce them. Heresy was a matter for the religious courts, and these courts were often poorly funded and lacked the administrative capabilities to investigate heresy. Papal inquisitors fervently pursued heretics in some regions, but often they were venal and ineffective: "[f]rom top to bottom from pope to bishop, church courts and canon law simply could not cope with the early Reformation" (Monter, 1999, 45). There was considerable regional variation in the numbers of heretics tried or executed. Some parlements (or local courts) were lenient to Protestantism, while others took a hardline position. However, the parlements everywhere struggled to enforce royal authority "in the more distant parts of their jurisdictions ...Pockets of immunity would therefore continue to exist for Protestantism almost everywhere within France, but particularly in the big cities and on the domains of the powerful nobility who protected their tenants from judicial enquiry" (Greengrass, 1987, 38).[31]

Reforms introduced by François I changed this. In particular, the Edict of Villers-Cotterêts of 1539 imposed common legal standards on what was a fragmented legal system. Villers-Cotterêts mandated the use of French in all courts and legal documents and standardized the use of the Roman-canon inquisitional model all across France.[32]

It was followed by the Edict of Fontainebleau in 1540, which asserted state control over the crime of heresy, making its suppression the responsibility of the regional parlements. All suspects were to be sent to the king's courts for sentencing regardless of their status. These alone were permitted to use torture and to pronounce capital sentences. It asserted royal control over the regional courts (which had to report to the king every six months) while at the same time granting those courts authority over religious affairs. Feudal lords were required to investigate heresy and to report to the king's officers (Knecht, 1982, 398). Heresy was identified with sedition and thus defined as a crime against the state, as opposed to the church. Those church courts that continued to exist were increasingly supervised by royal officials.[33]

Hersey was defined to make it easier for the courts to convict suspects; no longer based on theology (i.e., a judgment of the orthodoxy of one's beliefs), it became an assessment of whether an individual's behavior implied that they were heretical. It was now heretical for schoolmasters to interpret scripture a certain way, for individuals to damage or deface religion icons, to sell or distribute heretical books, or to speak words contrary to the Catholic religion (Greengrass, 1987, 34). This appears to have induced the majority of the population to continue to adhere to orthodox Catholic practices even if their actual beliefs were more sympathetic to the Reform movement.[34]

As in Mary I's England, the edicts of François I, created an "engine of repression" (Roelker, 1996, 211). Using trial data collected by Monter (1999), we illustrate in Figures 7.2a, 7.2b, and 7.2c, the effect the creation of this engine of judicial repression had on the both the number of individuals executed for heresy and the geographic scope of these heresy trials.[35] These figures show both the dramatic increase in heretic executions after 1540 and the accompanying increase in their geographic spread away from the center of judicial authority in Paris.[36] Before the Edict of Fountainebleau, most executions occurred either in Paris or Provence. After 1540 almost all the regions in France began to execute heretics.

"Inquisitors of the faith" were appointed and sent to the provinces in order to seek out and detect heretics.[37] Figure 7.3 depicts this increase by showing the geographic location of heretic executions in Provence. Squares show where executions occurred before 1540 (each symbol may represent multiple executions). Triangles show the location of executions after 1540. The seat of the high court in Aix-en-Provence is also marked. Figure 7.3 makes it clear that before legal centralization in 1540, executions clustered closely to the primary seat of legal power for the crown in Aix-en-Provence. However, after 1540, executions took place at a greater distance from the high court. In effect, the scope of royal authority, as measured by the willingness and ability of local courts to execute heretics, increased after 1540.

Figure 7.4 shows similar data for all regions between 1523 and 1560. Each point in the scatter plot represents the distance of a trial from its regional high court (parlement). The plotted line is the average distance of trials from their high courts in that year. The data confirm that François I's

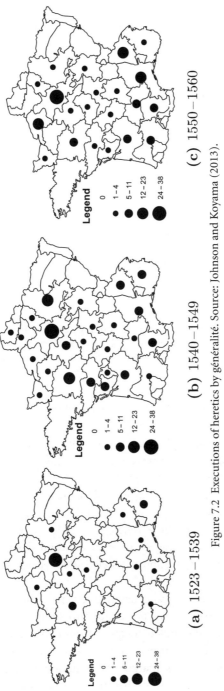

(a) 1523–1539   (b) 1540–1549   (c) 1550–1560

Figure 7.2 Executions of heretics by généralité. Source: Johnson and Koyama (2013).

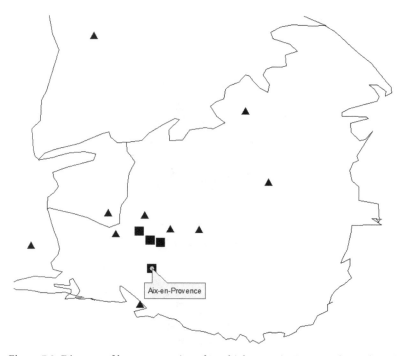

Figure 7.3 Distance of heresy executions from high court in Provence located at Aix-en-Provence. Squares represent executions before 1540. Triangles represent executions after 1540. Multiple executions may be represented by one symbol. Source: Johnson and Koyama (2013).

reforms between 1538 and 1540 increased both the number and geographic scope of heresy executions.

As we saw in Chapter 3, prior to the imposition of greater legal and religious centralization by François I in the late 1530s, the Waldensians in the Pays de Vaud had enjoyed decades of de facto toleration due to the fact that they occupied rugged upland territory far from Paris on the borderland with Savoy (Cameron, 1986, 49–61). Now, the French monarchy decided that these religious heretics should be brought to heel and a royal army ravaged the Pays de Vaud destroying 28 villages and killing or capturing approximately 4,000 villagers (Roelker, 1996, 212).

Although increases in legal capacity in France produced a tremendous growth in heresy trials, it was not enough to suppress Protestantism: the number of heretics continued to grow throughout the 1550s. Henri II (1547–1559) created the *burning chamber* – a special court devoted to prosecuting cases of heresy. This marked the peak of judicial repression. Many members of parlement themselves became suspects. It included twenty articles "covering in exhaustive detail all matters of censorship, the possession,

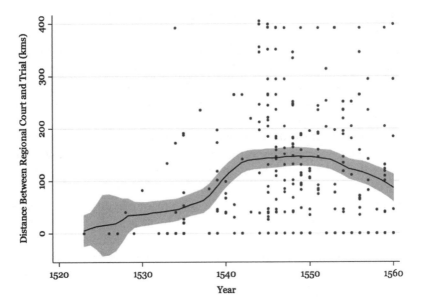

Figure 7.4 Distance of trials from regional Parlement, 1520–1560. Each dot represents a trial. Plotted line is a kernel weighted local polynomial regression of distance of trial on year (bandwidth = 2). 95% confidence interval shown. Source: Johnson and Koyama (2013).

production, sale, and dissemination of religious works; the rigid control of printing, and the inspection of bookshops. But even more vexatious and dangerous were the articles (27–33) relating to informing, which became mandatory" (Sutherland, 1980, 46).

Heresy had to expunged from the body politic. Metaphors contemporaries used included eliminating a disease, purging an infection, or amputating a gangrenous limb. Hence, death by fire was an appropriate fate for heretics. By burning their bodies to ashes, offenders were obliterated without possibility of burial. In the process society cleansed and purified itself.[38]

As in England, though, this intensification proved counterproductive. The execution of a single unbeliever or a small number of heretics could perform the cathartic societal role of exorcising evil that Michel Foucault ascribed to public forms of punishment. Large-scale executions, however, could delegitimize the state, especially if those punished were seen to be ordinary citizens.[39]

Public executions were theatre. And like a play or speech, they were designed to convey a specific message by humiliating and punishing the condemned, who were dragged to the place of execution either on carts or on a hurdle and often mutilated. Clerical heretics were stripped of their vestments. In some cases, the victims were dressed as fools prior to execution: "here the association of heresy with folly is clearly meant to be one more way of degrading the heretic" (Nicholls, 1988, 56–57). But the authorities could not always control how the audience would interpret the show. Persecution risked a backlash if it created a tradition of martyrs. The execution itself could become a testament to the faith, and according to adherents, the truth of the martyr's faith.[40]

Executions intensified "the impression of Protestants that they were recapitulating the experiences of early Christians," thereby consolidating "their view of themselves as belonging to the true faith, while their persecutions were enacting the will of the Devil" (Kelley, 1972, 1329).[41] A Catholic who had once been a Calvinist recalled the burning of one prominent Protestant who had been a councilor in the Parlement of Paris. He noted that all his colleagues wept at the sight and admired the victim's constancy and bravery, observing that "[h]is preaching on the gallows and on the bonfire did more harm than one hundred ministers would have known how to" (quoted in Shepardson, 2007, 30).

Finally, despite the administrative capacity built by François I, early modern states did not possess the ability of modern totalitarian states to systematically police the beliefs and ideas of the population at large. Completely suppressing Protestantism through force was beyond the means of the French monarchy once the new religion had become the faith of a sizable minority of the population.[42] The failure of the policy of persecution was apparent by 1560.

7.4 Temporary Religious Toleration

7.4.1 The French Wars of Religion

By the 1560s, rulers across Europe had failed to crush the Reformation. In Germany, secular rulers in conjunction with moderate reformers were successful in repressing the Radical Reformation, but all attempts to reintroduce Catholicism into northern Germany were acknowledged to have failed at the Peace of Augsburg. In England, and in France, heresy trials against Protestants in the 1550s backfired. Had Mary lived long enough, perhaps Catholicism would have been reestablished in England, but her death brought about a reversal of all of her policies.

Indeed, early modern states were extremely vulnerable when a monarch died unexpectedly. The deaths of Edward VI and Mary I destabilized England. Henri II's death in 1559 from a jousting accident threatened an already fragile political equilibrium. His 15-year-old son François II succeeded to the throne but he was ill and actual power devolved to Henri's

Table 7.1 *Brief chronology of the French Reformation*

Year	
1523	First heretic executed for "Lutherism" in France
1534	Affair of the Placards marks intensification of repression
1540	Edict of Fontainebleu; imposes secular and royal control over heresy trials
1547	Creation of the *Chambre Ardent*, a specialist court to sentence heretics
1560	Conspiracy of Amboise fails
1562	Edict of January promises toleration to Protestant
1562	Beginning of the French Wars of Religion
1572	St. Bartholomew's Day Massacre
1598	Edict of Nantes issued. Protection of civil liberties and toleration for Protestants
1685	Revocation of the Edict of Nantes
1724 onwards	Relaxation of the enforcement of the Edict of Nantes
1787	Edict of Versailles grants toleration to non-Catholics

widow, the Queen regent, Catherine de Medici, who was unpopular as both a foreigner and as a women. Factions within the nobility were soon jostling for power.

On March 10, 1560 a group of Protestant nobles attempted to kidnap François II. This plot, known as the conspiracy of Amboise, failed. Fear of a bloody response led to the formation of a Huguenot political party out of the Protestants religious movement.[43] In response, a party of intransigent Catholics led by Duke François de Guise also mobilized.

In December 1560, François II died and was succeeded by his 10-year-old brother Charles IX. But even after Charles IV attained his legal majority, policy continued to be made by Catherine de Medici. Catherine recognized the costs of the campaign against heresy and sought to decriminalize Protestant beliefs. The Edict of January, issued in 1562, achieved it. For the first time in French history, it recognized the right of private individuals to practice their own faith in their own homes. The pragmatic grounds for toleration were clear: too many people were "infected" with heresy to be tried and executed. If all heretics were punished there would be "a remarkable effusion of blood of people of all ages and sexes" (quoted in Monter, 1999, 175–176).

But events spiraled out of the control. In 1562, the Duc de Guise stumbled upon and killed 63 unarmed Huguenots praying in a barn. The leader of the Protestant party, Louis de Bourbon, Prince of Condé, seized upon this as cause for war. The resulting series of conflicts were not only or even primarily religious wars, they were also civil wars between rival noble factions and against the monarchy.

The death of the Duc de Guise and the capture of Condé allowed Catherine de Medici to issue the Edict of Amboise in March 1563, which promised a general pardon for all heretics, so long as they returned to the Catholic fold. She also appointed Michel de l'Hôpital – a pragmatist who favored compromise – as Lord Chancellor.

Civil war restarted at the end of the 1560s. Another peace attempt was made, this time by marrying the Prince of Condé's son Henri IV of Navarre to the sister of the king, Marguerite. However, within six days of the marriage, the peace was shattered by the attempted assassination of the Protestant leader Admiral de Coligny. To preempt retaliation, the order was given to kill all the Huguenots in Paris. This was the notorious St. Bartholomew's Day Massacre. Similar massacres occurred in cities across France and as many as 10,000 Protestants were killed.

As religion played a crucial role in upholding social order, the confessional crisis brought about by the civil war was thus a general social crisis. During the St. Bartholomew's Day Massacre, the "citizens of Paris ... responded with glee, grabbing 'suspects' and hacking them to bits with any means available ... With killing made legitimate, the killers broadened their targets. Many Catholics were killed as well as Huguenots." As is common in such episodes, people used religion as an excuse to settle old scores. "Those against whom someone bore a grudge or who were a barrier to an inheritance were speedily dubbed Huguenots and slain" (Moore, 2000, 50). The St. Bartholomew's Day Massacre did not destroy the Huguenot leadership, however, and the civil war continued.

By the 1580s, the Crown had come around to granting limited toleration to the Huguenots. However, the Guise family and the Catholic league opposed concessions. The final round of the French Wars of Religion was a three-way civil war between Henri III (r. 1574–1589), who had succeeded his brother in 1574, Henri duc de Guise, and the Protestant leader Henri of Navarre. After Henri III was assassinated by a Catholic monk in 1589, Henri of Navarre was the closest in line to the throne. To become King Henri IV, he abjured his religion and adopted Catholicism in 1593.[44]

Henri IV issued the Edict of Nantes in 1598 in an attempt to conciliate both the Catholics who remained suspicious of him and the Protestants whose faith he had abandoned. It was a compromise. Henri IV desired peace rather than toleration and the Edict envisioned religious concord and harmony without mentioning religious toleration explicitly. Henri IV himself described it as necessary, but not as good or desirable, and he envisioned reuniting Catholics and Protestants in the future.[45]

The Edict of Nantes was an important step toward obtaining religious peace. It was a recognition that religious unity was too costly to be imposed in a state as religiously fragmented as France. But it did not lead to religious freedom. By granting the French Protestants land and a considerable amount of autonomy, the Edict put in place institutional guarantees that the peace would be maintained. But these institutional guarantees were not the foundations for the development of religious freedom in the long run. Granting such political power to the Protestant nobility was bound to be galling to the monarchy. It was natural that Henri IV's successors and their ministers would wish to undercut and do away with the autonomous power of the Huguenots. Once they did this, the institutional factors maintaining religious peace would no longer be in place and this would set the scene for the eventual revocation of the Edict of Nantes.

7.4.2 The Act of Uniformity in England

In the aftermath of Mary's persecution of Protestants, her successor, Elizabeth, pursued very different policies. This was not only due to their different faiths, but also because of the failed example Mary left of attempting to enforce religious conformity through heresy trials and burnings. Elizabeth compromised between the traditionalists and the radical reformers of Edward IV's reign. During Mary's reign she had conformed as a Catholic and there was a degree of pragmatism and ambivalence in her attitude toward religion.[46] Elizabeth did not expect all Catholics to immediately abandon their religion and she declared herself uninterested in making "windows into people's souls." But if Elizabeth was largely indifferent to private beliefs, she also had no interest in religious freedom and there was no question that there should be a single compulsory faith.[47] Her position reflected the ubiquitous assumption "that some sort of religious uniformity was absolutely essential for the unity of a nation" (Russell, 1971, 38).

The Act of Uniformity of 1560 made church attendance compulsory and punishable by a sizable fine. It did not, however, inquire into an individual's actual beliefs. So-called Church Papists – those who conformed to Anglican worship but considered themselves Catholic – were tolerated (Walsham, 1993). Elizabeth did not execute anyone for being Catholic. During her forty-five-year reign, only non-trinitarian Protestants were burned as heretics. However, many individuals died *indirectly* for their religious beliefs. As geopolitical tensions between the Catholic powers and England intensified over the course of her reign and after the pope declared her overthrow licit, being a Catholic priest in England effectively became a capital crime. Jesuits and Catholic priests were hunted down, tortured for information, and then hanged, drawn, and quartered.[48] A surveillance state emerged to suppress these subversive elements.

Table 7.2 *Brief chronology of the English Reformation*

Year	
1523	Henry VIII awarded title "Defender of the Catholic Faith"
1533	Henry VIII marries Ann Boleyn
1534	Act of Supremacy makes Henry VIII head of the English Church
1536	Dissolution of the Monasteries
1549	Act of Uniformity
1550	Introduction of the Common Prayer Book
1553	Accession of Mary I and abolition of Edward's religious laws
1555	Burning of the Oxford Martyrs (Ridley, Latimer, and Cranmer)
1558	Accession of Elizabeth I
1559	Act of Supremacy makes Elizabeth I head of Church of England
1586	Execution of Margaret Clitherow in York
1612	Last executions for heresy in English history

In the town of York, tourists still walk by the house of Margaret Clitherow. Arrested for harboring priests, Clitherow was sentenced to be crushed to death when she refused to testify. Her execution took place on the bridge of the River Ouse, where a commemorative plaque now lies. Clitherow's fate horrified Elizabeth on account of her sex. This did not stop other executions, and religious coercion continued. Nevertheless, religious violence was markedly less intense than in the mid-sixteenth century.

The desire of the pope and the king of Spain, Philip II, to unseat her and to restore Catholicism enabled Elizabeth to portray herself as a champion of English freedoms and burnished her religious settlement with enough political legitimacy to ensure domestic peace. Her long reign enabled the Church of England to consolidate its position. Most people conformed to the new Church of England. Rather than relying on outright coercion and burnings, the Elizabethan government desired the Church of England "to be a nursery in which the masses were gently weaned, not roughly snatched, from popery" (Walsham, 1993, 17). A number of noble families, particularly those in the north, remained true to Catholicism. To overcome their resistance, the fines for nonconforming were increased. Those who could not pay had their land seized or were imprisoned. Had Catholicism been the only rival to the Church of England, this may have worked.

In the long run, however, the attempt to reestablish the religious legitimacy of the monarchy on Anglican foundations failed. Already by the end of Elizabeth's reign, it was clear that not only were religious divisions greater than they had been before her father's divorce, but that these religious divisions were there to stay. Confessionalization proved particularly problematic in states such as England and France that retained substantial religious minorities. The new religious equilibrium established in England after 1563 and France after 1598 proved to be *self-undermining* rather than *self-enforcing*. The destabilizing role played by Catholics and Protestant dissenters in seventeenth-century England and Huguenots in seventeenth-century France led to the political developments that would move Europe toward a more liberal religious regime.

Confessionalization failed because of the destabilizing influence of Puritans, Presbyterians, and other dissident Protestant sects for whom the English Reformation was not reformation enough. Already in Elizabeth's reign, there were Protestants who were dissatisfied with the failure of the Church of England to fully enact the Reformation program.[49] Religious diversity within the kingdom was greatly increased in 1603 when James VI of Scotland became James I of England (r. 1603–1625) as the population of Scotland, having undergone a Calvinist-influenced reformation, under John Knox, was predominantly Presbyterian.

The Reformation had other long-run consequences. The Catholic Church had held huge swaths of land across England. In an important sense, the authority of the medieval Church rested partly on its power and wealth as a major landowner. It had been richer than any monarch. And the archbishops and major prelates were the equivalent of great noblemen.

The seizure of Church lands and their sale at auction had two consequences. First, it enriched the gentry and middle classes. Their rise empowered Parliament.[50] Second, the dissolution of the monasteries reduced the authority and status of religion in English politics. Henry VIII's successors endowed the new Anglican Church with land, wealth, and status. But in the seventeenth century the economic problems facing the Church grew. No longer able to raise revenue through clerical fees and tithes, the income of clergymen declined. As it fell, so did the influence of the Anglican establishment and its ability to confer political legitimacy.[51]

7.5 Religious Peace Elsewhere in Europe

7.5.1 The Low Countries

The repression of religious deviancy was especially severe in the Low Countries. Between 1523 and 1565 more than 1,300 individuals were executed as heretics – an unusually high number (Greengrass, 2014, 375). This repression, on the face of it, appeared successful. However, the legitimacy of Habsburg rule in the Low Countries was weak. Food riots were seized upon by local elites to push for greater autonomy from Spanish rule. The response was brutal. The Duke of Alba was dispatched with a large army to occupy the Low Countries. Between 1567 and 1568 the Duke tried more than 12,000 people and executed more than 1,000 for rebelling against

Spanish authority (Greengrass, 2014, 400). This unprecedented violence sparked a general revolt against Habsburg rule.

The leader of the revolt, William of Orange, was initially in favor of religious toleration. But this proved infeasible and in the 1580s the northern provinces united under the Calvinist faith. However, there were many non-Calvinists within the new Republic. This led to the *de facto* emergence of religious toleration. Religious peace in the Dutch Republic required pillarization – a form of ideological and religious segregation involving the division of society into a number of highly organized "pillars," each based on its own denomination or ideology (van Eijinatten, 2003, 1). This was a form of conditional toleration, not religious freedom.

More than a third of the population were Catholic in the seventeenth century. But "[t]he toleration enjoyed by Catholics was tentative, and anti-Catholic sentiment remained widespread, especially among the populace and in Reformed synods and consistories. Until the end of the eighteenth century the Catholics paid a variety of taxes and thinly-disguised bribes, including 'recognition taxes', payments to prevent rescripts from being applied, and obligatory 'gifts' as a welcome to new administrators" (van Eijinatten, 2003, 22). Confessional divisions continued to matter into the twentieth century.[52]

7.5.2 Poland: "A State without Stakes"?

Sixteenth-century Poland, heralded as "a state without stakes" – an almost unique example of religious toleration and pluralism in a period of ubiquitous religious conflict – provides another interesting case (Tazbir, 1973). During the decades in which religious violence devastated much of Central and Western Europe, Catholic Poland did not prosecute Protestants, nor did it even prosecute anti-trinitarians who were denied toleration almost everywhere else. And, although Poland was not a state entirely without stakes – a woman was burned to death in 1539 for denying the divinity of Christ and attempting to convert to Judaism – it certainly did not go through a campaign of religious persecution on the same scale as did other parts of Europe.[53]

Poland nonetheless fits our framework. Significantly, the Polish state *did not* go through the same process of state centralization that accompanied religious prosecution in England, France, Spain, and the Netherlands. In Poland, the king was elected. His legitimacy was not grounded in as close a relationship with the Church as in Western Europe. Public order did not depend on religious conformity. For these reasons, Poland continued to be relatively tolerant toward both heretics and Jews in the sixteenth century, but this appearance of toleration was largely a reflection of the weakness of the state and its continued fiscal and legal fragmentation. It did not reflect a commitment to religious freedom.

The Polish king Sigismund I (1506–1558) passed edicts against heresy. But, unlike the actions of the kings of France, these were ineffective. The Polish state was decentralized and the monarchy was circumscribed by the *liberum veto*, which enabled the nobility to block policy.[54]

The religious diversity of Poland meant that the hardline Church position against heresy was unenforceable even prior to the Reformation. Consequently, the clergy in Poland advocated peaceful coexistence. In terms of our argument, the Polish-Lithuanian commonwealth survived in part because the bounds of toleration were set fairly widely. Religious policy remained the responsibility of ecclesiastical courts with limited jurisdiction – there was no Polish equivalent to the Edicts of Paris and Fontainebleau. The power of the Polish aristocracy was such that no noblemen was sentenced to death for his beliefs as "[n]o parliament could agree to any law invoking the death penalty for noblemen" (Tazbir, 1973, 73). This prevented the state from taking serious action against religious dissenters as long as they had protectors among the nobility.[55] The situation in sixteenth- and seventeenth-century Poland corresponded to the medieval conditional toleration equilibrium. It was not that dissimilar from the situation that obtained in the Ottoman Empire, except that during the course of the seventeenth century the Polish state's capacity to prevent foreign invasion and domestic civil wars deteriorated.

In 1648, Bohdan Khmelnytsky, a Ukrainian noble, led a revolt of Cossacks. This initiated a series of disasters for the Polish-Lithuanian Commonwealth that culminated in a Swedish invasion and the eventual annexation of the Ukraine by Russia. The Cossacks inflicted devastating pogroms against Jewish communities – remembered as the largest massacre of Jews between the Second Jewish Rebellion (115–117 CE) and the Holocaust. Out of an estimated Jewish population of 40,000 perhaps 18,000 to 20,000 died (Stampfer, 2003, 223). Furthermore, invasions by Lutheran Swedes spread religious intolerance among Poland's Catholic majority. Anti-trinitarians heretics were expelled on pain of death in 1658 and Protestants were stripped of legal and political rights. The toleration experienced by minorities in Poland was fragile; in a competitive and hostile state system, it did not provide robust protection for religious freedom.

Transylvania is another celebrated example of religious toleration. But the details suggest that political concerns were at the foremost in the decision to grant toleration. Politically and religiously fragmented from the late medieval period, Protestantism and anti-trinitarian views proliferated. Transylvanian elites were attracted to Protestantism following the defeat and death of the Catholic king of Hungary in the Battle of Mohács against the Ottomans.

The ruler of Transylvania, John Sigismund Zápolya, was himself a convert from Catholicism to first Lutheranism and then Calvinism. He passed the Edict of Torda in 1568, which prohibited religious toleration and allowed communities to choose their own religion. This Edict has been celebrated by modern liberals as a landmark in the history of religious toleration. But it was based on a premodern system of conditional toleration and was intended to limit conflict between groups and not on an individual's right to religious freedom.

7.6 Chapter Summary: The Impact of the Reformation

While the causes and consequences of the Reformation are difficult to disentangle, it is evident that Luther's 95 Theses were a shock to the belief structure of late medieval Europe. Humanists had criticized Church practices, but their criticisms had only influenced elites. The conjunction of Luther's critique with the new technology of printing meant that first the urban middle classes and then ordinary people and peasants began to agitate for religious change. In complex ways, the diversity of religious belief in Europe increased. New religious tensions emerged as different groups of believers disagreed and fought with one another.

At the same time, the Reformation was a challenge to state authority because the existing political equilibrium through which the church legitimated rulers was undermined. Governments initially attempted to deal with increased religious diversity by persecuting heretics. However, very often states lacked the capacity to suppress the burgeoning heretical movements.

All out repression proved too costly once the Reformation was established as proved to be the case in Germany, the Low Countries, England, and France. The violence required was itself destabilizing. As a fallback, governments tried to use the existing system of conditional toleration to compartmentalize religious sects away from each other. However, whereas this worked when religious deviants were either small and well organized (e.g., Jews) or when they were relatively unorganized and heterogenous (e.g., folk religions), the well organized and significant number of new heretics proved impossible to isolate. As the conditional toleration equilibrium began to break down, the self-reinforcing relationship between low state capacity and identity rules also ceased to operate. In subsequent chapters, we investigate the consequences of the increases in state capacity taking place in many parts of Europe after the Reformation.

Notes

1. The most famous argument is that attributed to Max Weber (1930). For recent work that emphasizes the Reformation as a turning point see Rubin (2017). Becker and Woessmann (2009) argue that the Reformation eventually boosted economic growth because it encouraged individuals to invest in human capital. Cantoni (2015) tests to see whether or not Protestant cities grew faster as a result of Protestantism in the early modern period and he finds no support for this thesis. Rather, the cities that adopted Protestantism were already growing in the centuries preceding the Reformation. See Becker et al. (2016) for an overview.

2. Acemoglu, Johnson, and Robinson (2005), for example, argue that Atlantic trade disproportionately benefited those states in which merchants had representation in parliament, as they were able to press for institutions that favored economic development and markets.

3. The transition from conditional toleration based on identity rules to religious liberty was gradual and, for a long time, fragile. In the French case, for example, limited tolerance for Protestants was reversed by Louis XIV's Revocation of the Edict of Nantes. The Revocation would come to be judged by the French themselves as a failure and it was eventually overturned, but it also illustrates how toleration could be revoked, even in centralizing states, so long as the ruler remained unconstrained. In England anti-Catholic violence remained an issue until the end of the eighteenth century. But, as we argue, the trends we identify reflect systematic patterns. Economic development and changes in the incentives facing political actors made it increasingly costly for rulers to impose systems of conditional toleration after the Reformation. Recognition of the self-undermining character of the old equilibrium eventually led to a transition to modern liberal attitudes toward religious diversity.

4. As they did, for example, in fifteenth-century Bohemia, where the proto-Protestant views of Jan Hus were adopted.

5. See Bossy (1985) for a statement of this position. It is widely acknowledged by recent historians. For example, Antonio de Beatis noted that "what was 'holy' in the Rhineland was different from what was 'holy' in his native Naples" (Greengrass, 2014, 316). There was "a cornucopia of local religious customs, voluntary devotional practices, specific ecclesiastical subgroups, particular jurisdictional privileges, divergent theological approaches, and syncretistic beliefs" (Gregory, 2012, 84). "The vision of a uniform Christendom under the leadership of a single Church," in the words of Cary Nederman, "barely concealed the heterogeneity of the peoples it embraced or the diversity of beliefs that they held." Instead she notes that "[b]eneath the veneer of religious singularity, European Christendom during the Middle Ages struggled endlessly with manifestations of difference" (Nederman, 2000, 4).

6. In the economics of religion literature, this argument has been developed by Ekelund et al. (2002, 2006), who view the Catholic Church as an incumbent monopolist that used its monopoly power to extract rents from believers. They argue that it was the rent-seeking activities of the Church that induced successful entry from a new religion – namely, Protestantism. Certainly it was in Germany that the papacy's attempts to raise revenue through the sale of indulgences were most egregious.

7. The centrality of the printing press to the Protestant reformation is forcefully argued for many historians. It has received rigorous empirical analysis from Rubin (2014). Tracy (1999, 5) notes that Jan Hus was at least as popular in Europe as Martin Luther and a martyr to his cause, but Hus lacked the printing press.

8. Gregory (2012) describes the shock of the Reformation as causing scales to fall "from long-clouded eyes" as previous attempts to reform the church were abandoned in favor of wholesale rejection.

9. For example, Nexon (2009) argues that the Reformation lowered the barriers to organizing resistance to the state among co-religionists thus increasing revolt probability. He also notes that it made it more costly for rulers to mobilize support among heterogeneous populations, "thereby eroding their ability to legitimate their policies on a range of issues, from religion to taxation" (Nexon, 2009, 4). Finally, it intensified potential resistance to the demands of the central state as religious issues became mingled with issues of taxation or domestic politics. Relatedly, it created new opportunities for the internalization of domestic politics as co-religionists in one state came to play prominent roles in the religious affairs of their neighbors.

10. Infant baptism was the last of two sacraments of the Church retained by Lutherans (along with the Lord's supper (Tracy, 1999, 67)).

11. Historians disagree about the timing of the Military Revolution and offer contending arguments for what factors were most important in driving it. It is best thought of as a series of evolutionary developments that took place over several centuries and increased the size of armies that were needed to achieve strategic objectives. The term military revolution originates with Michael Howard, who applied it narrowly to developments between 1560 and 1660. It was subsequently widened by Parker (1976, 1988) to encompass the entire early modern period. Recent research downplays the revolutionary nature of these developments (see Weigley, 1991; Arnold, 2001; Childs, 2001).

12. Medieval battles were comparatively small-scale. Agincourt, the decisive battle of the second phase of the Hundred Years' Wars, involved approximately 6,000 English archers and men-at-arms and perhaps 20,000 Frenchmen – the actual number is unknown. Other major engagements involved much smaller armies. The decisive battle in which the French reconquered Northern France, the Battle of Fromigny in 1453 was fought by armies roughly 5 or 6 thousand strong. Most battles in the sixteenth century remained relatively small scale by the standard of what was to come. The Battle of Pavia in 1515 was the decisive engagement between France and Spain for control of Italy, yet it was fought by armies roughly 25,000 strong. It was one of the largest battles between the major European powers of the century (battles involving the Ottoman empire tended to be larger). But by 1700 this had changed dramatically. Monstrously large armies contested the War of the Spanish Succession. Both French and Allied English, Dutch, and Imperial armies at the Battle of Oudenaarde in 1708 were more than 100,000 strong. This made them larger than the populations of all but the greatest of European cities. The combination of large armies; bayonets, which meant that every infantryman could be equipped with a musket; improved artillery; and linear formations that maximized firepower meant that causalities rose commensurately. At the Battle of Malplaquet, the bloodiest engagement of the eighteenth century, the victorious Allies lost between 20,000 and 25,000 men whereas their defeated French opponents lost between 11,000 and 15,000.

13. For example in the work of Waltz (1979), Mearscheimer (2001), Nexon (2009).

14. Hoffman (2015*a*) describes this as a military tournament. Gennaioli and Voth (2015) argue that the effects of the Military Revolution were asymmetric. An increase in the capital intensity of warfare induced some states to invest in state capacity. But this incentive was not uniform. More capital intensive warfare also made it worthwhile for other European states to drop out of great power competition. But this did not lead to the disappearance of all of Europe's small states, as Abramson (2017) shows. Europe's smaller states subordinated their foreign policies to those of the great powers, who were able to benefit from more capital intensive methods of warfare. Dincecco and Onorato (2017) argue that the intensification of warfare in this period encouraged the rise of urban centers, spurring economic growth.

15. Thereafter, the surviving Anabaptists embraced a policy of nonresistance to secular authorities; though continuing to face persecution, they diminished in political significance.

16. See MacCulloch (2003, 244–245). Calvin is said to have remarked of Servetus: "I shall never suffer him to depart alive" (quoted in MacKinnon, 1962, 131). Out of some measure of mercy, Calvin did ask for Servetus to quickly die by the sword rather than be burned alive. As it happened, the faggots were wet, so Servetus's death was a particularly slow one.

17. See Zagorin (2003, 93–144).

18. For a discussion see MacKinnon (1962).

19. Iyigun (2008, 2015) provides evidence that the timing of Ottoman invasions of Europe played a crucial role in the survival of Protestantism in the crucial middle decades of the sixteenth century.

20. Peter Wilson notes that "A fully secular *Pax Civilis* was not an option for the Empire as a whole. This solution was advocated two decades later by Jean Bodin in response to his own country's civil war; the state was still envisioned as broadly Christian, but disassociated from any particular confession, using its powers to preserve religious plurality and domestic order. Such a powerful secular monarchy was incompatible with both German freedom and the emperor's Holy Roman credentials" (Wilson, 2009, 41).

21. At a local level, people practiced "the tactics of toleration" that often characterize patterns of coexistence in religiously divided communities. These tactics in general ensured a measure of social peace (Spohnholz, 2011).

22. Henry authored *Assertio septum sacramentorum* against Luther, though it was likely edited by Thomas More. The English Reformation has been studied in immense detail. For a recent and comprehensive treatment see Marshall (2016).

23. Elton (1953) argues that this constituted a "revolution in government."

24. For a survey see Hall (2003).

25. See Edwards (2011, 253–265). See Hall (2003) for a discussion of Mary's intentions. Approximately 800 individuals fled Mary's persecution – they were predominantly members of the political and religious elite who had played administrative roles in Edward VI's reign (McGrath, 1967).

26. Though, as one historian notes, "the authorities had often little conception of what the term 'Lutheran' actually meant" (Greengrass, 1987, 11). Greengrass further notes, "The clarity between orthodoxy and heresy was, however, a long way off, even in 1530" (Greengrass, 1987, 10).

27. As Salmond observes: "There was no organized Protestant churches in France during this period of the préréforme" (Salmon, 1975, 87). Another historian comments: "it was to be a long time before heresy was adequately disentangled from humanism, a miscellany of advanced opinions, and a great deal of fluctuating confusion of thought and mind" (Sutherland, 1980, 11).

28. Collins (1999) observes that the French kings allocated their kingdom among their extended family members in the same way as the head of a prosperous peasant household. In the sixteenth century, the territory of the French kingdom became inalienable, a vital development in the movement toward a nation-state.

29. Many of the humanists who wished to reform the Church received the patronage of François I's sister, Marguerite of Angouleme.

30. See Holt (2005, 17–21). While the humanists never threatened the Catholic Church or the body politic, "the perpetrators of 1534 were not just heretics but rebels. It is thus no surprise that just a few years later Francis authorized the sovereign courts of the crown – Parlements as well as lower courts – to take over the prosecution of heresy from the inquisitional courts of the church" (Holt, 2005, 20).

31. As one historian notes, "the actions of the parlements were uneven. In Duaphinè only eleven cases of heresy in seven years were reported and only light sentences given. Yet there were certainly Protestant groups in that province. In Normandy the parlement were so lethargic that the king suspended it in 1540 and appointed commissioners to hold the Grand Jours at Bayeaux, specifically to deal with heresy. Even after the parlement had been reinstated it remained feeble" (Knecht, 1982, 401).

32. See Mentzer (1984). Villers-Cotterêts also was the first royal decree requiring marriages to be registered and ratified by a parish priest. The introduction of the Roman-canon inquisitional model had "a substantial impact on the trial of heresy. The adoption allowed the royal government to standardize criminal procedure and it forced upon all courts, secular and ecclesiastical, the practice and rules which had evolved in its own tribunals. The accused heretics, in whichever forum he appeared – officialité, Inquisition or parlement, found his case adjudicated according to trial procedures developed by royal magistrates in royal courts" (Mentzer, 1984, 11).

33. See Mentzer (1984, 10, 45), Sutherland (1980, 34), and Roelker (1996, 207). "At the same time, the number and proportion of heresy cases handled by the royal courts spiraled, with the bulk of this increased case-load passing to the parliaments" (Mentzer, 1984, 10).

34. This is consistent with Kuran's (1995) theory of preference falsification.

35. Monter (1999) collected the data on executions for heresy between 1523 and 1560 by combing through all of the parlementary criminal records in France. This was a significant undertaking considering the lack of an index system and that there were between eight and ten parlements operating at any time during this period. Monter reports the village of arrest for each trial. We geocoded this location as well the location of the closest regional parlement. We then used ArcGIS to measure the distance between these two locations for each trial.

36. We calculate the total number of trials by généralité for each period. The généralités were regions created by François I in 1542 in order to facilitate collection of royal taxes. For our purposes, they serve as convenient regional boundaries, but we don't suggest these boundaries were significant for religious belief.

37. See Roelker (1996, 208). The first inquisitor of the faith was Mattheiu Ory. He was not really an inquisitor, but rather a royal official. Other regional commissioners included Jacques Le Roux, who was sent to Sens, and Nicole Sanguin, who was dispatched to Meaux (Roelker, 1996, 208–212).

38. Even the "records of their trials were burned along with them and the ashes scattered to the winds, thereby preventing their burial. Guilty of the ultimate religious and political crime of *lèse-magesté divine*, even their memory was meant to be destroyed along with all physical evidence of their existence on earth and in this polity" (Nicholls, 1988, 50).

39. See Foucault (2012).

40. Historians note that "in his original *Institutes* of 1536 Calvin devoted only one short paragraph to martyrs, as one kind of witness among many others to God's working in history, whereas by 1552 he was urging the faithful to be prepared for persecution and martyrdom and if it comes to accept it joyfully, because faith should always be confessed and never denied, and witnessing the truth is more precious than life itself" (Nicholls, 1988, 66).

41. Protestant propaganda dwelt on this theme. Parker observes that "[o]ne of the central motifs within the *Histoire des martyrs* is the parallel between contemporary martyrs and the godly champions of biblical eras who attempt to console fellow Reformers, to explicate the endemic brutality of their situation, and to legitimize their cause" (Parker, 1993, 230).

42. Monter notes that the "great heresy hunt begun in mid-1540s … strained the resources of the Paris Parlement to their limits" (Monter, 1999, 120). Despite the imposition of royal control over the regional and church courts, enforcement of the laws against heresy continued to vary from region to region. In the south particularly, landowners sympathetic to Protestantism sheltered and failed to try individuals suspected of heresy.

43. Sutherland notes that "[b]y 1560 there were many contemporary names for describing Protestants: *les Luthériens, les Calvinists, les réformés ceux de la religion prétendu réformé* – often known as RPR – *les sectaires, les consistoriaux* and so forth" (Sutherland, 1980, 101). Thus, "the epithet Huguenot was not used before 1560; it then denoted a party, whose fortunes therefore became political" (Sutherland, 1980, 1).

44. In fact, it was the fifth time Henri IV of Navarre had changed his religion (see Labrousse, 1998, 35).

45. See Sutherland (1980, 330–332). One historian describes the Edict as "a more or less limp compromise – a poorly tailored cover which ardent believers on both sides deplored, but they were too much in the minority to prevent its implementation" (Labrousse, 1998, 35). Another notes "[t]here are no references whatever to philosophical ideas of tolerance. The Huguenots were indeed tolerated, in the limited sense of the word: they had to be accepted for want of a better solution. But they were expected one day to adopt the religion of the king" (Cottret, 2003, 119).

46. "There is considerable uncertainly about what Elizabeth I really did believe in religion, and she was not, it would seen, deeply committed theologically in the great disputes over doctrine which divided men at this time" (McGrath, 1967, 5).

47. See Marshall (2016). "Government policy was based on the premise that religious dissidence was to be punished only when it threatened national security and the

established order ... Catholics were ostensible persecuted not as heretics but as enemies of the state – not for their sinful opinions but for the potentially subversive consequences of holding them" (Walsham, 1993, 11).

48. See Jordan (1936, 20–23). In fact, a total 138 Catholic priests died as traitors and 60 laymen were executed for harboring them.

49. In 1600 a Puritan listed ninety-one problems with the Church of England. These included the use of Apocrypha, liturgies, and the set form of prayers; prohibitions during lent on marriages and eating meat; the rituals used in baptisms; "popish vestments" worn by the clergy; and the existence of bishops and archbishops with the powers to run courts and impose tithes (Morgan, 1963, 6).

50. Recent research reconsiders the arguments of R. H. Tawney (1926), linking it to the commercialization of agriculture and the eventual rise of manufacturing and industry (Heldrin, Robinson, and Vollmer, 2015).

51. The financial decline of the church is documented by Hill (1956). The decline in the legitimating power of the church is the focus of Greif and Rubin (2018).

52. For example, banking institutions were divided along confessional lines (Colvin, 2017).

53. See Teter (2006, 44) for details of the execution of Katarzyna Malcherowa in 1539.

54. Furthermore, Poland, unlike other Western European countries, was never religiously homogeneous and consequently, Catholicism played a much less important role in legitimizing the state than elsewhere in Europe. The state of Poland-Lithuania extended over a vast territory, and although its rulers were Catholic, its population included significant Greek Orthodox, Armenian, Jewish, and Muslim minorities (see Tazbir, 1973, 31). Poland had, for instance, more than 100 mosques in 1616 (Davis and Deaton, 1981, 190). As Davis notes: "The nobility believed what they wished, and protected whom they liked. The bourgeoisie and the Jews were secure within the framework of their autonomous estates ... the 'Golden Freedom' of the nobility, proved an obstruction to efficient government and to religious fanaticism alike" (Davies, 1981, 200).

55. Also see Lecler (1960).

8

The Inquisition and the Establishment of Religious Homogeneity in Spain

The Spanish Inquisition remains one of the most infamous institutions in European history. It has the reputation of ruthlessly suppressing dissent, hunting down Protestants, and freely resorting to brutal torture. Some elements of this "Black Legend" are exaggerated; others are rooted in fact. The Spanish Inquisition was an institution that was deeply tied up with the Spanish experience of the Reconquista. Established before the Reformation, its primary targets in its initial, and most active, decades were converted Jews.

In this chapter we document the rise of the Spanish Inquisition and relate it to the conditional toleration equilibrium that characterized medieval Europe. At the same time, though a product of the general medieval equilibrium we have described, the Spanish Inquisition was also a uniquely Iberian institution. First, it had its origins in a late medieval Spain that was much more religiously diverse than any other part of Europe. Second, we will emphasize that the key to the identity of the Iberian rulers and their claim to legitimacy was their status as crusader kingdoms reclaiming lands from infidel Muslims.

These two factors interacted with one another. On the one hand, the religious diversity of lands conquered by the monarchs of Castile and Aragon in the twelfth and thirteenth centuries made enforcing religious conformity impossible. During the Reconquista itself, largely pragmatic attitudes toward non-Christians held sway. As the Christian monarchs absorbed new territories, they allowed Jews and Muslims to continue their religious practices. On the other hand, the most important source of royal legitimacy and the means through which rulers could assert themselves over the nobility or independent cities was by stressing their identity as crusaders and as Christian monarchs.

These competing forces can be seen in the decision to establish a "royal" inquisition independent of the papacy in 1478. Opposition to heresy was a way the new rulers of a unified Castile and Aragon legitimated their rule and elevated themselves over their rivals. But, as with the persecution of Protestants in mid-sixteenth-century France, establishing an institution capable of investigating, imprisoning, and prosecuting large numbers of people created an "engine of repression." Unlike in England or France, however, the Spanish monarchy was successful in suppressing religious differences by the early seventeenth century: Jews and Muslims were expelled or compelled to abandon their old faith and Protestantism was eliminated. The Iberian peninsula was, as a result, truly Catholic for the first time since Visigothic times.

This attainment of religious unity was of little benefit, however, to Spain's status as a great power. Buoyed by the inflow of silver and gold from the Americas, Spanish monarchs hardly invested in fiscal capacity. Nor did they attempt to unify the different legal systems of the realms they ruled. As a consequence, the Spanish economy remained internally fragmented and beset by rent-seeking. Spain fell behind the leading Northern European economies. Fragmented and weakened by overexerting itself in near continuous warfare, Spain never made the investments in fiscal and legal capacity that England and France did. It remained in the conditional toleration equilibrium until the twentieth century and suffered for it.

8.1 The Conversos "Problem"

8.1.1 Religious Diversity in Medieval Spain

The famed *convivencia* that governed the three Abrahamic religions in early medieval Spain provided a measure of religious peace, but it has been exaggerated by modern scholars seeking an Islamic example of religious toleration. It was a classic example of conditional toleration. The Islamic conquerors were a small minority when they overthrew the Visigothic kingdom. They never succeeded in fully conquering the Iberian peninsula and remained in a state of semipermanent war with the small northern Christian kingdoms. As elsewhere under Islamic rule, Christians and Jews received *dhimmi* status, which granted them protection to continue to practice their religion in return for higher taxes and legal restrictions.

Religion was crucial in legitimating Umayyad rule in Spain. The ulama were more powerful and influential in Islamic Spain than was the case elsewhere in the Islamic world. As such, the Umayyad fiercely repressed threats to religious orthodoxy. Morera notes that

The Umayyads imposed brutal punishments on the *dhimmis* who dared to openly proclaim their religious beliefs. In the ninth century, *alim* Ibn al-Qasim asserted that if a Christian said, "Our religion is better than yours, for truly yours is the religion of the Ass," he must be punished. Al-Qaism cited imam Malik's view that when an infidel insulted the Prophet, he must be killed. (Fernández-Morera, 2016, 125)

Insults to Muhammad or Islam were violations of the "the covenant of protection" granted to *dhimmis*. These statements were not empty threats. Relatives of the ruler and members of the elite were on occasion executed for secretly practicing Christianity. In the mid-ninth century a spat of persecutions against Christians saw almost fifty individuals executed either as Christians or for reverting back to Christianity (having been born into families that had nominally converted to Islam). This system of religious repression was part of a more general system of social control.

As part of the Umayyads' effective system of social control, the powerful religious functionary known as the *muhtasib* policed the cities of Islamic Spain, enforcing *sharia* in everyday activities, including the marketplace. A central element of the job involved informing the Umayyad rulers of any potential subversion on the part of the masses. (Fernández-Morera, 2016, 134)

It was therefore a society that was both highly religious and highly religiously fragmented that was reconquered by the Christian kingdoms of medieval Spain.

As an urban and skilled minority, Jews played an important role in both the Muslim and the Christian states in medieval Spain. Nowhere else in Europe did Jews make up such a large part of the population. Numerous Jewish historians have celebrated the conditions of Jews under Islamic rule. The reality was more complex and ambivalent. On the one hand, Jews were economically successful. They rose to positions of prominence in government and Jewish communities flourished culturally. On the other hand, literary Muslim sources often express hostility and disdain for Jews. During the height of the "Golden Age" in Islamic Spain there were widespread massacres of Jews in Granada in 1066 and at various occasions in the twelfth century (see Cohen, 1994; Brann, 2002).

The Reconquista proceeded in three stages. The collapse of the Caliphate of Córdoba in the early eleventh century permitted the Christian kingdoms of northern Spain, which had never been conquered to win back large parts of territory. In 1085 Toledo was captured by the king of Castile and Leon. In response, the Berber Almoravids invaded Spain and took over the successor kingdoms of the Caliphate, imposing a much stricter and more intolerant form of Islam. In 1212, however, the kingdoms of Castile, Aragon, and Navarre decisively defeated the Berber Almohads. This began a second stage in the Reconquista and in 1248 the king of Castile captured Seville. From this point on, the majority of Spain was in Christian hands, although the rump Muslim state of Granda survived until 1492, the conquest of which marks the third and final stage in the Reconquista.

The graduated nature of the Reconquista shaped the patterns of religious and ethnic diversity in Spain. In the north, the small Christian kingdoms of Galicia, Asturias, Leon, and Navarre had retained their independence. Their populations were entirely Christian. The territories of New Castile and Aragon conquered during the first stage of Reconquista in the eleventh century had large Jewish populations. As the Reconquista proceeded south in the early thirteenth century, the Christian kingdoms occupied lands which had long been settled by Muslims.

Jewish communities were favorably treated by Christian kings of the Spanish Reconquista such as Alfonso X of Castile. As they conquered new territories, Spanish monarchs had granted rights to Jews and Muslims and allowed them freedom to practice their religion. But the relative religious peace that was maintained during the height of the Reconquista in the twelfth and thirteenth centuries was not a stable equilibrium. Medieval Spanish monarchs had little option but to offer toleration. They conquered lands that had been Islamic for centuries, and which were comprised of ethnically, religiously, and linguistically diverse communities. Toleration was a temporary and pragmatic expedient.

During the Reconquista, the Church played a crucial role both directly in the fighting (through military orders such as the Order of Santiago) and in administration. The Castilian monarchs distributed lands to the Church for this and, in return, they relied on the Church to collect taxes on its behalf. As a result, in the sixteenth century about one sixth of the land was owned by the Church (Drelichman and Voth, 2014, 80–81).

The resulting religious division of labor that characterized medieval Spain exemplifies the conditional toleration equilibrium. Accordingly, "the three communities performed quite different functions in Spanish society. The Christians were nobles, churchmen, and fighters, Jews were craftsmen, financiers, and intellectuals, and Muslims were predominantly agriculturalists and craftsmen" (Green, 2007, 24). As we noted in Chapter 1, Jews governed themselves through communal institutions such as the *aljama*. In Aragon, for example, they were a major source of income for the Crown. In return the crown protected them: "their prosperity was, in a way, the king's" (Assis, 1997, 32). As was the case elsewhere in Europe, this made the Jews targets of popular anger (Nirenberg, 1996).

In the long run, the diversity of medieval Spain was at odds with the ruler's reliance on religious legitimacy. In particular, the Church in Spain sought the long-term conversion of both Jews and Muslims. Anti-Jewish disputations in which clerics attacked the Talmud, which were in turn defended by Jewish Talmudic scholars, were one common technique in the arsenal of the clergy. Laws were implemented that limited social intercourse among Christians, Jews, and Muslims. Dress codes were promulgated for different religious groups and sexual intercourse between Christians or Muslims or Jews was punished by death by burning (Nirenberg, 1996, 130–133).

Until the end of the fourteenth century, anti-Jewish violence, however, remained comparatively rare in medieval Spain. This reflects the size and wealth of the Spanish Jewish community in this period and the degree to which Christian rulers relied on them as merchants, tax collectors, doctors, administrators, and financiers. As we saw in Chapter 6, the important economic role Jews played in medieval society helped to insulate them from the worst antisemitic violence. But this situation was unstable. Violent pogroms accompanied the Black Death. Much larger scale massacres followed in 1391, by far the worst in Spanish history up until that point. Tens of thousands submitted to forced baptism to avoid death.

Mass conversions did not solve the problem of religious diversity. So many were forcibly converted that this simply created another community in late medieval Spain: converted Jews or conversos, called *maranos* or swine by many Christians. Naturally these conversos had a similar economic profile to Jews. They played an important role in the urban economy, and as such they attracted resentment, now for largely economic reasons. Freed from the anti-Jewish restrictions and regulations, many conversos flourished more than they could have as Jews, becoming still more important in trade, finance, and government (Netanyahu, 1995).

Some converted Jews became fervent opponents of Judaism. They include Solomon ha-Levi who, under the name Paul of Burgos, advocated confining Jews to ghettos, restricting their trade, and imposing humiliating laws on them to encourage conversion. The majority of conversos, however, seem to have maintained close relationships with those Jews who had not converted, but with whom they shared cultural affinity and, in many cases, family ties. Many continued to abstain from eating pork and even to observe the Sabbath.

8.1.2 The Establishment of the Inquisition in Spain

Fifteenth-century Spain had been wracked by a series of wars and civil wars. These conflicts were only brought to an end in 1479 with the unification of the crowns of Castile and Aragon under Ferdinand and Isabella. To restore social and political order they established the Holy Hermandad as an internal police force and they petitioned the pope for the right to establish their own Inquisition.

The Spanish Inquisition was a different institution from the medieval Roman inquisition, founded to combat heresy after the Albigensian Crusade, as discussed in Chapter 3. The Roman inquisition was the responsibility of the Dominicans and subject to the authority of the Pope rather than the crown. In contrast, the Spanish inquisition was a tool of Ferdinand and Isabella – a royal inquisition that they could direct and control. It expanded into Aragon in 1483 and later became active across the Spanish empire.[1]

The Inquisition was one tool directed at achieving religious and cultural unity in Spain. A second tool was expulsion. By expelling the entire Jewish population in 1492, Isabella and Ferdinand hoped to break the ties that the conversos maintained with their old religion. Medieval England and France had "solved" their own diversity "problems" by expulsion, as we saw in Chapter 4. The rulers of Spain were unable to do this because Jews and Muslims formed larger minorities and they were culturally much more entrenched. Islam had been the ruling religion on much of the peninsula for many centuries, and the Jews had long been a prominent, rich, and influential minority. Expulsion alone could not rid Spain of this cultural diversity. And this cultural diversity was a problem so long as it was seen as containing within it the threat of potential religious diversity.

It was in its first few decades that the Inquisition killed the majority of its victims. Before 1525, the overwhelming proportion of victims of the Inquisition were converted Jews. In Barcelona, for example, 99 percent of the victims were conversos. Only a small minority were executed or otherwise punished for Protestantism. Henry Kamen observes that "The savagery of the onslaught against the conversos was without equal in the history of any tribunal in the western world: set beside it, the medieval Inquisition appears a model of moderation" (Kamen, 1985, 41).

Between 1480 and 1525 the Inquisition was at its most repressive. Half of those investigated were brought before Inquisitorial tribunals. About 15,000 individuals were "reconciled" after suffering nonfatal punishment and 2,000 individuals were executed (Rawlings, 2006, 15). This makes the Inquisition far more bloody than its medieval equivalent, but during these years it was roughly comparable to the French persecution of Protestants in terms of numbers executed (though it investigated and inflicted lesser punishments on a far larger number of individuals). However, unlike the *burning chamber* and its persecution of Protestants in France, the Inquisition was not disbanded after 1525; though the rate of executions slowed, the Inquisition continued to be active, finding new victims in the form of Protestants, converted Muslims, blasphemers, and homosexuals.

By the latter part of the sixteenth century even seemingly harmless cultural traits such as cooking with olive oil rather than butter or not eating pork could be grounds for suspicion. Tapas is said to have originated as a means by which tavern keepers could discover hidden Jews by placing hams and shellfish in front of their guests and observing those who did not partake. And its popularity was partly due to it being used as a way for those suspected of crypto-Judaism to signal that they were indeed good Catholics.

The Inquisition was fairly successful in repressing the conversos as an independent community. Spaniards of converso heritage continued to be prominent, but cut off from Judaism they lost their links to the cultural traditions that defined their independent identity.

8.2 The Threat of the Reformation in Spain

Spain's cultural and geographic distance to the center of the Reformation ensured that Lutheranism did not enter the Iberian peninsular until the late 1520s. The success of reforming Spanish bishops – notably Francisco Jiménez de Cisneros – in eradicating abuses within the Catholic Church in the early years of the sixteenth century also meant that there was less pent-up demand for religious change.[2] The first evidence of the influence of the Reformation can be seen in a small group of educated Spanish humanists, known as the Illuminists, who came under suspicion in 1529. The swift response of the Inquisition to any perceived religious deviancy, even from declared Catholics, stamped out any sparks of Protestantism before it could become a fire. Individuals were investigated for alleged Protestant beliefs, but there was "genuine ignorance and misunderstanding among Spaniards as to what actually constituted Protestantism ... The principal definition of a Lutheran where inquisitors were concerned was somebody who made a passing reference in praise of a reformer or his ideas. In the majority of cases 'Lutheranism' amounted to nothing more than a careless religious statement rather than a calculated attack on the Catholic Church" (Rawlings, 2006, 102).

Many of those Protestants brought before the Inquisition were foreigners – British sailors unlucky enough to fail into Spanish hands, for example. It was only in 1558 that a group of high level clergymen and nobles in Valladolid were investigated for Protestant sympathies. The severe suppression of this cell – between May 1559 and December 1560 a total of 218 individuals were accused, of whom 131 were Protestants, and of these 66 were burned – served as a deterrent and Spain thereafter remained almost entirely free from the Reform movement.

On the face of it, the Inquisition succeeded. Spain escaped the disruptive impact of the Reformation. Medieval Spain had had far greater religious diversity than other parts of Europe, but this diversity was reduced in the sixteenth and seventeenth centuries. In particular, the fact that the Inquisition was well established in Spain *prior* to the Reformation meant that it was possible to deploy the full force of its coercive apparatus at the first sign of Protestant ideas spreading among the populace. The Iberian peninsula followed a different path to other European countries which, as we saw in Chapter 7, experienced increased religious diversity after 1500. Spain succeeded in achieving religious homogeneity, but since the Enlightenment, historians have seen in this "success" many of the causes for Spain's subsequent economic and political decline.

Enlightenment critics of Spain charged that it had remained "medieval." This was not exactly accurate. The Spanish Inquisition was unlike any medieval institution in its repressive capabilities. This charge was true only insofar as Spain maintained the religious unity that had characterized the rest of medieval Europe (though, ironically, not Spain) throughout the early modern period.

Spain also differed from its rivals, England and France, because it had access to the gold and silver of the Americas. This liquid wealth fueled the Habsburg dream of global hegemony – a desire epitomized by Philip II's dictum *non sufficit orbis* "the world is not enough" (Parker, 1998).[3] The resources of the New World relaxed the budget constraint of the Spanish monarchy in the short-run. In the long run, however, it reduced the need for investment in fiscal or legal capacity. At the same time, it led to inflation and rent-seeking, which undermined Spain's domestic economy.[4] These factors, as well as the over expansion of Spanish military power and its subsequent collapse in the wake of the Thirty Years' War, ensured that Spain followed a very different trajectory to Northwestern Europe.

A second critical factor in Spain's historical development was the premature death of the heirs of Ferdinand and Isabella. This resulted in the Habsburg Charles V inheriting the Spanish empire in addition to the Habsburg territories in Austria and the Low Countries, and a strong claim to the Holy Roman Empire. Viewed as a foreigner in Spain, Charles was committed to Habsburg dynastic interests, which included the suppression of Protestantism in Germany and the Low Countries. Charles and his son, Phillip II, involved Spain in large-scale and extremely costly warfare across the breadth of Europe.

As foreigners who lacked the legitimacy of native rulers, both Charles II and Phillip II were highly sensitive to domestic opposition. In particular, their decision to commit Spanish resources to warfare in Northern Europe was unpopular among Spanish elites. As a result, they willingly granted the Inquisition increasing autonomy which resulted in subcontracting ideological repression to the most ardent Counter-Reformation elements in the Spanish Church. When the crown committed to overseas war, the Inquisition was used to suppress and terrify domestic opposition (Vidal-Robert, 2013).[5]

Despite increasing military commitments – not least maintaining a large, highly trained, professional army in the Low Countries – the Habsburg monarchs made no significant investments in state capacity. The marriage of Ferdinand and Isabella fused the monarchies of Aragon and Castile, but did not create a single unified political entity. Within Castile, Ferdinand and Isabella built an extremely effective military and state by the standards of the early sixteenth century. Charles V crushed the Revolt of Communeros in 1522, ending opposition to his authority and destroying Spain's medieval republicanism. American silver and the distractions of wars across Europe meant Charles V and Philip II did not need to create a fiscal system capable of sustaining Spain's imperial ambitions in the long run. The consequences of this failure became apparent in the seventeenth century as Spain fought states that had begun to modernize their fiscal and financial systems.

The state-building efforts that were attempted were largely confined to Castile. Elsewhere, in Aragon, for instance, "semi-independent lords exercised numerous feudal rights to the detriment of the crown and their vassals, where Castilians were debarred from office, where laws were different and independently administered, and where taxation was checked by the cortes" (Lynch, 1992, 290). Thus the reason for the ultimate failure of the Spanish empire lay not with profligate borrowing or overspending, as argued by traditional historians, but was on the revenue side and the failure to create a unified fiscal state.[6] This failure went hand-in-hand with the Spanish government's continued reliance on identity rules.

Political and legal fragmentation had adverse economic consequences. Internal custom barriers impeded trade preventing the formation of a unified market. High transportation costs compounded this problem, as did the absence of any means of coordinating investment in improving roads. Indirect taxes were collected and spent at the local level. Regina Grafe (2012), characterizes early modern Spain as a confederation of urban republics that were able to maintain their "liberties."

The crown negotiated lump-sum taxes with each city or territory; tax exemptions were commonplace. In Castile, while the *cortes* decided on the amount of taxes that each city had to pay, all decisions about how to collect or allocate the tax were taken by members of the town council. Unlike in England or France, there were few serious attempts to centralize or standardize tax collection. Drelichman and Voth (2014) note that "The persistence of these ancient 'freedoms' are not only responsible for the continuation of economically harmful rules; they also serve to illustrate a particular type of internal weakness, and one that goes to the heart of Spain's early modern failure to build a more capable state." Officials in

Spanish territories often ignored royal commands citing ancient privileges. As the monarchs had agreed to uphold these privileges and liberties, legally they had a good case. And because Spanish rulers had access to American silver, they lacked the pressing need to override these privileges in the way that their French rivals did.

8.3 The Decline of Spain and the Continuation of the Inquisition

Spain provides an hypothetical alternative path that the rest of Europe could have followed in the absence of a Reformation. The Inquisition successfully imposed religious homogeneity in Spain – something that rulers failed to achieve in England, France, or the Holy Roman Empire. The conversos were terrorized into cultural oblivion. The Moriscos were suppressed and then expelled. Protestantism was stamped out before it could gain any kind of foothold. But the benefits of achieving Catholic unity were fleeting, at least in material terms. Overburdened by taxes, suffering from a decline in export markets, and deteriorating agricultural conditions, from 1600 onward Spain gradually fell behind in both relative and absolute terms.[7]

This economic decline had deep roots. In the late Middle Ages, the cities of the kingdom of Aragon played an important role in the commercial economy of the Mediterranean; Castile was a leading wool exporter and cloth producer. Urbanization rates in the sixteenth century were comparatively high and a significant proportion of the population was engaged in nonagricultural activities. Álvarez Nogal and De La Escosura (2007, 2013) find that medieval and sixteenth-century Spain was a relatively affluent economy with comparatively high per capita income.[8] But the proportion of the population living in towns declined starkly in the seventeenth century.[9] Whereas medieval Spain had grown rich on wool exports, the post-1600 economy was a low-wage agricultural economy based on cereal production that would prove to be ill suited to the new technologies of the Industrial Revolution after 1800.

North (1981, 1990) attributed the decline of Spain to political institutions that encouraged economically inefficiency such as granting monopoly rights to guilds, failing to tax the nobility, defaulting on debts, and confiscating property. Bad political institutions thereby undermined the foundations of commerce: the "structure of property rights that evolved in response to the fiscal policies of the government simply discouraged individuals from undertaking many productive activities and instead encouraged socially less productive activities that were sheltered from the reach of the state" (North, 1981, 151–152). But this explanation does not give the full picture. As we have seen, in practice, the reach of the Habsburg monarchs was limited (Grafe and Irigoin, 2006; Grafe, 2012).[10]

In general, however, institutional explanations for Spain's decline remain persuasive and complement other important factors. Institutional factors exacerbated the overvaluation of the currency caused by inflows of American silver, which helped to price Spanish goods out of export markets (Drelichman, 2005). But contrary to North, it was the weakness of the Spanish monarchy more than its strength that was responsible for the problems that overwhelmed the region after 1600. The failure of the Spanish monarchy to fiscally unify the country helped to perpetuate the fragmentation of Spanish markets, as documented by Grafe (2012). Drelichman and Voth (2008, 2014) argue that the resource curse associated with large inflows of American silver afflicted the Spanish economy by increasing the returns to rent-seeking and undermining the institutions that limited the power of the monarchy. The silver boon undermined the bargaining power of the Cortes, who were unable to threaten the crown by withholding tax revenues. Thus the "development of Castilian institutions was in many ways the exact opposite to that in Britain and the Netherlands, whose constitutional arrangements were a consequence of the need to grapple with scarcity" (Drechlichman and Voth, 2008, 141).

Spanish economic decline was still more striking because it was bound up with a rapid collapse in political power after 1640 (Elliott, 1961). The nadir of Spain's political fortunes were reached in the late seventeenth century during the last Habsburg king Charles II (r. 1665–1700). As Spain declined, religious legitimacy remained key to maintaining political order. The elaborate ritual of the auto-da-fé that saw the Spanish monarchs oversee the punishment of heretics remained prominent. The importance of religion for political legitimacy did not lessen over the course of the seventeenth century as it did in Northern Europe. An intense persecution of Portuguese conversos took place in the 1650s. The largest auto-da-fé in Spanish history was in 1680. As late as 1691, thirty-seven conversos were burned in Majorca.[11] In 1700 a damning report of the Inquisition was produced, but by this period the Inquisition had become a powerful political player. The Grand Inquisition persuaded the king to burn the report and, thereafter, it was not in the interest of Spain's new (French) Bourbon dynasty to dispense with it.

After 1700 the new Bourbon dynasty partially modernized the Spanish state. But during the first part of the eighteenth century, the Bourbon rulers were predominantly interested in the possibility of succeeding to the French throne. It was only in the reign of Charles III (1759–1788) that large-scale reforms were pursued in Spain and in the colonies.

During this period, the Inquisition remained a powerful tool of social control. By the eighteenth century, it was primarily concerned with "minor heresies" such as bigamy, blasphemy, and sodomy. The Inquisition often punished individuals for "careless talk." The majority of such individuals were punished lightly. The Inquisitors continued to complain about the numbers of pagans and atheists. Barely educated peasants and craftsmen often had irreligious views. But it was only when individuals continued to publicly maintain deviant beliefs or to intentionally subvert the teachings of the Church that they faced capital punishment. Nevertheless, the institution remained oppressive. As late as the eighteenth century, English merchants trading in Spain could become entangled in its clutches.[12]

Early modern Spain remained in the conditional toleration equilibrium. The state remained dependent on religion for legitimation; there was no movement toward religious freedom. The Inquisition continued to police personal morality. One example of this was that it saw bigamy as a form of heresy and sentenced such individuals to 3 years hard labor (Pérez, 2006, 90). In a world of poor transport and communication technology, it was easy for peasants to slip into bigamous relationships. A woman could believe her husband to be dead and then remarry, only to have her first husband reappear.[13] This continued until the Inquisition finally disappeared in 1834, by which time, Spain had long since fallen from the ranks of major European powers.

8.4 Chapter Summary: The Legacy of the Inquisition

Medieval Spain was both the most religiously diverse part of medieval Europe and home to a particularly militarized Catholicism. Given the prominence of its Jewish and Muslim populations, Ferdinand and Isabella faced a very different situation from that of rulers in France, England, and the Holy Roman Empire.[14]

Once they established the Inquisition to deal with the perceived problem of conversos reverting to Judaism, they put in place an institution that was uniquely capable of suppressing religious diversity, albeit at a high cost in blood and treasure. The argument of this book suggests that they did so because they were highly dependent on Catholicism for their legitimacy and feared that converted Jews might relapse to Judaism or lure Catholics into Judaizing heresies. This would, in turn, threaten the religious foundations of the Spanish monarchy. Once established, the Inquisition helped to insulate Spain from the disturbances associated with the Reformation in Central and Northern Europe. But it did so at a huge cost. In the long run, the Inquisition had a pervasive and negative impact on Spanish culture and society.

Many have argued that the Inquisition created a polarized culture that was hostile to innovation. Jordi Vidal-Robert (2014) studied the Inquisition's long-term legacy using data from Catalonia. He found that it reduced population growth during the early modern period. The mechanism Vidal-Roberts hypothesizes was that Inquisitions reduced innovation, technological progress, and productivity growth and that this translated into slower population growth. Even today Vidal-Roberts finds people living in areas with historically more intense levels of inquisitorial activity are more likely to think that new technologies will harm them.

The trajectory of the Spanish state points to an alternative path to that taken by the major European powers. Confronted with religious heterogeneity, Spain chose to force groups to assimilate or eliminated them altogether. Religiously unified and flush with the resources of the New World, Spain then sustained ambitious overseas military commitments without investing in fiscal or legal capacity. Its domestic industries stagnated and declined; urbanization and total population fell, and as a result, the average Spaniard was poorer in 1800 than in 1500.

This alternative path could easily have become the fate of the rest of Europe. Had Mary I sired an heir, a unified Anglo-Iberian Habsburg monarchy could have dominated Western Europe, crushed the rebellious Low Countries, kept France weak and divided, and contained, if not entirely reversed, the Reformation. Had this occurred, there may have been no movement toward constitutional monarchy, liberalism, or religious freedom.

Notes

1. The introduction of the Inquisition into Aragon, where Jews and Conversos played particularly important social roles, faced greater resistance than in other regions. Prominent conversos were able to persuade Pope Sixtus IV to issue a bull to stop the Inquisition, but Ferdinand forced him to withdraw it (Monter, 1990).
2. In particular, Cisneros reformed the mendicant orders, rigorously enforcing celibacy among friars.
3. This motto was originally applied to Alexander the Great and was seen by contemporaries as a mark of Spanish ambition (Parker, 2014, 276).
4. See Drelichman (2005), Drechlichman and Voth (2008), and Drelichman and Voth (2014).
5. He suggests that there was an inverted U-shaped relationship between the intensity of the Crown's military commitments and the intensity of Inquisitional activity.
6. The view that the decline of Spain was due to excessive borrowing is present in many traditional accounts such as Kennedy (1987) but it has been overturned by Drelichman and Voth (2010, 2011, 2014).
7. Henry Kamen expressed skepticism over this decline on the grounds that "Spain never rose. So-called decline was nothing less than the operation and persistence over an extended period of basic weaknesses in the Spanish economy" (Kamen, 1978, 25). But more recent quantitative evidence has overturned this revisionism and reaffirms the reality of decline.
8. On the more optimistic estimates, Álvarez Nogal and De La Escosura (2013) estimate that in 1348, per capita GDP in Spain may have been twice that of England.

In 1570 it was still almost 28 percent higher. But by 1850, it was only 64 percent of British output per capita. On more pessimistic estimates, Spanish per capita GDP was only 46 percent of British levels in 1850.

9. In Andalusia, Aragon, Asturias, Navarre, Old Castile, and Valencia, the number of people living in towns of 5,000 or more inhabitants declined by half or more between 1590 and 1700 (Álvarez Nogal and De La Escosura, 2007, 338).

10. Similarly, the long-criticized institution of the Mesta has been reevaluated by economic historians (Drelichman, 2009).

11. It is true that the proportion of death sentences relative to non-capital sentences fell over time. The Inquisition no longer had to police a large community of converted Jews, and Protestant beliefs were no longer spreading rapidly.

12. As vividly documented by Lea (1907, 5).

13. The picture in Portugal was similar. The Portuguese inquisition remained active, sentencing a total of 30,000 individuals between 1536 and 1821. See Anderson (2013).

14. There are no exact numbers of the number of Jews in Spain on the eve of the expulsion. Estimates of the number expelled have been revised downward from up to 400,000 to around 50,000 (Kamen, 1988). But this was due to many Jews converting to Christianity. Kamen (1988) suggests that Jews were perhaps 1.6 percent of the population of Castile and 1.2 percent of the population of Aragon. The number of conversos, however, was much greater (see Netanyahu, 1995). The number of Moriscos on the eve of their expulsion in 1609 was 300,000, but they were concentrated in certain parts of Spain, especially the Kingdom of Valencia, where they made up one-third of the population (Chaney and Hornbeck, 2016).

9

From Confessionalization to Toleration and Then to Religious Liberty

On May 23 1618, three men could be seen hurtling the seventy feet from the third floor of the Bohemian Chancery tower to the ground below. They were all representatives of the Catholic Habsburg Emperor. Despite all of them surviving the fall, either because they fell in manure (as claimed by Protestants) or because of the divine intervention of angels (as claimed by Catholics), this "Defenestration of Prague" became the precipitating event of the great European conflagration known as the Thirty Years' War. It marked the breakdown in the political modus vivendi that, since 1555 and the Peace of Augsburg, had allowed Protestants and Catholics to avoid war. This equilibrium, described in the Latin as *cuius regio, eius religio,* or "whose realm, his religion" allowed for peace by permitting the princes of Germany with conflicting religious beliefs, literally, to live in separate realms. This is one of the more salient examples of the identity rules that characterized early modern Europe. The Peace of Augsburg did not enforce religious freedom but rather avoided conflict by allowing intolerance to be legislated at the local level – this was conditional toleration par excellence.[1]

The conditional toleration equilibrium that was shattered in Prague in 1618 was also uniquely suited for the highly fragmented political system of the Holy Roman Empire. As we have seen in earlier chapters this loose political agglomeration had lacked strong centralized government since the eleventh century controversy over investiture of priests that pitted the secular authority against the Church and had ended up weakening both.

This chapter studies the failure to reconstitute the conditional toleration equilibrium in Europe after the crisis brought about by the Reformation. In the aftermath of religious conflict, attempts to impose conditional toleration on their populations resulted in a fragile political-religious equilibrium. This equilibrium eventually undermined itself. And the intensification of interstate competition and state building saw the rise of mercantilist states like France and Prussia.

On the one hand, these states, like their predecessors, sought religious legitimacy as a key pillar of their authority. On the other hand, they also came to see economic development as crucial to political success. Pragmatic and mercantilist considerations led Cardinal Richelieu to offer de facto toleration to Portuguese Jews who could finance war against Spain and encouraged Jean Baptiste Colbert to tolerate Huguenots – a policy that was reversed after his death. Economic considerations also led the rulers of Prussia – the rising power in the Holy Roman Empire – in the late seventeenth century to accept both Jewish settlements and the Protestants who fled France after Louis XIV revoked the Edict of Nantes. Similar concerns drove mercantilist policymaking in Britain. These policies reflected institutional changes in the structure of European states.

We first consider the last major crisis associated with the wars of religion: the Thirty Years' War. Then we turn to France where the Edict of Nantes succeeded in maintaining religious peace for almost a century before being overturned by Louis XIV. Despite this major reversal in religious freedom, in the long run, there was a gradual movement toward greater religious liberty in France during the eighteenth century. Finally, we study England, where attempts in the seventeenth century to enforce religious conformity failed. This failure paved the way to greater religious freedom in the eighteenth and nineteenth centuries.

9.1 The Breakdown of Conditional Toleration in the Holy Roman Empire

9.1.1 The Thirty Years' War

The Peace of Augsburg brought Germany peace for sixty-three years. However, ever since the seventeenth century numerous scholars have attributed the outbreak of the Thirty Years' War to the contradictions of the peace of 1555. In the words of one historian, the Peace of Augsburg "created a machinery of conflict which ultimately precipitated the outbreak of the Thirty Years' War" (Whaley, 1985, 4).

The issues involved were complex. One of the most important had to do with the fragmented political and religious character of the Habsburg lands: in Tyrol and Lower Austria the position of the Habsburgs was strong and the population was majority Catholic, whereas in Bohemia and in Hungary, Habsburg authority was conditional on the support of the estates and the elite was largely Protestant. In the aftermath of the Peace of Augsburg, unlike in most of the Holy Roman Empire, the Habsburg rulers did not implement *cuius regio, eius religio*. It was only in the Tyrol, under Archduke Ferdinand, that the Counter-Reformation was embraced fully and policies put in place to marginalize and convert Protestants. The accession of Ferdinand was feared by Protestants because they were concerned that he might implement similar policies in the rest of the empire.

Following the Defenestration of Prague, the conflict within the Habsburg lands engulfed the rest of the Holy Roman Empire. After his army's resounding success on the battlefield at the Battle of White Mountain, the Habsburg ruler Ferdinand II extended the Counter-Reformation into the German states that had allied with Protestant rebels. This attempt to reverse the Reformation threatened to overturn not only the Peace of Augsburg, but also the European balance of power. Denmark, then Sweden, and finally France intervened, ostensibly to defend German liberties, but really to prevent Habsburg hegemony over central Europe. This widened the scope of the war, leading to decades of brutal but inconclusive fighting. Millions of deaths resulted from the disease and devastation brought about by the movements of large armies.[2] The cessation of fighting in 1648 ended Habsburg ambitions to build a confessional state in the Holy Roman Empire where *cuius regio, eius religio* was now cemented into legislation.[3]

9.1.2 The End of the Conditional Toleration?

The conclusion of the Thirty Years' War and the Treaty of Westphalia are often seen as marking the end of religious war in Europe. In many respects this is not entirely accurate. Religion continued to shape geopolitics. And religious violence remained a fact of life across Europe. Nevertheless the second part of the seventeenth century marked a turning point.

The Reformation and the Thirty Years' War shattered whatever was left of the unity of the Holy Roman Empire. And in its aftermath, states such as Brandenburg Prussia began to invest in fiscal and military capacity. As they did so, they followed mercantilist policies, religion ceased to play as important a role in legitimating their authority, and they invited Huguenots exiled from France and Jews from Eastern Europe to settle in their territories. This set the scene for the transition away from the medieval equilibrium of conditional toleration in Central as well as Western Europe.

9.2 The Fall and Rise of Religious Toleration in France

9.2.1 The Revocation of the Edict of Nantes

The failure of the Habsburgs to build a state in the Holy Roman Empire and the exhaustion of Spain led to France becoming the leading power in Europe. The Edict of Nantes reduced religious tensions. It made it possible for Protestants and Catholics to live side by side peacefully for almost a century. It ended the "crown's ancient function of forcibly extirpating heresy within the realm" (Church, 1972, 88–89).[4] But the Edict of Nantes was "predicated on confessional co-existence" based "on separation and exclusion mitigated only by those 'liberties' specifically guaranteed for Huguenots by the crown" (Wolfe, 1998, 17).

The problem with the Edict of Nantes was that the freedoms it granted Huguenot elites were bound to be unacceptable to the monarchy in the long run. Cardinal Richelieu crushed the independence of the Huguenot nobility during the 1620s, ending their status as a state within the state. But he maintained the rights of Huguenot worship. In the words of his biographer: "Richelieu hated the Huguenots as heretics … but was willing to tolerate them and allow them to live unmolested as long as they remained loyal subjects of the crown" (Church, 1972, 87). Richelieu sought to incorporate the Huguenots into the state. When Richelieu directed royal policy against the Huguenot nobility it was as rebels, not as heretics. The "king would treat all his subjects equally regardless of religion, merely requiring all to remain in their stations as reason required" (Church, 1972, 88). He believed this would bring the Protestants back into the Catholic fold whereas persecution would be counterproductive.

During the civil war known as the Fronde (1648–1653), the Protestants supported the monarchy and Jean-Baptist Colbert, Louis XIV's powerful finance minister, continued the policy of royal protection. Nevertheless, the conditions facing Protestants in France gradually deteriorated and Louis XIV came to believe he could end the religious split that had marred the kingdom for more than a century.

Between 1679 and 1685, Louis XIV signed 100 edicts against heresy (Ocibal, 1976, 157). Conservative estimates suggest that there were perhaps 900,000 Protestants in the country in 1685, less than 5 percent of the population.[5] The measures Louis XIV took against the Huguenots had support from Catholic thinkers and elite opinion. Louis's ministers, however, greatly exaggerated the number of conversions to Catholicism. As a consequence, Louis become convinced that only a few thousand heretics remained and that a policy of conversion (and expulsion of the obdurate) could be imposed at little cost.

Local initiatives by the intendant René de Marillac began the process. He requisitioned Protestant homes in Poitou in 1681 to billet soldiers. This policy, known as the *dragonnades*, aroused local opposition as the soldiers assaulted and robbed those families who provided them shelter. François-Michel le Tellier, Marquis de Louvois, who had succeeded Colbert as Louis XIV's chief minister, was upset at the disorder, but saw its potential as an instrument for encouraging mass conversions. Throughout the summer of

1685, this policy was effective in attracting large numbers of conversions. In Bérne, the king was told that 21,500 out of 22,000 Protestants converted in June and July (Bernard, 1956).

The perceived success of these coerced conversions convinced Louis XIV that the time was ripe to reunify the country religiously. In October 1685, the Edict of Nantes was revoked and Protestant worship was made illegal. The Revocation was the policy

... of a monarchy that had grown considerably in strength since the sixteenth century, could imagine that the eradication of heresy was within its grasp with few of the costs that had been associated with pursuing the goal a century earlier, and was pleased to carry out a policy that the great majority of the Catholic majority continued to consider fitting for a Most Christian King (Benedict, 1996, 74).

Protestant churches were pulled down and religious leaders went into hiding. In the months following the Revocation, 200,000 Huguenots left the country while the remaining 700,000 were either prevented from fleeing, coerced to attend Catholic worship, or attempted to disguise their faith. The majority of Huguenots stayed in France and conformed to Catholic worship but far more fled than Louis had anticipated. Converts to Catholicism were labeled *new converts*, who had to pay special taxes, and their behavior was monitored to see if their conversion was genuine. The potential punishments for obdurate Protestants were harsh "ranging from death or a life term rowing the King's galleys to confiscation of property or loss of inheritance rights" (Adams, 1991, 35).

This policy faded from prominence as France became embroiled in the Nine Years' War (1688–1697). The first year of peace, 1698, saw a renewed campaign against Protestants. Large-scale migration briefly revived. But Protestantism proved impossible to root out entirely. Enforcement required cooperation from local Catholic elites. Where this was not forthcoming, officials were unable to eradicate Protestantism. Despite the efforts of the state, the "goal of confessional unity remained unrealized, making the Revocation a failure" (Wilson, 2011, 7). In remote regions, Protestant worship never ceased (Sutherland, 1980, 36).

To take one example, Wilson (2011) studied the consequences of the Revocation in the majority Protestant town of Loriol in the Rhône Valley. Protestants in Loriol experienced hardship and downwards mobility as a result of Revocation. But they did not leave en masse. Many outwardly conformed while maintaining their Protestant faith. Despite tensions and incomplete or reluctant participation in Catholic duties, the new converts of Loriol did not go far enough in their resistance to warrant intervention (Wilson, 2011, 83). In Paris, after the initial Revocation, there was little active enforcement as the "authorities largely turned a blind eye to individual Protestants who did not try to leave the kingdom and who kept a low profile" (Garrioch, 2014, 46).

The distinction between old Catholics and new converts was removed in 1700. Royal officials like Marc-René d'Argenson, the police chief of Paris, adopted a new attitude, one that was more concerned with law and order than with religion (Garrioch, 2014, 48–51). By 1715, the Revocation's failure was clear: "[s]imply removing the official existence of Huguenot worship in France and legislating participation in the Catholic Church was obviously not enough to achieve true religious unity. Much of the Protestant minority was poorly integrated into the Catholic Church" (Wilson, 2011, 109).

Despite everything, a Protestant minority remained. By the 1760s, they numbered around 700,000. Although their religion remained illegal until 1787, "administrative laxity mitigated the severity of the laws" (Merrick, 1990, 139). This was particularly true in the south of France, where the authorities tacitly colluded with Protestant worship. After the 1760s, laws against Protestantism ceased to be enforced.[6]

The Edict of Toleration in 1787 acknowledged this by recognizing Protestantism legally. It stopped short of granting religious freedom: Protestants were recognized legally as individuals who were free to worship but prohibited from organizing in groups.[7] The Edict was acknowledgment that the imposition of religious unity had failed and thus played a major role in redefining the role of the king; it suggested that "the unity of the realm resided not in the putative Catholicity of his subjects but in their common civil status" thereby presaging the transformation of the French state that would occur after 1789 (Merrick, 1990, 164).

9.2.2 The French Revolution

The French Revolution brought about full civic equality for all Frenchman irrespective of whether they were Protestant or Catholic. Huguenots who had fled in the preceding century were offered the right to return. This is often seen as a radical change in policy.

As Tocqueville (1998) noted, many of the changes brought by the Revolution were prefigured in the preceding decades, and much that happened after the Revolution was a continuation of prior trends. It would take years for Protestantism to be treated equally with Catholicism. Even though Protestantism was legally recognized after 1791, it remained legally inferior. After the restoration of 1814, Catholicism remained the state religion. The defeat of Napoleon was associated with a "White Terror" as groups of royalists attacked Protestants who fled to Switzerland or to Paris for protection (Encrevé, 1999, 75). Protestants faced local opposition when they conducted missionary activity and in the 1820s they were fined for not participating in Catholic festivals. Napoleon III (r. 1852–1870) relied on the support of conservative Catholic elites and hence did not push for complete civic equality for Protestantism. This only came in 1879, though, even then, fierce debates continued over issues such as secular education (Franck and Johnson, 2016).

9.3 The Emergence of a Modern State in England

The English Civil War 1642–1651) saw Parliament openly challenge the authority of the crown and in so doing set England on a path toward both limited and democratic government.[8] Throughout the seventeenth century, the English monarchy strove to reestablish a stable political-religious equilibrium based around the Church of England. But every attempt failed.[9] What accounts for this failure to restore the old conditional toleration equilibrium?

The political influence of bishops such as Archbishop Laud was resented, especially by Puritans. Laud suppressed religious dissent by flogging, mutilating, and imprisoning his opponents. But this simply strengthened opposition to him. Laud's forced imposition of a common prayer book on Scotland led to outright war and the end of Charles I's (r. 1625–1649) personal rule.[10] The resulting political crisis brought civil war.

The Civil War saw the rise of a commercial, nonreligious elite. To defeat Charles I, Parliament raised tax revenues to build a professional "new model" army.[11] After the victory of Parliament, Presbyterians and Independents fought, partly over religious toleration. Presbyterians wanted a Calvinist state church. The Independents opposed bishops and favored toleration for dissenting Protestants. The Commonwealth established by Oliver Cromwell lacked legitimacy beyond that of military success. It rapidly collapsed following Cromwell's death, setting the scene for the restoration of Charles II (r. 1660–1685).[12]

A dissolute crypto-Catholic, Charles II was personally amenable to a religious accommodation with various dissenting Protestants. But he depended on a Royalist parliament determined to restore the privileges of the Anglican Church and to punish both Protestant dissenters and Catholics. Harsh punishments were imposed on nonconforming Protestants. According to the 1664 Conventicle Act, a first offense of worshiping in a nonconformist meeting led to a £5 fine. A second offense brought about a fine of either £10 or a six-month spell in jail. A third offense, a £100 fine or transportation to the colonies. Anyone convicted who did not conform within three months lost all land and goods to the church. In theory, though not in practice, failure to comply with these laws entailed the death penalty

(Marshall, 2006). This criminalized a substantial minority of the English population as, despite the legal restrictions, about 4 percent of the population or 200,000 people belonged to the four largest nondenominational Protestant sects.

The number of Quakers imprisoned in England between 1660 and 1685 has been estimated at over 11,000. Thousands of others were fined and financially ruined. The death toll was in the hundreds, if not in the thousands (Marshall, 2006, 95). It was only the fact that the laws were often laxly enforced by local officials that prevented these persecutions from being even more severe.

Protestant dissenters were not the only group who faced persecution. Even though England was ruled by a king who was privately a Catholic, priests continued to be killed as traitors. Between 1600 and 1680, seventy priests were executed in England. The Titus Oates affair led to the death of 22 Catholics for their alleged involvement in the fabricated Popish Plot.[13] The last judicial murder of a Roman Catholic was the execution of the Jesuit Oliver Plunkett in 1681.[14] But these executions did not strengthen the partnership between state and church; rather, they *destabilized* it. While Catholic priests were indeed aiming to assassinate Elizabeth I in the sixteenth century, they no longer posed this kind of geopolitical threat in the late seventeenth century. The executions and panics underscored the fact that in a religiously diverse environment, the Church of England was unable to provide the level of religious legitimacy that the pre-Reformation Catholic Church had done.[15]

Charles II largely avoided constitutional conflicts by ruling in tandem with a royalist Parliament. In administrative terms, his reign saw several important developments. The figure responsible for these reforms was Sir George Downing, who as a former ambassador to the Dutch Republic was acutely aware of England's financial backwardness compared to the Netherlands.[16] In 1665, Downing attempted to reform the Treasury by centralizing the different revenue streams and standardizing accounting procedures. He was particularly interested in finding alternative "parliamentary-based" sources of credit for the king (Ashworth, 2003, 17). Tax farming was replaced by a permanent bureaucracy of tax collectors (Johnson and Koyama, 2014*a*). Nevertheless, the major constitutional questions raised by the first English civil war were not resolved. The prospect of the succession of Charles II's openly Catholic brother, James, provoked a second crisis.

9.3.1 The Glorious Revolution

To gain recognition for Catholics, James II (r. 1685–1688) was prepared to grant toleration to dissenting Protestants. This was opposed by the Anglican establishment.[17] James II, however, also had ambitions to build a Catholic absolutist monarchy along the pattern of Louis XIV (Pincus, 2009). Once he sired a Catholic heir, opposition solidified from both the successors of the Parliamentary tradition of opposition (the Whigs) and from Anglican Royalists (Tories). James's Protestant son-in-law, William of Orange, the stadtholder of the Netherlands was invited to invade with a Dutch army. As soon as William landed, James's support crumbled and he fled to Ireland abandoning the royal seal. In England, as this revolution was almost bloodless, it was soon hailed as the Glorious Revolution.[18] William of Orange became William III and ruled jointly with his wife Mary as constitutional monarchs.

One of the first acts of the new reign, the Act of Toleration, brought relief for dissenting Protestants. But it did not relax the recusancy laws against Catholics nor did it apply to non-trinitarians or to atheists. It was a compromise necessitated by England's geopolitical situation. As Sowerby observes, the key drivers in the move toward greater religious toleration were "more political than intellectual" (Sowerby, 2013, 251). The Act of Toleration only ended the repression of dissenting Protestants. William III attempted to obtain a much broader measure of toleration, but this was struck down by Parliament. In practice, he was, however, able to reduce sentences passed against Catholics and persecution against Catholics diminished over time (Marshall, 2006, 135).

Tensions between Anglicans and dissenting Protestants continued after 1689. Meeting houses for Quakers and other dissenters were attacked into the 1710s (Sowerby, 2013, 254). The last person to die for their religious beliefs in the British Isles was a student in Edinburgh executed for blasphemy in 1697. Anti-Catholic legislation continued to be enforced: "[i]f 1689 marked the end of the persecutory society, it did not mark the beginning of the secular state" (Coffey, 2000, 201). The old order based on an alliance between church and a persecuting state unraveled slowly.

The Glorious Revolution was associated with a broader package of institutional reforms. In particular, Douglass North and Barry Weginast (1989) argued that the Glorious Revolution led to both an improvement in the ability of the state to borrow but also a transformation in the security of private property rights.[19] In fact, as we have seen, many important institutional changes occurred prior to the Glorious Revolution.[20]

The Glorious Revolution enabled the British state to access outside credit. Parliament gained control of expenditure and, from 1693 onwards, guaranteed loan repayment. The formation of political parties in Parliament in the decades following 1688 secured lenders a commitment that parliament would not default on the new debt (Stasavage, 2002). Moreover, establishment of ministerial responsibility curtailed the king's ability to enter into costly wars that Parliament disapproved of (Cox, 2011, 2015, 2016).

Did the Glorious Revolution secure property rights? Clark (1996) found that the returns on farmland and land prices were unaffected by the political turmoil of the English Civil War and the Glorious Revolution. But perhaps a better barometer is the efficiency rather than the stability of property rights? The preexisting property rights regime in England was feudal. Many of the stipulations of feudal property rights involved the obligations tenants owed their lords to supply military service. They sought to maintain the property in its entirety because if the land fragmented into numerous smallholding this might prevent a single tenant from being able to supply a mounted man-at-arms. Ownership of land often carried feudal entails, which meant that potential heirs could veto anything that might affect the future capital value of the land (such as cutting down a forest or draining a lake).[21] Divided but *secure* property rights hindered projects to improve the quality of the land.

Bogart and Richardson (2011) argue that after 1688, Parliament became a forum where property rights could be renegotiated and made more flexible. This flexibility allowed land to be profitably reallocated for commercial and industrial purposes. Parliamentary supremacy loosened constraints on how land could be used. Parliament eliminated many of the customary rights held by smallholders. Absent this many profitable opportunities for investment would have been lost.[22]

The Glorious Revolution marked a point of no return in the institutional development of the fiscal state in England (Pincus and Robinson, 2014).[23] Taxation increased and was approximately twice as high in per capita terms as in France. The main taxes in eighteenth-century England were the customs, the excise, and the land tax; on average these accounted for 90 percent of revenue. From the Middle Ages through to the seventeenth century, the customs had been an important source of royal revenue. However, customs revenue was volatile and hence could not provide a stable foundation of the establishment of a fiscal military state. Numerous attempts to raise revenue, via first the hearth tax and then the land tax, also brought in disappointing yields due to collection costs. Consequently, after 1700 the excise tax became the mainstay of the British tax system. From 1720 onwards, reliable and growing revenue from the excise enabled the British state to secure its debt at low rates of interest – a transition crucial to the formation of a modern fiscal state (Hoffman, 2015b; Brewer, 1988).[24]

Figure 9.1 depicts the rise in British tax revenues after 1700 on a logarithmic scale. GDP grew by roughly a factor of 3 between 1688 and 1815, but total tax receipts by a factor of 15. The most dramatic rise in state power

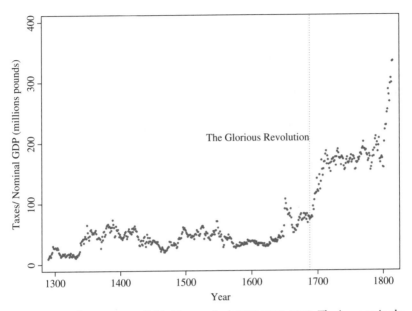

Figure 9.1 Total tax revenue divided by nominal GDP, 1290–1815. The increase in the size of the British tax state after 1700 dwarfed the increase in the size of the overall economy. Sources: O'Brien (1988) and Broadberry et al. (2011).

came during the major periods of war with France of 1688–1713, 1792–1815. With each conflict there was a ratchet effect that increased the size of the fiscal military state.

Eighteenth-century Britain was governed by a very different kind of state than Tudor England had been. Not only were taxes higher, authority was more centralized; violence was no longer privatized but concentrated in the hands of state officials. Even in its internal organization, the state was gradually moving away from patrimonialism.[25]

The establishment of a fiscal-military state diminished the importance of religious identity. Eighteenth-century Britain was not fully committed to the principles of religious freedom. It remained a proudly Protestant state: the Anglican Church was the established Church. Dissenters were excluded from political offices, the universities, and from many of the professions. While Jews were economically and socially free from the types of restrictions that afflicted them elsewhere, they were far from being equal citizens. In some respects, restrictions on religious freedom were tightened after 1689: the monarch could not marry a Catholic, for example. Nevertheless, Britain was one of the first states to dismantle the old equilibrium based on identity rules, religious legitimacy, and conditional toleration.

This attitude carried over to colonial policy. Geloso (2015) documents how British policy changed as it acquired land settled by French Catholics in Canada. Initially, British colonial authorities were wary about how to deal with Catholic populations of French descent, and in the 1750s they acquiesced to local decisions to expel Catholic Acadians who refused to sign an oath of allegiance from Nova Scotia. But this policy proved both costly and counterproductive, and on the conquest of Quebec in 1760, they allowed the Catholic population to continue their religious activities unmolested. This was, Geloso argues, a pragmatic policy motivated by fiscal considerations:

Constrained by a large public debt, expenditures at record high levels, and a still powerful French empire, the British had received a lesson from the Acadian upheaval. In a compromise between the domestic, colonial, and strategic needs, the British adopted toleration in a bid to sustain the empire both financially and strategically (Geloso, 2015, 73).

The successful incorporation of Catholic Quebec into the British empire showed that religious homogeneity did not have to be a precondition for political stability and further developments toward full religious freedom occurred in the 1790s.

Margaret Jacob argues that the key to the emergence of cosmopolitanism was the state becoming "a non-combatant" in religion (Jacob, 2006, 76). This occurred gradually. The Anglican Church went into slow decline. The Toleration Act was associated with "a decline in Church congregations, an increase in the number of Dissenters' chapels, the spread of latitudinarianism, deism, and even atheism" (Gilmour, 1992, 37). By the time of David Hume and Adam Smith, the Anglican Church was a byword for religious laxity.

Voltaire and Montesquieu celebrated Britain's comparative religious liberalism. They were right in so far as England remained *relatively* free compared to France or Spain. Voltaire justly celebrated the London Stock Exchange as an expression of religious freedom:

Go into the Exchange in London, that place more venerable than many a court, and you will see representatives of all the nations assembled there for the profit of mankind. There the Jew, the Mahometan, and the Christian deal with one another as if they were of the same religion, and reserve the name of infidel for those who go bankrupt (Voltaire, 1964, 26).

Voltaire's argument exemplifies the Enlightenment emphasis on commerce's role in securing greater religious freedom.[26] Importantly, the environment described by Voltaire was a fairly recent one and still precarious. Jacobs notes that "Presumably Voltaire did not know that he could not have waxed as eloquently about his Quaker's word had he written before 1689"

(Jacob, 2006, 76). Even in the eighteenth century David Hume attracted widespread condemnation for his religious skepticism and suspected atheism. He did not publish his *Dialogues Concerning Natural Religion* until after his death because he feared public outcry. His friend Adam Smith was widely condemned for posthumously describing Hume as close to the perfect embodiment of virtue and wisdom, as this was seen to be a celebration of atheism.[27] Nonetheless, the very fact that this statement could be made publicly was made possible by a withdrawal of the British state from regulating religious affairs.

9.4 Chapter Summary: The Rise of the State and the Abandonment of Religious Regulation

The long history of religious intolerance in post-Reformation England is documented by historians, but often ignored by those who argue that religious freedom was a product of the Protestant Reformation. Louis XIV is rightly condemned for expelling French Protestants in 1685, but late seventeenth-century England was also a persecuting society in which Quakers could be imprisoned, Catholics hounded to their deaths on trumped up charges, and Jesuits publicly dismembered.

The slow demise of religious persecution in England and France after 1700 was the result of a series of factors, including the erosion of the ability of the church to legitimate political authority, the rise of commercial society, and the emergence of a modern state that was based on general rules and no longer needed religion to govern.

It does not appear to have been preceded by any decrease in animosity toward religious dissidents. There was little popular enthusiasm for religious toleration in England, particularly for Catholics. In 1778 Parliament passed a Catholic Relief Bill that enabled Catholics to officially inherit property. But just this small measure toward official recognition for Catholics helped to spark the Gordon Riots in which 210 were killed outright and 245 wounded (Zamoyski, 2015, 27).

Further piecemeal steps toward toleration followed. In 1791 The Catholic Relief Act granted freedom of worship and education for Catholics in England and Wales. The actual number of Catholics in England in the eighteenth century was very small.[28] But this number grew rapidly in the nineteenth century, partly due to Irish immigration. Anti-Catholic sentiments and violence took on a different color as they became associated with anti-Irish feelings. Violence and riots against Catholics became a routine feature of English urban life.

William Pitt was blocked from offering Catholic emancipation in 1800 by King George III largely due to concerns over the Irish situation. It was pushed through in 1829 despite substantial opposition from those who saw Britain as a confessional, that is, Anglican state. The Lords and Commons received 896 petitions opposing it compared to just 147 in favor (Machin, 1963, 471). Numerous anti-Catholic societies formed in response. Moreover, while the act of 1829 allowed Catholic members of parliament and was a measure of greater religious freedom to come, it did not grant full civic equality to Catholics. They were unable to graduate from Oxford and Cambridge until the 1850s (Machin, 1999, 21). In some respects, so long as there is a state church, religious equality between Catholics and Protestants in England cannot be declared fully achieved, but from the 1870s onward, the members of the two faiths can be said to have enjoyed civic equality. In the next chapter we show that the same dynamic can explain why Jews in Europe acquired civic rights after centuries of persecution.

Notes

1. Individuals within each jurisdiction were, technically, allowed the freedom to migrate.
2. See Greengrass (2014, 595–621), Parker (1984), and Wilson (2009).
3. The 1648 Treaty of Osnabrück was modified by the Peace of Augsburg by recognizing Catholicism, Lutheranism, and Calvinism. "Three types of religious worship emerged from this complex legislation. The dominant religion alone enjoyed the *exercitium religionis publicum*; the other recognized Churches were granted *exercitium religionis privatum*. Members of the recognized religions without rights before 1624 were only allowed an *exercitium religionis domesticum*. Public worship meant churches with spires and bells; private worship meant chapels without either; domestic worship meant prayers in the family home and the right to visit churches in neighboring states" (Whaley, 1985, 5).
4. While some historians have seen the Edict as failing to heal the wounds of the Wars of Religion (Benedict, 1996), others have noted that "even if the provisions of the Edict of Nantes made no mention at all of religious toleration, that is precisely the legacy it eventually procured" (Holt, 1998, 31).
5. See Benedict (2001). This estimate is lower than previous estimates of 1.5 to 2 million given by Scoville (1960).
6. The last Protestant minister hanged for his religion was Francois Rochette in 1762, and the last Protestant to be condemned to the galleys was in 1775 (Encrevé, 1999, 61).
7. In this last aspect, it was considerably more restrictive than the Edict of Nantes. See the analysis of Merrick (1990), who notes that "[t]he edict disturbed some magistrates, displeased many bishops, and disappointed most Protestants" (Merrick, 1990, 156).
8. There is a vast historiography of the causes of the English Civil War. Historians in the Whig tradition emphasized the constitutional issues at stake in the Parliamentary debates of the 1620s and 1640s (Russell, 1971), whereas historians in the Marxian tradition have long emphasized the role of economic factors such as the increase role of merchants and the economic decline of the great landowners brought about by a century of inflation resulting in part from a great inflow

of Spanish Silver (Brenner, 1993). Since the 1980s, scholars have increasingly pointed to the religious divide between the High Church Anglicanism espoused by the crown and Archbishop Laud, and the position held by Puritans like Oliver Cromwell as a source of irreconcilable difference that splintered the political body of the realm. For the role of demographic pressure, see Goldstone (1991).

9. See Hill (1964, 2002).

10. Recent trends among scholars have also pointed to the importance of contingent factors in the immediate lead up to civil war, pointing out the numerous opportunities Charles I had to pull back from the brink and conciliate at least some of his leading opportunities and also the extent to which the Parliamentary opposition to Charles was close to fracturing at several points (such as during the impeachment of Stafford). They see the Bishops' War, caused by the attempts of Charles to force the English prayerbook on Scotland, as chief among the proximate cause of the English Civil War.

11. Brenner (1993) argued that merchant interests were crucial in Parliamentary success in the conflict with the crown. Saumitra Jha (2015) finds that Members of Parliament (MPs) with financial interests in overseas trade were more likely to support Parliament in the conflict with the crown. Shares in overseas ventures aligned the interests of nonmerchants with those of merchants. To test this theory, Jha matches investor MPs to noninvestor MPs along a range of endowed wealth and locational characteristics to estimate the effect of shareholding. He finds that the measured effect of shareholding on support for parliamentary supremacy was considerable.

12. Cromwell ruled as a nonroyal monarch, governing England effectively for several years before his death in 1658. Had he taken the title king he might have founded a dynasty; as it was, his son proved ineffective so Parliament invited Charles II to return to England as king in 1660.

13. But see Coffey (2000, 183), who notes that "[e]ven at the height of the Popish Plot, there was never 'an all-out persecution of the Catholic peers and gentry in the shires.' Partly this was due to the complexity of the prosecution procedures, but it also reflected the lack of enthusiasm for persecution felt by local officials."

14. Periodic violence against Catholics was common. "On 30 September 1688, the Jesuit Charles Petre was dragged from the pulpit at the Catholic chapel in Lime Street, London, by a crowd. On the following Sunday, they pulled down the pulpit and broke the alter, and he fled. Other crowds attacked Catholic chapels throughout England on many occasions in late 1688. In Norwich, a 'mob' of over a thousand 'ill-used' the priest and had to be dispersed by soldiers; a mass-house in Newcastle was 'sacked' and a chapel in York was destroyed. In Oxford, there was an anti-Catholic riot, while in Bristol there were attacks on the houses of Catholics" (Marshall, 2006, 134).

15. Greif and Rubin (2018) document the declining importance of religious legitimacy in this period. They argue that the post-Reformation Anglican Church was not able to provide the same level of legitimacy as had medieval Catholic Church. They document the rise of Parliament as an alternative source of legitimacy following the Reformation.

16. See Rosevere (1991). According to Scott: "Downing's astonishing subsequent impact upon the reform of royal finances owed everything to his previous republican experience ... he was instrumental in adding to these innovations the first

English imitations of Dutch republican structures of public credit. This occurred despite Clarendon's vociferous protests that these were incompatible with monarchy" (Scott, 2003, 337).

17. Sowerby (2013) provides a detailed account of this "repealer" movement.

18. There was widespread bloodshed in Scotland and Ireland. And historians observe that "[t]he foremost legacy of the Glorious Revolution was the initiation of a long period of war with France and its allies that lasted nearly half of the following 130 years. During this period the state became the largest employer, borrower, and spender of money in England/Britain" (Ashworth, 2003, 20).

19. Historians such as Thomas Macaulay celebrated and endorsed what became known as the Whig view of history according to which the Glorious Revolution marks a decisive break in the institutional history of England (and after 1707, Britain) (Macaulay, 1967, 1848).

20. See O'Brien (2001), Rosevere (1991), Braddick (1996), Ashworth (2003), and Johnson and Koyama (2014a). It is also true that prior to 1689, "England was something of an exception among European states in the weakness of its instruments for long-term borrowing" (Stasavage, 2002, 60). Dickson notes that "By 1688 private and public finance both in England and abroad had therefore developed and improved and had already moved on to a longer-term basis" (Dickson, 1993, 1967, 45). Epstein (2000) provided evidence that the English Crown paid much higher interest rates than did other borrowers such as the Italian city-states or the Dutch Republic; the fall in rates that North and Weingast (1989) document was a convergence to the European norm. Stasavage notes "One potential reason why English monarchs before 1688 did not develop a regularized system of borrowing was that after the end of the Hundred Years' War in 1453, England faced fewer pressures from external military threats than did its continental neighbors" (Stasavage, 2002, 60). Critics of North and Weingast (1989) contend that the ability of the king to borrow after 1688 was grounded less in the commitments embodied by the new political settlement and more in the greater ability of the state to collect taxes. The contrast drawn in the traditional literature between the constrained English constitutional monarchy (after 1689) and the unconstrained absolutist French kings may also be overdrawn. Throughout the early modern period, French monarch could borrow from regional corporate bodies, estates, and tax farmers (Root, 1989; Potter, 1997, 2000, 2003; Johnson, 2006; Balla and Johnson, 2009). These bodies served as "a kind of commitment technology designed to expand the state's fiscal capacity" (Root, 1989, 243). Thus in the eighteenth century the power of the French monarch was not unconstrained. The French king could borrow money despite the fact that he was above the law and could freely default on his loans. Corporate bodies like the Company of General Farms acted as an important intermediaries (Johnson, 2006; Balla and Johnson, 2009).

21. This analysis draws on the work of Dan Bogart and Gary Richardson (2009 and 2011). See also Finley, Franck, and Johnson (2017) for the inefficiency of (secure) property rights in pre-Revolution France and the efficiency gains from the Revolutionary *re-allocation* of those rights during the nineteenth century.

22. See the related discussion in Lamoreaux (2011).

23. Brewer (1988) coined the term fiscal-military state to describe the Hanoverian polity that emerged in the wake of the Glorious Revolution. More recent work has traced back the origins of this fiscal military state to the 1680s (Pincus, 2009) or the 1640s (O'Brien, 1988, 2001, 2011).

24. The excise was particularly efficient in imposing duties on luxuries such as coffee or tea and alcohol. When extra revenue was required as between 1793 and 1815, the British government could increase the amount of revenue they received in taxation by up to 60 percent. Over the period 1770 to 1810 the government more than doubled the share of national product taken in taxes (Mathias and O'Brien, 1976). This required high tax compliance by preindustrial standards.

25. Allen (2011) calls this process the Institutional Revolution and attributes it to changing monitoring technology after 1850. Historians tend to view it as a more gradual process. Until the late seventeenth century, tax collection was typically in the hands of tax farmers and highly decentralized. See Brewer (1988, 91) and Johnson and Koyama (2014*a*).

26. We consider the *doux commerce* thesis in Chapter 16.

27. For the friendship between Hume and Smith see Rasmussen (2017). For a more general discussion of how cautious writers continued to be on the subject of irreligion into the late eighteenth century see Melzer (2014).

28. In 1767 there were only 67,928 Catholics in England and Wales, and a further 16,490 in Scotland (Machin, 1999, 14).

10

From Persecution to Emancipation

The corporate political character of the medieval European Jewish community ceased to exist. Rabbis were no longer civil magistrates with police powers. Instead, they exercised authority only among those they could persuade to obey.

Ellenson (1994, xii)

The treatment of Jews in medieval and early modern Europe has provided a case study with which to examine the conditional toleration equilibrium under a finer microscope. This has provided an in-depth portrait into how important religion was and how European states governed on the basis of discriminatory and restrictive identity rules. In this chapter we study how at the end of the eighteenth century states across Western Europe began to dismantle these rules.

First, we examine the reasons for the decline in persecutions and violence against Jews. Though expulsions, riots, and pogroms still took place, the number of acts of violence against Jews markedly diminished after 1600. We review evidence that the rise of state capacity that took place during this period played a crucial role in extending protection to Jewish communities.

Second, we study the legislative changes, collectively known as Jewish emancipation, that transformed the status of Jews across Western and Central Europe, bringing them legal equality. Inspired by mercantilistic concerns, rulers in the Habsburg empire and Germany slowly freed Jews from many of the restrictions that governed their existence during the medieval period. The French Revolution and the armies of Napoleon then spread emancipation across Europe. These shocks swept away much of what remained of the conditional toleration equilibrium and set the stage for the emergence of economic and political liberalism in the second half of the nineteenth century.[1]

10.1 The Decline in Jewish Persecutions

Expulsions remained in the repertoire of European rulers. Jews were expelled from Vienna in 1669/70, Munich in 1715, and Stuttgart in 1731. Over 12,000 Protestants were expelled from Salzburg in 1731. As late as 1744 Maria Theresa (r. 1740–1780), ruler of the Habsburg empire, expelled the Jews of Prague. But this was one of the last such occurrences and, other rulers, including George II of England, pleaded with her to retract the order.[2] Though legal and social discrimination remained in place across continental Europe, violence against Jews declined after 1600. What factors can account for this decline?

To investigate how the conditional toleration equilibrium evolved over time, we can return to the analysis in Chapter 5 where we looked at supply shocks driven by the weather and persecution probability. Instead of summarizing this relationship with a single estimate for the entire period, we can generate separate estimates for each century. Figure 10.1 presents these results. A one degree decrease in growing season temperature increased the likelihood of a persecution by between 5 percent and 7 percent between 1200 and 1600.[3] However, by the sixteenth century, the estimated effect had shrunk to about 2.5 percent, and by the seventeenth and eighteenth centuries there is, in effect, no relationship between supply shocks and persecution. This suggests a change in the conditional toleration equilibrium sometime after 1600.

Why did this occur? Attitudes toward Jews did not became less hostile as a result of the Renaissance or Reformation. Erasmus, the leading advocate of Renaissance humanism, is often viewed by historians as an advocate of greater religious toleration, at least for trinitarian Christians. But he was not in favor of religious pluralism and "would have had no patience with the modern, enlightened idea of toleration (i.e. of religious freedom) – of individual rights that extend to every race and creed" (Oberman, 1981, 39). In particular, his lenient attitude toward other Christians did not mean that he favored extending better treatment to Jews, for whom he had an "unbound hatred" suspecting them of a "collective conspiracy" and viewing them as "culpable as the wirepullers of the German Peasant's War" (Oberman, 1981, 38). Erasmus noted that antipathy toward Jews is the one thing all Christians share.[4]

Luther's position on the Jews was complex and ambiguous. Initially Luther was favorable to Judaism. He published a book entitled *That Jesus Christ Was Born a Jew,* and he saw the Jews as fellow opponents of the Catholic Church. But once he realized that the Reformation would not win over Jewish converts, Luther's attitudes changed and he developed increasingly antisemitic views (Kaufmann, 2017).[5] This culminated in his book

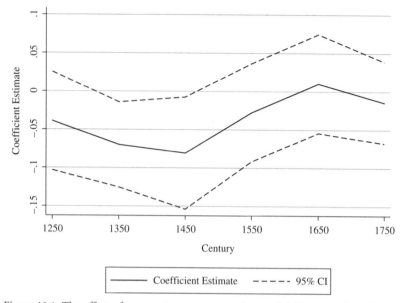

Figure 10.1 The effect of temperature on persecution probability over time. Source: Anderson, Johnson, and Koyama (2017).

The Jews and Their Lies in 1543. He wrote that "they [the Jews] are nothing but thieves and robbers who daily eat no morsel and wear no thread of clothing which they have not stolen and pilfered from us by means of their accursed usury." Luther became an advocate of expulsion: "eject them forever from this country. For, as we have heard, God's anger with them is so intense that gentle mercy will only tend to make them worse and worse, while sharp mercy will reform them but little" (Luther, 1553). His preaching led to numerous expulsions in Protestant Germany cities. Luther was on his way to insist a Jewish community not be settled in Eisleben when he died. Scholars continue to debate the nature of Luther's antisemitism but there is no doubt that it continued to inspire antisemitic views all the way to the Nazi period.

Becker and Pascali (2016) provide evidence that in Germany Protestants were more intolerant of Jews than were Catholics. This, they claim, reflects the fact that Catholics continued to rely on Jewish moneylending, whereas Protestants were able to lend money at interest and hence had less need for Jews.

In contrast to the Reformation, the Enlightenment is a more plausible explanation of the decline in antisemitic attitudes. By downgrading the value of revealed religion, the Enlightenment created a neutral sphere where Christians and Jews could meet on an equal footing. Nevertheless, many Enlightenment figures including Voltaire, Edward Gibbon, and Edmund

Burke voiced anti-Jewish views. John Locke was in favor of granting toleration to Jews, but this was because he believed it would encourage their conversion to Christianity. Voltaire described the Jewish nation as "the most detestable ever to have sullied the earth." Moreover, the Enlightenment came too late to explain the decline in Jewish persecutions that is observed after 1600.[6]

Another possibility is economic growth. Could an increase in agricultural productivity explain the breakdown of the relationship between supply shocks and persecutions? Though this argument is plausible, the European economy remained Malthusian and agricultural output did not increase until the eighteenth century. Market integration did improve after 1600 and the European economy became less vulnerable to shocks. This was certainly a factor weakening the link from climate shocks to pogroms. Nevertheless, the increase in market integration was modest. Hence, it cannot fully explain the decline in the relationship between supply shocks and persecutions.[7]

In this case, what explains the transition from the persecuting societies of the Middle Ages to the liberal states of the nineteenth century that, by and large, tried to protect minority communities? The most persuasive explanation is that the terms on which Jews were accepted in European society began to change in this period; the conditional toleration equilibrium began to weaken.

The conditional toleration equilibrium first broke down in the Dutch Republic and England. The Dutch Republic offered permanent protection to Jews after its declaration of independence from Spain, with large numbers of so-called crypto-Jews arriving in 1593. The rights of Jews to practice their religion was codified in 1619. Jews were invited to return to England in 1655 by Oliver Cromwell. In both cases, economic reasoning and reasons of state played a role. The Jews who arrived in Amsterdam were largely Portuguese or Spanish and they were fleeing the Inquisition. They were ready to lend money and financial expertise to aide the Dutch rebellion from Spanish rule. Cromwell in speaking to Parliament in favor of allowing Jewish settlement noted that "[t]he Merchants vehemently insisted upon it" (quoted in Katz, 1991, 217).[8]

The terms on which Jews were accepted into the Dutch Republic and England in the seventeenth century were different to those of the old conditional toleration equilibrium. While their status was initially uncertain, the Jews who came to England did not face religious persecution nor were they confined to a particular part of London. There were tensions; Jews were suspected of pro-Dutch sympathies during the Anglo-Dutch Wars. They were not granted full political rights. But they came to enjoy a measure of social and economic freedom, especially after 1689. Despite the existence of popular antisemitism, they were no longer subject to persecutions and violence.[9]

The equilibrium based on conditional toleration was no longer self-enforcing in the Dutch Republic of the 1590s or the England of the 1650s. Both the Dutch Republic and the England of Commonwealth were investing in fiscal capacity; the Dutch, to preserve their independence in the face of first Spanish and later French power; the English, as they became embroiled in great power competition. Figure 10.2a depicts the rise of state capacity in England as measured by tax revenue and the increase in legislative activity by Parliament. Figure 10.2c plots the relationship between toleration offered to the Jews and the rise of the Dutch state as measured by taxation per capita over real wages and by the wartime strength of the Republic's armed forces.

These new fiscal-military states were different than their medieval predecessors. They were governed by ministers whose outlook was explicitly mercantilist: men who sought to use policy in order to enrich their economies and thereby raise greater tax revenues. Though religion remained a powerful force in both countries and Cromwell, in particular, characterized his rule in explicitly theological terms, both states were also less reliant on religion as a source of legitimation. The English state was quite capable of protecting the small Jewish community from popular anger.[10]

Anti-Jewish sentiment was widespread and commonplace as demonstrated in the opposition to the so-called Jew Bill of 1753.

In 1747 an anonymous poem put in words what some others, too, must have thought. It attacked the exchange for being a place where Jews, of all people, had liberties: "What Liberties have Freemen, when a Jew/ Shall in the Citys Heart his Trade pursue?" (Jacob, 2006, 77)

Antisemitism was visible in those who opposed the new commercial and industrial society and who disdained liberalism and in particular, political economists (Levy, 2002).

Though in many respects a liberal and an advocate of Catholic emancipation, Edmund Burke railed against Jews and "sophisters, economists, and calculators" in his *Reflections on the Revolution in France*. He regretted the decline of a more orderly society in which status and nobility were respected. He noted that "the next generation of the nobility will resemble the artificers and clowns, and money-jobbers usurers, and Jews, who will be always their fellows, sometimes their masters."[11] Other prominent critics of industrial and commercial society such as radical William Cobbett also openly displayed antisemitic attitudes, as did Charles Dickens in his early fiction.[12]

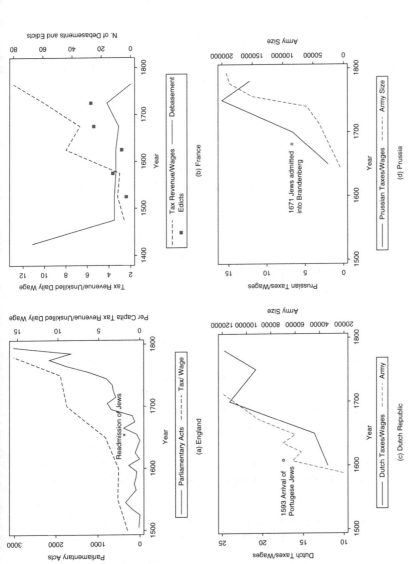

Figure 10.2 The rise of state capacity in early modern Western Europe: tax revenue data are from Karaman and Pamuk (2013); data on English Parliamentary Acts are from Bogart and Richardson (2011). Data on Royal Edicts are from Johnson and Koyama (2014a); data on debasements is from Shaw (1896). Army size data are from van Nimwegen (2006). Source: Anderson, Johnson, and Koyama (2017).

Even among advocates of religious toleration, the presence of Jews was welcomed in part because Protestants hoped to convert them.[13] While Jews were economically successful in nineteenth-century England, the issue of their political representation was extremely contentious. Opponents argued that Jews were compromised by their dual loyalty to their people as well as to their country and that they could not be full citizens in a Christian kingdom. It was in spite of this opposition that they eventually achieved civic equality alongside Catholics in 1833. Jewish entry into Parliament was obtained in 1858 and it was only in 1860 that they were admitted into the House of Lords.

In England it is difficult to disentangle the importance of state capacity in protecting the Jews from persecution from the role Parliament may have played in protecting them. However, a similar process also took place in France under the auspices of an absolutist monarchy.

As we document in Chapter 11, tax revenues in France grew after 1630. Figure 10.2b traces the increase in state capacity using tax revenues and counts of royal edicts issued. At the beginning of the seventeenth century, Portuguese conversos petitioned for the right to settle in Bordeaux. Following a similar logic to the Dutch Republic, Cardinal Richelieu appreciated their value as merchants and financiers and they would play an important role in financing France's ongoing conflict with Spain. Israel describes this as "a classic instance of *raison d'État* politics and mercantilism," the result of which allowed the Portuguese communities in France to cast off all remaining pretense of being Christians and to openly organize Jewish religious services (Israel, 1985, 96–97). By 1722, the right of all French Jews to openly practice their religion was recognized in law.

While there had been a long history of Jewish settlement in lands controlled by Prussia, it was only in the late seventeenth century that Frederick William (1650–1688) gave the Jews a charter, which established their permanent residency. This occurred at the same time as the Elector invested in fiscal capacity and built a professional standing army that would propel Prussia to the status of a major European power (Figure 10.2d).

10.1.1 Court Jews and The Conditional Toleration Equilibrium in Central Europe

The situation in the rest of central Europe was different. Many German states invited Jewish communities to return in the wake of the Thirty Years' War. They were invited because they were expected to provide credit and revive local economies devastated by war and plague. But they did not obtain any measure of religious or social freedom. German rulers preferred to reconstruct the conditional toleration equilibrium and to grant specific privileges to individual Jewish financiers, known as "court Jews."

Court Jews were a product of the conditional toleration equilibrium. They were individuals who were given special privileges to live and work outside of the ghetto and to wear Christian clothes. They were also exempt from the taxes that were incumbent upon the rest of the Jewish community. They obtained these favors because of the role they played in lending to local rulers, organizing their finances and collecting taxation.

The role of court Jews was not substantively different from other Jews who worked in moneylending or tax farming, except that they operated on a larger scale. Their prominence was a function of the restrictions on economic activity created by the regulations imposed by early modern European states: "the unique identifying characteristic of this partnership between Jew and ruler was the fact that profits depended upon state sponsorship" (Katz, 2000, 46). They were a product of the restrictions that hedged in trade across Central Europe. In Saxony, the linen trade was typically an urban monopoly in this period. Different guilds controlled and restricted each part of the production process. Weavers in Wüttemberg were obliged to sell their output to a specified guild of dyers at artificially high prices. Local tariffs and regional industrial policy abounded and resulted in waste, inefficiency, and stagnation (Ogilvie, 1996, 285–292).

Samuel Oppenheimer (1630–1703) and Samson Wetheimer (1658–1728) were prominent court Jews. Their treatment was characteristic of the conditional toleration equilibrium. No matter how rich they became, they were always vulnerable, particularly if the ruler who favored them died unexpectedly. Perhaps the most ill-fated court Jew was Joseph Süss Oppenheimer (1697–1738) who was executed after the death of his backer, the Duke of Wüttemberg. Oppenheimer was killed for alleged corruption and for sexual relations with Christian women. His body was then hung in cage until it rotted away (Mintzker, 2017). The fate of Oppenheimer suggests the limitations of peaceful coexistence with the conditional toleration equilibrium. Jews who became too prominent, too financially successful, and too integrated into Christian society, continued to face the risk of violence or even death.

We focus on the Habsburg empire to observe how the treatment of religious minorities changed over the course of the eighteenth century. Maria Theresa was committed to the goal of converting the Empire's Protestants, Orthodox Christians, and Catholics to Catholicism. Described as "the last Habsburg of the Counter-Reformation," she strove to maintain Catholic uniformity prosecuting both Catholics who left the church and Protestants (O'Brien, 1969, 12). As late as 1771, when a village of hidden Protestants were discovered, all the young men were forcibly enrolled in the army, families were broken up, and children taken to be brought up by Catholics.

Nevertheless, at the same time other developments were undermining the purpose of these persecutory policies. Non-Catholics could be viewed as potentially useful economic assets. Moreover, O'Brien writes: "The rise of a modern state under Maria Theresa contributed notably to this decline in the political significance of religious dissent. Not only did the state weaken several of the main bastions of intolerance, especially the estate of the clergy, but it also created a modern army, a bureaucracy, and other institutions that lessened its need for support from the church" (O'Brien, 1969, 13).

The leading economic thinkers in the German-speaking world, the Cameralists, argued for policies to increase population by attracting migrants regardless of their religious affiliations. The most important Austrian Cameralist was Joseph Sonnenfels. According to one historian: "Throughly secularist, Sonnenfels taught a generation of government servants that increasing a country's population was fundamentally more important than religious uniformity, persuading many that religious toleration could prevent the flight of non-Catholics from the monarchy as well as encourage immigration" (O'Brien, 1969, 14). He thereby implicitly advocated for greater religious freedom.

Sonnenfels' policies influenced Joseph II who, though personally religious, saw the state as a secular institution. The state's attitude to the religious faiths of its subjects had to be determined by essentially pragmatic considerations. Rather than being concerned with their salvation or with their impact on the religious conduct of Catholics, he viewed religious minorities through the lens of economics and realpolitik. They were a potential economic asset to the monarchy. When he was co-regent during his mother's reign he encouraged the immigration of Protestants to help resettle war devastated lands in Hungary. He was inspired by the example of Trieste, where religious toleration had been the official policy since its founding.

The Habsburg state under Joseph II also took control of many aspects of society, intruding on the traditional domain of the church. At the same time, Joseph's government faced resistance from local elites, including the provincial court chancellors whose role it had been to monitor religious conformity (O'Brien, 1969, 14). Nonetheless, after initiating toleration for Protestants, Joseph II took the radical step of becoming the first ruler of a major continental monarchy to campaign for religious toleration for the Jews.

10.2 Jewish Emancipation

Jews experienced a considerable degree of social and religious freedom in eighteenth-century Britain and in the Dutch Republic even though they did not possess full civic rights. In the rest of Europe, Jewish rights remained heavily circumscribed until the end of the eighteenth century. Joseph II's Edict of Toleration of 1782 (*Toleranzpatent*) was the first act of emancipation by a large continental European state.[14]

Joseph II was influenced by Christian Wilhelm Dohm's 1781 work, entitled *Über die bürgerliche Verbesserung der Juden* (*On the Civic Improvement of the Jews*). Dohm argued that the Jews could be more usefully employed so as to benefit the body politic if they were freed and integrated. Writers in this tradition were not necessarily inspired by philo-semitic sentiment. Dohm "would go so far as to concede that the Jews were more morally corrupt, criminally inclined, and antisocial than other peoples ... Using 'sophistic artistry,' rabbinical exegesis had falsified Mosaic Law and had introduced 'narrow-minded and petty regulations' to the Jewish religion" (quoted in Berkovitz, 1989, 26). Dohm was anything but a liberal. He wanted to grant the Jews full civil rights but not necessarily full political rights (Rose, 1990, 72). He accepted that the state might legitimately choose to favor Christians over Jews and he intended them to have rights only insofar as it benefited the state.[15]

The Edict of Toleration was an act of partial emancipation that granted certain civic rights to Jews provided that they attended secular schools and learn German; it did not grant Jews legal equality with Christians.[16] Jewish settlement in Vienna, for example, remained restricted and no public synagogues could be built (Low, 1979, 15–23). This reduced discrimination against Jews, but was not full religious freedom. Moreover, in the reign of Joseph II's successor, new restrictions and taxes were imposed upon the Jews and in Galicia Jews were confined to ghettos for the first time.[17]

Maria Theresa had been a staunch opponent of granting rights to any religious minority. As we have seen, she expelled the Jewish community of Prague in 1746 in spite of strong protests from elites and her fellow rulers. What was responsible for her son's shift in policy? Joseph's policies were unpopular; he was not responding to a rise in support for Jewish rights (Beales, 1990, 46). Instead, he hoped that the Jews could be more profitably employed by the state. Joseph II's reforms aimed at making the Jews productive. Past policies had restricted Jews to particular sectors of the economy. Now Joseph and his advisors hoped to switch Jews away from moneylending or small-scale retailing to agriculture and manufacturing.[18]

More radical change came with the French Revolution. After a long debate in 1791 the National Assembly granted Jews full citizenship. This policy was spread across Europe with French armies during the Revolutionary and Napoleonic wars.[19] Jewish Emancipation in France was a part of a package of reforms – one inspired by Enlightenment thinking – to remake the state by abolishing all special privileges and restrictions. As Kaplan puts it: "No more than Louis XIV, though for entirely different reasons, could they brook a 'state within the state' or, as the Count of Clermont-Tonnerre recast it, 'a nation within the nation'" (Kaplan, 2007, 328).

The old equilibrium based on restricted rights and conditional toleration was hard to displace. Across much of Germany, emancipation was reversed after the defeat of France in 1815. Jews were expelled from Bremen and Lübeck in 1816. Frankfurt, Hamburg, Hanover, Nassau, and other territories also reinstated settlement regulations (Jersch-Wenzel, 1997, 29).

Nevertheless, despite these backward steps, the shock of the French Revolution and the military defeats of Austria and Prussia demonstrated that the old European order was moribund. Rulers across Central Europe sought to imitate French reforms in order to match their enemy militarily. Greater economic and social rights for Jews were part of the reform package. Prussia granted Jews a limited form of citizenship in 1812 as part of the modernization program imposed in the aftermath of Napoleon's victory at Jena in 1806. Jews in Prussia were still prevented from working in government and Judaism was not recognized as a religion. Nevertheless, the partial emancipation of Prussian Jews was significant, because they were viewed as "the culturally most advanced community of Jews in Western Europe" and because it was not subsequently revoked (Katz, 1974, 170).

More substantial moves toward legal equality in the rest of Germany recommenced in the 1820s. Jews were granted partial but not full civic rights in Frankfurt and Hamburg in 1824 (Adler, 1960). New constitutions in Belgium, the Netherlands, and Greece codified Jewish equality. Emancipation occurred throughout Italy during the revolution of 1848.[20]

The rest of this process was drawn out over subsequent decades. In Central Europe the revolutions of 1848 promised full emancipation but their defeat delayed this. Figure 10.3 depicts the major dates of complete political and social emancipation. Full Jewish emancipation in central Europe came only in 1867 in Austria-Hungary and 1871 with the ratification of the Germany Empire. Further east, in the empire of the Tzars, Jews remained confined to the Pale of Settlement from 1804 onward. They faced strict restrictions on their movements and economic activities outside the Pale and, from the 1870s onwards, renewed risk of persecutions and pogroms.[21]

Prior to emancipation, Jewish communities were self-governing communities. Their leaders were civil magistrates. Communities imposed rules on their members that governed all aspects of their behavior including religion (Katz, 1974; Israel, 1985; Kaplan, 2007). While there was some leeway for disagreement, too fervent dissent or open religious skepticism was not tolerated. Jewish religious authorities were effectively monopolists as secular authorities permitted only a single synagogue and religious organization

Important Dates of Jewish Emancipation in Europe

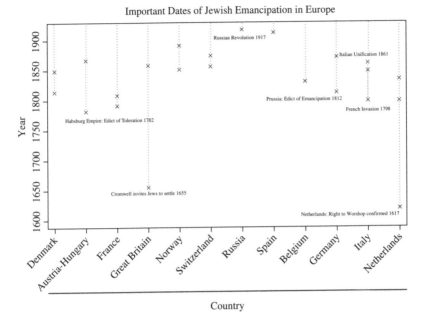

Figure 10.3 Partial and full emancipation of Jews across selected European countries. This figure distinguishes between the first act of emancipation (first cross) and the final act of full emancipation (second cross). Sources: Bates (1945); Adler (1960); Rürup (1969); Sorkin (1987); Meyer (1997).

per community. Costs of exit were high: violating the laws of the community was extremely costly as "deviants could not persevere in their deviation and live both in Jewish society and in the surrounding society" (Graetz, 1996, 5). Jews who left Judaism in early modern Europe had no secular or religiously neutral arena into which they could enter.[22] Even if they converted to Christianity, they often faced hostility and suspicion.[23] This was the fate of Spinoza who was expelled from his own Jewish community and viewed as an atheist by most Christians. As Jews who left their community continued to face discrimination, Jewish religious authorities did not have to concern themselves with the possibility of large-scale exit from their communities.

This changed with Jewish emancipation. Many Jews left Judaism altogether. Others developed more liberal strands of the Jewish religion such as Reform Judaism, which relaxed traditional dietary rules and restrictions on the working on the sabbath or eating with non-Jews.[24] According to Meyer "[b]y 1871 the great majority of the German Jews were no longer observant of Jewish ritual law in its totality" (Meyer, 1997, 352).

But nor were they secular. Reform Judaism was distinct from secularization: "It was perfectly possible for an individual to work on the Sabbath, eat non-koscher food, and neglect other traditional regulations without feeling the need for a 'modernized' religious service or for changes in the Jewish ritual" (Lowenstein, 1981, 256). While previously, Jews who had wished to participate in mainstream society had to leave Judaism altogether, Reform Judaism made it possible for Jews to enter secular society while retaining their religion. Meyer observes that "[w]ithin the urban communities, which now boasted lavish new synagogues and attractive liturgical music, some Jews continued to worship in the old manner but most attended synagogues that installed elaborate organs and used a modified liturgy" (Meyer, 1997, 352). This indicates how religious traditions can respond to accommodate institutional and economic change.[25]

10.2.1 Emancipation and Antisemitism

The emancipation of Europe's Jewish communities and their entry into mainstream European life can be seen as a singular success for political liberalism. As we detail in Chapter 12, following emancipation Jews became successful in numerous professions across society – as lawyers, doctors, businessmen – so the policy was more successful than Joseph II and Christian Dohm could have anticipated.

But there was a dark side to emancipation: modern antisemitism, which emerged in the late nineteenth century. We have thus far used the word antisemitism to describe a persistent set of anti-Jewish tropes and stereotypes about Jews. But the term itself originated in the second part of the nineteenth century and was itself in part a response to the success of Jewish emancipation.

Like other forms of racism, antisemitism was largely about status. It rose in late nineteenth-century Europe because previous policies of discrimination had given non-Jews what economists would call non-pecuniary rents: they gave any non-Jew a degree of status purely because they were Christians or Germans. In a similar way, racist ideas were popular among poor and uneducated whites in the nineteenth- and early twentieth-century United States because it ensured that there was a large group of individuals that they dominated in terms of status. Emancipation and the economic and social rise of Jews across Europe after 1800 eroded this status. The displeasure this caused is evident in a petition in Bavaria in which eighty-three citizens of Hilders opposed emancipation on the grounds that they did not want to "humble" themselves before the Jews (see Hayes, 2017, 23). The persistence of antisemitism suggests that greater social freedoms for Jews did not directly lead to a more tolerant culture or reduced xenophobia. These antisemitic sentiments would play out fatefully in the twentieth century.

10.3 The Argument Thus Far ... A Summary of Part II

We can now take stock of the argument we have advanced thus far. Part 1 of this book described the conditional toleration equilibrium that characterized European society for most of its history. In Part 2 we documented how this equilibrium began to unravel after 1500. This was due to a confluence of forces, the most important of which was the Reformation.

Chapter 7 outlined how the combination of religious change with political and economic upheaval made the Reformation period so transformative. The new teachings of Luther and Calvin coincided with the advent of new technologies, the discovery of the Americas, and with the rise of powerful states such as England and France as well as states in Scandinavia and Germany willing to utilize the new religion for geopolitical purposes. It was the conjunction of these factors, coming after the weakening of Church authority in the fourteenth and fifteenth centuries, that made the Reformation such an important event in European history.

As a result of the spread of new religious ideas, European rulers faced more "heretics" than they had to deal with in the past. Their response was guided by a mixture of religious ideology, past experience with heresies, and political pragmatism. Ideology and past experience suggested that a fierce response based on the public execution by burning of open heretics would be effective; ruthless repression had eradicated the Cathars and driven the Lollards underground. However, in France, the Low Countries, the Holy Roman Empire, and England there were simply too many religious dissidents to execute. This problem was most acute in the most politically and economically developed regions of Europe.

Chapter 8 turned our attention to the Iberian peninsular where thanks to the Spanish and Portuguese Inquisitions, early modern rulers were able to attain religious homogeneity. This achievement – something that all early modern rulers aspired to – did not avail them, however. As military competition intensified, Spain went into decline. While England and France invested in state capacity, the Spanish monarchs became ever more dependent on American silver. By 1650, Spain lacked the fiscal system to sustain armies and navies large enough to meet the geopolitical ambitions of their rulers.

Chapter 9 returned our attention to England and France. In both countries there was temporary religious peace after 1600, but in neither case did it last long. By the end of the seventeenth century, the foundations of the conditional equilibrium of the medieval world was destroyed. In England, while discriminatory laws against Catholics and Jews would remain in place, these discriminatory laws ceased to be at the center of the state.

In France, the Edict of Nantes achieved peace between Catholics and Protestants at the expense of making the Protestant community a state within a state. This independent polity was reduced by Cardinal Richelieu whose policy dictated toleration for the Protestants and private individuals but the elimination of all special privileges, religious or feudal, that stood in the way of an extension of state power. But the religious peace was overturned by Louis XIV. Louis XIV benefited from the centralized state established by his predecessors and he sought to use it to dismantle the system of conditional toleration by attempting to eliminate all Protestants. This greatly damaged French society and the French economy. And, by 1715, the revocation was tacitly acknowledged to have failed. Over the course of the eighteenth century, France moved toward gradual de facto toleration before granting Protestants civil rights on the eve of Revolution.

European rulers came to appreciate that old, feudal systems of governance were unable to generate the tax revenues they needed to wage war on a large scale. Identity rules were recognized as a source of inefficiency and administrators such as Colbert and Vauban in France and Downing in England sought to establish more general rules. They were not always successful but they pioneered the policies that would later be used to reform old regime states. Cameralists in Germany, Physiocrats in France, and political economists in Britain sought to make their economies more productive. They supported greater religious freedom as a means to reform society at large. These policies found favor with Europe's rulers who recognized the economic and political gains that could result. As a result, the late eighteenth and early nineteenth centuries saw increases in religious freedom for dissenters and Catholics in Britain, Protestants in France, and Jews across Europe.

Expelled from much of Europe by the sixteenth century, Jews began to return to Western Europe in the seventeenth century. In England and the Dutch Republic, they were able to live and work free from the restrictions that had hemmed in their existence elsewhere. In the rest of Europe, they remained in ghettos or in communities where they had local autonomy but faced harsh discriminatory laws. This changed with Jewish emancipation at the turn of the nineteenth century, a critical development in the history of religious freedom. It was one thing to extend rights to other Christians, but quite another to extend full civic rights to members of a different religion. We document how, with the exception of the French Revolution, Jewish emancipation was not driven by ideological change, but by concern for revenue and economic productivity by rulers influenced by mercantilism.

The final part of the book considers the consequences of this transformation for the rule of law and economic growth. We first examine the European witch hunt that took place between 1550 and 1700. The witch hunts occurred for many reasons but they were more severe in regions which were politically and legally fragmented. We document how investment in fiscal and legal capacity in France gave rise to a process of legal centralization and helped bring the witch trials to an end before 1700.

Next, we consider the economic consequences of Jewish toleration by studying the relationship between Jewish communities and city growth. We find that Jews made a positive contribution to city growth, particularly in the period after 1700.

In Chapter 13, we consider the declining role of religion in European economies after 1700. Premodern thinkers viewed religion as an essential ingredient for political order. We focus on the rise of national identity as an alternative source of political order. We provide evidence for how the rise of modern states based on general rules was conducive to economic growth. The rise of higher capacity states, the switch from identity rules to general rules, and the expansion of trade and commerce were thus complementarity processes that helped to inaugurate the modern world. In Chapter 14, we discuss the applicability of our argument to other parts of the world. Chapter 15 discusses the totalitarian regimes of the twentieth century. Chapter 16 summarizes our argument and concludes.

Notes

1. The section on Jewish emancipation draws on research in Carvalho and Koyama (2016) and Carvalho, Koyama, and Sacks (2017).
2. See Katz (1974, 12–13) and Vital (1999, 1–4).
3. These sorts of estimates should be interpreted relative to some baseline – which is the twelfth century here; as such there is no coefficient reported for it.
4. See Zagorin (2003, 50–63). Whether Erasmus's anti-Judaism was sufficiently virulent to represent antisemitism is a subject of scholarly debate (see Markish, 1986).
5. Kaufmann (2017) provides a detailed and judicious account of Luther's evolving views toward Jews.
6. See Low (1979), Sutcliffe (2000), and Matar (1993).
7. We discuss this in more detail in Anderson, Johnson, and Koyama (2017).
8. As early as the reign of James I, there had been those citing the "great benefit and commodity which would redound to your majesty and to all your subjects … by the great commerce in trade and traffic both of Jews and all people; which for want of liberty of conscience, are forced and driven elsewhere" (quoted in Bainton, 1941).
9. See Katz (1994, 140–141 and 188). For details on the survival of antisemitic stereotypes and attitudes in England after the re-admittance of Jews into the country see Poliakov (1955, 203–209) and Felsenstein (1999).
10. In any case most popular anger was directly against Catholics – the growing rivalry between France and England gradually transformed Protestant–Catholic tensions into national rivalries.
11. In fairness, in more temperate times prior to the Revolution, Burke's attitudes toward Jews were humane (see Baron, 1947, 33).

12. Cobbett was openly antisemitic. He defended medieval persecutions of Jews and described Jewish religious services as hateful (see Osborne, 1984, 89). As Osborne (1984, 90) notes, Cobbett's argument was: "Thus, if only the corrupt politicians, fundholders, commercial interests, Jews, East India merchants, and political economists could be swept away, England would once again be serene and happy, blessed by a rich and substantial agriculture: a land of roast beef and plenty and a sure and exact relation between the classes." Scholarship suggests that Dicken's attitudes toward Jews evolved over time, from the relatively crude antisemitic portrayal of Fagin in Oliver Twist toward a more sensitive and sympathetic position in his later work (see Stone, 1959).

13. Summarizing this state of affairs, Cesarani notes: "Jews were tolerated precisely because they were despised: they necessarily served as a foil for Christian triumphalism and as objects for missionary activity. Those who welcomed them into English society and promoted their cause did not do so out of love for the Jews or Judaism but in expectation of their eventual demise" (Cesarani, 1999, 40).

14. Prussian emancipation was limited and other German states had preceded Prussia in offering emancipation. The Margrave of Baden, Karl Friedrich had issued an edict of toleration granting Jews some rights but not citizenship in 1781 (Goldstein, 1984, 47).

15. Rose writes that while Dohm is often taken for a liberal his views were only "an expression of his fundamental principle of raison d'état. For Dohm, all rights exist at the discretion of the state. There is no axiom or principle in Dohm that Jews have by right exactly the same rights as other Germans – only the quite different proposal that in a prudent state a class of useful Jews should be made equal with German Christians (Rose, 1990, 73–74)."

16. It was not in fact the first Edit of Toleration, the Margrave of Baden, Karl Friedrich had issued a similar document, granting Jews some rights but not citizenship in 1781 (Goldstein, 1984, 47).

17. See Katz (1974, 163–164) and Mahler (1985, 3–10).

18. See Wistrich (1990).

19. See Berkovitz (1989, 111–114).

20. In Rome, however, the Jews remained unemancipated until 1870 when the Holy City was incorporated into the new Kingdom of Italy.

21. See Greenberg (1976). See Grosfled et al. (2013) for an economic analysis of the persistent consequences of the confinement of Jews to the Pale of Settlement in Eastern Europe. For an analysis of these pogroms see Grosfeld et al. (2017). For a detailed assessment of the role played by pogroms in encouraging Jewish migration to the United States see Spitzer (2015).

22. As Katz writes: "Slight though his ideological training may have even, the Jew at least knew that Judaism and Christianity were mutually exclusive and therefore that defection to Christianity meant a complete abandonment of the true faith for a false one" (Katz, 1974, 25).

23. Jewish converts were often suspected of "rejudaizing" if they maintained contact with Jewish family members or continued Jewish dietary practices. Jews who attempted to integrate found themselves "between nations" to use Adam Sutcliffe's phrase (Sutcliffe, 2000).

24. See Plaut (1963), Steinberg (1965), and Meyer (1988).

25. The rise of Reform Judaism and the backlash it provoked is discussed and analyzed in detail in Carvalho and Koyama (2016).

PART III

IMPLICATIONS OF GREATER RELIGIOUS LIBERTY

11

The Persecution of Witchcraft

Prolonged witch hunting is as good a barometer as any for measuring weakness in a state.

(Soman, 1989, 17)

In 1670, a strange sight occurred repeatedly in the villages located at the base of the Pyrénées mountains in western France. A young weaver's apprentice named Bacqué could be seen in the middle of the village square – flanked by two agents of the local *parlement*, or, high court. While this, in itself, was not so strange – apprentices and agents of the court were not so rare – the actions of Bacqué and the villagers certainly were. The entire village would line up and file past the young weaver, and he would declare each villager either a "witch" or "not a witch," for the local magistrates in the region of Pau were convinced that Bacqué had the "gift" of seeing into people's souls to determine if they were tainted by the devil. The court agents and Bacqué would do this for as many as 30 villages, in the process identifying 6,210 "witches" (Mandrou, 1979, 236).

What happened next illustrates how the rule of law emerged in a society that was steeped in superstitious belief and clung to identity rules at the local level, but that was increasingly ruled by governments committed to maintaining order. Louis XIV's minister, Colbert, heard of what was going on and decided that it could not stand. He had Bacqué arrested and thrown in the Bastille and commanded the local magistrates to cease their search for witches in the area. On what grounds did he do this? Colbert objected to the irregularity of the judicial proceedings and annulled the prosecutions while issuing a royal proclamation (edict) that "...prevents the courts and averts the disorders that would be caused by a procedure so irregular that it would envelop the majority of the inhabitants of the aforementioned province, trouble the repose of families and violate the rules of justice" (Mandrou, 1979, 241). Colbert's objection to the violation of the "rules of justice" was about as close to a proclamation in favor of the rule of law as one gets in early modern Europe.

We have seen how medieval Europe became a "persecuting society." It did so not because of the religious bigotry of its leaders nor because of any intrinsic fanaticism within Christianity, but because of the deep structural forces responsible for maintaining order. Over the course of the Middle Ages, rulers came to rely on enforcing religious conformity in order to legitimate their rule. This equilibrium gradually undermined itself, however, as states grew larger and as religious beliefs became more diverse. As described in Chapter 7, the Reformation shocked the conditional toleration equilibrium. When states eventually realized that they could not kill all the heretics in their midst, they were forced to abandon religion as their primary source of legitimization. The shift away from religious legitimization was accompanied by a shift away from the identity rules based on religion. This, in turn, undermined the equilibrium described in Chapter 2, in which identity rules were used to create easily expropriated rents. In their stead, states were forced to invest in fiscal capacity and this was accompanied by the adoption of general rules that were more likely to advance religious liberty and, ultimately, rule of law.

The situation facing individuals accused of witchcraft had similarities to that facing Jews and heretics, but there were also important differences. Unlike Jews or heretics, the majority of convicted "witches" did not perceive themselves as belonging to a different religion than Christianity; many, or perhaps most, of those accused denied being witches, at least until put to torture. Nevertheless, a common thread connected antisemitic violence to the persecution of heretics and then the persecution of individuals for witchcraft. In the argument of Moore (1987), persecution became habitual in late medieval Europe, with many groups being victimized, including heretics, lepers, Jews, sodomites, and witches. Witches were classic scapegoats who could be blamed for natural disasters, disease, or general misfortune.

The persecution of witches required a legal system that treated those suspected of witchcraft *differently* from those suspected of more mundane crimes. It required torture and coercion to be brought to bear on alleged witches in the absence (or indeed impossibility) of direct evidence for their guilt. This was possible only in an environment in which some individuals – those considered inherently more susceptible to being seduced by the devil – could be singled out for special treatment by the legal system.

The decline in European witch trials offers an example of how the rise of modern fiscal states led to the imposition of more general rules. Earlier chapters have explored why the conjunction of the Reformation and state building efforts brought about religious persecution and violence. Out of this conflict, however, new types of state emerged that were more willing to offer first greater toleration and then eventually religious freedom.

11.1 Explanations for the European Witch Panic

11.1.1 Belief in Witchcraft

Peasants and elites alike believed in the reality of magic, and therefore in witchcraft, into the early modern period. These beliefs had been common in ancient Rome. Legislation was passed in Roman and Carolingian times condemning witchcraft.[1] Nevertheless, despite legislation against sorcery, we have no record of witchcraft trials in the early Middle Ages. Of course, it is likely that occasionally faith-healers or unpopular individuals did fall afoul of this legislation or were lynched by their neighbors. But, in general, as noted in Chapter 2, neither religious nor secular authorities pursued crimes of this kind. Until the fifteenth century, witchcraft trials were rare, and when they did occur they were often politically motivated and the accusation of witchcraft was understood by all as a way to camouflage or embellish other offenses.[2] Large-scale witch hunting did not emerge until the Renaissance and peaked during the sixteenth and seventeenth centuries, the age of Shakespeare, Cervantes, Bacon, and Descartes.

Far more individuals were killed for witchcraft than for heresy. Between 1450 and 1750, approximately 100,000 individuals were put on trial for witchcraft, of whom 30,000–40,000 were executed (Levack, 2006, 21–24). The largest number of executions were concentrated between 1580 and 1630 and took place in the Holy Roman Empire.[3] This was where witch trials became large-scale, panic-driven hunts, largely ignoring formal legal procedures (Midelfort, 1972).

There was tremendous variation in the number of trials across and within different countries. Both Protestants and Catholics killed witches. Few witches were killed in Catholic Spain – the land of the Inquisition. But large numbers died in the Catholic parts of Germany. Calvinist Scotland also killed large numbers of witches while the Calvinist Dutch Republic killed very few. Large-scale witch-hunts also took place in Lorraine, Savoy, and parts of Switzerland.

Why did Europeans persecute witches? And why did they persecute them with particular ferocity in the sixteenth and seventeenth centuries? Belief in witchcraft, that is, in maleficia or harmful magic, is not a sufficient explanation. This was almost universal in premodern society. In Europe, these beliefs did not generate large-scale trials before 1450, and would persist after the end of the witch trials of the sixteenth and seventeenth centuries.

Belief in witchcraft was a precondition for the witch craze. Such beliefs involved the hypothesis that some or perhaps most misfortune has social origins. Bad things happened because malevolent individuals used magic in order to intentionally cause harm to their acquaintances and neighbors.[4]

Cooperation over mutual aid, usage of common-pool resources, and the provision of public goods was beset by potential free-rider problems, and many of the customs of village life were institutional responses to the problems posed by free-riding. Managing the commons or ensuring that insurance systems were functioning became more important in periods of population growth or economic uncertainty.[5] Hence, neighborly relations mattered because of the overwhelming importance of maintaining cooperation.

If bad neighbors were a common problem in premodern societies, witches were bad neighbors who had become *demonized*.[6] Robin Briggs observes that the "popular image of the witch was that of a person motivated by ill-will and spite who lacked the proper sense of neighborhood and community. Witches were always close by; the bewitched invariably accused an acquaintance. Suspects were often alleged to have shown themselves resentful in their dealings with others and unwilling to accept delays or excuses in small matters" (Briggs, 1996, 23). The accusation of witchcraft was a libel against someone's character since to be a witch was to be utterly antithetic to all human society (Douglas, 1991). As they regulated individual actions and deterred unneighborly behavior, these beliefs may have had a functional role in premodern societies.[7] Belief in witchcraft was not a sufficient condition for the European witch-hunts. What factors, then, contributed to the sparks that set the bonfire of the witch-hunts alight?

11.1.2 Heresy Trials

Numerous scholars have drawn comparisons between the persecutions of heretics and witches (Moore, 1987; Jenson, 2007; Waite, 2009). Witches and heretics were both punished by burning, as these were "[c]rimes for which this purification was necessary where those believed to infect or pollute a community with their 'enormous' sin: heresy, witchcraft, sacrilege, blasphemy, infanticide, homosexuality, the murder of a spouse, incest, and poisoning" (Waite, 2009, 19). Moreover, the great European witch-hunts began after 1560, the period that followed the end of the great heresy persecutions of the mid-sixteenth century. But many aspects of the witch-trials differed from those of heresy trials. Different kinds of individuals were targeted. Heresy trials seldom involved panics and hysteria. Witches had no opportunity to confess their errors and return to orthodoxy.

11.1.3 Economic Stress

A classic attempt to explain the timing of the witch trials was pioneered by Thomas (1971) and Macfarlane (1970). They asked why the worst witch-hunts occurred during the early modern period and not earlier. Building on work by historians dating the birth of capitalism to the sixteenth century, Thomas and Macfarlane argued that this was period of particular economic turbulence.

Rapid population growth reduced real wages from the post–Black Death period and led to the cultivation of more marginal lands. It was, in the words of Henry Kamen (1971), "an iron century." These Malthusian forces acted in conjunction with the decline in average temperatures and increased temperature variability to generate greater volatility of agricultural output. As rural hardship and opportunities in the cities drew people away from the countryside, disrupting local systems of insurance and public good provision, inequality increased.

Drawing on English evidence, Thomas (1971) and Macfarlane (1970) conjectured that it was the combination of economic growth on the one hand and increased economic misery on the other hand that gave rise to witchcraft accusations. They suggested that the accused were usually poor, often elderly, women, who were partially dependent on charity and aid from their neighbors. They relied on the kinds of informal systems of mutual insurance typical in agricultural societies.[8] Thomas and Macfarlane hypothesized that witchcraft accusations were a mechanism through which more prosperous villagers sought to free themselves from the burden of supporting the poor.

Under this hypothesis, bad weather and other economic shocks could generate trials without being the underlying cause – bad weather simply increased the burden posed by the old and poor and hence led to more accusations and trials. Macfarlane stressed that in Essex it "was usually the person who had done the first wrong under the old ideals of charity who felt himself bewitched" (Macfarlane, 1970, 196). Poor individuals were accused as witches by their richer neighbors who did not want to provide them with aid or give them charity. Thus, "an accusation of witchcraft was a clever way of reversing the guilt, of transferring it from the person who had failed in social obligation under the old standard to the person who had made him fail ... witchcraft was a way not of conserving traditional values of mutual reciprocity, but of destroying them" (Macfarlane,

1970, 197). As economic change brought social differentiation within the village, the demands of charity remained theoretically boundless. For this reason, Macfarlane (1970) and Thomas (1971) speculated that charitable obligations were often felt to be increasingly oppressive in the century after 1550.

One problem is that often the accusers were not richer than the accused. Moreover, often "there was no link between local destitution, bad harvests, famine or general agricultural dislocation and suspicion of witchcraft... The burden of supporting the community's dependents in times of acute economic crisis and personal economic difficulties was not critical in inciting suspicion" (Quaife, 1987, 165).

Research on continental Europe developed a variant of the economic stress hypothesis without the specific predictions made by Thomas and Macfarlane. Studying witch-hunts in south-western Germany, Eric Midelfort observed that "misfortune of one sort or another provided the occasion for most witch hunting," singling out the role of storms, plague, and famine (Midelfort, 1972, 73). Behringer (1995) argued that the upsurge in witchcraft persecutions in the second part of the sixteenth century was partly a response to "unnatural" weather conditions. For instance, he argues that the "prerequisite" for the witch-hunts in southwest Germany in the 1590s was "a series of storms damaging crops and resultant crop failures, as chronicled for the regions near Kempten, Memmingen, and Augsburg, culminating in peasant unrest" (Behringer, 1995, 7). This resembles the link in Chapter 5 between weather shocks and Jewish pogroms. It is still more direct as witches were sometimes held responsible for strange or particularly harsh weather.[9]

The economic shock hypothesis has empirical support. Oster (2004) tested Behringer's claims for a relationship between witchcraft trials and broad correlates of economic growth such as urbanization and population growth. She found that witch trials were negatively correlated with urbanization and population growth, and occurred more frequently during cold spells. Nevertheless, while this economic stress explanation of witchcraft sheds light upon some of the proximate causes of witch killings, it does not fully resolve the puzzle. There were economic shocks before the European witch-hunts as well as after. The economic stress hypothesis is an institutions-free analysis that does not posit a mechanism through which economic variables affected the number of witchcraft prosecutions. Nor does it explain why the witchcraft prosecutions peaked in the early modern period rather than in earlier years of economic stress or why witchcraft trials declined during the early eighteenth century, a period that experienced cold temperatures comparable to those in the late sixteenth century.

11.1.4 State Building and Religious Legitimacy

While Thomas and Macfarlane focused on England, others scholars, drawing on evidence from Scotland, Lorraine, and parts of Germany, emphasized an alternative cause of the European witch-hunts: state building.

A major feature of the European witch-hunts was the distinction between evil magic, or maleficia, and diabolism, which meant conspiring with the devil. Maleficia could range from harming cattle or causing a blight on grain to murder. For example, in 1611 Jacques Jean Thiébaud in Montbéliard was accused of killing the livestock of neighbors and making them sick (Tuetey, 1886, 9). Diabolism – having dealings with the devil or his agents – could involve attendance at a "Devil's Sabbath" and making a pact with satan (Cohn, 1975; Roper, 2004). Norman Cohn argued that belief in maleficia alone was not sufficient to support large-scale witch-hunts because it usually involved an individual witch, whereas diabolism implied the existence of a conspiracy involving many individuals (Cohn, 1975). It was diabolism that led European elites to license widespread torture in the belief that there existed a hidden cabal of witches conspiring against society. Once elites became convinced of this threat, they imposed it on the testimonies of the accused.[10]

There are problems with this hypothesis. There is plenty of evidence from across Europe that accusations of witchcraft were made by villagers and that the pressure to prosecute frequently came from below. Behringer notes that "[v]illagers demanded that their superiors should follow the example of their neighbors and burn witches" (Behringer, 1997, 157). The mass trials in Würzburg were preceded by rumors about witches eating a child and witchcraft was mentioned in a general petition of the townsfolk to the Bishop (Roper, 2004, 28).

Another problem is that it is not clear what rulers stood to gain from witch-hunting. James VI of Scotland and I of England, author of a book on witch-hunting and a fervent believer in the reality of witches, found himself curbing the witch-hunting of his local lords. Weak and insecure rulers like the Archbishop of Trier could and did exploit witch panics to cement their power. But the rulers of the major European states gradually came to see witch panics as a nuisance and almost an embarrassment. Witch panics discredited witch trials long before elites became skeptical of the actual existence of witches.

A related explanation of the witch panics centers on the importance of religious legitimation in early modern states. Allied with the state-building hypothesis, the religious legitimization hypothesis predicts that witch trials will be most intense in regions where rulers needed religious legitimacy the most. For example, where Protestants and Catholics lived side-by-side, there should have been a greater frequency of witch trials. MacCulloch (2003) stressed the importance confessional divisions played in legitimizing large-scale judicial executions for religious deviants.

Peter Leeson and Jacob Russ (2017) explore this argument using a dataset of witch trials. They argue that witch trials reflected non-price competition between Catholic and Protestant churches for market share in religiously contested parts of early modern Christendom. In those parts of Europe where the Catholic Church was an effective monopolist such as in Spain and Italy, there was little need for rulers to demonstrate their religiosity by persecuting witches. But in regions where Catholicism was challenged by the Reformation, Leeson and Russ argue that there were more likely to be witch trials. This was also the case in Protestant areas where Catholicism was a genuine rival.

As a measure of religious contestation, Leeson and Russ use data on battles fought during the Wars of Religion. They find a correlation between religious contestation and witchcraft trials. Each additional battle is associated with approximately a 3 percent increase in the number of people tried for witchcraft and each additional battle per million, to a 7.5 percent increase in the number of people tried for witchcraft per million.

11.1.5 Legal Fragmentation and the European Witch-Hunt

Together these hypotheses provide reasonable explanations of the timing of the European witch-hunts. They help us understand why persecutions peaked in the late sixteenth and early seventeenth centuries. However, they do not fully explain the variation in intensity of persecution across different regions of Europe.

Small and fragmented jurisdictions such as Cologne, Würzburg, Luxembourg, Ellwangen, and Bamberg experienced the most severe witch-hunts. In contrast, while more centralized territories did try individual witches, they often avoided mass panics. Behringer argues that "strong governments in developed secular states tended to establish a legal system that would not allow for irregular witch-hunts" (Behringer, 2004, 126). The Inquisition in Spain, a "highly centralized, national institution," controlled local witch prosecutions and prevented large-scale or widespread trials (Levack, 1999, 15).[11] To explain why the Holy Roman Empire was so prone to witch-hunts, Levack argued that the "prevailing pattern of jurisdictional particularism in Germany meant that witch-hunting could easily go unchecked" (Levack, 2006, 212).

Levack observes that "judges of local or 'inferior' jurisdictions usually demonstrated much more zeal in prosecuting witches than did the central authorities, and when left to their own devices they generally executed more witches than when they were closely supervised by their judicial superiors" (Levack, 2006, 97). Central governments were, on the other hand, "a moderating influence" (Levack, 1996, 14).

Individuals demanded trials for a variety of reasons; crop failure, disease, bad weather, declining wages, population growth, greater economic insecurity, increased religious tension, and political pressure from local elites may all have played a role. In well-governed states, these factors only led to sporadic witch trials; they were not sufficient to generate widespread conflagrations of accusations as occurred in the areas worst hit by the witch panic of the early modern period. The legal fragmentation hypothesis accounts for why the most intense witch trials were concentrated in Germany, Lorraine, Switzerland, and Scotland.

It is an empirical question as to whether investments in fiscal capacity and the rule of law were causally linked. To evaluate this claim, we focus on the decline in witchcraft trials in seventeenth-century France.

11.2 Legal Fragmentation in France

France was characterized by extreme legal fragmentation at the beginning of the sixteenth century. Judicial and financial officials had a large amount of latitude. There was "a lack of a coherent and common set of laws for the realm; and, one might add, the absence of unified laws even within each governmental region" (Moote, 1971, 8).

The costs of legal fragmentation were evident in the administration of justice. France did not possess a single criminal code and the concept of equality before the law was "unknown." The absence of a common criminal code placed discretion in the hands of local elites who staffed the courts and who used this power to extract rents (Beik, 1985). Nepotism was common, corruption was widespread, and standards were lax. The latitude judges possessed in deciding what constituted a crime and how to punish it meant that local courts had enormous discretionary authority. Even in ordinary criminal cases, defendants could wither in prison for months before their cases were heard. Local magistrates could decide to deny them counsel or employ torture (Hamscher, 1976, 161–162). Reporting directly to Colbert, Nicholas Potier de Novion described the conduct of local judicial officials as "worse than one can imagine" as "all the cases that have been brought before us have been poorly prepared and judged" (quoted in Hamscher, 1976, 168–169).

Fiscal and legal fragmentation were intertwined.[12] Legal fragmentation produced fiscal fragmentation, and vice versa. The "administration of justice was closely tied to venality of office, a system in which officeholders purchased their posts and provided revenue for the state" (Trout, 1978,

117). To raise revenues, rulers had created and sold venal offices. This produced "perennial jurisdictional conflicts among the courts and great expense to litigants who faced a vast judicial hierarchy if they were entitled to appeal a decision from a lower court" (Hamscher, 1976, 160). In turn, legal fragmentation was a source of fiscal weakness. "Prior to the improvement of the fiscal machine, for example, it was comparatively easy to purchase relief from the taille in the form of deferments from the receiver. This official, using government funds, often assumed the role of a local banker and extended credit throughout the region. When conditions were poor, it was to his interest to protect his jurisdiction from ruinous taxation" (Trout, 1978, 140).

The extent of fiscal fragmentation in France was evident in the division between the pays d'état and pays d'élection. The pays d'élection made up two-thirds of France – those regions where local estates had been suppressed. The remaining pays d'état comprised later additions to the monarchy, notably Brittany, Burgundy, Languedoc, and Normandy. Direct taxes – the most important of which was the *taille* – were collected differently in the pays d'état than in the pays d'élection. In the latter, tax collection was the responsibility of agents of the crown who were typically local venal office holders. In the former, the burden of the taille was determined through bargaining between the king and the estates, and assessed and collected by provincial courts staffed by members of the old nobility.[13] In pays d'état such as Brittany or Burgundy the provincial nobility retained discretion over the allocation of the tax burden and they used this power to resist increases in direct taxation.[14]

11.2.1 Centralization and the Growth of the French State

Cardinal Richelieu forcefully made the case for centralization in 1629:

Reduce and restrict those bodies [for example, the parlements] which, because of pretensions to sovereignty, always oppose the good of the realm. Ensure that your majesty is absolutely obeyed by great and small. Fill the bishoprics with carefully selected, wise, and capable men. Repurchase the royal domain and increase your revenue by one half, as far as may be done by harmless measures (quoted in Church, 1969, 30).

As a result, taxes went up. Direct taxes in the pays d'élection were increased by 65 percent between 1627 and 1634 (Collins, 1988, 233). New offices were created so that the state could sell the rights to collect these new taxes.

To collect the new taxes, agents of the crown, called intendants, were sent into the countryside. Intendants were granted the power to ensure that taxes were collected, revolts put down, and appeals against impositions settled quickly. They coopted, or if need be overruled, local elites.

In the sixteenth century, the French monarch mobilized an army of around 50,000 men during wartime. The French army grew dramatically in size following entry into the Thirty Years' War in the 1630s. It grew again in the 1660s as Louis XIV's Secretary of War, Michael Le Tellier, created a professional royal army. This army ballooned in size as Louis XIV embarked on a series of expansionist wars. More than 400,000 soldiers were mobilized in the early 1700s (Lynn, 1997, 8). The new ability of the French monarch to project military force was accompanied by a consolidation of power internally. Louis XIV and his ministers had a much greater ability to influence the lives of their subjects than had his predecessors.

This army had to be paid for. Figure 11.1 shows the growing fiscal capacity of the French state in the seventeenth century.[15] The dashed line shows the per capita value of all revenues collected in silver equivalents. These include both ordinary tax revenues in addition to loans and temporary financial expedients. The solid line shows the revenues coming from the primary direct tax collected by the crown known as the taille. There was a marked increase in the amount of taxes collected following France's

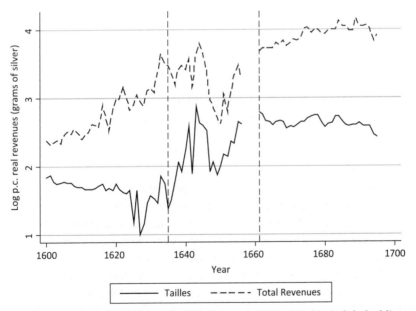

Figure 11.1 Total tax revenues and tailles revenues, 1600–1695. Vertical dashed lines indicate the dates France entered the Thirty Years' War (1635) and the beginning of Louis XIV's personal rule (1661). Source: Johnson and Koyama (2014*b*). © 2014 by The University of Chicago Press.

entry into the Thirty Years' War. Moreover, whereas increases in revenues between 1600 and 1635 tended to come from so-called "extraordinary" sources, such as loans (voluntary and forced) and temporary taxes, after 1635 there was a dramatic rise in revenues coming from "ordinary" sources, such as the taille. These two trends: the shift from extraordinary toward ordinary sources of revenue and the increase in revenues being collected, both represented an increase in fiscal capacity.[16]

Fiscal centralization was accompanied by a shift from decentralized to centralized rent-seeking. Old clientelistic networks were broken up and reorganized along new lines. The pacification of the country and the increased professionalism of the army greatly reduced the ability of the provincial nobility to provide patronage, particularly military patronage. Relationships with the crown, became more important (Black, 2004, 27). Ministers such as Richelieu, Mazarin, and Colbert controlled political networks in the provinces, and thereby gained influence in peripheral regions that had traditionally been largely independent such as Provence, Languedoc, Guyenne, Burgundy, Alsace, and the Franche-Comté (Kettering, 1986, 7–9). As a consequence of royal policy, these client networks were centralized: "there was finally a single line of command at the top and a unified network in the provinces, accompanied by the administrative channels to make it function properly" (Beik, 1985, 338). In particular, after 1660 Colbert transferred power from venal officers and local notables to the central government (Sargent, 1968, 51).

11.2.2 Prosecuting Individuals for Witchcraft in France

Legal standards across Europe required that a witch must be shown to have engaged in both maleficia (evil magic) and diabolism (devil worship). Maleficia may have sometimes actually occurred and, in rare cases, may even have left evidence. However, diabolism was, by its nature, beyond the pale of rational legal procedure because dealings with the devil existed only in the fantasies of accusers and (sometimes) the accused. To get around the difficulty of prosecuting a suspected witch according to traditional standards of legal proof, and to convict individuals of diabolism, local judges turned to the theories of the demonologists.[17] These writers claimed witchcraft was an "exceptional crime" (*crimen exceptum*) (Larner, 1980). For demonologist Henri Boguet, "[w]itchcraft is a crime apart ... Therefore the trial of this crime must be conducted in an extraordinary manner; and the usual legalities and ordinary procedures cannot be strictly observed" (Boguet, 1929, 211–212). The Devil was seen as extremely cunning and endowed with the ability to enable witches to resist interrogation. As Soman writes, "[i]n order to prosecute witches cheaply and efficiently the crime needed to be redefined and the rules of evidence relaxed ...Learned demonological theory came to the rescue and found ready acceptance within the ranks of subalternate magistrates" (Soman, 1992, 13).

Influenced by the ideas of the demonologists, suspected witches were tried using evidence that was poor in both quantity and quality.[18] To break the hold of Satan it was also often deemed necessary to resort to torture, since the application of standard rules of evidence would result in the majority of accused witches being acquitted. The dangers associated with using torture to extract confessions were recognized both in legal codes and in the attitudes of professional legislators and judges at the state level (Langbein, 1977).[19] Judicial torture required at least "half-proof" that the individual had committed the crime. Half-proof was defined in the Lex Carolina as half of the evidence necessary for a conviction. Thus, for a crime requiring two eyewitnesses, if the prosecutor only had one eyewitness, he could proceed to put the accused to the "question." Even then, however, torture was intended to be used to obtain information that could be externally verified, information that "no innocent person can know" (quoted in Langbein, 1977). The magistrates conducting the interrogation were to refrain from suggestive questioning and torture could be repeated only a certain number of times. Had these rules been adhered to, witchcraft cases would have been infrequent.[20] However, legal restrictions on the use of torture were often ignored in witchcraft cases, especially when judges were pressured by popular opinion.

One highly publicized trial could stoke fear of witchcraft, and hence increase demand for further trials. One mechanism that can explain this is that of information cascades. An information cascade occurs when people with incomplete information on a specific matter base their own beliefs on what they perceive to be the beliefs of others (Kuran, 1998, 86).[21] In the case of witchcraft, an information cascade can explain why a judge in one region might find it optimal to convict a witch (or allow a witch suspect to be tortured into producing a confession) simply because the number of convictions in nearby regions had increased the perceived threat posed by witchcraft.

Suppose local courts attached an a priori probability to the possibility that witches exist and pose a large threat to society. Based on this probability, the courts determined what evidence could be accepted in court and whether torture could be used. If the danger posed by witches was truly great then this could justify departing from the legal rules concerning what kind of information can be elicited from a suspect during interrogations. Hence, the higher this perceived probability, the more witches that would be executed by the local court.

But this perceived probability was itself affected by local information including perceptions of the dangers posed by witchcraft. Fear of sorcery and satanic pacts were spread by court transcripts that reported lurid confessions of devilish crimes.[22] This could generate a positive feedback loop as trials begat more trials.

Local authorities either ignored, or were unable to internalize the effect that trials in their region had in reinforcing belief in witchcraft in other regions. Central authorities, however, faced stronger incentives to internalize this externality. Hence, central authorities and higher courts often upheld stricter legal standards than did lower or local courts and well-organized states did not "tolerate genuine witch-hunting for very long" (Briggs, 1996, 190–191).[23]

11.3 Legal Centralization and the Decline in Witchcraft Trials

Many individuals were tried for witchcraft trials in late sixteenth- and early seventeenth-century France. However, from the mid-seventeenth century onward the number of trials began to fall. We argue that part of this decline can be explained by the process of legal centralization that accompanied the growth of the fiscal state.

A crucial factor in stopping witchcraft trials was the Parlement of Paris. Compared to local courts or regional parlements, it upheld strict legal standards. In 1588 trials by water were banned by the Parlement. In March 1588, magistrates proposed making all witchcraft cases subject to appeal. The Catholic League intervened, however, and Paris was under siege for five years. After 1596, however, the Parlement succeeded in preventing several local legal authorities from declaring witchcraft to be a *crimen exemptum* and thus not subject to the jurisdiction of the Parlement (Soman, 1992, 5).

In the words of Soman, evidence was "elevated" among the magistrates of the Parlement of Paris. This emphasis on evidence was not restricted to witch trials. For example, women were required by the Parlement to register any children to whom they gave birth and to have a witness to the birth itself. These rules were designed to ensure that infanticide could be properly prosecuted, as it could be readily ascertained whether or not a child was alive at birth from the testimony of a witness. As a result, the number of death sentences confirmed in cases of infanticide by the Parlement was as high as 70 percent. It was impossible to do this in the case of witchcraft. There simply were no criteria that could be invoked to prove the existence of a witch. As a result, trials of witches increasingly became legally impossible. Soman finds that through 1600 the Parlement only approved 74 out of 249 death sentences. Between 1611 and 1640 there were only 18 executions, that is, 4.7 percent of the total.

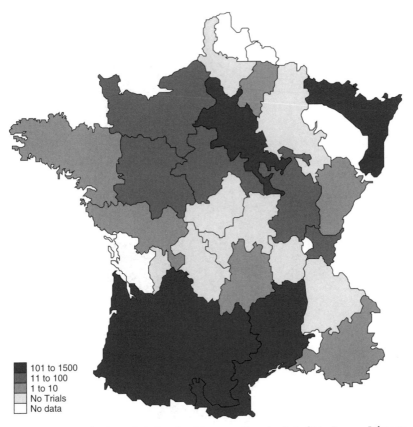

Figure 11.2 Distribution of witchcraft trials across French généralités. Source: Johnson and Koyama (2014*b*). © 2014 by The University of Chicago Press.

To explore the relationship between increases in fiscal capacity and greater adherence to rule of law we create a dataset spanning the years 1550–1700 for witchcraft trials and tax revenues in France.[24] Figure 11.2 plots the total distribution of witchcraft trials in our data for the entire period. Figure 11.3 plots average taille revenue for the entire period. Together they suggest that where taxes were higher, there were fewer witchcraft trials.

Does this correlation between low fiscal capacity and witch trials reflect a causal relationship? We exploit the fact that fiscal capacity increased at different rates across regions to test whether increases in state capacity led to fewer witchcraft trials. That is, we adopt a difference-in-differences approach similar to that in Chapter 5. In effect, we are comparing the difference in the difference in number of trials between two groups of regions over time. The monarchy had low fiscal capacity in both groups of regions initially. Over time, however, its capacity increased in one of the groups (the treatment group) while staying unchanged in the other group (the control

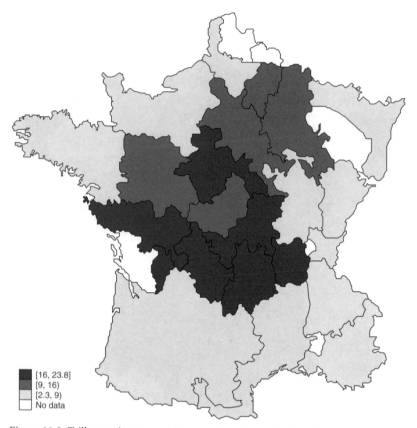

Figure 11.3 Tailles receipts per capita across French généralités. Source: Johnson and Koyama (2014*b*). © 2014 by The University of Chicago Press.

group). Suppose the control group had, on average, 35 trials in the first period and 30 in the second period. Further, assume the treatment group, which has higher fiscal capacity in the second period, has 25 trials in the first period and 0 in the second period. The difference-in-differences estimate would then be $(0 - 30) - (25 - 35) = -20$. We would infer from this that the causal effect of the increased fiscal capacity of the state on witch trials was 20 fewer trials.

Notice that our estimate of a reduction by 20 trials is less than the overall reduction in the treatment regions of 25 trials. This is because we are taking into account that in *all* regions the number of trials fell by 5. Attributing those 5 trials to increases in state capacity would be inappropriate, because in the control group state capacity did not increase. Another explanation, common to both regions, must account for the 5 trial reduction – for example, maybe incomes went up reducing the incentive to accuse rich widowers of being witches.

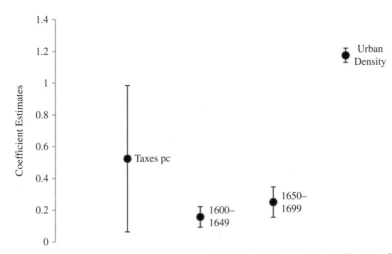

Figure 11.4 Incidence rate ratios from negative binomial regressions indicating the effects of our key variables on the number of witch trials. Specifications also include region fixed effects and are based on our maximal dataset. 95% confidence intervals are shown.

Figure 11.4 presents the results of our regression analysis.[25] The first coefficient is for taxation per capita. This coefficient is reported as an incidence rate ratio. If we assume one region has taxes per capita increase by 1 and the other regions experience no increase, then the incidence rate ratio is equal to the number of trials in the high-tax region divided by the number of trials in the low-tax region. Thus, the coefficient of 0.44 in Figure 11.4 indicates that a 1 unit increase in taxes collected is associated with a region having only 44 percent as many trials as in the region experiencing no increase in state capacity. As the mean number of trials across all regions and periods is 36, this suggests that a 1-unit increase in fiscal capacity in a given region leads to about 20 fewer trials.[26]

We also report the coefficients for the periods 1600–1649 and 1650–1699.[27] The sign and size of these coefficients indicates that over time there was a general decline in witch trials. The coefficient on 1600–1649 is 0.15, indicating that, on average across all regions, the number of trials in 1600–1649 was about 15 percent of what it was in 1550–1599. Similarly, between 1650 and 1699 there were only 24 percent as many trials as in 1550–1599. Surprisingly, the coefficient on urban density is above 1, which means that regions with higher urban density actually had slightly *more* trials than less urbanized areas.

Figure 11.4 indicates that while many factors played a role in the decline of witch trials over time, fiscal capacity was one of the more important ones. As fiscal capacity increased across regions, the discretion local magistrates had to depart from de jure law to pursue witches decreased.[28]

An alternative explanation for the decline in witch trials is that central courts were more skeptical and less likely to believe in the existence of witches. However, there is little evidence for this. The idea that the decline in the European witch trials was caused by changing beliefs is rejected by historians.[29] Educated elites continued to *believe* in witchcraft: "[f]rom the viewpoint of 1700, the possibility of another bout of witchcraft prosecution was not safely dead and buried as those with hindsight may assume" (Bostridge, 1996, 310). As late as 1769, the celebrated jurist William Blackstone could, while deploring the legal abuses that took place when witches were prosecuted, still assert that "to deny the possibility, nay the actual existence of witchcraft and sorcery is at once to contradict the revealed word of God" (quoted in Bever, 2009, 279).

11.4 The Growth in Legal Capacity

Increases in fiscal capacity lead to greater adherence to rule of law – as proxied by a decline in witch trials. Now we investigate whether there was a relationship between increases in fiscal capacity and spending on legal capacity. While there are no systematic data on spending on courts during the sixteenth and early seventeenth centuries, Hamscher (2012) has collected data on court expenditure for thirty-four regions during the eighteenth century.

Figure 11.5 illustrates the relationship between average taxes collected per capita in a region between 1661 and 1685 and spending on the courts between 1700 and 1790.[30] Regions that invested in fiscal capacity also invested in courts, lawyers, and the infrastructure required for the rule of law. A 10 percent increase in fiscal capacity during the late seventeenth century was accompanied by a 6 percent increase in court spending in the eighteenth century. This suggests that increases in fiscal capacity were indeed related to fewer witch trial through the mechanism of greater legal capacity.

11.5 Other Parts of Europe

Evidence from the Holy Roman Empire supports our argument. The most severe witch-hunts occurred in small and fragmented jurisdictions and in the lands ruled by the archbishops of Mainz, Cologne, and Trier – "areas of notoriously loose (central) government control" (Monter, 2002, 17).[31] These trials were associated with the indiscriminate use of judicial torture. In contrast, the more powerful and centralized states within the

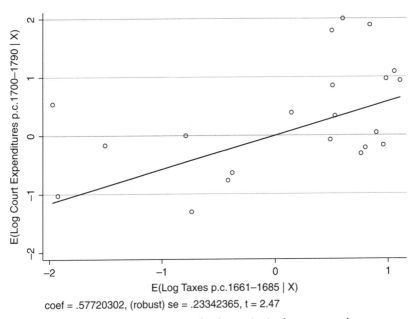

Figure 11.5 The effect of investment in fiscal capacity in the seventeenth century on legal expenditure in the subsequent century.

Empire tried notably fewer witches and the judicial institutions of large states such as Bavaria and Brandenburg exerted a moderating influence (Levack, 1999, 18).

One reason why trials were so frequent and continued for so much longer in the Holy Roman Empire compared to France was that unlike in France, there was no higher court like the Parlement of France to which cases could be referred.[32] Monter contrasts centralized French courts "which generally rejected village testimony" (at least after 1600) with "the 550 villages and eleven small towns which today comprise Germany's Saarland." Between 1580 and 1630, "these virtually autonomous rustics executed 450 per cent more witches than the Parlement of Paris, in a corner of the Empire divided among four principal overlords, two Protestant and two Catholic" (Monter, 2002, 9–10).

Three times as many individuals were executed as witches in Scotland as in England. One reason was that local judges in Scotland had much more discretion. Judicial torture was often employed in Scotland even though it "was administered illegally, without warrant from the privy council." Levack observes that "the main difference, therefore, between the English and the Scottish use of torture is not that the laws of one country allowed its use, whereas the laws of the other did not, but that the central government of one country was generally able to enforce its own strict rules regarding

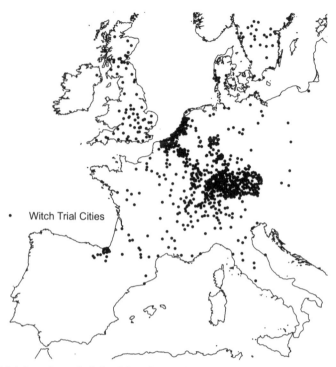

Figure 11.6 Locations of witch trials and executions, 1300–1850. Data from Leeson and Russ (2018) and Nussli (2011).

the use of torture whereas the government of the other could not" (Levack, 2008, 23).

Data Leeson and Russ (2017) collected on 29,400 witch trials and 9,736 executions across 1,070 locations in Europe between 1300 and 1850 allows us to test some of our hypotheses accross all of Europe.[33] The spatial distribution of these trials can be seen in Figure 11.6.

In the absence of disaggregated data on state capacity, we employ several proxies. Figure 11.7 depicts state boundaries in Europe in 1500 (Nussli, 2011). We draw buffers with a 25-kilometer radius around each city or region centroid and then count how many political boundaries fall within these circles. The more boundaries there are, the more fragmented political authority likely was, and the lower we expect state capacity to be.

The other proxy we use is the elevation around a city or region under the assumption that cities at higher elevation are more difficult to govern. We use data that measure elevation at the 90-meter resolution for the entire world (Jarvis, 2008) (Figure 11.7). We extract the median elevation within 25 kilometers of a city or region.

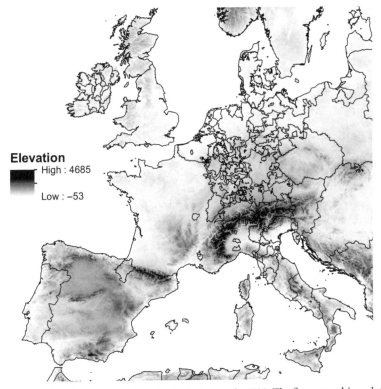

Figure 11.7 Elevation and state boundaries in Europe in 1500. The figure combines data on elevation from Jarvis (2008) with data on political boundaries from Nussli (2011).

Do our two proxies for the cost of investing in state capacity predict whether a city tried witches? Figure 11.8 illustrates the estimated coefficients from four regressions.[34] Our prediction is that territories at a higher altitude may have been harder to rule and, consequently, state capacity would be lower and witch trials more likely in those areas. The coefficient is 0.28, which means that one standard deviation increase in elevation around a city was associated with an increase in the probability of a witch trial of 14 percent. Similarly, the correlation between having a witch trial or execution and the number of nearby borders is 0.26. In this case, a one standard deviation increase in the number of borders is associated with a 29 percent greater chance of the city or region having a witch trial.

These correlations tell us about the relationship between the cost of investing in state capacity and witch trial probability on the *extensive* margin. But they do not shed light on the intensity of the persecutions. To investigate the *intensive* margin, we restrict our sample to those regions that had a trial or execution at one point. We find a modest impact of our

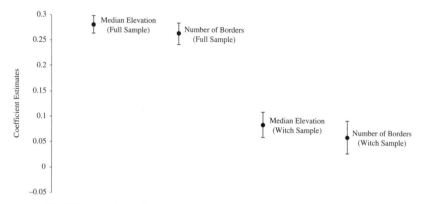

Figure 11.8 The correlation between witch trials and proxies for the costs of investing in state capacity across Europe. 10% confidence intervals based on robust standard errors are also shown.

proxies on witch trial intensity. The coefficient on elevation of 9 percent suggests that a one standard deviation increase in elevation of a region is correlated with three additional executions (relative to the average number of executions of nine). The coefficient on borders of 6 percent means that one additional border is associated with two more executions.

Overall, the analysis witch trials across Europe is highly suggestive. There is a strong positive correlation between the cost of investing in state capacity, as proxied by geographic isolation or political fragmentation, and the probability of a witch trial.

11.6 Chapter Summary: Legal Centralization and Rule of Law

The increased size of the fiscal state in early modern France probably brought little direct benefits to the ordinary population. Taxes were spent on warfare or on conspicuous consumption of the king and his nobles at Versailles. Incomes stagnated during the seventeenth century. This increased peasant vulnerability to agricultural crises, which continued to occur, particularly in times of war.

Nevertheless, investments in fiscal capacity were accompanied by investments in legal capacity and in legal centralization. Legal centralization was associated with more standardized and general rules. It limited the responsiveness of local legal institutions to popular fears of witchcraft and restricted the arbitrary use of torture.

The case study of seventeenth-century France thus illustrates the link from greater fiscal capacity to greater legal capacity and the adoption of more general rules. This reliance on general rules was incompatible with the old equilibrium that was based on identity rules grounded in feudal obligations and local privilege. Clearing away this old system helped lay the foundations for the modern state and for the eventual rise of religious freedom.

Notes

1. See Tacitus on the bewitchment of Germanicus (Tacitus, 1931, 499).
2. Prior to his execution by treason in 1330, Edmund Earl of Kent was accused of consulting with the devil (Childs, 1991, 155). Similarly, Joan of Arc was tried as a witch and a heretic. In 1441 Eleanor Cobham was accused of witchcraft as a part of a ploy to undermine the power of Humphrey, Duke of Gloucester, uncle of king Henry VI (r. 1422–1461 and 1470–1471).
3. Fifty percent of the total number of witches killed in Bavaria between 1400 and 1700 were killed in thirteen hunts between 1586 and 1631.
4. "There are evil forces around, and they try to cause harm. Some people, who are essentially anti-social, either incorporate such forces involuntarily, or form alliances with these forces intentionally in order to inflict harm by mystical means, mostly on their relatives or neighbors" (Behringer, 2004, 12–13). These beliefs continue to exist in many sub-Saharan African countries today as work by Boris Gershman has documented (Gershman, 2016). See also Platteau (2000).
5. Neighborliness does not just include mutual aid but included "the maintenance of solidarity in dealing with those outside the community; and secondly, the reduction of dissension within, in order to establish a social environment conducive to mutual help and solidarity ... failure to maintain a adequate level of neighborliness, or disagreements about what that level should be, could have exacerbate major factional divisions within the community as a whole. Accusations of witchcraft were one means of expressing and acting upon such conflicts" (Gregory, 1991, 34).
6. Behringer (2004, 2) observes that "witchcraft is often a *synonym* for evil, characterized by the inversion of central moral norms. It is the antisocial crime *par excellence*, the ultimate form of human depravity and male, or the quintessence of immorality."
7. For speculations along these lines see Posner (1980).
8. More recent research indicates that these forms of mutual insurance in fact had been replaced by credit markets as early as the thirteenth and fourteenth centuries. See Briggs (2006, 2008).
9. "The nexus of causality between agrarian crisis and persecutions is based upon four supports. First, witches were held directly responsible for weather damage and crop failures, despite the official teachings of theologians ... Second, illness and death multiplied in the wake of crop failures, especially among children, who were also held accountable as witches. Third, latent conflicts emerged virulently because shortages of resources during agrarian crises increased social tensions, adding a psychological dimension that needed to be resolved. Fourth, witch-trials provided 'positive' feedback, leading to further accusations in the region" (Behringer, 1997, 26).
10. Other historians have also argued that elites utilized the witch trials for their own purposes. Larner (1981) studied the Scottish witch trials, arguing that the pursuit of witches was part of the process of building a confessional state. This is called the Rise of the Godly state hypothesis.
11. For a detailed analysis see Henningsen (1980).

12. The term composite monarchy was coined by John Elliot. On the organization of the French monarchy in 1610 see Moote (1971, 3–35). For analysis see Root (1987).

13. For this reason, the pays d'état paid the *taille réelle* assessed on real property whereas the pays d'élection typically paid the more extensive and burdensome *taille personnelle* assessed on personal wealth.

14. As Collins writes: "[e]veryone wanted access to peasant stocks of cash: the king obtained the cash through the direct taxes, the landlords through higher entry fees for leases or in higher rents. Higher direct taxes meant less liquid capital for paying entry fees, rents, and perhaps most critically of all, for investment." The local nobility, moreover, "stood to lose financially if their tenants could not pay their rents due to overtaxation" (Collins, 1994, 13).

15. All data come from Bonney and Bonney (2011). Total Revenues are equal to the sum of extraordinary revenues and ordinary revenues. "Tailles Revenues" are simply the value of the tailles, which is a subset of ordinary revenues (usually about two-thirds of ordinary revenues). All series are converted into silver equivalents. We use généralité level taille receipt data from Malet. We use population data from around 1700 contained in Dupâquier (1988) to create per capita values. We then converted these numbers into real values using data on the silver content (in grams) of the livre tournois provided by Wailly (1857).

16. Our assessment of the growth of tax revenues in seventeenth-century France does not depend on the old historiography that took the French monarch's claims to absolutism at face value and depicted the bureaucracy created by Colbert in proto-totalitarian terms. Revisionist accounts stress the limitations that Louis XIV faced as well as the continued importance of clientism and personal relationships and the extent to which the power of the king remained mediated by his relationship with the elites. See Kettering (1986) for the continued importance of patronage networks and clientism during this period.

17. In France, the most well-known demonologists and the dates of their tracts were: Jean Bodin (1579), Nicolas Rémy (1595), Martin Del Rio (1599), Henri Boguet (1602), and Pierre de Lancre (1612 and 1622).

18. As with torture, evidence taken from children was not admissible in normal criminal cases but judges like Pierre de Lancre in the Labourd justified relying on statements from children as young as six because doing otherwise would be "very dangerous for the republic, and especially for a country as infected as Labourd" (quoted in Williams, 1995, 119).

19. The *Lex Carolina* of 1532 in Germany and The *Ordinance of Villers-Cotterets* of 1539 in France required adherence to Roman Canon Law when trying accused witches and, as such, limited the use of the judicial torture [see Roper (2004, 46) and Levack (1996, 82–88)].

20. Torture was not generally used in England and the number of witches tried in England was comparatively low (Sharpe, 1996). The exception that proves the rule is the East Anglian witch hunt of the 1640s, where witch hunters exploited the breakdown in central authority and generated a witch panic (Gaskill, 1996).

21. For applications and detailed discussion of such information (and other kinds of) cascades see Kuran (1989, 1998) and Bikhchandani et al. (1992).

22. "The news of witch-hunts and executions in other parts of a country could easily fan popular fears and create a mood that was conducive to witch-hunting in a village or town. It was because of such communications that many hunts spread

from village to village, even when confessing witches did not implicate accomplices outside their communities or when witch-hunters did not move from place to place" (Levack, 2006, 178–179).

23. We use the term "stricter" as specifically meaning that central authorities were less likely to allow a deviation in legal procedure due to the influence of superstitious belief reinforced by popular opinion.

24. There are data covering twenty-one regions over three time periods. The fragmented nature of the tax system in early modern France means that variation in fiscal capacity between regions at any given time was significantly higher than the variation within a given region over time.

25. We estimate negative binomial regressions with region fixed effects and period dummies. We report incident rate ratios in Figure 11.4. We control for changing levels of economic development across regions using city population data compiled by Bairoch (1988) and Bosker et al. (2013). It includes cities with populations of at least 5,000 inhabitants and provides estimates of the populations for 84 French cities.

26. A 1 unit increase in taxes collected per capita in this context is equivalent to a move from about the 50th percentile of regions to the 84th percentile. A standard deviation in log taxes per capita also happens to be 1 in our sample.

27. These are binary variables for each period. 1550–1599 is the omitted category.

28. In Johnson and Koyama (2014*b*) we show that our results are robust to dropping Paris and the Metz-Alsace region from our analysis and to using alternative estimates for tax revenues.

29. See Levack (1999), Bostridge (1996), and Bever (2008). "Historians of witchcraft now reverse the traditional assumption and see the decline of witch beliefs as – at least in Western and Central Europe – an important cause, not an effect, of the change in elite mentalités" (Bever, 2009, 264). While we cannot fully disentangle this, the negative time trend we find can be interpreted as capturing declining belief in witchcraft over time. But this time trend only explains a portion of the decline in trials.

30. Nominal expenditures are converted into silver equivalents and we match the thirty-four regions to our data on taxes collected per capita during the seventeenth century. We report the results of a simple bivariate regression. We choose these dates because 1661 marks the beginning of the major expansion of the French fiscal state under Louis XIV and the Hamscher data start in 1686. We experiment with different time periods and get the same results as we report here.

31. "The Prince-Abbot of Ellwangen alone accounted for one-ninth of the 3,229 known executions for witchcraft throughout Baden-Württemburg. Two other smaller Catholic prelates also instigated genuine witch-hunting panics: the monastery of Obermarchtal (whose territory of ten tiny settlements contained barely 350 adults) executed over 50 witches between 1586 and 1588 and 30 more afterwards; the Teutonic Knights at Mergentheim executed 114 witches between 1628 and 1630 during a panic inspired by developments in the neighbouring bishopric of Würzburg. But if a handful of Catholic prelates compiled the highest death totals in south-western Germany, a few self-governing cities, ruling territories no larger than the Teutonic Knights at Mergentheim, were not far behind. Rottenburg executed at least 150 witches between 1578 and 1609; Rottweil executed 113 in thirty different years between 1566 and 1648" (Monter, 2002, 17).

32. The *Reichskammergericht* or imperial supreme court sat at Speyer but it lacked the ability to compel lower courts to direct cases to it (Levack, 1999, 18).
33. The vast majority of these trials (about 90 percent) occurred between 1500 and 1700. 929 of the locations are given as specific cities. 141 are regions. When geocoding regions (e.g., the Department of "Moselle" in France) we use the centroid of the geographic unit. In some cases, where a region and a city share the same name (e.g., "Trier" in Germany) we use the coordinates of the major city.
34. Each variable is standardized by subtracting its mean from it and then dividing by its standard deviation. We include the longitude and latitude of the city or region as controls.

Religious Minorities and Economic Growth

12.1 Minorities and Economic Development

Religious freedom is an end in of itself, desirable because it enables greater human flourishing. However, it was also part of a package of reforms that were associated with the rise of modern liberal states and economic growth. This chapter asks whether religious freedom was good for economic growth. We focus on the relationship between religious minorities and long-run economic development.

Specifically, we focus on the case of Jewish communities and city growth, as this allows the use of econometric techniques to undercover a *causal* relationship between the presence of a religious minority and subsequent economic growth. We find a strong relationship between a city having a Jewish community and urban growth in the subsequent century. This growth premium is driven primarily by the period after 1600.

We argue that the most persuasive interpretation of the results is that Jews brought tangible economic skills to the cities in which they settled including financial services, access to trading networks, and higher human capital. However, under identity rules, the benefits associated with these skills were often captured by political elites (Chapter 4). Moreover, restrictions on Jewish participation in trade and commerce attenuated the positive growth effect of a Jewish community. However, as cities abandoned identity rules and moved toward more liberal economic regimes, they reaped the rewards of having a Jewish community.

12.1.1 Minorities and Economic Development

Interest in the role played by religious minorities in economic development goes back to the work of Max Weber, who identified the spirit of capitalism with Calvinists who viewed worldly success as a sign that they were part of the elect. Subsequent scholars such as Fernand Braudel observed that religious minorities such as Jews, Armenians, Parsees, Russian Old Believers, and Christian Copts played crucial roles in long-distance trade throughout the preindustrial world.[1]

One example are the French Protestants who fled France after the revocation of the Edict of Nantes in 1685. Approximately 16,000 to 20,000 Huguenots went to Prussia. Many were skilled workers and they brought with them technical know-how unavailable in Prussia.[2] Hornung (2014) found that they substantially increased firm productivity in the locations where they settled.

Another example are the Quakers, who suffered severe persecution prior to 1688 but played an important role in British economic development after 1700. While they still faced legal discrimination and were barred from positions in government and universities, the Quakers thrived in business. Quakers comprised around 17 percent of London's overseas merchants in the 1690s despite constituting at most 1.6 percent of the population (Sahle, 2017, 1). Mokyr notes that "[a]mong successful Quaker industrialists, the Darbys are the first to come to mind, but there were many others: the eighteenth-century banker David Barclay, the coco and chocolate pioneer John Cadbury, the biscuit manufacturer Jonathan Carr, railroad entrepreneur George Pease, the Welsh iron and tinplate tycoon James Halford, and the Welsh bankers Joseph Gibbins Sr. and Jr." (Mokyr, 2009, 362).

Why were the Quakers successful in business? One argument is that they specialized in business because conventional arenas for advancement were closed to them. They could not become politicians, soldiers, academics, or churchmen. They were also denied access to many professions and trade guilds (Raistrick, 1968).[3] The strict religious practices of the Quakers may also have given them an economic edge. As a tightly knit, culturally homogeneous group, they were better able to enforce informal agreements. Quakers were able to signal trustworthiness because being associated with their religion was costly and hence could screen out potential cheats.[4]

The question of whether a particular religious culture was conducive to development confronts analytical challenges. In particular, there is the problem of assessing the direction of causality: "The fact that a correlation existed between certain religious beliefs and cultural traits proves little about the direction of causation ... Did religion lead people to behave in a certain way, or did certain cultural features or economic attainments help make people choose certain religious beliefs?" (Mokyr, 2009, 364). We can gain insight into the mechanisms linking religious minorities to economic success by looking at the relationship between the presence of Jewish communities and city growth.

12.2 Jewish Communities and City Growth

There are several reasons why Jewish communities might have had a positive effect on economic growth in premodern Europe. Simon Kuznets (1960) found that Jews were a market-dominant minority in the late nineteenth century. Acemoglu, Hassan, and Robinson (2011) found similar results in Eastern Europe before the Holocaust. However, the fact that the economic role of Jews varied over time and across space suggests that their presence in a community need not have had the same effect in all places and at all times.[5]

Botticini and Eckstein (2012) document that Jews in medieval Europe had higher levels of human capital than did Christians. Higher human capital might be one channel through which the presence of a Jewish community could affect economic growth. However, as documented in previous chapters, Jewish settlement was always conditional. Their economic role was restricted. These restrictions meant that it was likely Jewish human capital was not allocated to its highest-value use. Moreover, the practice of regulating Jewish moneylenders generated economic rents that were then extracted by rulers. This had negative consequences for overall economic efficiency, as it impeded Christians from entering the financial sector and drove up the overall costs of capital. Therefore, the net impact of Jewish presence in medieval Europe was likely mixed. On the one hand, Jews had much needed commercial skills, expertise, and capital. On the other hand, they were often exploited as part of a system of rent-extraction that impeded capital markets (Bein, 1990, 100–107).

Another channel through which Jewish communities could have generated economic growth was through the transmission of cultural values.[6] Weber (1930) claimed that Calvinism played a role in building a spirit of capitalism. The evidence for this is weak (see Becker et al., 2011; Cantoni, 2015). However, the idea that religious cultural traits can play an important role in spurring economic growth needs to be taken seriously.

Weber also noted a resemblance between Jewish values and the Calvinism he saw as giving rise to the spirit of capitalism (Weber, 1930). Weber, however, downplayed the importance of Jewish communities for sustained economic growth as they were limited to what he called "pariah capitalism" – a phenomenon he deemed "speculative" in contrast to the Puritan "bourgeois organization of labour" (Weber, 1930, 245).[7] In Weber's words:

The Jews stood on the side of the politically and speculatively oriented adventurous capitalism; their ethos was, in a word, that of pariah-capitalism. But Puritanism carried the ethos of the rational organization of capital and labour. It took over from the Jewish ethic only what was adapted to this purpose. (Weber, 1930)

In contrast to Weber, the controversial historical economist Werner Sombart, who began his career as a socialist and later became a National Socialist, argued that the Jews were central to the rise of capitalism. In *The Jews and Modern Capitalism*, Sombart argued that Jewish communities, because they were excluded from the formal institutions of medieval commerce (such as guilds), developed a true capitalist outlook. Sombart emphasized the role Jewish traders played in developing credit instruments in the Middle Ages and as financiers in the early modern period. He attributed the economic decline of Spain and Italy as due in part to the expulsion of Jewish communities and the economic success of Amsterdam and London to their acceptance of Jewish communities in the seventeenth century.

A final channel we investigate is market integration.[8] Jews were disproportionately involved in trade and commerce, in no small part because they had cultural, linguistic, and religious ties across the continent. In Amsterdam, Portuguese Jews were heavily involved in the Atlantic trade, particularly in sugar, tobacco, and diamonds (Bloom, 1936). In Poland, they were involved in river trade with Russia, the Ottoman Empire, and the Baltic. In Germany, Jews were closely associated with cattle trading (see Bell, 2008, 127–129). Thus, one channel through which the presence of a Jewish community might benefit a city economically may have been through Jews' ability to build trade networks with other communities.

12.2.1 City Population as a Measure of Development

City population is a widely used measure of economic development.[9] City population data provide information on technology and productivity in commerce and agriculture (de Vries, 1976). Cities were centers of productive activity but they were also disease ridden and unhealthy – urban death rates almost always exceeded rural death rates. As preindustrial cities rarely grew via natural increase, they had to attract migration from the countryside by offering higher wages and greater economic opportunities. Their ability to do so reflected the productivity of their surrounding farm land.

12.3 The Relationship between Jewish Communities and City Growth

We use the same information on the presence of Jewish communities at the city level over time as in Chapter 5. We combine them with data on urban populations from Bairoch (1988). Figure 12.1 shows the distribution of cities in the Bairoch dataset and Jewish cities. We create two samples. The first, which we call the "Main Sample," consists of only cities that at some point in their history possessed a Jewish community. We consider

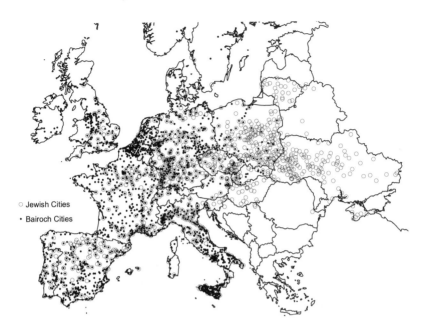

Figure 12.1 Matching the cities in the Bairoch dataset and Jewish communities. Location of the cities in the Bairoch dataset are solid black dots. Locations of Jewish communities are shown as circles. Source: Johnson and Koyama (2017).

this to be the most appropriate sample because we will, in effect, be comparing city growth in cities with and without a Jewish community, under the assumption that both groups are "the kind of places willing to host a Jewish community." The second sample, the "Extended Sample," consists of all of the Bairoch cities and, as such, includes many cities that never possessed a Jewish community between 1400 and 1850.

We begin by investigating the correlation between Jewish community presence in a city and that city's subsequent population growth. As we have repeated observations of city population and Jewish presence over time, we are able to implement a difference-in-differences strategy as in Chapters 5 and 11.[10] This allows us to control for potentially confounding variables that do not change over time (e.g., the fact that a city is land-locked or near a major river) and shocks common to all the cities that do vary with time (e.g., the inflow of silver from the New World post-1492). In addition, we control for time-varying factors that might affect city population and Jewish presence through separate channels – thereby generating a spurious relationship between the two.[11] We find that between 1400 and 1850 cities with Jewish communities grew faster than cities without Jews. The estimated effect of a Jewish community on the growth in the level of a city population is about 35 percent (Figure 12.2).

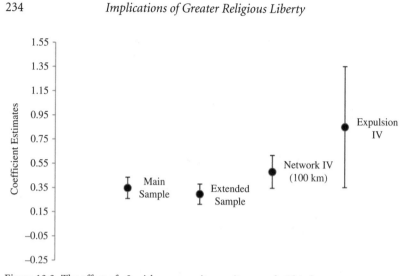

Figure 12.2 The effect of a Jewish community on city growth. This figure reports regression coefficients for the effect of a Jewish community on city growth for both our main and extended samples and for our two instrumental variable strategies. 95% confidence intervals are shown.

12.4 Access to the Network of Jewish Communities

Jewish settlement was influenced by a range of economic and political factors. Rulers sometimes allowed Jewish settlement because they "anticipated Jewish contribution to the economy" (Chazan, 2010, 102). This could result in Jews settling in less prosperous locations where they were expected to boost local economic development. Such was the case, for example, in Germany after the Thirty Years' War (1618–1648) (Israel, 1983, 19–22).[12]

Jewish settlement was also shaped by expulsions. Jews could be excluded from cities by merchants who saw them as direct competitors as occurred in Turin, Florence, and Milan (Roth, 1950).[13]

If Jews were invited to settle in declining cities and expelled or excluded from prosperous ones it would mean that we are, if anything, underestimating the impact of a Jewish community on city growth. But if Jews could decide to selectively migrate to cities that were more prosperous, then we would be in danger of overestimating the positive impact of a Jewish community on growth.[14]

One way to overcome these selection issues is to introduce a source of variation in Jewish presence that is unrelated to other factors driving a city's growth. We generate such a source of variation by modeling the network of Jewish communities over time in Europe.[15]

The idea is that there were cultural and economic linkages that made it more likely for a given Jewish community to settle close to other Jewish communities. This might be driven by a desire to be part of an existing trade network or simply due to the fact that new Jewish communities wanted to avoid settling too far from their origin cities. Consequently, we can use a measure of how dense the Jewish network is nearby a city to predict the likelihood that it possesses a Jewish community.

A problem with this approach is that it runs straight into the First Law of Economic Geography – things that are close to each other tend to be similar. A city that is close to another city with a Jewish community will probably resemble that city in terms of its economic, cultural, or institutional characteristics. To the extent that we are unable to control for these characteristics, they can be a source of bias, potentially confounding our estimates of the effect of a Jewish community on city growth. To mitigate this problem, we exclude cities that are close to the city we are interested in. For example, when calculating the network density for London, we only include cities that are greater than 100 or 250 kilometers away from London.

We measure the distance between cities as the least cost travel path. We allow for four different transportation technologies: seas, rivers, roads, and portage (i.e., walking). We then split Europe into 10 × 10 kilometer grid cells and assign a value to each cell equal to the least cost travel technology contained within it (see Figure 12.3).[16] The resulting "least cost travel map" along with an example of the route calculated between Paris and Rome is presented in Figure 12.4.

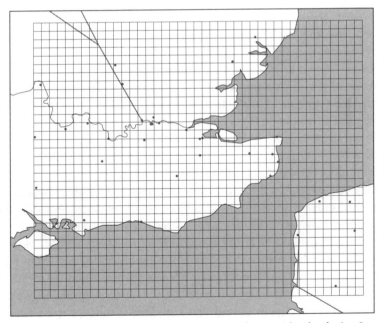

Figure 12.3 Example of a 10 × 10 kilometer grid with four travel technologies. Source: Johnson and Koyama (2017).

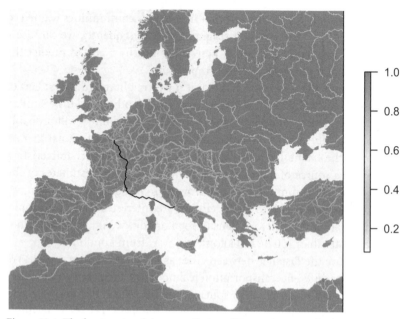

Figure 12.4 The least cost path between Paris and Rome. Source: Johnson and Koyama (2017).

We use our measure of Jewish Network Access, excluding nearby cities, to predict whether a city has a Jewish community for every year in our sample. We then use the predicted values of Jewish community presence to reestimate the effect of a Jewish community on city growth. This procedure is known as instrumental variables analysis. It produces a causal estimate of Jewish communities on growth provided that the Jewish Network Access variable is uncorrelated with city population growth *other than through its correlation with Jewish presence*. The Jewish network instrument estimate suggests that the population of cities with Jewish communities grew between 47 percent and 52 percent faster than cities without Jewish communities between 1400 and 1850 (see Figure 12.2).

One concern is that the Jewish Network measure may affect population growth through a mechanism other than Jewish presence. For example, if the Jewish network density were correlated with non-Jewish trading networks, this would be a problem. Thus, we construct another variable to predict Jewish presence that is based on expulsions of Jews from locations more than 100 kilometers away. The assumption is that the expulsion of a Jewish community far away from a given city will "push" Jews along the least cost travel path toward that city. These estimates will be causal so long as the expulsions taking place more than 100 kilometers away are

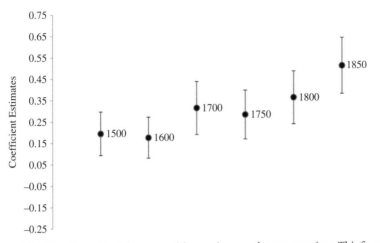

Figure 12.5 The effect of Jewish communities on city growth rates over time. This figure plots regression coefficients on the effects of the presence of a Jewish community on city growth. 95% confidence intervals are shown.

unrelated to factors driving city growth in the target city. The estimate we arrive at using the expulsions instrument suggests that cities with a Jewish community grew about 80 percent faster than cities without a Jewish community (Figure 12.2).

Another natural concern with our results might be that they are driven by a purely mechanistic relationship between the presence of a Jewish community and the size of a city's population. This would be a major issue if Jewish communities were large. However, this was not the case during the medieval or early modern period. Jews made up only a small proportion of the population of the cities where they lived.[17]

The Timing of the Impact of Jewish Communities on City Growth

The results so far suggest that there was, on average between 1400 and 1850, a positive effect of Jewish community presence on city population growth. What explains this?

As a first cut, let us look at how the effect of a Jewish community on city growth varied over time. We estimate the effect of a Jewish community for each time period (Figure 12.5). The positive association between a Jewish community and city growth is driven primarily by the post-1600 period. Before 1600, the difference in growth rates between cities that had Jewish communities and those that did not was only about 20 percent. After 1600, it became noticeably larger, however, growing to 30 percent in 1700 and 50 percent in 1850. It was only after governments started abandoning identity rules that a large growth premium emerges for cities that had Jewish communities.

12.4.1 Mechanisms Linking Jewish Communities Presence with City Growth

We now consider some specific factors that the historical literature suggests may explain why Jewish communities contributed to city growth. First we consider the role of the Sephardic Jewish trading diaspora. The expansion of Jewish trading activity after 1600 is often associated with the rise of Sephardic Jewish communities that migrated from Spain and Portugal after 1492 and settled across Europe in Amsterdam, Bordeaux, Hamburg, Livorno, and London.[18]

According to Israel (2005, 11), the Sephardic diaspora created "a new phenomenon ... a new type of Jewish commercial system" that was based not on local markets, or on trade in agricultural products but on the transportation of luxury goods over long distances. Trivellato (2009) argues that the Sephardic diaspora was remarkable for its "geographical breadth" and "stability" (Trivellato, 2009, 149).[19] Sephardic merchants formed long-lasting partnerships and employed long-distance agency relationships relying on both formal courts and on reputation-based mechanisms of the kind we encountered in Chapter 3.[20]

Sephardic merchants were involved in a variety of mercantile activities. The Sephardic community in Amsterdam was heavily involved in the silk trade (until it was closed to them in the 1650s), in sugar, and in the trade with both the Levant and with the Portuguese colonies in the Americans and in Asia. They were a significant presence in the colonial trade between the British West Indies and the England from the 1650s onwards (Fortune, 1984).[21] We find that Sephardic Jewish communities were particularly beneficial for city growth. Cities with Sephardic communities grew between 38 and 48 percent more quickly than non-Sephardic communities (which could be either Jewish and non-Sephardic or have no Jewish presence).[22]

Another channel through which the presence of Jewish communities could help accelerate growth in a city was through trade. To explore this, we construct a measure of market access for all of the cities in our data. The difference between our market access measure and the Jewish network access measure is that, instead of multiplying the travel cost weights by the Jewish community presence variable, we multiply them by all city populations (both cities with and without Jewish communities). The resulting variable measures the "embededness" of each city within the urban network.

Greater market access means both easier access to inputs of production as well as larger markets in which to sell final goods and services.

Our estimates suggest that cities with a Jewish community benefitted from market access more than non-Jewish communities. In particular, in 1400 market access can explain about 15 percent of the growth difference between Jewish and non-Jewish cities (i.e., about 75 percent of the total growth difference of 20 percent given in Figure 12.5). By 1850, market access explains about 40 percent of the difference in growth between Jewish and non-Jewish cities.

One natural question concerning the market access results is whether these growth differences across cities were being generated on the *extensive margin* of trade or on the *intensive margin*. Did Jewish communities grow faster because they developed higher values of market access over time, or did Jewish communities use the market access they had to greater effect? Market access was virtually identical for Jewish and non-Jewish cities throughout the period. Cities with Jewish communities benefited from market access on the intensive margin – there was something about Jewish communities themselves (or the willingness to allow Jews to live in one's city) that caused potential trading opportunities to be realized.

Chapter 10 documented the importance of Jewish emancipation as an intellectual and social event. To investigate its impact on economic development, we code whether a Jewish community was emancipated.[23] The growth effect associated with a Jewish community increases greatly with Jewish emancipation. This suggests that institutions played a crucial role in determining the contribution that Jewish communities could make to economic growth. Prior to emancipation, Jews were concentrated in either moneylending or trade or else were involved in retailing, peddling, or informal commerce. In the wake of emancipation, Jews began to enter universities and professions such as law.

12.5 Chapter Summary: Liberalism and Markets Enabled Religious Minorities to Contribute to Growth

Cities with Jewish communities grew faster than cities that did not have Jewish communities, and this growth advantage was stronger in the early modern period. There is less of a discernible impact of a Jewish community on city growth in the Middle Ages. This is consistent with the importance of identity rules in determining the role of religious minorities in premodern Europe. Jews had more human capital than their Christian peers. They specialized in trade, retail, banking, and finance. However, in the Middle Ages these skills were exploited by political elites who, for example, often licensed and taxed Jewish moneylending. The net effect was that the presence of a Jewish community did not translate into economic growth – at least as measured by city growth – in the Middle Ages.

This changed after 1600. Greater economic freedom and the diminished importance of identity rules, enabled Jewish communities to put their human capital to uses that generated positive spillovers and faster city growth. This effect was strengthened where there were Sephardic communities as their wide-ranging trading networks knit together the Atlantic and Mediterranean economies and where market access was already growing. It was also strengthened by Jewish emancipation. The transition from identity rules to general rules thus accelerated urban development and economic growth.

What about the Enlightenment? As discussed in Chapter 10, many Enlightenment thinkers expressed antisemitic views. However, the Enlightenment also created a sphere free from religion in which Christians and Jews could interact. This was true, for instance, in the Berlin salons where Moses Mendelssohn became a celebrated member of the Enlightenment movement (Graupe, 1978; Bach, 1984; Goldfarb, 2009; Finer and Naimark-Goldberg, 2011).

The Enlightenment had an effect on Jewish communities that it did not have on non-Jews. While in the Middle Ages, Jews had possessed higher human capital than non-Jews, this was no longer the case in the early modern period. As we saw in Chapter 12, Jews were not prominent inventors or scientists. Jews were excluded from the universities and few Jews were members of the Republic of Letters that Mokyr (2016) describes. Jewish communities in many parts of Europe in the eighteenth century provided religious education but little or no secular education (Katz, 2000).[24] It was very difficult for Jews to acquire modern secular education. In his autobiography, Solomon Maimon (1753–1800) recalled that

to gratify my desire for scientific knowledge, there were no means available but that of learning foreign languages. But how was I to begin? To learn Polish or Latin with a Catholic teacher was for me impossible, on the one hand because the prejudices of my own people prohibited languages but Hebrew, and all sciences but the Talmud and the vast array of its commentators; on the other hand because the prejudices of the Catholics would not allow them to give instruction in those matters to a Jew. (Maimon, 1954, 68)[25]

Elon describes Moses Mendelssohn's (1729–1786) trek from Dessau to Berlin as a march "through a time machine, a journey across centuries, from the hermetic insularity of the medieval ghetto into which he was born to the relative enlightenment of eighteenth-century Berlin …Mendelssohn's education had been exclusively religious. He was still unable to speak German or read a German book" (Elon, 2002, 2–3).[26] Mendelssohn was plunged into the "modern" world of Enlightenment

Germany. He survived this transformative experience and succeeded in becoming an Enlightenment thinker while retaining his traditional Judaism. Those who followed him often were not able to do this. Many, as we saw in Chapter 10, adopted more liberal forms of Judaism. Others left Judaism altogether.

In the decades following Mendelssohn's arrival in Berlin, the Enlightenment and Jewish emancipation transformed economic and social opportunities for Jews. Emancipation freed them from constraints that had previously prevented them from deploying their human capital where it could earn its highest return. Jews "were seized with a hunger for the new education. To belong to the educated classes became for the German Jews especially the watchword of life, which sometimes threatened almost to take the place of religion" (Kober, 1947, 211–212). Baden in 1809 allowed Jews to establish they own primary schools. From the 1820s onward, Jews were authorized to build new primary schools in the Rhineland and Württemberg. In Bavaria 140 Jewish schools were built in the first half of the nineteenth century (Kober, 1947, 212). The adoption of secular education cumulated with the "surge of Jews into secondary and higher education, which began as early as the 1840s and which was a most conspicuous aspect of the entry of Jews into the secular world" (Pulzer, 1992, 6).[27]

Cinnirella and Streb (2017) provide further evidence that religious toleration can spur innovation. Looking at late nineteenth-century Prussia, they find that cities with more religiously diverse populations produced a higher number of valuable patents. They argue that religious diversity and the practice of day-to-day religious tolerance that developed in religiously fragmented parts of Germany created conditions that favored the development of breakthrough inventions after 1850.

The well-documented flowering of Jewish intellectual achievement after 1850 attests to the costs of the conditional toleration equilibrium that restricted Jewish economic and educational activities. Charles Murray (2003) attempted to quantify human accomplishments in the arts, science, and culture. He documented a surge of Jewish achievement after around 1830. Barring some exceptional figures, Jews were not especially well represented in art, culture, or science prior to emancipation: "In all of those 26 centuries, the roster of Western significant figures includes not one Jewish artist, scientist, physician, or inventor, and just one writer (Fernando Rojas), one composer (Salamone Rossi), and one mathematician" (Paul Guldin) (Murray, 2003, 275). This was transformed following emancipation. Murray notes that sixteen significant Jewish figures appear between 1830 and 1870 and then from 1870 to 1910 the number rises to forty (Murray, 2003, 277).[28] After 1910 this rate of growth accelerated further. The success of European Jews in the sciences, philosophy, mathematics, and the social sciences is so well known that we hardly need to elaborate further.

Notes

1. See Braudel (1979, 1982, 165).
2. Innovations associated with the Huguenots include new methods of dying, the art of printing on cotton, and the hosiery knitting loom. Huguenots had particular expertise in silk farming.
3. Raistrick argues that "[t]he natural energy of the Quakers, penned up under a savage persecution and by rigorous disabilities, religious, political, and economic, responded by extra assertion and effectiveness in non-political spheres; the external pressures of adverse conditions served as a constant stimulus. It was incumbent upon Friends to demonstrate in their lives and activities that if, in the eyes of the law they were compelled to be poor and disobedient citizens in some things which they considered to be allowed, they could not only be as serviceable as others, but could 'go the extra mile' and give a service of unquestionable quality" (Raistrick, 1968, 338).
4. See the discussion in Mokyr (2009, 368–388). Sahle (2017) argues that the formal institutions of the Quakers did not play an important role in enforcing contracts prior to 1750.
5. It is important to recognize that not all Jews in medieval and early modern Europe were traders and merchants and that the occupational distribution of Jews likely varied from place to place. In early modern Germany, for example, the majority of Jews were poor.
6. A growing literature emphasizes the importance of cultural values in shaping economic outcomes (Greif, 2006b; Guiso et al., 2006; Doepke and Zilibotti, 2008; Tabellini, 2008). See Alesina and Giuliano (2015) for a recent survey of the connection between culture and institutions.
7. In the original German: *Paria-Kapitalismus*. This concept is developed further in Weber (1927). Note that this concept has been criticized (see Cahnman, 1974; Momigliano, 1980).
8. Market integration has been widely studied as a potential driver of urbanization and subsequent economic growth during that time. See Shiue and Keller (2007), Bateman (2011), Chilosi et al. (2013), and Bernhofen et al. (2015). Within this literature numerous economists use the law of one price and other measures of price dispersion as tests of the level of market integration. The evidence suggests that grain markets became increasingly well integrated from the late seventeenth century onwards. Bateman (2011) argued that levels of market integration were stationary between the medieval period and the onset of the Industrial Revolution. However, by expanding the sample of cities considered, Chilosi et al. (2013) show that northwestern Europe had significantly more integrated markets by 1750.
9. For example see, De Long and Shleifer (1993), Dittmar (2011), Nunn and Puga (2012), Bosker et al. (2013), and Dincecco and Onorato (2016).
10. Our outcome variable is the log level of the population of a city. The variable of interest is an indicator variable that takes a value of 1 if there was a Jewish community in the city during the previous century and a 0 otherwise. We have observations in 1400, 1500, 1600, 1700, 1750, 1800, and 1850.
11. In all specifications we include controls for how local geography (cereal suitability, proximity to rivers, proximity to coast) and local infrastructure (presence of university and distance to Roman road intersection) affect city growth in each century.

12. Israel carefully documents the revival and expansion of many German Jewish communities during this period, concluding that "the terrible upheavals of the Thirty Years' War mostly worked in favor of German and all Central European Jewry, appreciably enhanced the Jewish role in German life, and prepared the ground fort the 'Age of the Court Jew' – the late seventeenth and early eighteenth century – the high-water mark of Jewish influence on Central European commerce and finance" (Israel, 1983, 30).

13. For instance: "it was either small or middle-sized communes (which had to call on outside financiers) or strong governments (concerned with public order) who turned first and from choice to the Jews. In the plutocratic towns, on the other hand, coalitions of local interests opposed to their admission were able to delay it" (Poliakov, 1977, 1965, 58). Foa writes: "Not all Italian cities accepted or solicited settlement by Jews. Cities in which Christian bankers were numerous and organized in guilds were generally hostile to Jews, in whom the former saw dangerous competition" (Foa, 2000, 111).

14. The historical evidence does not suggest that there was such positive selection. Jewish traders and merchants sought to establish communities in as many cities as possible. As moneylenders, Jews had an incentive to settle new areas, as it enabled them to build more extensive credit networks and to smooth local shocks (see Botticini, 1997).

15. To do this we use tools drawn from the market access literature (e.g., Donaldson and Hornbeck, 2016).

16. There is no closed form solution to the mathematical problem of finding a least cost travel path through a grid like the one we construct. There is, however, a well-known procedure known as Djikstra's Algorithm, which is recognized as producing very close approximations to the least cost path (van Etten, 2017).

17. Furthermore, individual Jewish communities remained small throughout this period. There were only a small number of exceptions to this generalization. One of the biggest communities was in Amsterdam, where the size of the Aschkenazim community was approximately 5,000 in 1674 or 2.5 percent of the total city population. It grew rapidly to 22,000 by 1795 or approximately 10 percent of the population but this was exceptional. The largest community in Germany was Frankfurt, with a population of 3,000 in 1610. Prague also had a large Jewish community 6,000 in 1600 and more than 11,500 by 1702 (Bell, 2008, 36). At its peak, the Jewish population of Venice numbered 4,800. But the vast majority of Jewish communities were much smaller.

18. See Braudel (1972, 1949), Israel (1985), and Trivellato (2009).

19. There was a widespread perception in Amsterdam and in other cities such as Hamburg that the Sephardic Jews were significantly more prosperous and entrepreneurial than were Ashkenazi Jews. For example, Bloom writes: "Unlike their Sephardic brethren the Ashkenazic Jews, because of different background and tradition, were not concerned with secular matters but were deeply engrossed in the study of the Talmud." He notes that though "the Ashkenazic community by dint of sober industry and thrift had acquired a certain degree of prosperity...It is self evident that, as compared with the Sephardim, the Ashkenazic group was poor indeed" (Bloom, 1936).

20. Community organizations strove to uphold the collective reputation of local merchants, excommunicating members found guilty of trading in counterfeit coins or

goods or acting in such a way that would "discredit the commerce of the Jewish nation" (Trivellato, 2009, 166).

21. See Bloom (1936). Sephardic Jews came to play a similarly important role elsewhere in Europe, in the Venetian economy, for example, where they imported Spanish wool and Spanish American dyestuff for the Italian textiles industry (Fusaro, 2015, 261). Livorno, in particular, grew in importance as an entrepôt for trade with the Levant; it was the fastest growing port in Italy in the seventeenth century (Trivellato, 2009, 71).

22. These results are obtaining by running regressions where we interact proxies for each of these mechanisms with our main Jewish presence variable. They are reported in Johnson and Koyama (2017).

23. This is based on the proportion of years in the previous century that they were emancipated. For example, the Jewish community of Berlin was emancipated in 1812 so they receive a value of 0.76 for the period 1800–1850. Though in practice Jewish emancipation was rarely binary, our results are not sensitive to how we code emancipation. For example, in our baseline analysis we code all Jewish communities in the Habsburg empire as emancipated following the Toleration Edict of 1782, giving them a value of 0.36 for 1800 and 1 for 1850. As a robustness exercise, we employ an alternative and more restrictive coding that counts the Jewish communities in the Habsburg empire as not emancipated. This does not affect our results.

24. Eisenbach comments that the "curricula of religious schools of various grades did not yet include secular subjects. The schools did not impart to the young people knowledge of the surrounding world, of the society in which they lived, its history and culture" (Eisenbach, 1991, 42).

25. Maimon describes the typical school as "a 'small smoky hut' in which children were tyrannized by their school masters, often went unfed, read Hebrew without understanding it or its grammar, and learnt the scriptures without being able to interpret them" (see Maimon, 1954, 31–34).

26. Of course within two decades "almost entirely self-taught, he had become a renowned German philosopher, philologist, stylist, literary critic, and man of letters" (Elon, 2002, 2–3). Mendelssohn is both a driver and an exemplar of the phenomenon we analyze in this chapter.

27. According to Richarz, by 1840 the proportion of Jewish students was twice that of Christians (Richarz, 1975, 71). Carvalho, Koyama, and Sacks (2017) model the impact of Jewish emancipation in Western Europe on the incentives for Jews to either embrace or resist secular education.

28. While Murray (2003) is a pioneering attempt to quantify this topic, his approach has unsurprisingly come under criticism. For our purposes, issues of selection or bias are largely irrelevant, as we are interested in the variation in various measures of accomplished among Jews over time.

13

The Emergence of Modern States, Religious Freedom, and Modern Economic Growth

Religious freedom emerged gradually in Europe in the period after 1600. Before the seventeenth century, these things were seen as either impossible or undesirable by all but the most radical and marginalized thinkers. By the end of the nineteenth century, however, a commitment to liberalism became the default position of elites across Western Europe. The question we now turn to is: "What made this transformation possible?"

In modern societies national identity came to replace religion as a source of political legitimacy. Nationalism today has a bad reputation, and we are all familiar with its various pathologies. But the breadth and widespread appeal of nationalism should not be dismissed. In the nineteenth century, for example, nationalism helped pave the way for the emergence of both stronger and more liberal states. We discuss the coevolution of arguments for religious liberty with stronger states and provide detailed evidence from late eighteenth-century France for how state capacity played a role in generating support for national identity and for general rules over identity rules. Lastly, we consider the relationship between the breakdown of the conditional toleration equilibrium and the onset of sustained economic growth.

13.1 The Idea of Religious Freedom: Hobbes, Hume, and Smith on the Role of Religion in a Commercial Society

As we saw in Chapter 7, isolated voices argued for religious identity to be voluntary rather than compulsory throughout the period we study. These included Anabaptists such as Michael Sattler and Menno Simons, and a small group of more intellectually oriented reformers whom historians label evangelical rationalists, most notably Michael Sevetus.[1] Their arguments, however, had little impact on their societies.

For most, the idea of religious freedom was inconceivable because the link between political and religious authority underpinned the entire social order. In his survey of the Reformation, Carlos Eire observes that the Anabaptists were seen by their persecutors as "inherently evil." They were perceived as a mortal threat to the social order because of, and not despite, their impeccable personal morality. They were dangerous precisely because they were seemingly so good. And it was their belief in a voluntary church that made them especially subversive and in need of eradication: "How could one hope to hold society together without magistrates, execution-ers, and soldiers, or the oaths that bound people to one another, not just as Christians, but as Citizens?" (Eire, 2016, 262).

Niccoló Machiavelli and Thomas Hobbes argued in favor of a civic religion and against religious freedom on pragmatic grounds. Neither Machiavelli nor Hobbes were themselves conventional Christians. Nev-ertheless, they believed that the sovereign had the authority to compel outward religious conformity. Religious freedom was to be sacrificed for social stability. They provided theoretical reasons for coercion in religious affairs, while at the same time recognizing that rulers had to accept religious fragmentation and diversity when they were too weak to stamp it out, as in much of Europe at the end of the wars of religion.

The arguments for religious compulsion advanced by Hobbes are con-sistent with the evidence reviewed in Chapter 2. Religion supports social stability. The pragmatic case for religious compulsion he offered, however, was not the only school of thought. Politiques such as Michel de L'Hôpital and mercantilists such as Joseph Sonnenfels and Christian Dohm argued that religious diversity did not, in fact, undermine social stability and that the attempt to enforce religious conformity could be more costly than an acceptance of religious differences. Mercantilists argued in favor of some form of lasting religious accommodation on the grounds that religious peace was good for economic growth, and that religious minorities could play a key role in the economy.[2]

The mercantilists set out a negative argument for religious freedom, one based on the costs of religious persecution. Their case was seemingly borne out by Louis XIV's attempts to enforce the Revocation of the Edict of Nantes. Eighteenth-century liberal writers built on these arguments to argue the positive case that social flourishing was in fact consistent with religious diversity.

To what extent was the move toward greater religious freedom influenced by intellectual developments during the Enlightenment? A famous debate between David Hume and Adam Smith provides clues. The two great Scot-tish philosophers and economists agreed on much but had quite different positions on religious freedom. Hume deplored religious extremism and viewed religious sects as dangerous and potentially subversive of the social order. He was deeply influenced by Hobbes's account of the role religious factions played in the English civil war.[3] Thus, though a skeptic in religion, in the *History of England*, Hume defended established state religion. He argued that a market in religion generated perverse incentives because each "ghostly practitioner" aims to maximize the number of his adherents and puts aside "truth, morals, or decency" and appeals to the "passions and credulity of the populace." In a religious marketplace, competition breeds extremism. The state, Hume argued, could regulate this competition reducing such extreme passions in the interests of social stability. Political liberty for Hume could be guaranteed only if there was some way of "regulating party zeal" (Herdt, 1997, 14).

This argument built on previous liberal thinkers. Locke argued for religious toleration for dissenting Protestant sects, though not necessarily for Catholics or atheists. Bernard Mandeville, a skeptic most famous for *The Fable of the Bees*, was critical of the established Anglican Church and an advocate for mutual toleration (Mandeville, 1924, 1714). But like Locke, in print at least, he argued for toleration only for those who owed no allegiance to a foreign sovereign, hence excluding Catholics.[4] Like Mandeville's, Hume's attitude toward religious freedom was pragmatic. He was opposed to religious persecution and in favor of toleration, but not ready to embrace full freedom of religious belief.[5]

Hume wished to make society safe for philosophy. He celebrated living in a liberal age and in a commercial republic where he was free to write what he wished. But he also feared that superstition could undermine such a liberal order and wished to educate elites to be cognizant of this danger. In this view, "societies dominated by a monotheistic religion may approximate the conditions of polytheism by instituting a state church (in which ministers are government employees with no incentive to recruit members intensively) and enforcing religious toleration of religious dissenters. This, Hume believes, will tend to diffuse religious zeal and secure the peace" (Herdt, 1997, 14).

Toleration was favored by Hume because he believed that, in the long run, it would lessen religious passion: "a mutual toleration would in time abate the fury of religious prejudices" (Hume, 1983, 1778, 54). But in the absence of such moderation, he preferred a state church to religious freedom.

In contrast, Adam Smith argued that religious sects tended toward extreme positions only because they were persecuted. Smith was opposed to "superstition" and "enthusiasm," but he believed that education and philosophy were better able to combat "superstition" than a state church. Religious competition had the potential to moderate extremism:

The teachers of each little sect, finding themselves almost alone, would be obliged to respect those of almost every other sect, and the concessions which they would mutually find it both convenient and agreeable to make to one another, might in time probably reduce the doctrine of the greater part of them to that pure and rational religion, free of every mixture of absurdity, imposture, or fanaticism. (Smith, 1776, 793)

A competitive religious marketplace would improve the quality of the religious experience provided by both mainstream and dissenting churches by providing incentives for religious organizations to better serve their congregations. Moreover, religious diversity could be a source of social stability. Competition would lead to both greater religiosity and greater civility and temperance. This set Smith apart from his liberal predecessors.[6] It aligned him with more radical thinkers such as Pierre Bayle. That said, Smith was favorable toward the established church in Scotland. This may suggest "unwarranted complacency about the church in his native land" (Graham, 2016, 316). Or it may be mere exoteric cover for his more radical views of allowing a market for religion.

Smith's views on religion did not have an immediate impact. Restrictions on the political rights of Catholics and Jews continued into the middle decades of the nineteenth century. However, in the long run they have proven influential.

13.2 Nationalism and General Rules

Charles Taylor (2007, 392) describes a shift from a vertical to a horizontal model of social order in the past few hundred years. The vertical model was based on a feudal hierarchy in which social and political order emanated from the monarch, who sat at the apex of society. This was replaced with a horizontal model in which society is composed of "equal-rights-bearing individuals, related so as to further mutual benefit."

The emergence of national identity, substituting for earlier identities that were either religious and supranational or local and subnational, played a crucial role in this. Precisely dating the rise of a sense of national identity across Europe is difficult; it was a slow, uneven, process. On the one hand, medieval historians have argued that the Hundred Years' War created a sense of nascent national identity in England and France. On the other hand, historians of modern Europe argue that it was not until late in the nineteenth century that there was a sense of nationhood outside metropolitan or elite circles (Weber, 1976). To understand this process better, we need a definition of nationalism.

Ernest Gellner (1983) defines nationalism as the principle that the political and the national unit should be congruent. Even the smallest nations encompass many more people than one can possibly meet and know. Nationalism, therefore, requires identification with a highly abstract concept, that of the country. Benedict Anderson stressed the importance of print media in this process (Anderson, 1983). The spread of pamphlets and newspapers created the imagined community required for disparate individuals to believe that they were part of a common endeavor, and to identify with being French or English.

National identity superseded the previous notion of an unified religious community – Christendom. Christendom formed what Anderson calls a "sacred community." As an ideal, it possessed a tremendous power. Even a century and a half after the Reformation, intellectuals such as Leibniz dreamed of reunifying Europe under one religion. The discourse of this sacred community employed a language that meant that the realm they governed could be vast in scope and encompass many of millions of people. In practice, however, this language was possessed only by a small number of educated elites. As most people in premodern agrarian societies were illiterate, their relevant community was their town or village. Christendom was a meaningful concept to clerical Latin speaking elite; ordinary people had more local aspirations and identities.[7]

This changed with the rise of larger imagined communities that we call nations. Nations emerged from and replaced dynastic states. National identity need not be exclusive. It can coexist and overlap with local, religious, or ethnic identities, but in modern societies it is the master identity, what Lieh Greenfeld calls the "fundamental identity," the one that is believed to define the very essence of the individual, which the other identities may modify only slightly, and to which they are consequently considered secondary (Greenfeld, 2006, 69).

For scholars such as Greenfeld nationalism is modern and modernity itself is defined by the rise of nation-states. National identity, moreover, was not simply a one-for-one replacement for religious identity. It is incorrect to simply call nationalism a modern religion. Rather nationalism "resides in the earthly national community. There is no higher arbiter. In expropriating divine authority, nationalism endows this world with ultimate meaning." Hence it implies secularization. "With nationalism, the heavens, so to speak, descend to earth; this world becomes the sphere of the sacred. Religion, whatever its stripe, carries a very different world-image. The authority of any power of this world is essentially limited. Most importantly, all truly religious world-images include a belief in some other world beyond this one: the essence of the religious world-image is the belief in some sort of transcendence of this, corporeal, world" (Greenfeld, 2006, 69).

If in premodern societies religion was the core identity, after 1800 this was largely replaced by national identity. Many factors can be enlisted to explain this transformation including capitalism, Protestantism, and industrialization. Among these, perhaps the most interesting explanation for the creation of national identity was what Greenfeld calls "status inconsistency" among the elite. According to Greenfeld: "In France, the architects of the national identity came from the ranks of the traditional aristocracy, as it became increasingly discontented with its position and the manner in which its place in society was defined, and, in the process of redefinition, admitted into its ranks the most prominent of the non-noble intellectuals" (Greenfeld, 2006, 73).

Greenfeld's argument that nationalism arose because of the crises that affected the old order in Europe can be folded into our account of the institutional crisis that faced European states after the Reformation. The old order based on a tight relationship between religious and political authority became less tenable. Holding to religious legitimation and attempting to suppress all religious dissent led either to mass persecutions and civil and religious war as in France, England, and the Holy Roman Empire or to economic stagnation as in Spain.

In contrast, nationalism as an ideology was at odds with caste, class, or religious distinctions. The only relevant criteria for full membership in the body politic was membership of the nation. This was inconsistent with identity rules that were not based on national distinctions. "The modern state as an abstract bearer of sovereignty and the creator of legal norms – emerged after and because of the development of the idea of the 'nation' which redefined populations as uniform and diffused sovereignty within them" (Greenfeld, 2006, 79).

Nationalism contained the seeds of imperialism, racism, and oppression – a theme we take up in Chapter 15 – but relative to what came before, it was an emancipatory creed, and until the second half of the nineteenth century, it was accompanied by liberalism. This liberalism allowed for a proliferation of identities that could accompany and enrich nascent national identity.

13.3 Fiscal Capacity and National Identity in Ancién Regime France

The previous sections suggested a link between increases in state capacity and the development of national identity. Furthermore, we argued that the development of national identity helped support the adoption of more general rules. In this section we provide evidence for these claims by drawing on Johnson's (2015) study of national identity on the eve of the French Revolution.

In 1664 Colbert created a customs union known as the Cinq Grosses Fermes (CGF) that included about half the provinces of the kingdom.[8] The provinces that formed the basis for this union were structured around five "great" tax farms created during the Hundred Years' War.[9]

In creating the CGF Colbert hoped to unify the French economy by facilitating domestic trade, eliminating internal tariffs and feudal regulations that empowered local nobles but impeded economic integration.[10] Trade would increase and with it tax revenues for the crown. Indeed inside the CGF, taxes collected per capita in 1784 were between 30 and 40 percent higher than outside.[11]

To assess how this increase in state capacity shaped national identity, Johnson (2015) considers the Cahier des Doléances. On the eve of the calling of the Estates General in 1788, every town in France was required to submit a list of grievances that would be discussed. Separate cahiers were prepared for each of the three estates: the clergy, the nobility, and everybody else. Using the district level cahiers which aggregate the village-level documents to 200 geographic regions, Hyslop (1934) coded 46 different topics covered in the documents. For example, Hyslop recorded whether a given cahier requested more uniform weights and measures, asked for the abolition of feudal dues, or petitioned for a more uniform legal code.[12]

Figure 13.1 shows the correlation between national affiliation in the cahiers with membership in the CGF. The CGF is the region on the map

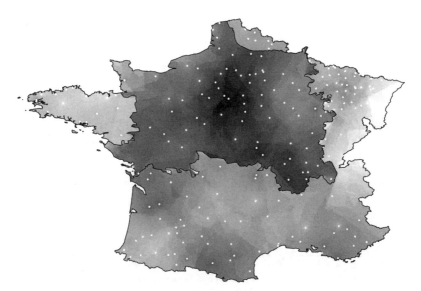

Figure 13.1 National identity in the 1789 General Cahiers. Darker shading represents greater identification in the Cahiers by the Nobility and Third Estate with either the "King" or "France" according to Hyslop (1934). Each grid point in the map is assigned a value based on the inverse-weighted distance of surrounding twelve cities that sent in Cahiers. The Cinq Grosses Fermes region is delineated in bold. Source: Johnson (2015).

within the bold border. Each white dot represents the capital of a district for which there is a cahier. The shading represents the average of the national affiliation index for the cahiers in the surrounding districts.[13]   Darker shading represents greater affiliation with national identity in the cahiers.

There is a positive correlation between a region being in the CGF and affiliation with national identity. However, there are many reasons why this correlation could be spurious. For example, maybe proximity to Paris – with its cultural and economic influence – made it easier for Colbert to get a region to join the CGF in the seventeenth century. However, the influence of Paris could also generate a greater affiliation with the monarchy or national, as opposed to local, identity.

To estimate the causal effect of greater state capacity we focus on the difference between districts close to the CGF border. Comparing average tax collected per capita, national identity, and economic development in the nineteenth century in districts within 150 or 75 kilometers of the CGF border, controls for many variables that we cannot observe. This approach is known as regression discontinuity design.

Figure 13.2 fits a line to the data on average national identity in the cahiers for all districts as a function of their distance from the CGF border. For example, Rouen is a little over 200 kilometers inside the CGF border whereas Montauban is about 200 kilometers outside the border.[14]   If we

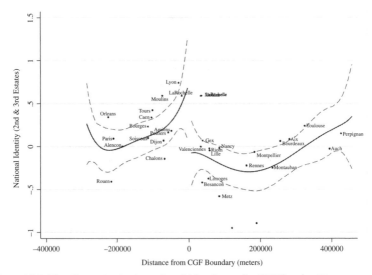

Figure 13.2 The discontinuity in national identity at the CGF border. Nonparametric estimate of effect of distance from CGF border on identity estimated for both sides of the border after partialling out all control variables. 95% confidence intervals are shown by dashed lines. Source: Johnson (2015).

compare the average value of national identity of the districts in these two provinces, they appear relatively similar. But there are also many differences, other than state capacity, between them. For example, Rouen is closer to Paris, closer to the sea, and it's inhabitants spoke Langue d'Oil (modern French) rather than the Langue d'Oc spoken in Montauban.

To overcome this concern, we compare districts that are very close to the border. For example, cities in the province of La Rochelle are split by the CGF boundary. Their inhabitants spoke the same language, shared the same geography, and, for all intents and purposes, had similar access to political institutions. Comparing cities located very close to the border, there is a large difference in affiliation with national identity between CGF and non-CGF regions (Figure 13.2). This gap survives after we control for many observable factors. Moving a city that was in the 50th percentile on the national identity scale from just outside the CGF border to just inside it shifts its ranking up to the 68th percentile.

The grievances raised in the cahiers reveal stronger support for general rules within the CGF and greater support for identity rules outside. Within the CGF, 10 percent more of the cahiers called for greater uniformity of the administrative and legal system than outside the CGF.[15] Similarly, 20 percent more cahiers called for economic uniformity (e.g., taxation and government spending) inside the CGF. There were 11 percent more cahiers asking that the same laws be applied to all estates and 7 percent more requesting that feudal dues be abolished. Overall, people in areas where state capacity was greater were also more likely to prefer general rules over identity rules.

Membership in the CGF also increased the level of agreement between different classes of people. Differences in our national identity measure between the nobility and the third estate shrink closer to the CGF border – reflecting greater agreement between the two groups. If a region was outside the CGF and in the 50th percentile of cooperation between the second and third estates but of we move that region just inside the CGF border, then it would move to over the 95th percentile. Together these findings suggest a causal relationship between state capacity and support for general rules over identity rules.

13.4 Modern States and Modern Economic Growth

Now we turn to the relationship between general rules, markets, and modern economic growth. Growth prior to the Industrial Revolution was slow and sporadic. There were meaningful differences in living standards and incomes per capita across different societies, but the vast differences that exist today were not present, simply because no premodern society had yet experienced sustained increases in per capita income.

Simon Kuznets labeled such sustained increases in per capita income "modern economic growth." The miracle of compounding means that in a society like the United States that has grown by roughly 2 percent per year in per capita terms since 1800, average living standards double roughly every 35 years. Hence the average American is roughly 25 times richer than in 1800. This is what Deirdre McCloskey calls the "Great Enrichment."[16]

Such sustained economic growth (as opposed to temporary periods of catch-up growth) is possible only in a market economy. But the existence of markets is not sufficient to explain why modern economic growth began. Markets existed in all premodern societies.[17]

Markets, for example, were common in medieval Europe. But they were also highly fragmented and suffered from numerous information problems. Transport costs were high, particularly on overland routes: it was rarely economical to move bulky goods like grain far by road as the price would double every 250 miles (Masschaele, 1993). These barriers were not only technological, they were institutional. Internal trade barriers and tolls impeded trade.[18]   Moreover, religious barriers impeded the division of labor and trade. Reliance on identity rules created barriers to entry and monopoly power, and resulted in high prices and inefficiency.

Market prices not only signal relative scarcity or abundance, but also provide the incentive to correct such imbalances. However, if transaction costs are high, then markets will be fragmented and provide only blunt incentives to market actors. This was the case in much of premodern Europe. Profits could be extraordinarily high. But so was the risk. Indeed it is these characteristics of medieval trade that help to explain the prominence of many medieval institutions such as guilds, fairs, and trading leagues.

Markets for goods like grain in Europe only became integrated in the nineteenth century.[19] Technological developments and improvements in transportation played an important role. But institutional developments were also crucial. Two of the most important developments involved France and Prussia consolidating tariff barriers.

Commerce flourished along the Rhine during the Middle Ages when it was an important conduit for trade between the North Sea and western Germany (Lopez, 1971). But over time, this trade was stifled by the proliferation of tolls established along the river by the numerous political entities. Such tolls played an important role in generating revenues for local rulers and princes within Germany who lacked the fiscal capacity to directly tax land. It was difficult to tax agriculture because the output was low and consumed locally, and powerful landowners sought to keep the surplus for themselves, while economic activity in urban areas was also difficult to tax because cities were strong enough to assert their independence from the territorial rulers. The river traffic was an accessible source of revenue as traders "could not well conceal the quantity or value of their cargos; if they had no money to pay, the toll-man took payment in kind" (Clapp, 1907, 6).

The number of tolls multiplied as the power of the Holy Roman Empire waned. By the late seventeenth century, it reached the point where local rulers possessed free reign to extract as much as possible from the river trade. This generated an inefficiently low amount of trade. Individual toll collectors ignored the effects of their toll on the total level of river commerce. Consequently, the volume of trade was much lower than if a single ruler had set the revenue maximizing tax.

The rates charged were unpublished. They varied unpredictably with the "judgement and corruptibility of the officials," making it difficult for merchants to plan as they could not anticipate what they would have to pay (Clapp, 1907, 7).[20] The proliferation of tolls also diverted trade to more costly inland routes. It was cheaper to send goods overland and then along the river Weser to Bremen than along the direct route north (Clapp, 1907, 10).

The old regime was shattered by the French Revolution and the occupation of the Rhineland by French troops that followed in 1794. This invasion marked "a decisive break with the past, as centuries of traditional institutions, ways of thinking and acting were swept away" (Diefendorf, 1980, 23).[21] The French eliminated the majority of tolls and standardized the regulation of the river. They created a modern fiscal bureaucracy to collect the taxes. As a result trade boomed. Between 1789 and 1807 the volume of trade increased by as much as 400 percent (Spaulding, 2011, 217). After the French defeat, this centralized administration was continued by the Prussians and the Rhine became a vital commercial artery as Germany industrialized.

The consolidation of tolls along the Rhine provides one example where the rise of modern states complemented the expansion of markets. The period after 1815 saw mercantilist restrictions dismantled across Europe. In Germany, Prussia pioneered the path toward a free trade zone, the Zollverein. This reduced price differentials in grain by almost one third.[22]

State building efforts in ancién regime France also benefited economic performance. This is evident from data on direct taxes per capital (a proxy for income per capita, as the tax rate on income was identical for everyone) and taxes on notary contracts (a proxy for use of formal contracting institution). Figures 13.3 and 13.4 show a strong positive relationship between affiliation with national institutions as measured using the cahiers in 1788 and both measures of economic development.[23]

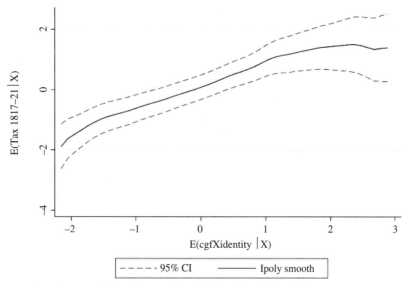

kernel = epanechnikov, degree = 0, bandwidth = .72, pwidth = 1.08

Figure 13.3 Direct tax receipts 1817–1821 and national identity. Dashed lines show 95% confidence intervals. Source: Johnson (2015).

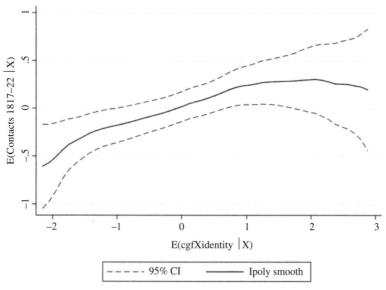

kernel = epanechnikov, degree = 0, bandwidth = .59, pwidth = .89

Figure 13.4 Tax on notary contracts and national identity. Dashed lines show 95% confidence intervals. Source: Johnson (2015).

13.5 Innovation and Modern Economic Growth

Market development is an important precondition for sustained economic growth. But on its own, is not a sufficient condition for the economic growth we observe after 1800. Modern economic growth is driven by innovation. The difference between premodern growth rates of around 0.1 percent per year and the modern growth regime in which mature economies grow can around 1–2 percent per year is due to productivity growth, which ultimately depends on innovation. Innovation was rare before 1700; it accelerated during the First Industrial Revolution, taking off after 1850 as modern scientific principles were applied to economic problems.

Innovation involves not just the application of new ideas to industry; it also requires ideas to "have sex."[24] Ideas and inventions need to beget new ideas and inventions, and entrepreneurs have to find it useful to experiment with new ideas and inventions in new and different ways. Innovation requires a mindset open to new ideas, new ways of doing things, and to the idea that things can be changed and improved upon.

Sustained growth requires more than the inventiveness of one individual thinker. It needs a culture of innovation (Mokyr, 2016). It flourishes when people share ideas and is less likely when legal and social barriers limit interactions between different groups of individuals. Identity rules were an impediment to the development of a culture of innovation.

Innovation did occur under the equilibrium of identity rules and conditional toleration, but the incentives to innovate were subdued and the dissemination of information limited. Islamic Science flourished from the eighth through to the eleventh century (Huff, 1993).[25] Medieval thinkers like Roger Bacon developed important ideas in astronomy. Indeed there are numerous scholars who have attempted to push back the origins of modern science, innovation, and growth to earlier centuries. But these are not fully convincing. In particular, until the early modern period, scientific invention was often not cumulative – pioneering developments were rarely seized upon by others. New ideas were not widely disseminated, making it harder for progress to take place. The decisive breakthrough came after 1600.[26]

The direct role played by the Church in blocking scientific innovation is sometimes exaggerated. There are clearcut instances of the Church prosecuting individuals such as Galileo. Even in the case of Galileo, however, the opposition of the Church to his findings was far from inevitable (Mokyr, 2016, 260). Nevertheless, indirectly, the suppression of Copernican astrology cowed scientists across Southern Europe.[27]

What role did the dismantling of the conditional toleration equilibrium play in the upsurge of innovative activity? Goldstone (2002, 374) highlighted the importance of a "peculiar engine-based scientific culture in seventeenth-century Britain." Mokyr (2002, 2009) argues that the Enlightenment was the crucial turning point. The Enlightenment was the product of a cultural change, a new willingness to question established authorities, to experiment, and to put forward new explanations of the world; this cultural attitude is summarized by Kant's adage *sapere aude* (dare to know). Mokyr describes how a practical, hands-on variant of the Enlightenment that he calls the Industrial Enlightenment took root in Britain prior to the Industrial Revolution. The Industrial Enlightenment favored experimental and practical science and the application of new ideas to industrial problems, what Mokyr calls a focus on "useful knowledge."

The breakdown of the conditional toleration equilibrium was critical to this development. As Mokyr observes, by modern standards eighteenth-century Britain was not especially tolerant. But "few Britons got into serious trouble because they proposed new ideas about theology that some regarded as blasphemous, or chemistry that went against the grain" (Mokyr, 2009, 97). Britain had evolved a competitive market for a ideas.

The development of the Republic of Letters, as a transnational meta-institution, was vital in fueling innovation and scientific thought in early modern Europe (Mokyr, 2016). Previously innovators were often silos: brilliant individuals working in isolation such as Leonardo de Vinci, whose ideas about anatomy, flight, and engineering were not developed by his peers. Or they were dependent on the patronage of a monarch, who they might offend or displease. Individual genius was not enough to produce a culture of innovation.

The Republic of Letters allowed scientists and scholars to engage with one another in the pursuit of knowledge. It crossed national and religious borders. It also followed strict rules of intellectual engagement, making possible a marketplace where ideas could be refined, tested, rejected or accepted, and built upon. Despite the famous stories of clashing egos and feuds, in general, the Republic of Letters was open to new scholars advancing ideas that overturned existing orthodoxies, while also vetting quacks and charlatans, and advancing best practice methods. Participants in the Republic of Letters practiced an important form of analytic egalitarianism and hierarchy of merit whereby individuals were judged on the basis of their ideas and not their social pedigree.

The Enlightenment created a new secular cultural space that made it easier for individuals of different religions to interact. The coffee shops of Amsterdam and London, the salons of Paris and Berlin: these were places where individuals could discourse relatively freely about new ideas. Importantly, the Republic of Letters that Mokyr describes spanned all of Europe, Catholic and Protestant.[28]

The Enlightenment and the Industrial Enlightenment were part of a more general cultural change studied by McCloskey (2006, 2010, 2016). This involved the revaluation of attitudes toward commerce, the market, and the application of new ideas to industrial and entrepreneurial purposes. Crucial to what McCloskey calls the spirit of bourgeois equality was a change in rhetoric. How people talked about commerce, trade, and human betterment changed in the Dutch Republic and England after 1600. Previously traders and merchants had been scorned. Fernand Braudel coined the term "the treason of the bourgeoisie" to describe this phenomenon: "everywhere, rich bourgeois of every origin were irresistibly drawn towards the aristocracy as if toward the sun" (Braudel, 1972, 1949, 729). This betrayal meant that successful merchants and traders aspired to the aristocracy: the capital they accumulated in commerce was squandered preparing their children to be noblemen.

The cultural allure of the aristocracy did not disappear instantly after 1800. It was still powerful in late nineteenth-century England. But over time, aristocratic virtues were replaced by bourgeois virtues that were consistent with the new world of commerce. Integrity came to replace honor; enterprise was more valued than courage, and to be trustworthy was viewed as more important than loyalty. Examples of this transformation include the fairly rapid switch from Roman numerals, which had associations with the classical world but were difficult to use in practical applications, to the much more useful Arabic numerals, a change that occurred in England during the seventeenth century. These instances of cultural change thus complement our story of institutional change.

13.6 Chapter Summary: The Demise of Conditional Toleration and Modern Economic Growth

We have considered why mainstream thinkers in medieval and early modern Europe all favored religious compulsion. Even David Hume, a notorious free thinker and a liberal, supported an established church. What changed after 1750 was evidence that religious freedom was indeed compatible with stability and prosperity.

An important factor in this transformation was the emergence of nationalism as a substitute for religious identity. Nationalism meant that the religious authorities no longer had as much power to legitimate rulers. The formation of national identities also facilitated a shift toward government based on general rules as we saw when examining France on the eve of the Revolution.

Finally, we considered what effect the breakdown of the conditional toleration equilibrium had on modern economic growth. The switch from reliance on identity rules to general rules helped to facilitate market integration across Europe. The expansion of trade and markets were a necessary precondition for modern economic growth to begin but they were unlikely to be sufficient. Innovation was also necessary. The breakdown of the medieval conditional toleration equilibrium aided the development of a culture of innovation and invention that recent scholars point to as critical for the onset of modern economic growth.

Notes

1. See Eire (2016, 260–285).
2. As we have seen, it was on these terms that both Richelieu and Colbert were prepared to make accommodations to Jews and Protestants in seventeenth-century France.
3. Merrill (2015, 34) draws attention to the significance of the historical background provided by the European wars of religion and the English Civil War in Hume's analysis. While this has often been neglected in modern accounts, every contemporary reader of Hume was aware of Wars of Religion that had devastated Europe in the previous century.
4. Locke's exclusion of those who owed loyalty to a foreign ruler may have been intended to exclude the Catholic supporters of James II rather than all Catholics (see Pincus, 2009). We are grateful to Jacob Levy for this clarification.
5. Sabl (2009) provides a rational reconstruction of these arguments. Hume's argument was first and foremost against the negative consequences of persecution.
6. See Anderson (1988) and Leather and Raines (1992). This debate is reviewed in detail by Whelan (1990). Smith's views were very different from those of Burke, for instance, who held that atheists should never be tolerated (see Baron, 1947, 34).
7. Anderson (1983) and Gellner (1983). On Leibniz, see his *Letters to Boussuet*, where he argues that a unified Church under the auspices of the Catholic Church might be achieved in clerical abuses are eliminated an if certain doctrines are left unspecified (Leibniz, 1972).
8. The Provinces excluded from this customs union were Angoumois, Artois, Auvergne, lower Navarre, Béarn, Brittany, Cambrésis, Foix, Dauphiné, Flanders, Forez, Franch-Compté, Gascony, Guyenne, Hainaut, Ile-de-Rhé, Ile d'Oléron, Languedoc, Limousin, Lyonnais (in parts), Marche, Provence, Roussillon, Rouergue, Saintonge, and Vivarais.
9. These tax farms were called the (1) traite foraine, le rêve et le haut passage de Champagne et de Normandie, (2) la traite foraine de Normandie, (3) le traite domaniale de Champagne, Picardie, Normandie, et Bourgogne, (4) la douane de Lyon, and (5) les droits d'entrée sur l'épicieries, drogueries et grosses denrées. During one of the most destructive periods of the Wars of Religion, Henri III (r. 1574–1589) needed to raise money fast and allowed the consolidation of the five great farms by the financier René Brunet (Roux, 1916, 70–73).
10. See, e.g., Heckscher (1955, 103–106) and Bosher (1964).
11. Data from 1784 are used because this is one of the only years in the eighteenth century for which these data were collected. The other years were all at the beginning of the century.
12. Johnson (2015) uses an index of these variables that summarizes whether a region's cahier is more likely to mention national or local concerns. This index runs between 1 and 3, with a score of 1 representing more local concerns and 3 a more national outlook.

13. Johnson (2015) uses the average of the cahiers from the second and third estates – the clergy are excluded because they expressed more concerns with the church than with national and local institutions. However, the results are robust to including the clergy. The map is created using an inverse distance weighted averaging procedure. The CGF border is treated as a boundary for the averaging.

14. The plotted cities are capitals of provinces. Plotting all 200 districts contained within the provinces would have cluttered the figure.

15. These numbers correspond to the cahiers of the nobility, though similar patterns are observed for the first and second estates.

16. See McCloskey (2006, 2010, 2016). For Kuznet's discussion of modern economic growth, see Kuznets (1966).

17. The notion, inspired by Karl Polanyi, that markets are an invention of the nineteenth century, is entirely wrong. But the issue at hand is less the existence of markets than how well they functioned. See Hejeebu and McCloskey (2004) for a systematic critique.

18. See Heckscher (1955), Epstein (2000), and Dincecco (2010).

19. For example, Shiue and Keller (2007), Bateman (2011), and Chilosi et al. (2013). The same is true for international markets, which began to become integrated only after 1820 (O'Rourke and Williamson, 1999).

20. "A cargo upstream from Rotterdam could never tell what new toll stations had been erected or what would be charged this trip at the old ones" (Clapp, 1907, 7).

21. This is in line with the argument of Acemoglu, Cantoni, and Robinson (2011) that the French invasion of Germany provided the conditions required for sustained economic growth by replacing wholesale the extractive institutions of the ancien regime.

22. See Keller and Shiue (2014). Ploeckl (2013) studied the impact of the Zollverein on market access and investment in Baden.

23. The data presented in Figures 13.3 and 13.4 also control for population density, geography, religion, education, and political institutions. In Figure 13.3, the slope of the fitted line suggests that a one standard deviation in the CGF-identity variable leads to about a third of a standard deviation increase in income per capita. The slope of the line for notary contract usage in Figure 13.4 suggests similarly large effects.

24. The coinage is due to Ridley (2010).

25. For a recent attempt to quantify the rise and decline of Islamic science see Chaney (2016).

26. See Wooton (2015) and Mokyr (2016). Wooton (2015) argues that prior to the voyages to the Americas, there was no concept of discovery in the medieval world – only the notion that previous knowledge had been lost or misplaced.

27. See Benabou, Ticchi, and Vindigni (2015) for a theoretical model of the situations when religious authorities will attempt to block scientific innovation and when they will instead attempt to "repair" religious doctrine in the face of new ideas. Also see Benabou et al. (2015b).

28. It did not penetrate Spain or Portugal. Howes (2017) traces the rise of a new culture of innovation in Britain during the eighteenth century. He documents a surge in the number of innovators in eighteenth-century Britain. He describes as an almost contagious meme, a sprits of inventiveness that could cross disciplinary boundaries. See also the discussion in Goldstone (2000) and Goldstone (2002, 359–379).

Applying Our Argument to the Rest of the World

Thus far our argument has focused on Europe. What about the rest of the world? To address this question we consider the evolution of religion and the state in the Middle East, East Asia, and the United States.

14.1 The Middle East

Islam emerged as the monotheistic faith of Arab tribesmen, who, under Muhammad unified the Arabian Peninsula, and then, under his successors, conquered the entire Middle East. In the process, the Byzantine empire was severed from its richest provinces and Sassanid Persia was destroyed entirely. The polities that rose and fell over the centuries in the wake of these conquests were similar to those in the Europe in that religion played a key role in legitimizing authority. However, a key difference is that, unlike most of the states we have discussed so far, polities in the Middle East never went through the transition from identity rules to general rules. This fact is reflected in the institutions and policies of states in the Middle East today.

From its inception, Islam was a religion associated with empire. It was therefore shaped by a pragmatism unusual in nascent religious faiths, as it was intended to bind together the Arab people and to inspire their conquest of new lands to the north, west, and east. The practice of offering toleration for Jews and Christians began in the Arabian Peninsula itself and, as Arab armies expanded into new territories, they continued this policy.[1]

The Islamic Caliphate was pluralistic for pragmatic reasons. Even within the Arabian Peninsula, Muhammad and the early caliphates received support from Jews, and later Christians and Zoroastrians, who "stood firm over their own faiths but were friendlily disposed toward the Prophet and his new creed" (Bosworth, 1982, 41–42).[2] What was later known as the Pact of Umar – a "contract in which the non-Muslims agree[d] to a host of discriminatory regulations in return for protection" – was in fact a rationalization of these ad hoc arrangements (Bosworth, 1982; Cohen, 1994). The pact of Umar was a preeminent example of conditional toleration. Indeed, there was actually a distinct term under Muslim rule for a community that was granted special or separate status – *dhimmi*.

As Arab armies continued to conquer new regions, their political leaders found themselves extending conditional toleration first to "people of the Book," then to Zoroastrians, and then, during the conquest of northern India in the eighth century, to polytheistic Hindus.[3] This religious pluralism was continued by the Ottomans after they conquered Eastern Europe (Runciman, 1970; Braude, 1982).

In contrast to Western Europe where, as we observed in Chapter 3, the collapse of Roman authority and the rise of successor kingdoms saw the end of the Roman tax state, the Arab conquerors of the Middle East took over and maintained existing Roman and Persian fiscal systems. At first, the Muslims were a tiny military elite who could be supported by a system of permanent taxation. A poll tax (*jizya*) on non-Muslims was introduced. The details of how this tax was assessed and collected varied greatly across the Middle East, but it was an important element of the fiscal system of the early Islamic polities. It provided a strong incentive for Islamic rulers to deter forcible conversion to Islam, as this would hurt revenues. At the same time, as Platteau (2017) notes, Umayyad and Abbasid Caliphates continued to rely on Roman and Persian systems of governance and political legitimation.

The tax on non-Muslim had the effect of incentivizing conversion. As it was an important part of the tax base, over time, the Caliphate had an incentive to adjust this tax (Saleh and Tirole, 2018). The importance of this fiscal incentive to tolerate minorities is consistent with our overall argument. The attitude of the Arab empire, and the Islamic states that succeeded it, was not one of religious freedom. The celebration of Islamic toleration in comparison to Christian fanaticism, though not without a kernel of truth, is often exaggerated by modern historians. Recent scholarship has emphasized the extent to which medieval Christianity, Islam, and Judaism confronted similar problems when it came to maintaining religious orthodoxy and suppressing religious deviancy. Throughout Islamic history, "the ideal singularity of the unified community (*umma*) was, in reality, in tension with its plurality and diversity. 'Muslim' polities, ethnicities, and religious groups had differing levels of commitment to Islam and differing senses of Islamic identity" (Ames, 2015, 20).

The maintenance of religious conformity was an important task for all medieval Islamic rulers. The repression of heresy was thus a duty incumbent upon Muslim rulers. Sufi mystics suffered frequent persecution. Caliph al-Qadir (r. 991–1031) suppressed the rationalist Mu 'tazilites. The punishment for heresy ranged from exile or imprisonment to death, often by crucifixion (Ames, 2015, 86–87). As the Abbasid Caliphate weakened, the importance of religious orthodoxy grew. And as political authority fragmented in the Islamic world after 1000, the new states "themselves attended to heresy, particularly for the purposes of establishing legitimacy." Ames (2015, 169) concludes that "[i]n the distinct religious-political contest of medieval Islam, protecting the state was to combat heresy (and vice versa), just as political rebellion was bound up with heresy (And vice versa)."

Jews did not face the systematic and intense antisemitism in the Muslim Middle East that they experienced in post-crusades Europe. But they did encounter both discrimination and occasional violence. Bernard Lewis notes: "[v]iolent persecution, forced conversion and banishment were rare, though not unknown. They usually occurred at times of stress and danger, when the Islamic world was threatened from within or without, by pestilence or famine, religious division or foreign invasion" (Lewis, 1986, 124). As discussed in Chapter 8, Jews and Christians were sometimes subject to persecutions. Christian communities in Spain were expelled wholesale to North Africa in the twelfth century and pogroms occurred.[4] This religious violence and conflict, however, was fairly rare. Virulent antisemitism arrived in the Middle East only in modern times.

But calling the relationship between Muslims and non-Muslims religious toleration risks confusion. The system of community autonomy that characterized Muslim treatment of Christians and Jews permitted these minorities to survive and sometimes flourish so long as they remained within their confined sphere. But the autonomy granted to officially recognized communities permitted intolerance and the enforcement of religious conformity within each community. In Islamic Spain, for example, the leaders of Rabbinical Judaism carried out a persecution of Qariates (Rustow, 2008). Non-Abrahamic faiths faced greater risk of persecution. The Yazidis in Iraq, for example, suffered intermittent persecution during Ottoman times. They survived because they lived in remote, infertile, and economically unimportant land. The Middle East throughout its history has been characterized by conditional toleration in which non-Islamic minorities have been left to largely govern themselves and have been subject to only occasional persecution.

There was no transition from identity rules to general rules in the Islamic Middle East. Rubin (2017) argues that this stagnation of institutions can be explained by the historical context in which Islam emerged. In the Arabian Peninsula there was a political vacuum. There was no strong organized state capable of imposing a general system of laws as Rome was at the time when Christianity emerged. Consequently, Islamic law became a more important component of everyday life. Muhammad and his followers laid the groundwork for the Muslim doctrines that would be enshrined in the Koran and the Hadiths during the seventh and eight centuries. As a consequence, religion was a more significant source of legitimacy in the Middle East than in Europe. Islamic religious authorities could impose both religious and temporal sanctions on rulers who deviated from religious law. Secular rulers lacked alternative sources of legitimacy and hence had to rely on religious authorities to shore up their rule. According to Rubin, the Islamic Middle East's conservative equilibrium had important consequences. It meant that the Islamic prohibition against interest (*riba*) remained in force while the Christian prohibition on usury fell into disuse after 1400. It also helps to explain why the Ottoman Empire chose to prohibit printing in the Arabic script. These two bans impeded economic development in the Middle East. The ban on interest limited the types of corporate forms that could develop. The ban on printing slowed the spread of new ideas and meant that when the Ottoman empire tried to modernize in the late eighteenth and nineteenth centuries it was far behind Europe. In particular, Rubin notes that the economic implications of the ban on interest and printing put the Islamic Middle East on a divergent path from that of Western Europe; the full costs of this development became apparent only gradually.

Another key factor in the political development of the Middle East was the absence of institutional constraints on state power. Blaydes (2017) notes that while the initial geographic conditions of the Middle East were conducive to the formation of strong states, developments in the intervening centuries impeded the process of state centralization and development of executive constraints. In particular, the rise of military systems based on slave soldiers meant that Islamic rulers did not need to bargain with a nobility as in Europe. In the absence of a stable propertied elite, representative institutions did not develop. The consequences are visible in the divergent tenure of rulers in the Middle East in comparison to Europe documented by Blaydes and Chaney (2013). After 1000 CE, European rulers enjoyed longer reigns, a divergence that they attribute to the emergence of institutions that constrained executive power in Europe.

These insights complement the work of Timur Kuran (2010, 2018), who argues that the system of conditional toleration that emerged in the Muslim Middle East imposed long-run economic and social costs on the Ottoman Empire. Kuran argues that while Islam is neither inherently conservative nor hostile to commerce, institutions that emerged during its first two centuries retarded the development of impersonal exchange.

The institutions that arose in the early centuries of Islam were not inherently inefficient. Islamic attitudes toward inheritance and partnerships helped limit inequality. The prohibition on interest was intended to prevent debt slavery. Islamic partnerships were an effective way to share risk when trade was relatively small-scale; and they were not inferior to the contractual forms developed by Christian or Jewish merchants at the same time. The economy of the Middle East was ahead of that of Western Europe at least until 1200.

The institutions of the Islamic world were sufficient to enable the Middle East to flourish during the medieval period. But, as new opportunities to trade and produce on a larger scale emerged after 1500, they failed to evolve as did institutional and organizational forms in the West. This was partly due to the fact that they were highly stable because they were supported by Islamic religious institutions. Islamic partnerships allowed merchants to pool assets for a single voyage, but they impeded the emergence of more complicated organizational forms such as the corporation. Such complex and long-lasting organizational forms were critical to European colonial and trading ventures. Similarly, Islamic restrictions on usury prevented the emergence of investment banking. This limited the size of firms and long-term commercial endeavors. It also meant that Muslim states did not develop institutions such as central banks or a system of national debt.

Another important example of an Islamic institution that may have been initially efficient, but failed to evolve, was the highly egalitarian inheritance system. Islamic inheritance rules fixed how much each heir would receive. In so doing, these laws elevated the status of women and younger sons who could not be written out of a bequest. However, by specifying an even division of property, these laws prevented successful merchants from passing down their entire business intact to the next generation. As a result, organizations in the Islamic world remained relatively simple. Innovations that emerged in Europe to deal with larger-scale and more impersonal trade could not easily be adopted in the Middle East. This long institutional divergence helps to explain both why the Industrial Revolution did not originate in the Middle East, despite the relative prosperity that the region enjoyed in the early Middle Ages, and why the Industrial Revolution did not spread as quickly in the Middle East relative to other parts of the world after 1800.

It also explains why constraints on political authority did not emerge from merchant interests in the Middle East. This was a prominent feature of the emergence of representative government in Europe.[5] In the Ottoman Empire, however, the institutions of inheritance and the lack of a concept of corporate personhood made it very difficult to pool capital in a way that could coordinate the actions of private interests to check autocratic rule (Balla and Johnson, 2009).

For instance, Kuran (2016) discusses how the institution of the Islamic waqf hindered the development of civil society in the Middle East. Waqfs allowed individuals to endow mosques, charities, schools, fountains, or other similar organizations. They were an important and uniquely long-lived form of organization in the Islamic world. However, as Kuran documents, they were also highly rigid and hierarchical. The funds could be used only for the explicit purpose of the waqf as laid down by the founder. In particular, waqfs could not be used for a political purposes. Thus while the corporate form was crucial in enabling the rise of an independent civil society in Western Europe (North et al., 2009), this did not occur in the Middle East.

The Ottoman state allowed minorities considerable autonomy. Kuran (2010, 187) notes that the Ottomans endowed minority communities with collective rights when convenient. For example, "in 1596, an impoverished Jew appeared before a *kadi* (judge) to complain that he was ordered to repay part of a debt incurred for the collective benefit of his community." The court upheld the right of the Jewish community to legal personhood and to effectively tax its members in order to repay a collective debt. The reason was that:

The Jews borrowed mostly from Muslims, and some of their creditors were dignitaries. For this reason alone, the restitution of Jewish debts was of concern to officials. In addition, both intercommunal harmony and financial markets benefited from the orderly repayment of debts. The state thus gained from having a communal leader allocate debt burdens among his constituents. As with taxation, he would possess the local knowledge necessary to exact resources; the state's own agents would not. (Kuran, 2010, 187)

As a result of institutional stagnation within the Islamic world, economic developments after 1750 disproportionately benefited Christian and Jewish minorities in the Ottoman empire. Christians and Jews became successful merchants and traders, mediating between Western firms and Muslims. As they were not subject to Islamic law, they freely adopted Western organizational forms. By 1900, Christians and Jews were overrepresented in all of the modernizing sectors of the economy such as insurance, finance, electricity, gas, and the building of railway lines (Kuran, 2010, 194). Hence, Kuran (2010, 208) notes "[i]mposed initially to benefit Muslims, the Pact of Umar thus had the unintended effect, more than a millennium later, of seriously harming Muslim economic opportunities."

Recent research consistently confirms these negative consequences of the reliance on identity rules in the Islamic world. In Egypt, the discriminatory poll tax charged on non-Muslims encouraged poorer Christian minority Copts to convert to Islam. This produced a better-off, higher human capital, minority who were disproportionately represented in white-collar jobs in the nineteenth century (Saleh, 2018). This differential between Christians and Muslims grew in the modern period. Industrialization in nineteenth century Egypt benefited the Coptic population who were overrepresented in urban and skilled work. At the same time, industrialization, particularly in the textile industry, harmed traditional artisan workers, who were predominantly Muslim (Saleh, 2015). These legacies of the Ottoman millet system remain relevant today.[6]

14.2 China and Japan

Two thousand years ago China and Europe closely resembled one another in their political structures. Both were unified under the rule of emperors who combined both political and religious authority. Chinese and Roman rulers raised permanent taxes, governed through bureaucracies, and commanded professional armies that were large by premodern standards. Religion played an important role in legitimating political authority. But religious authority was subsumed to political authority.[7]

The trajectory of Western Europe diverged from that of China following the failure of the Eastern Roman empire to reconquer its western half on a permanent basis in the sixth century. While a centralized empire was rebuilt in China under the Sui and Tang dynasties, in Europe there was a collapse in political authority that could not be arrested even by the vigorous kingship of Charlemagne. In the wake of this collapse, the Church became a powerful independent force.

No equivalently powerful religious organization ever emerged in China. The processes that generated a persecuting society in Europe, therefore, were absent in China. Allied to the state, Chinese religious traditions remained syncretist rather than exclusive. The comparative weakness of Chinese religious organizations also meant that religion was subordinated. In this setting, there could be no religious freedom. All Chinese dynasties from the Tang (618–907) onwards registered and monitored religious groups. A Board of Religious Rites was responsible for supervising temples and religious organizations (Bayes, 2004).

The situation in Japan was similar. Japanese rulers used syncretic Shinto-Buddhist-Confucian beliefs to legitimate their authority. Unlike in China, Japanese political authority became divided during the Middle Ages as shoguns took over the business of governing while the emperor in Kyoto increasingly became a figurehead. But it was only during periods of state weakness that religious organizations (such as Buddhist temples) gained any independent authority.

In one such period of political disunity in the sixteenth century, Christianity spread rapidly throughout Japan. Rival daimyo welcomed Portuguese and Spanish traders and missionaries. They were eager as the foreigners brought handguns, which proved crucial in the ongoing warfare of the period. For their part, both the Jesuits and the Franciscans devoted considerable resources to converting a country that they saw as among the most advanced in Asia. A few prominent daimyo, particularly in the southern island of Kyushu, converted to Christianity.[8]

However, just as political fragmentation was conducive to the spread of Christianity, unification proved fatal to it. There were three "great unifiers" in late sixteenth-century Japan; these warlords were willing to make use of Christian knowledge and weapons but had no interest in converting to Christianity or allowing the religion to destabilize the existing order. The second great unifier, Hideyoshi crushed independent Buddhist monks who opposed him, ordered the expulsion of all missionaries in 1587, and then crucified twenty-six Japanese Christians in 1597.[9]

A systematic program of repression was introduced only by the third great unifier, Tokugawa Ieyasu in 1614. Hideyoshi and Tokugawa Ieyasu initially were willing to tolerate Christian missions as the price of access to the lucrative trade in silk and precious metals between Macao and Japan. Warned by Dutch and English Protestants, the Shogun feared that the missionaries in general and the Jesuit priests, in particular, were a fifth column who aimed to convert Japan to Catholicism in anticipation of a Spanish invasion. Furthermore, the arrival of the Dutch meant that the Spanish and Portuguese were no longer indispensable from the perspective of maintaining trade. As a result, and provoked by a series of minor conspiracies involving Christian daimyo, the Shogun's attitude toward Christianity hardened.

Under the second Tokugawa Shogun, the repression of Christianity became part of a general policy of isolation and eradication of Western influences. It was justified as follows: "the Kirishitan (i.e., Roman Catholic) band have come to Japan not only sending their merchant vessels to exchange commodities but also longing to disseminate an evil law, to overthrow true doctrine, so that they may change the government of the country, and obtain possession of thee land ... This is the germ of great disaster and must be crushed" (quoted in Boxer, 1951, 318). Everyone had to become a member of one of the main Buddhist sects and the head of the family became responsible for the religious choices of all individuals under his authority.

The Tokugawa state that Ieyesu created was powerful enough to conduct one of the most thoroughgoing religious persecutions in history.[10] It sealed the country to foreigners and missionaries and prevented Japanese who traveled abroad from returning. As in sixteenth-century France and Spain, an administrative machinery was created to investigate religious beliefs and induce Christians to abjure. Christians had to apostatize by treading on a picture of Christ. Those who were suspected of not doing this wholeheartedly, or found with Christian symbols, were subject to torture until they openly apostatized in full. Failure to do so meant death. As in contemporary Europe, the executions were carried out in public with great fanfare and deliberate cruelty. For example, at Nagasaki in 1622, there was a mass burning of twenty-five foreign priests and the execution of thirty Japanese Christians, including twelve children. This spectacle was followed by a series of other public executions. But because the fate of the condemned inspired many Christian onlookers, from this point onwards the government switched to imprisoning and executing Christians in private (Boxer, 1951, 343).

The Japanese persecution of Christians was perhaps the most successful attempt to eliminate an entire religion in history. By around 1630 Christianity had been forced underground. However, even in Japan, persecution did not entirely succeed. Hidden Christians survived until the nineteenth century. Nevertheless, this example shows that in certain circumstances, early modern states could successfully crush religious dissent if they were able to pay the huge costs that it entailed. In the Japanese case, these costs involved secluding the country from the rest of the world for more than 200 years.

The issue of religious toleration arose once again after Japan was opened to the West following the arrival of Captain Perry's Black Ships in Yokohama. The introduction of religious freedom involved an entire overhauling of Japanese society. In nineteenth-century Japan, there were no direct translations for the words "religion" and "liberty." The Japanese recognized freedom of thought in the private sphere. In the public sphere, however, they prioritized the maintenance of political order and had no desire to countenance potentially destabilizing religious freedoms.

In English, the word liberal evolved gradually – in the Middle Ages it came into use to refer to a liberal mind or a liberal education – and first developed in parallel with the concept of "liberties," such as the liberties of a city, or of a privileged group. Liberty acquired its political meaning in the fifteenth century and the word liberal came into use to describe individuals who championed the value of liberty only in the late eighteenth century, largely as a consequence of Adam Smith's advocacy of a liberal system of trade. As Howland (2001) documents, this long development had to be condensed as Japanese reformers and constitutional thinkers struggled to incorporate Western political concepts into the Japanese intellectual tradition in the 1860s and 1870s. He traces the efforts of Fukuzawa Yukichi (1835–1901) and Nakamura Masanao (1832–1891), both of whom contrasted the classical liberal position based on individual freedom that they encountered in writers such as John Stuart Mill with traditional Japanese society with its basis in status and privileges.

When the Meiji government lifted the ban on practicing Christianity in 1873, they did so for predominantly pragmatic reasons (see Burkman,

1974). Religious intolerance was an issue that the Western powers emphasized when they forced a series of trade agreements on the Tokugawa Shogunate in the 1860s. As part of these negotiations, the Japanese government was initially prepared to grant religious toleration to Westerners who practiced Christianity in the treaty ports, but they were less willing to concede religious freedom elsewhere in the country. In 1867 Christians in the village of Urakami were imprisoned and their chapels destroyed. This episode revealed the existence of so-called hidden Christians to missionaries who raised this issue with the major Western powers. French and Prussian protests about the treatment of Christians secured their release.

The British Foreign Minister Lord Stanley advised the Japanese government that renewed persecution of Christians was likely to backfire and that "it would be better to tolerate the exercise of their religion within certain limits rather than acquire throughout Europe and America the reputation of persecuting the faith accepted in those continents and so incur the ill will of all civilized nations to whose feelings religious persecution is now abhorrent" (quoted in Burkman, 1974, 162).

This appeal to pragmatism was convincing and Meiji Japan thus adopted a measure of religious toleration. But it did not become a religiously free society overnight. The Meiji government deliberately cultivated a religious cult around the emperor. They utilized the religious and spiritual legitimacy that they obtained by elevating the emperor in order to push through a costly and ambitious reform program overcoming numerous vested interests and using the full force of the state to crush open resistance.[11] In particular, they elevated Shintoism into a state religion, separating it from the Buddhist religious tradition with which it had coevolved for centuries. This process involved closing down Buddhist shrines and destroying temples. Full religious freedom was only instituted in Japan 1946.

The fate of Christianity in China was less dramatic than in Japan. Jesuits arrived in the late sixteenth century and focused on converting the political elite and the emperor. The most successful Jesuit, Matteo Ricci, become an advisor to the emperor. Nevertheless, as in Japan, they were most successful in obtaining converts among servants and women, and in general, they had no lasting success. Their mission ultimately depended on the attitude of the reigning emperor. The Kangxi Emperor (r. 1661–1722) initially welcomed Jesuits because of their knowledge of astronomy, languages, and artillery, and issued a general order of toleration.[12]

The Jesuits did not attempt to impose Christianity on the Chinese. Rather there were attempts to blend Confucianism and Christianity into a syncretic creed that could gain adherence among the Chinese literati class. However, this aroused opposition from other religious orders, notably the Dominicans, and at their urging, Pope Clement XI prohibited Chinese

Christians from performing Confucian rites in 1704. In retaliation, the Kangxi emperor prohibited Christian missions in China in 1721. The Yongzheng Emperor (r. 1722 – 1735) continued this policy, explicitly proscribing Christianity in an edict of 1724. Christian missions only returned to China as the Qing state weakened in the early nineteenth century.

In general, there was less tension between religion and the state in imperial China. S. N. Eisenstadt writes that to account for this, "there developed in China a very strong emphasis on civility, or a mixture of civility and sacrality, as the central legitimating criterion, of the sociopolitical order. Such civility tended to be formulated in a mixture of sacral and legal terms, with relatively weak charismatic elements, focused mostly on the office of the emperor. In this scheme, the purely sacred or primordial criteria of legitimation were secondary or incorporated into the hegemonic discourse, and in China – unlike other axial-age civilizations – the tensions between them tended to be relatively weak" (Eistenstadt, 2009, xiii).

Chinese emperors rarely persecuted religious minorities because they were not a threat to political order. However, this does not mean that persecutions never occurred. The Qin Emperor (r. 220–210 BCE) was famous for burning books and the mass execution of Confucian scholars.[13] The eighteenth-century Qing state was a persecutory state but the persecutions it conducted were political rather than religious in nature. Confucianism mandated obedience to political authority while also offering a set of values against which the political authorities could be held to account, thereby providing a set of beliefs that legitimized political authority so long as the emperor was capable of providing peace and social order – the "mandate of heaven."[14]

The Qing had a particular problem: the Confucian principles they relied on for ideological legitimation had the potential to undermine their claim to authority. The Confucian classics denigrated non-Chinese as barbarians and praised the role of the emperor in subduing them. It was vital, therefore, for Qing authority that the "correct" interpretation of the classics be upheld. The legitimacy of the Qing emperors depended on them not being viewed as "barbarian interlopers from beyond the pale of civilization," but as being civilized: "a concept consistently phrased in terms of *wen* or literate expression" which "meant, among other things, the recording of knowledge, and those who controlled that record held the keys to state legitimacy" (Brook, 1988, 177–178).[15]

Alternative sources of textual interpretation were prohibited. The Shunzhi Emperor (r. 1643–1661) purged the officials and closed independent academies that were suspected of encouraging factionalism and fostering discontent.[16] In their place, imperial academies were founded that focused on teaching official interpretations of Confucian texts.[17]

The imperial examination system played a vital role in producing educated scholars for service in the Chinese bureaucracy. Chinese emperors, furthermore, sought to legitimate their position through control of the examination system. This relationship became particularly tense during the Qing period. The emperors used the threat of persecution to exercise a form of intellectual control on the Han ruling elite: "Whatever their status – officials, students, or private individuals – intellectuals had to familiarize themselves with special works championing the imperial cause written by the Yung-chen Emperor or sponsored by him" (Huang, 1974, 19). Individuals who, for whatever reason, fell foul of this system faced the risk of persecution.[18]

Individuals could be investigated for variety of reasons, many of which appear opaque to modern eyes. Alleged crimes for which individuals were punished included writings that were deemed to implicitly criticize the dynasty, for use of words such as the name of an emperor that could be seen as lacking respect, for statements that were deemed to reflect negatively on the achievements of Qing emperors, for writing positively of the previous dynasty, and for actual or alleged factionalism (see Huang, 1974, 208). Individuals were liable, not only if they wrote suspect literature, but also if they kept silent about the existence of such literature or owned copies themselves. Individuals were punished for distributing and selling books written by those found guilty by the literary inquisition.

From the reign of the Yongzheng Emperor onwards, individuals could be investigated on the basis of anonymous denouncements from their peers and, in response, a wide network of informers emerged. Timothy Brook observes that the literary inquisition "grew into a hydra of suspicion and denunciation because the Chinese (as opposed to the Manchu) elite found in the project's hazy guidelines opportunities for pursuing personal vendettas. Scholars began to denounce each other, both to settle old scores and to attract the attention of regional officials" (Brook, 2005, 178). The houses of scholar-officials were searched for suspect material; at the "same time brutal measures were taken against the authors and their relations – execution, exile, forced labor, confiscation of property, and so on" (Gernet, 1972, 506). Therefore, even though the number of individuals actually persecuted for literary crimes was relatively small, large numbers of scholar-officials saw themselves as potential victims of a literary persecution. Victims were publicly executed and their families enslaved.[19]

Xue and Koyama (2017) investigated the impact of the literary inquisition on social capital. China had a rich tradition of voluntary organizations that historians alternatively call benevolent associations, voluntary societies, charity halls, or charitable organizations. These were small-scale, nonpartisan, institutions that aided widows, looked after orphans, ran soup kitchens, and helped the poor. Historians note that this philanthropic activity reflected a "clearly articulated concept of a 'public' or 'communal' sphere, as opposed to a 'state' or 'private' sphere, as both the agent and the beneficiary of philanthropic activism" (Rowe, 2009, 119). Xue and Koyama (2017) found that an episode of political repression brought about an immediate and permanent decline in the number of charities. After the first persecution, the number of charitable organizations in a prefecture fell by an average of 38 percent, compared to prefectures that never had a persecution, or prefectures that had not yet experienced a persecution. This reflected changes in the willingness of individuals to organize and to invest effort to aid their neighbors in an environment of mutual mistrust. These persecutions had a persistent impact on trust and political participation today (Xue and Koyama, 2017).

Nor was China immune from the types of panics that engulfed Europe during the age of witch-hunts. In 1768 a scare arose as some individuals in Chekiang were accused of "soul stealing" (Kuhn, 1990). These individuals were imagined to be sorcerers, who roamed the land, and were able to steal the souls of individuals, by clipping off the top of the ends of men's queues (the braids worn by royal decree). As in Europe, belief in sorcery was widespread in Chinese society. What transformed these beliefs into wholesale panic and mass trials was the willingness of officials to investigate these cases and the use of torture to extract confessions. Unlike in Europe, this episode was an isolated one in China, largely because China was governed by a single powerful state.

To Chinese eyes, religion was closely associated with the threat of popular revolt. The Shangong Rebellion (1774), for example, was linked to the White-Lotus sect of Wang Lun. Hong Xiuquan was a failed examination candidate inspired by the Christian teachings he obtained from Western missionaries.[20] The rebellion Hong inspired – the Taiping rebellion (1850–1864) – is often estimated to have been the second most bloody conflict in human history with conservative estimates placing the number of dead at around 20 million (Platt, 2012).

With the exception of Christianity, Qing China and Tokugawa Japan rarely persecuted religious minorities. But this did not reflect a commitment to religious freedom. Social order was prioritized. To maintain stability, all East Asian states were committed to the use of coercion and were perfectly willing to use violence to encourage outward conformity of religious belief. It was only the comparative weakness of Asian states in the nineteenth century that led to the imposition of religious toleration from outside.

In China today, religious markets remain heavily regulated. Religions are categorized according to those which are officially tolerated, those that are officially banned, or those whose legal status is ambiguous. Religious toleration is an official part of Communist Party policy (Grim and Finke, 2011, 133). However, religious groups that meet the disapproval of government can find themselves labeled evil or dangerous cults. Government agencies have a wide remit in shutting down such religions and arresting and persecuting their members. The most well known example is the persecution of Falun Gong.

14.3 The United States

Colonial America inherited its social and political institutions from England. Nevertheless, the early American colonies varied greatly in culture, social norms, and political institutions. New England was settled by Puritans from eastern England. Tidewater Virginia, on the other hand, was settled by Anglican royalists from the southwest of the country (Fisher, 1989). Despite these differences, all of the colonies "utilized religion to support a social hierarchy, an intolerance of dissent, and a communitarian emphasis premised at least in part on concepts of moral duty and Christian brotherhood" (McGarvie, 2005, 21). Religious establishments across most of North America were characterized by compulsory church attendance and were supported by taxes. The legal system was shaped by religious norms and enforced religious prohibitions not only against sins such as bestiality, witchcraft, and homosexuality, but also against idleness, card playing, and music.

In fact, in part because the state was less present and powerful in colonial American than in Europe, churches took on an even more important role in the colonies as an enforcer of the moral and political order. Criminal sanctions were applied to those who did not attend church. In New England, in particular, churchmen enjoyed tremendous authority and respect. Blasphemy continued to be punished severely into the eighteenth century.

In the New England colonies, the only major development toward greater religious freedom in the colonial period was the rise of multiple Protestant establishments. As a result, parishioners gained the ability to choose which church they wished to support with their taxes. Nevertheless, this hardly amounted to a tendency toward religious liberalism: "it is a mistake to regard the religious pluralism of seventeenth-century America as indicative of an unusually high degree of tolerance among the colonists themselves" as at the same time "nearly all American colonies enacted laws to deter deviant religious practices or beliefs" (McGarvie, 2005, 25).

This was particularly true in the Massachusetts Bay colony. However, religion was also crucial to enforcing the social order in Rhode Island, which was founded on the notion that the political authorities should not coerce belief. McGarvie (2005, 27) observed that "Roger Williams' commitment to religious freedom was derived not from the rights of man to be free from state interference but from a belief in the supremacy of God and the depravity of man's created churches." In practice, Rhode Island struggled to live up to the ideals of religious toleration espoused by its founder. Pennsylvania grew out of the land grants made to William Penn, a celebrated Quaker, and was settled by religious dissenters. But even Pennsylvania restricted the civic rights of non-Christians and Quakerism enjoined tremendous moral authority over people's lives.

Nor was colonial America characterized by liberal markets. As in Europe, economic activity was buried in regulations, many of which were religious. Religion informed notions about the "just price" of a good and continued to form the basis for laws that regulated trade and commerce throughout colonial America. In general, colonial America remained in the conditional toleration equilibrium that prevailed in early modern Europe. After the Revolution, however, the United States became celebrated as embodying the ideal of religious freedom and the separation of church and state. How did this happen?

Traditional accounts emphasize the influence of the writings of Locke. No doubt Lockean discourse was influential, particularly in elite and enlightened circles. But Locke himself did not argue for the disestablishment of the Anglican Church and it was facts on the ground, unanticipated by Locke, that made Americans receptive to Lockean themes.

Several developments put pressure on the religious establishments of colonial America. The first was economic growth, the expansion of long-distance trade, and increased migration from the Old World to the New. This further increased religious pluralism and pragmatic concerns further undermined the positions of the established churches at the state level.[21]

Second, there was a further proliferation of religious sects in the eighteenth century as a result of the religious movement known as the First Great Awakening in the 1730s and 1740s. The influence of the Enlightenment saw many elites adopt deist or skeptical views about religion. A consequence was that over time the establishment churches increasingly lost parishioners and influence. As society became more fluid and urbanized, it became impossible to enforce church attendance.

During the Revolutionary War, religious dissenters pushed for greater religious freedom. State constitutions written in the 1770s embodied these developments, and states like New Jersey outlawed a tax to support religious establishments (McGarvie, 2005, 43).[22] However, other states, such as Massachusetts, continued to retain an established church. It was one thing, however, to legislate for religion at the state level, and quite something else to establish laws governing religious freedom at the national level.

The First Amendment – the prohibition of making laws establishing a church or intervening in the free exercise of religion, freedom of speech, and freedom of the press – was a radical statement. Historical scholarships suggests that there was nothing inevitable in its passing. Numerous established churches existed at the state level. The question was whether an established church would exist at the federal level. This was opposed not only by deists and religious skeptics like Thomas Jefferson, but also by dissenting Protestants.

What led to the First Amendment was, less the secularism of Jefferson, but rather the realization that the creation of a powerful federal government posed challenges to religious establishments across America. For Feldman the "motivating political reality that pushed liberty of conscience onto state and then federal agendas: the sudden increase in religious diversity that resulted from bringing the states together into federal union" (Feldman, 2005, 26). "Religious diversity" he notes "drove this push for a constitutional amendment on religious liberty. The new form of government under consideration was intended to bind together the states into a union that was more complete – 'more perfect' – than under the Articles of Confederation. The resulting bound-together union would contain a degree of religious diversity much greater than existed in any of the several states. Under these conditions, various religious groups worried about the possibility – unlikely, to be sure – of the federal government coming under the control of some other particular denomination" (Feldman, 2005, 43–44). Religious diversity among the states both made a national established church impossible and made an explicit statement of religious separation from the state desirable. The guarantee of religious freedom, therefore, accompanied the birth of a modern state in North America.

The main justification for religious freedom in the US context was the desire to protect the church from the state rather than to protect the state from religion. Fear of state intervention in religious affairs made religious freedom attractive in late eighteenth-century America. In this, as in other respects, the American settlers were the inheritors of the long European evolution of economic and political institutions. The authors of the Constitution wanted a framework that would preserve both existing liberties and at the same time ensure that the state was strong enough to ward off foreign powers (Hamilton et al., 1788, 2004).

The unique status of the United States as the birthplace and home of religious freedom is part of the country's civic identity. The historical reality is more complex than this civic myth. Blasphemy laws remained in place in nineteenth-century America and individuals continued to fall afoul of them. As late as 1886, Charles B. Reynolds was indicted and fined by a grand jury in New Jersey for holding a meeting of free thinkers and distributing pamphlets advocating agnosticism.[23]   The reason for this is that religion continued to play a crucial role in upholding and legitimating the social order. Religion, specifically Protestantism, was the glue that held together the moral order and criticism of religion that threatened this moral order could be legally sanctioned.[24]   In America, therefore, as in Europe, the emergence of genuine religious liberty was a gradual process.

14.4 Chapter Summary

Arthur Versluis views the inquisitorial mindset as a specifically Christian pathology. In *The New Inquisitions* (2006) he draws a link from the Roman and Spanish inquisitions to the horrors of modern totalitarian states. He contends that the concept of heresy is a product of the historical development of the Church and it is the concept of heresy – and the desire to eliminate it – that leads to totalitarianism.[25]   But (Versluis 2006, 3) argues, "another model is quite possible ... When one looks East, to Eastern Christianity, or even farther East, to the religions of India, China, and Tibet, for example, one sees some more pluralistic models."

In contrast, we have argued that no indelible characteristics of Western Europe or Christianity made it more likely to develop into a persecuting society. Nor did any fatal decision, made by Tertullian or Augustine, set the Church down the path toward religious coercion. Rather, religious coercion and conditional toleration were features of all premodern societies. China and Japan differed from Europe only insofar as they lacked indigenous monotheistic religious traditions of their own but as we have seen in this chapter, they had no notion of religious freedom or liberalism.

Similarly, no special features made America uniquely hospitable to religious freedom. As in Europe, chance events and long-run institutional and economic developments played the most important role in the growth of religious freedom in United States.

Notes

1. One should not get the impression that these conquests were peaceful affairs, however. The Islamic conquest of Spain, for example, was accompanied by the destruction of the church, wide spread massacres, and enslavement (Fernández-Morera, 2016, 48).

2. Muhammad viewed Jews and Christians as potential allies against the pagan established elite in the city of Mecca who opposed him and his new religion. Jewish Arab tribes were part of Muhammad's early alliance against Mecca before he turned on them and had them destroyed. As a result of this mixed history, there are Koranic verses that preach toleration and those that celebrate the killing and forced conversion of non-Muslims.

3. The granting of *dhimmi* status to Zoroastrians was justified because it was claimed that they had been granted a revelation from God but the Holy Books has not survived. However, "[w]hen the Muslims first acquired a foothold in the Indian subcontinent through the conquest of Sind in the early eighth century, a situation arose similar to that of Persia; the teeming populations there could not be slaughtered *en bloc*, but how in the absence of any Quranic *nass* (legal injunction), could the pagan Hindus be assimilated to *dhimmi* status? On the evidence of Balhduri's account of the conquest of Sin, there were certainly massacres in the towns of Sind when the Arabs first arrived." But, eventually "[p]eace treaties were made with the local communities ... on what had been the standard conditions during the overrunning of the Fertile Crescent and Persia" (Bosworth, 1982, 43).

4. Fernández-Morera (2016) deconstructs the myth that Islamic Spain was especially hospitable to religious minorities or free-thinkers. The Islamic conquest of Spain was accompanied by the destruction of churches and the marginalization of Christians. As was the case elsewhere under Muslim rule, Christians and Jews were not allowed to proselytize or convert Muslims and faced a host of discriminatory barriers.

5. See Jha (2015) and Acemoglu, Johnson, and Robinson (2005).

6. Armenians and Greeks prospered in the late Ottoman empire but were expelled from Turkey following the First World War. Using data on the distribution of Armenians and Greeks from 1893, Arbatli and Gokmen (2016) find that districts with greater Armenian and Greek concentration before the expulsions are today more densely populated, more urbanized, and have greater levels of economic development as measured by the intensity of lights at night.

7. See Scheidel (2009) for a comparison of Han China and the Roman empire.

8. The classic account of the spread of Christianity in Japan is Boxer (1951).

9. In general, Hideyoshi's attitude to Christianity up to this point had been ambivalent. Alessandro Valignano noted that "Hideyoshi had on the whole done more to foster Christianity than to suppress it, since his exclusion edict was more than outweighed by his keeping the Buddhist church in its place and by his support of the Christian daimyo. His motives in this policy of toleration were undoubtedly somewhat mixed, but that Mammon was his lodestar rather than God is clear" (Boxer, 1951, 177).

10. The power of the Tokugawa state rested on the indirect way that the Shogun and the Daimyo could police rural society. The Shogun himself directly controlled and taxed only a part of the Japanese islands and the Daiymo remained rulers in their own domains.

11. See the discussion in Koyama, Moriguchi, and Sng (2018).

12. Christians sometimes faced persecution at a local level (as, for example, in Shandong between 1663 and 1669).

13. This event, widely known as *fen shu keng ru* (210 BCE), has had a lasting effect on Chinese culture ever since.

14. Confucianism is sometimes described as a religion. However, this is problematic for a variety of reasons (not least the problem of providing a usable definition of "religion"). Kung and Ma (2014) provide empirical evidence that Confucianism did legitimate political authority and had an effect in reducing the likelihood of peasant rebellion in Qing China.

15. Brooks goes on to argue that "[t]he Manchu leaders realized that they needed to dominate discourse about the past so as to be able to project certain historical interpretations that would justify Inner Asian rule over the Chinese people" (Brook, 1988, 177–178). The Qianlong emperor, in particular, displayed "a hypersensitivity to ethnic slurs from the subject literati, who soon learned that words, especially their allusive edges, could be fatal. The faintest hint of disrespect toward Manchu domination could bring a writer's neck under the axe" (Kuhn, 2002, 9).

16. For example, Wakeman writes: "The public activities of the literati heroes of the and Fushe movements were looked upon with alarm by the new Qing rulers, who pointed out that the Ming empire had fallen so easily to them because of political factionalism at court and literati bickering in the cities of the South" (Wakeman, 1998, 172). See discussion in Xue and Koyama (2017).

17. See Eistenstadt (2009, xv).

18. The material that follows is based on Xue and Koyama (2017).

19. The extent to which these persecutions resembled the religious persecutions that occurred in Europe is highly debatable. Historians have, however, explicitly made this comparison: China had little in the way of religious persecution, but her literary persecutions amounted at times to inquisitions. The worst persecution came under the Manchus (Han, 1947).

20. See Grim and Finke (2011, 128).

21. Gill, for example, argues, it seems that "the primary factors driving the movement to deregulate religion were immigration, trade, internal migration, and the continued growth of pluralism (due to the difficulties in enforcing conformity), which meant a rise in new constituencies demanding tax relief from general religious assessment" (Gill, 2008, 91).

22. But the New Jersey Constitution of 1776 only guaranteed the civil rights of Protestants and denied public office to non-Protestants (Sehat, 2011, 21).

23. Sehat (2011, 1, 58–59, 65) documents this and numerous other cases.

24. In general "non-Christians were 'tolerated' so long as they did not criticize Christianity, violate moral norms, or expect to be treated equally. Toleration is considerably more liberal than outright persecution, but it does not entirely comport with the usual laudatory narrative of American religious liberty" (Sehat, 2011, 68).

25. This link is conceptual and is most apparent in the relationship between Tertullian – who Versluis holds most responsible for demonizing heretics – and Carl Schmitt. See Versluis (2006, 52–57).

15

Modern States, Liberalism, and Religious Freedom

The twentieth century saw totalitarian states repress freedom on a previously unimaginable scale. Did the same developments that produced the modern state also give rise to totalitarianism? In this chapter we discuss why the rise of more powerful and capable states was a double-edged sword. The existence of a parallel path to totalitarianism is consistent with our argument. It also serves as a reminder of the fragility of liberalism and its dependence on shared prosperity.

Premodern states were weak – they lacked the capacity to raise taxes and to enforce general laws – and illiberal. They governed through identity rules and relied on religion to provide legitimacy. In some cases this led them to tolerate a measure of religious diversity. But this toleration was always conditional. In other times and places, these same factors gave rise to religious persecution. The absence of religious freedom was "built in" to the structure of all premodern states.

The kinds of polities that emerged for the first time in Europe after 1600 changed this. These were modern states that had the ability to both raise large amounts of tax revenues and to legislate behavior.

The shadow of the twentieth century looms large over any discussion of state power. The totalitarian states of the mid-twentieth century not only conducted mass slaughter on an industrial scale, but also presaged the elimination of the possibility of private life and independent thought. Outside North Korea, there are no such states in the world today, but modern technology opens up the possibility of states restricting offensive or risky behaviors by private individuals. There is no doubt that the power of the modern security state poses a threat to liberty. Genuine commitment to freedom of speech and freedom of thought is rare among politicians even in societies that pay lip service to liberal values.

Progressives celebrate the power of the managerial state to improve the lives of ordinary people. They are opposed by classical liberals and conservatives who wish either to preserve a sphere of freedom for individuals or communities, or disagreed with the direction of economic and social policies. This contemporary debate between advocates of state power as a mechanism for social improvement and its opponents, while crucial for understanding twentieth- and twenty-first-century politics in the developed world, may not be the best lens for viewing developments in premodern Europe or in the developing world today. Many of the distinctions we rely on, such as the political connotations of the designations left and right, stem from the French Revolution. And they do not help us understand the political landscape prior to that point.[1] There is little sense in which we can describe Adam Smith, Voltaire, or Spinoza as left or right wing. Political configurations were simply different before the rise of the modern state.

The transformation of European states was associated with economic, social, and religious liberalization. These policies were imposed from above by political elites. Liberal and pro-market reforms came about because ruling elites came to favor these policies and to see them as being in their own best interest (Mokyr and Nye, 2007; Nye, 2007). This was the case both in France and in Britain.[2]

In Britain, governments after 1828 dismantled the fiscal-military state that had been built up after 1689. They repealed laws that made apprenticeships compulsory (in 1814), overturned the ban on trade union organization (in 1824–1825), removed all usury restrictions (in 1833), weakened and then dispensed with the prohibition on exporting machinery (in 1825 and 1844, respectively), and relaxed and then repealed the Navigation Acts (in 1823 and 1849) respectively.[3] The East India Company's monopoly on trade was withdrawn in 1833. The harsh laws used to protect property in eighteenth-century England, reviled as the Bloody Code, were moderated; the slave trade followed by slavery itself were abolished, and something close to religious freedom was established for the first time in British history.

Nineteenth-century British Parliaments cut government spending and reduced the national debt. After 1815 government expenditures were brought under control and public spending was reduced by 25 percent in real terms between 1815 and 1835 (Harling and Mandler, 1993, 56). They also reformed the legal system and created a professional police force, first in London and then across the entire country.[4] Eventually, they came to embrace a policy of more or less free trade (Irwin, 1993; Nye, 2007).[5] All of these reforms took place before Britain became a full democracy in the modern sense of granting universal suffrage. This liberal epoch was made possible by the prior establishment of a strong but limited state.

Elsewhere in Europe similar liberal reforms took place. In Prussia, following the defeats of Jena and Auerstedt, statesmen such as Heinrich von

Stein abolished serfdom, ended guild privileges, and (partially) emancipated the Jews. These reforms laid the foundation for German economic growth after 1850. Following the defeat of Napoleon, the pace of political reform slackened (and in some places went into reverse), but economic liberalization continued. The justification was not liberal ideas (which were distrusted following the French Revolution) but the demands of "sound economy" (see Gray, 1986).[6]

The move toward economic freedom was closely related to the rise of religious freedom. Religious freedom came about as the result of a gradual process of economic and political change which undermined the old system based on conditional toleration and identity rules in western Europe; a shift from reliance on religious legitimation to other sources of political legitimacy.

Economic growth, the Reformation, the Scientific Revolution and Enlightenment, the rise of a bourgeois culture, and other developments in the intellectual sphere were also important factors in these developments. But their importance should not obscure the transformation that occurred at the level of government. These changes did not rest on the actions of any single individual. Nor were these developments the natural consequence of the writings of specific thinkers or advocates of liberal ideas. Our argument is that it was the rise of modern states that led to the collapse of the old equilibrium of conditional toleration and made it possible to envision an alternative liberal model of state action.

Preserving religious freedom and freedom in general requires constraints on state behavior, so it is natural to think of states as the enemy of freedom. But the idea of limiting the state makes sense only in the presence of a state powerful to enforce rules for society at large. Samuel Huntington was correct to observe that "Authority has to exist before it can be limited" (Huntington, 1968, 8). Acemoglu and Robinson likewise distinguish among weak states, despotic leviathans, and shackled leviathans, arguing that it is only in the latter that human freedom can flourish.[7] There was no religious freedom when state power was weak or absent, as was the case in early medieval Europe.

In modern liberal societies, constitutional limits, rule of law, and judicial oversight evolved in tandem with powerful states to prevent state power from being directed against unpopular groups and minorities. A strong civil society evolved that was capable of holding state power in check. Frequently, of course, the constraints imposed on the state were breached or observed in a biased fashion. But this fact should not prevent us from recognizing the extent to which modern liberal states (for all their manifest flaws) differ from their predecessors.[8]

Modern states have frequently been repressive and indeed murderous; we have documented many examples of state violence. But they are not the only source of violence. Some of the worst episodes of mass murder, inspired by either religious or ethnic conflict, have taken place in the absence of functioning states. For example, this was the case with the persecution of Christians in post-invasion Iraq and the killings of the Yazidis by ISIS.

15.1 Exclusionary versus Inclusive Nationalism

Modernity brought about a heightened sense of nationhood – the rise of the imaginary communities discussed in Chapter 13. This nationalism was a unifying and liberal force for much of the nineteenth century. In the twentieth century, however, it became harnessed to an exclusionary ethnonationalism that was autarkic and illiberal.

Ethnonationalism defines membership in the national community along ethnic lines. In contrast with civic nationalism, the national body comprises all those who actively identify and participate as citizens. The French Revolution was based on the liberal principle of civic nationalism. It was this principle that led to religious freedom for Protestants and the emancipation of the Jews. But this liberal movement that dominated much of Europe in the first part of the nineteenth century provoked an immediate backlash, particularly in Germany, where liberalism had been introduced at the point of a French bayonet.

Thinkers like Gottfried von Herder and Johann Gottlieb Fichte promoted a romantic ideal of German nationhood based on a distant, pre-Christian past. This nationalist and romantic response to the liberal Enlightenment entranced many writers and thinkers throughout the nineteenth century. From the start, however, it was premised on the idea of a coherent and unified national identity, a German nation that to many necessarily excluded outsiders such as Jews.[9]

Civic nationalism is fully compatible with liberalism. The duties owed to one's fellow citizens are predominantly negative ones – the promise not to interfere with their private lives, intrude on their property, or infringe on their rights. Fellow citizens are deserving of respect and equality of treatment, but they are not your brothers or sisters, and a liberal society draws a sharp distinction between the moral obligations you may have to friends and family, and the obligations toward strangers that the state can coerce you to fulfill. Ethnonationalist states, by contrast, elide the distinction between private and public loyalties. They emphasize the idea that ties of kinship underly the political unit. Your fellow citizens are your brothers. You owe your nation a debt of blood. While a liberal nation state may indeed attempt to draw on some sources of instinctive loyalty during warfare, the ethnonationalist state tries to cultivate such sentiments in peacetime.

Ethnonationalism lends itself to exclusionary politics because ethnic identities and state borders never perfectly align. To overcome this inevitable disjunction, there arises the need to construct a myth or myths of national origins (i.e., the notion that identities such as German, English, or Han Chinese are rooted in the deep historical past). Nineteenth-century thinkers expended tremendous energy trying to reconstruct these identities, anachronistically tracing back, for instance, a sense of German nationhood to the revolt of Arminius against the Romans in 9 CE. The sources of political legitimacy in premodern Europe had been predominantly religious. But while anyone can become Christian, for the new theorists of nationhood and race, it was increasingly seen as impossible to *become* German.[10]

15.2　Power States

Though the rise of modern states was accompanied by a process of pacification, modern states themselves developed the ability to wage war on a scale hitherto unimaginable. Internal pacification was thus accompanied by greater risk of external destruction in a global war. This danger was evident to some thinkers even prior to the cataclysms of the world wars. Ever since those disasters, liberal thinkers have been aware of the fragility of the liberal democratic order and worried about the possibility of mutual destruction.

Max Weber called the strong states that emerged at the end of the nineteenth century *Machtstaats* or power states. The key point he made was that when such *Machtstaats* seek to either go to war or to eliminate a minority group, they can do so much more effectively than any premodern state could. Perhaps the preeminent theorist of mid-twentieth century *Machtstaats* was Carl Schmitt, the Weimar and Nazi jurist and political theorist. For Schmitt, the essence of the political was the distinction between friend and enemy. Differences between groups generate enmity. This enmity was not to be ameliorated by economic growth, and might even be heightened under conditions of modernity because it was not rooted in material living standards but in identity. The role of the state was to establish who was inside the political community, and hence to be protected, and who was outside the political community, and hence to be treated as an enemy.

Modern antisemitism, the rise of "power states," the Great Depression, and the crisis of liberalism in the wake of World War I produced circumstances that made possible the rise to power of a rabid antisemite in

Europe's most powerful state. The policies of Hitler and the Nazi party then led to the greatest genocide in history, the Holocaust. There is no shortage of high-quality research on the subject so we can hardly provide a comprehensive treatment of the Holocaust here. Nevertheless, in providing an account of how the rise of modern liberal states and the rule of law helped give rise to religious liberty, it is incumbent on us to explain how things went so wrong in the mid-twentieth century.

We do *not* argue that the rise of the modern state made religious freedom inevitable. Rather, there are important complementarities between the rise of modern, high-capacity, states and the adoption of general rules that makes religious freedom more likely. Thus, a powerful state like Nazi Germany that intends to repress a minority like the Jews will do so by reintroducing identity rules and dismantling the rule of law. This, in turn, leads to administrative balkanization and creates opportunities for individuals with power to exploit. From the perspective advanced in this book, it is unsurprising that historians have documented that, far from being the efficient totalitarian state of popular imagination, the Nazi state became increasingly incoherent over time – captured by overlapping interests and fought over by semi-feudal satrapies.

The Nazi Party was an explicitly antisemitic party, one that campaigned in the 1920s on reversing Jewish emancipation. It also fed upon the wave of antisemitism that was unleashed during World War I. Germany's defeat saw the creation of the myth of the stab-in-the-back – the *Dolchstoßlegende* – a particularly potent source of modern scapegoating. The German army was said to have been betrayed by the November Criminals who comprised the liberals and Social Democrat politicians who negotiated the subsequent armistice. But in the antisemitic mythology that emerged, this betrayal was associated with the Jews. The myth of the stab-in-the-back thus became embodied with a wider set of conspiracy theories that held Jews responsible for German misfortune. Whereas medieval communities could scapegoat outsiders like Jews for local calamities such as the Black Death or poor harvests, modern states could create scapegoats on a much larger scale. The Nazi state made the Jews the scapegoat par excellence.

The other great totalitarian state of the mid-twentieth century, the Soviet Union, also repressed religious freedom and persecuted minorities. The Communist Revolution proclaimed freedom of religion and separation of church and state while persecuting religious leaders and priests as members of the old reactionary regime. Among the first victims of the Communist regime were Orthodox Christian priests, who were singled out during the Russian Civil War along with kulaks and "White Guards" for imprisonment in concentration camps. In 1922 this policy of persecution escalated and became more systematic. Churches were stripped of precious materials.

Thousands of priests, monks, and nuns were arrested and killed in 1922 – the church reports estimates of 8,100 killed in that year alone.[11] Prominent religious leaders were put on public trial and many were sentenced to concentration camps.

The early 1930s saw a second campaign against organized religion. Church bells were seized and melted down and churches closed. In the 1930s more than 13,000 priests were persecuted or dekulakized as the economic edifice of the Orthodox Church was systematically dismantled. The Great Terror intensified this policy of persecution. Ninety-five percent of churches in operation in 1936 were closed by 1941. Thousands of priests and clergy were killed or sent to camps. The higher levels of the clergy were more or less eliminated (Werth, 1997).

This campaign against religion eased only with World War II, when Stalin, seeking to depict himself as a traditional Russian leader defending his country from foreign invasion, revived the Orthodox churches. But in Soviet-occupied Eastern Europe after World War II, the Catholic Church was targeted for political repression, and again the Communists killed or imprisoned churchmen. There were major repressions of Muslims and Lutherans in the Soviet Union on the grounds that they had collaborated with the Germans. Moreover, after the formation of the state of Israel, the Soviet Union embraced antisemitism. The Doctors' Plot, for example, saw the revival of the age-old libel of the Jew as poisoner. Thus it is important to recognize the bloody symmetry of both mid-century totalitarian governments.

15.3 The Holocaust

The Holocaust was not an inevitable consequence of Nazi ideology. It was also the result of a confluence of other factors, most notably war. The Holocaust occurred the way it did because of the accidents and chaos of global war. The Nazi's declared aim was to make Germany Jew free (*Judenfrei*). But they did not initially plan on annihilation.

On coming to power the Nazis rapidly reversed Jewish emancipation. Thereafter, Nazi policies toward the Jews evolved gradually. At all times, the Nazis sought to move as strongly against the Jews as was possible given potential domestic or international opposition. Their policy was often stop-start, involving the initiation of anti-Jewish legislation, gauging the reaction, and sometimes stepping back or pausing for a few months before initiating the next round of anti-Jewish policies. This strategy was evident in the boycott of Jewish shops organized in 1933 that initially proved to be unsuccessful, and later, in the passing of the Nuremberg Laws in 1935. The latter were particularly momentous, as they stripped Jews of German citizenship. From then on, the rule of law did not to apply to Jews. The Nazis slowed the pace of antisemitic legislation in 1936 to avoid adverse international reactions during the Berlin Olympic Games. Antisemitic policies were accelerated again in 1938. But the extent to which the regime was dedicated to making life impossible for Jews in Germany became fully evident only after Kristallnacht in November 1938.[12] This was a return to the world of conditional toleration and identity rules, a world in which the rule of law was absent and Jews were subject to arbitrary violence and persecution.

The return to religious repression, and the reversals suffered by liberalism in the mid-twentieth centuries, extracted a cost that is measurable in terms of lost economic and scientific output. The destruction of European Jewry after 1933 had a large negative effect on intellectual activities and science, particularly in Germany – a scientific leader in 1930. More than 1,000 academics were dismissed from their posts between 1933 and 1934 for non-Aryan descent. This amounted to between 13 and 16 percent of all physicists in Germany and 18 percent of all mathematicians (Waldinger, 2012). Many of these scientists were at the top of their relative fields and would go on to win Nobel Prizes; mathematicians who left included David Hilbert, John von Neumann, and Richard von Mises (Waldinger, 2010). The dismissals followed by the emigration of many prominent Jewish scientists had both a direct effect on scientific output and an indirect effect via collaborations and partnerships, worse outcomes for PhD students, and other peer effects. Furthermore, Waldinger (2012) shows that even those scientists who remained in Germany were negatively affected by the dismissal of Jewish scientists.

Another important study is Moser et al. (2014), who examined the impact of the expulsion of Jewish scientists on innovation in chemistry in the United States. They estimated that the arrival of German Jewish émigrés led to a 31 percent increase in innovation after 1933 in the research fields of émigrés.[13] The return of religious intolerance and conditional toleration to Europe hastened the transfer of scientific leadership from Germany and Europe to the United States. The return to identity rules in Nazi Germany serves as yet another piece of evidence of the economic costs of abandoning general rules. It reminds us that the evolution we describe in this book, from identity rules to general rules, need not be permanent.

The antisemitic policies of the 1930s did not inevitably lead to the death camps and the Shoah, however. Extermination was not the goal of Nazi policy during the 1930s. While Nazis killed and terrorized individual Jews, the aim of policy was to create an institutional environment that was designed to impoverish and humiliate Germany's previously prosperous Jewish community. On the one hand, this aimed at making the majority of Jews want to leave Germany. On the other hand, the Nazis endeavored to fleece Jews of their possessions as they attempted to emigrate. Absent the onset of total war in 1939, it is possible that they may have been satisfied with a policy that forced the Jews out of Germany but did not result in mass killings.

However, the other policy aims of the Nazi state – the desire for living space in Eastern Europe – conflicted with the policy to make Germany *Judenfrei*. Nazi military success in 1939–1941 brought far more Jews into the orbit of Nazi power than had ever resided in the German Reich. Having occupied Austria, Czechoslovakia, Poland, the Netherlands, Belgium, France, Yugoslavia, Greece, and then the Soviet Union, and currently at war with Britain, there was nowhere the Nazis could deport the Jewish populations they now had under their control.

In the place of mass deportation, the Nazi leadership considered forcibly relocating the Jews within their empire, a policy that would have led to many, perhaps the majority of them dying from starvation or hardship. But even as they were deliberating, the murderous character of the total war waged by the Germans on the Eastern Front had already led to large-scale massacres of Jews in summer and autumn 1941 in which hundreds of thousands were killed. This policy of ad hoc killings initially aimed at Communists and Jewish males rapidly embraced the mass murder of all Jews, including women and children. They were killed not by the bureaucratic machinery of a modern state, but by small groups of *Einsatzgruppen* and local militias armed with pistols. These mass killings had been taking place for more than six months before the Wannsee Conference confirmed, as official policy, the Final Solution for all Jews in Europe.

The widely accepted image of the Holocaust is of a powerful bureaucratic state using sophisticated modern tools to systematically annihilate its Jewish minority. In one respect, this is correct. The Nazi state was much more powerful than any premodern state and able to kill far more effectively. However, in other respects it is quite misleading.

Timothy Snyder (2015) notes that the "dominant stereotype of Nazi Germany is of an all-powerful state that catalogued, repressed, and then exterminated an entire class of its own citizens" is inappropriate, as the vast majority of the victims of the Holocaust did not die in these circumstances (Snyder, 2015, 337). The main victims of the Holocausts were not German Jews (who had been subject to systematic and escalating state repression during the 1930s) but Jews who lived in territories where states had been destroyed, first by the Soviet Union and then by Nazi Germany.[14] Other recent research contests the emphasis on the "modernity" of the Holocaust. Hayes (2017, 330), for instance, argues that "[f]ar from being modern in either conception or means, the Holocaust was an outbreak of extraordinary primitivism, a fitting product of an ideology that believed that all life is governed by the law of the jungle."

Snyder contrasts the experience of Jews where states were destroyed such as Estonia, where 99 percent of Jews died, with those of Jews in territories with sovereign states recognized by the Nazis such as Denmark, which was able to preserve the lives of most Danish Jews. The pattern of the data supports his thesis: the Holocaust was most complete "[w]here Germans obliterated conventional states, or annihilated Soviet institutions that had just destroyed conventional states." The destruction of state institutions "created the abyss where racism and politics pulled together toward nothingness. In this black hole, Jews were murdered" (Snyder, 2015, 319–320). In these stateless areas nineteen out of twenty Jews died compared to an average of one out of two Jews in those countries occupied or allied to the Nazis that were able to maintain some measure of sovereignty.[15] It is therefore clearly true that the rise of modern states made genocide on an industrial scale possible. But it is also the case that this genocide was most effective in areas where there was little organized political authority.

15.4 Chapter Summary

In this book we have charted the crucial, but often overlooked, part religion played in the development of modern states. The path to modern liberal states required the dismantling of the conditional toleration equilibrium. It was driven by the rise of states that invested in fiscal and legal capacity but also states that were constrained by institutions such as parliaments and by civil society. These changes made *possible* the rise of modern liberal states but they did not make it inevitable.

There is no ineluctable link between high capacity states and a liberal society. This chapter has traced the rise of both the modern liberal states that emerged in nineteenth-century Europe and the modern totalitarian that arose in the twentieth century. Studying the fate of societies governed by Communist and Nazi regimes brings to mind Nietzsche's warning that the state is the coldest of cold monsters.[16] But this does not mean that liberalism can be secured in the absence of a powerful modern state.

The examples reinforce the point that there are many paths to state development. And not all these paths lead to a liberal state. Some societies such as Britain and the United States followed what Tilly (1990) called a capital-intensive path in which economic development and state building complemented each other. Others such as Russia and China followed a coercion-intensive path in which state building preceded economic development. Acemoglu and Robinson (2019) use the metaphor of a narrow corridor to describe the conditions required for the development of states that are both powerful but also constrained. Certainly many scholars have attempted to diagnose why societies like Germany, Japan, and Russia developed autocratic modern states (see Moore, 1966). Regardless of whether that question has a definite answer, it is evident that when ideologues in control of power in modern states are beholden to illiberal ideologies such as ethnonationalism and Marxism unimaginable human suffering results.

Notes

1. See Rothschild (2001).
2. After 1776, Adam Smith's writings came to be part of elite discourse and his influence spread across Europe in the work of translators and through the next generation of political economists – Jean-Baptiste Say, David Ricardo, and Dugald Stewart. Smith's *The Wealth of Nations* was translated into German in the same year that it was published. It was translated into French in 1778, into Danish in 1779, and into Italian in 1790 (Lai, 2000, xvii). For the rise of elite political opinion in favor of freer trade see Irwin (1996). Also see the discussion in Rothschild (2001).
3. See Beales (1928).
4. For details of the creation of the modern police force in this period see Koyama (2014).
5. Irwin (1989) provides a discussion of the relative importance of ideas verses economic interests in determining this decision. Peel was aware of the intellectual case for free trade his entire career. His decision to move toward free grain in grain was that of a practical policymaker who came to see agricultural protection as unsustainable rather than either an ideological shift or simply a reflection of economic interests.
6. Gray observes that in general the "Stein ministry led Prussia in the direction of free markets and individual freedom of action" (Gray, 1986, 139).
7. See Acemoglu and Robinson (2017, 2018).
8. None of this is to say the future preservation or extension of human freedoms requires the enlargement of the state. In fact, powerful arguments suggest that the future of human freedom requires us to constrain the state's ability to, for example, collect information on private individuals. But this argument rests on an assessment of the technological and social possibilities of the future and not the past. Similarly, in the economic realm it seems likely that we still require the heavy hand of the state to provide law and order and defense, though we can plausibly envision a future in which many current state services are provided privately (Stringham, 2015). It would be ahistorical, however, to read this analysis back to the premodern period.
9. See Rose (1990) and the discussion in Chapter 10.
10. Ethnonationalism drew on many of tensions that had previously animated religious violence – the desire to exclude outsiders and to elevate membership of an in-group. For a superb analysis see Baron (1947).
11. See Werth (1997, 73 and 16).
12. See Friedländer (1997) and Johnson (1999).
13. Due to concerns that the scientists who went to the United States may have been negatively selected due to higher profile scientists choosing to migrate to Britain or due to antisemitism in the United States, Moser et al. (2014) use the pre-1933

fields of dismissed chemists as an instrument for the fields of émigrés to the United States. These instrumental variable estimates suggest that a 71 percent increase in patenting.

14. The view that the Jews were made particularly vulnerable by the dissolution of nation-states is not novel to Snyder. It was advanced by both Hannah Arendt (1951) and Ellis Rivkin (1971). The latter notes that "The Jews were trapped in a very special kind of way by the disintegration of nation-state capacity" as it was the nation-state that had given them a political identity, and stripped of this, they had only their racial or economic identity, which left them particularly exposed to either Nazi or Communist persecution (Rivkin, 1971, 212).

15. Snyder shows that this pattern cannot be easily explained by resorting to other factors such as prewar levels of antisemitism, which was evident in countries like Poland, Romania, and France, but not evident in either Lithuania or Estonia, whose Jewish populations were annihilated.

16. "State is the name of the coldest of all cold monsters. Coldly it lies; and this lie slips from its mouth: 'I, the state, am the people.' " (Nietzsche, 1999, 1911, 30).

16

Conclusions

The best things on religious liberty were said in the sixteenth century but not practiced until the nineteenth.

Roland H. Bainton (1951, 253)

Religious beliefs and practices emerged as a consequence of the deep-seated desire for meaning that characterizes humanity. For anthropologists, the desire to seek meaning in the world distinguishes *Homo sapiens* from earlier hominids. The quest for meaning led to the creation of myths and cultural beliefs and that, in turn, enabled human communities to band together into groups larger than extended kinship networks.

As religion is coeval with large-scale society, it is unsurprising that the relationship between religion and political authority that arose in early agricultural societies was close. Religion was not a separate sphere from politics. The two were intricately related in every aspect of life as religion was a source of group identity and shared social meaning.

Early human societies existed on the edge of subsistence. They could be threatened by natural disasters, climate change, or invasion by a neighboring group. Given the dangers they faced, and given their beliefs, it is natural that they enforced religious worship because impiety could endanger the entire community. There was no notion of religious freedom.

Over time, agrarian civilizations became more complex. Empires rose and fell. As more sophisticated forms of governance arose, the close relationship between religion and politics strengthened. The most successful religions encouraged pro-social behavior. During the Axial Age (c. 700–200 BCE), Judaism, Buddhism, and later, Christianity developed, each responding to the concerns of ordinary people in highly unequal agrarian societies. These religions were initially radical and destabilizing, but they were soon accommodated into the preexisting political equilibrium, an equilibrium based on a partnership between religion and the state.[1]

293

This book has examined how this equilibrium first broke down in Western Europe. It has studied the transformation from a world where religion and politics were inseparable to a world where both religious and broader social and intellectual freedoms became both worthy of respect and deserving of protection. Our argument does not imply that modern liberal societies have attained full religious liberty. Today, modern liberal states are committed to the ideal of religious freedom, but this commitment is often observed in the breach. Tensions and unresolved problems remain, and new issues will always arise.

To take one example, liberal societies struggle to deal with extremist religious organizations such as radical Islamist groups. These organizations may be committed to the use of political violence, discriminate against women, or inculcate undemocratic and illiberal values. In certain respects, tensions between liberal democracies today and Islamist groups resemble the struggles of the past between the state and dissenting religious groups such as Catholics and Mormons. But they also resemble the challenge liberal democracies faced in the early and mid-twentieth century from Fascists and Communists committed to overthrowing democracy.

Another problem stems from our understanding of general rules and equal treatment. Classical liberalism holds that private individuals and firms have a fundamental right to freedom of association even when some individuals choose to exercise that right in ways that are expressive of non-liberal values, as for instance when a baker refuses to decorate a cake with a message endorsing homosexual marriage. Modern progressives argue that a state's commitment to principles such as equality of treatment can override the right of freedom of association. Conservative and classical liberals often disagree.

We do not suggest easy answers to the problems of tolerating the intolerant or of reconciling freedom with equality.[2] But by providing an historical account of how societies have wrestled with the problems posed by religious diversity, we gain new insights into the dilemmas facing liberal states today.

16.1 A Summary of Our Argument

The link between religion and political authority is ancient. Throughout history, religious leaders have denounced the corrupting influence of politics on religion; but all successful religions have invariably become tangled up in worldly affairs and allowed themselves to become the foundations for power in this world rather than in the next. They have become the basis for political theologies that legitimated existing power structures.

It is this connection between religion and politics rather than the characteristics of specific religions that explains the pervasiveness of religious restrictions and persecution through history. The principle of religious freedom was more or less absent throughout much of history, even in societies that did not regularly persecute individuals for religious reasons. The religious toleration that did exist in past societies was based on conditional toleration, not genuine religious freedom.

Religious dissent was often tolerated in premodern societies, but religious differences were accepted only so long as they did not undermine the political authority of those who wielded power.

We have charted the transition from conditional toleration to religious freedom. In particular, we have examined the mechanisms that led Western Europe from one social-political equilibrium to another quite different one, an equilibrium characterized by open liberal societies that embrace general rules.

Chapter 1 established the fundamental dichotomy between conditional toleration and religious liberty. We distinguished between two ways of organizing society. The first is the form of social organization that emerged with the first settled agrarian societies, and which remained ubiquitous in all parts of the world until a few centuries ago – what Karl Popper (1945) called the closed society, and what North, Wallis, and Weingast (2009) call the natural state – a social order that was reliant on identity rules. Identity rules treat individuals differently based on their social identity. The second way of organizing society is using general rules. General rules treat all members of society equally.

Identity rules were ubiquitous throughout the world because they enabled rulers to grant or sell special privileges to particular social groups. The consequent rents that were generated helped maintain order. Identity rules thus were "cheap" ways to sustain a social order. They did impose a cost, however, both in terms of personal liberty and economic development.

In contrast, general rules are "expensive." They require investments in institutions capable of enforcing the law equally on all members of society. This may involve courts, a judiciary, and a police force. But general rules are crucial for maintaining sustained economic growth because they allow for disruption, entry, and innovation. The dismantling of the old identity rule equilibrium and its replacement with a system of general rules is a critical ingredient in modern economic growth.

Chapter 2 provided a framework for understanding the relationship between church and state. The influential role of religion in society gave religious authorities social and political influence. They used this influence to partner with secular authorities, granting them political legitimacy. In return, stronger states enforced religious conformity. States too weak to enforce conformity "bought" support in other ways.

Chapter 3 focused on the institutions that underlay conditional toleration. We examined how political and economic incentives shaped attitudes toward religious dissent. In line with the logic laid out in Chapter 2, the rise of more coherent political organizations in medieval Europe was accompanied by persecution. Stronger states enforced religious conformity in exchange for legitimacy. The result was the other side of conditional toleration: persecution, as experienced by Cathars, Lollards, and other "heretical" groups.

Chapter 4 focused on the socioeconomic conditions governing Jewish settlement in medieval Europe. This conditional toleration equilibrium was based on the economic rents generated by Jewish moneylending. As such, it was fragile in the extreme. It broke down during times of economic distress. Chapter 5 studied the relationship between extreme weather and Jewish persecution. Chapter 6 showed that Jews were especially vulnerable where political authority was contested.

The medieval Church defeated countless heresies. But it was unable to defeat the Reformation. Chapter 7 studied the impact of the Reformation. We view the Reformation as a shock to religious preferences that disrupted rulers claims to political legitimacy.

This shock led to short-lived, but intense, religious persecution (Chapter 7).[3] The degree of religious persecution varied according to the capacity and coherence of states. Persecutions were intense in England, France, and the Low Countries. In contrast, the attempts of the Polish-Lithuanian Commonwealth to enforce religious conformity were ineffectual. As a consequence, the impact of the Reformation was heterogenous. The greatest disruption was where state building had gone furthest.

Where state capacity was high and persecutions most intense, new institutions emerged. These new institutions were incompatible with the conditional toleration equilibrium. The rulers of England, France, and the Netherlands after 1600 depended less on religion. Moreover, with economic development, the cost of persecuting economically valuable minorities became apparent.

There was no inevitability to the rise of modern liberal state. Chapter 8 considers a case where a polity chose another way to deal with religious heterogeneity. In the Iberian Peninsula, the Inquisition successfully achieved religious conformity. Partly as a result, the economic and political power of Spain declined after 1600.

The Reformation led to the collapse of the medieval conditional toleration equilibrium in much of Europe. Attempts to repair it during the seventeenth century failed. What arose in its place were states that relied less on religion for legitimation, but rather invested in fiscal and administrative capacity and replaced identity rules with general rules.

Chapter 9 followed developments in France and England after 1600. Rulers in both countries attempted to restore the conditional toleration equilibrium, in France on the basis of Catholicism and in England on the basis of Anglicanism. But they were of limited success in what were now much more fragmented religious economies. Louis XIV attempted to solve this problem by expelling the Huguenots. But this failed to make France fully Catholic and came at considerable economic cost. England also persecuted nonconforming Protestants in the seventeenth century before abandoning its attempts to achieve religious conformity after 1689. But eighteenth-century Britain moved toward a new equilibrium with a diminished political role for religion.

Chapter 10 tracked the decline in antisemitic violence after 1600. This decline was not the direct result of the Reformation or Enlightenment. Rather, greater state capacity both freed European states from dependence on Jewish moneylending and meant that they did not have to respond to antisemitic agitation. We then examined the factors that gave rise to Jewish emancipation after 1780. In France, Enlightenment notions of the equality of man played a crucial role in lifting discriminatory barriers. But elsewhere pragmatic concerns with tax revenue and the economy were more important.

Chapter 11 studied the relationship between state capacity and religious violence from another perspective: that of witch trials. The Europe-wide panic about witches offered a case study of the link between fiscal capacity and rule of law. The witch trials reflected a broader disruption in the religious-political equilibrium of early modern Europe caused by the Reformation. Decentralized legal systems permitted torture to exact confessions and hence generated convictions in response to popular fears about witches. Self-perpetuating witch crazes emerged, resulting in the trials of hundreds, or on occasion, thousands of individuals in a single locality. We track how this changed in seventeenth-century France. The establishment of a tax state was accompanied by investment in legal capacity and the imposition of stricter evidentiary standards. As a result, courts became less receptive to local fear of witches.

What were the economic consequences of greater religious freedom? Chapter 12 showed that cities that were tolerant of Jews grew faster than those that excluded Jews. This effect was larger after 1600, and we argue that it was driven by the complementarities between Jewish religious minorities and the expansion of markets.

As religious legitimacy waned in importance, what took its place? Chapter 13 examined nationalism as an alternative source of political legitimacy. Civic (but not ethnic) nationalism is consistent with government based on general rules. We considered how the rise of civic nationalism helped European states replace identity rules with general rules.

While our focus has been on Europe, our framework applies elsewhere. Chapter 14 studied the Middle East, East Asia, and the United States. The Middle East and East Asia had very different religious traditions and histories. In the Middle East, religion was crucial for political legitimacy. Conditional toleration of Christians and Jews was consistent with the material incentives facing Muslim rulers. But this conditional toleration was underpinned by identity rules. Over time reliance on identity rules impeded economic growth. Failure to invest in state capacity resulted in the conditional toleration equilibrium persisting until modern times.

In East Asia the charismatic monotheistic religions of the Fertile Crescent never became majority religions. State authority was also more secure. As a result, religion never acquired the same power to legitimate political authority that characterized Europe or the Middle East.

The dark side of the modern state is illustrated by Nazi Germany and the Soviet Union. Both Nazi Germany and the Soviet Union repressed religion. They saw religious authorities as rival sources of political authority and targeted specific minorities for destruction. Chapter 15 examined why these totalitarian states repressed religion.

The remainder of this chapter takes a thematic approach. We consider how our argument stands in relationship to other work by historians and social scientists.

16.2 Alternative and Complementary Hypotheses

16.2.1 Economic Development and Doux Commerce

The *doux commerce* thesis developed by Enlightenment thinkers such as Montesquieu (1748, 1989) and elaborated by modern scholars like Albert Hirschman (1977) holds that the rise of markets led to religious toleration.[4]

Commerce has the power to soften both laws and social mores. Commerce leads to liberalism and undermines despotism. As Thomas Pangle puts it: "Commerce impresses upon men and women the fact that they share these needs with the inhabitants of other nations, regardless of their conflicting beliefs and customs" (Pangle, 2010, 100).

Doux commerce operates through several channels. The first channel suggests that self-interest alone can generate tolerance among merchants.[5] Individuals who stand to gain from trade with those of a different religion will rarely favor religious persecution. Certainly the rise of commerce in the early modern period may have been one factor weakening religious persecution. This parallels Gary Becker's explanation (1971) of how the profit motive erodes discrimination. Individuals with a preference for discrimination will end up paying higher wages than their color-blind rivals and in the long run, if the market is competitive, they will be weeded out.

Opposition to persecution based purely on self-interest is unlikely to generate support for religious liberty per se. It is likely to be easily overawed – a merchant *qua merchant* is unlikely to stand-up for religious liberty if doing so comes at a cost to him.

A second mechanism linking trade with greater religious toleration is via preferences. Adam Smith developed a theory of human sociability based on sympathy in *The Theory of Moral Sentiments*. He drew on this theory in *The Wealth of Nations* in arguing that the proclivity to trade was a uniquely human trait. Exchanging goods requires understanding the point of view of another individual. Merchants cultivate that part of their personality that enables them to understand individuals from different backgrounds. Hence, trade between individuals with different religious backgrounds reduces mutual antipathy.

A third mechanism proposes that trade and economic growth can help individuals generate new social identities. This proliferation of different lifestyles can make religious identity less salient. This offers another channel through which trade might diminish religious persecution.[6]

Saumitra Jha argues that economic complementarities are crucial for the peaceful coexistence between different groups (Jha, 2013; Diaz-Cayeros and Jha, 2017; Jha, 2018). He contends that a minority group is more likely to enjoy toleration if it provides nonreplicable and nonexpropriable economic services. In contrast, minorities who either directly compete with the majority group or provide easily substitutable economic services are more likely to be expropriated.[7] To substantiate this argument, Jha examined cities in southern India where Muslim merchants played a role in trade in the medieval period. He then looked at how this historical legacy of economic interaction affected intolerance (as measured by religious violence) between 1950 and 1995. He found that religious toleration is indeed more prevalent in cities where the minority group provided nonreplicable and nonexpropriable economic services.[8] Trade does lead to greater religious toleration when the benefits of trade accrue to the majority as well as to the minority community.

However, this argument also means that merchants may be in favor of repression and persecution if they see it as profitable. Jews were excluded from Florence until the 1430s because Christian bankers saw them as competitors (as substitutes).[9] While in early modern Hamburg, the richest Hanseatic merchants who comprised the city's senate and were involved in international trade were favorable to Jewish settlement, other merchants such as the goldsmiths frequently agitated for their expulsion.[10]

16.2.2 Changing Values

We focus on how institutional developments led to the rise of religious freedom. But this does not mean that a cultural shift did not occur. The details of this cultural transition vary, and historians disagree about its timing. In general, however, there is no denying that it took place. To tolerate religious differences in medieval Europe was to place the possibility of salvation at risk. This was no longer the case by the nineteenth century. Religion receded into the private sphere, and religious diversity was no longer seen as posing an existential threat to a community. How did this change take place?

One explanation is the secularization thesis. This claims that economic development diminishes the importance of religion in peoples' lives (Chadwick, 1975). Taken crudely, the secularization thesis is an alternative hypothesis, because it argues that a change in beliefs about religion led to subsequent institutional change. In our account the first mover was not religious beliefs but institutions.

The original version of the secularization thesis has been criticized and does not describe many parts of the world.[11] Religious identity remains strong in many countries. In response, scholars of religion have reformulated the idea of secularization to have several components. It can refer to the decline in religious beliefs and practices. It also refers to the retreat of religion from the political sphere – i.e., the privatization of religion. Finally, it can mean the rise of a secular sphere free from religion (Casanova, 1994).

We argue that the separation of religion from politics resulted from institutional change. More capable states needed religious legitimation less. Their state-building agenda was often in conflict with religious authorities having an active political role. Moreover, economic growth often encouraged more "private forms of religions" – that is, religions more conducive to participation in a modern market society (such as Reform Judaism, Episcopalianism, and Methodism). However, these developments also produced a backlash. Fundamentalist movements that explicitly rejected modernity arose.[12]

Another claim is that there was a shift from valuing souls to valuing lives (Pinker, 2011, 143–144). The former led to the view that death was simply a passage to the afterlife and thus justified killing individuals in order to save their external souls. This shift was linked with the Enlightenment and to secularization. Pinker finds it present in Erasmus and in Spinoza. But, beyond identifying it, he does not provide an explanation for this specific shift in values. Though he provides evidence for a general tendency toward pacification and moral improvement, Pinker does not disentangle changing values from institutional change.

We approach this question as economists. The economic approach takes individual values, tastes, and preferences as given, and sees how choices are affected by changes in the implicit prices, or constraints, that individuals face.[13]

This approach may seem reductionist. By holding preferences constant, it denies the richness of the historical experience. There is no doubt that preferences do change. The challenge is that we lack a barometer of these changes. We don't know if people became more adverse to heresy in the eleventh century or more comfortable with religious heterogeneity in the eighteenth century. This reveals the problem with placing explanatory weight on changing values: it is nearly impossible to reliably measure such changes. For every piece of evidence that supports claims of a radical change in cultural values, it is possible to find evidence of persistent hostility to different religions.

None of this refutes the argument that changes in values were important drivers of increased religious freedom. Instead, it foregrounds several issues that such a theory needs to account for.

First, if there was a change in cultural attitudes, why did it take hold? An argument that relies on exogenous cultural change as a *deus ex machine* does not generate additional insights into how a liberal social order came about. A useful theory has to shed light on the conditions which made possible such a change in cultural values.

Second, what determines the pace of cultural change? At present, social scientists do not have a theory of why cultural change is extremely rapid in some contexts and very slow in others. Recent research suggests that at least some cultural values are both deep rooted and persistent. Voigtländer and Voth (2012) show that towns in Germany that persecuted Jews during the Black Death of the fourteenth century were more likely to have anti-semitic riots, vote for the Nazi Party, and denounce or deport Jews in the 1920s and 1930s than were those towns that did not persecute their Jewish communities during the Black Death.[14] Grosjean (2014) found that high homicide rates in the US South are partly the result of a culture of honor and violence transmitted from Scots-Irish herders who emigrated there in the seventeenth and eighteenth centuries. Xue (2017) shows that the rise of high-value opportunities for women in premodern China has left a persistent legacy of more favorable gender attitudes and higher female labor force participation today.[15]

Thus sometimes cultural values are resistant to change. But changes in values may also be difficult to detect because individuals have an incentive to misrepresent their opinions (Kuran, 1995). For this reason, when social norms shift it can often appear to be very rapid.[16] At present we do not know whether attitudes toward religious freedom or toleration in early modern Europe changed quickly or slowly or how the pace of this change varied across regions and over time. Future research, perhaps drawing on tools from machine learning, may give us a better understanding of the pace and nature of changing attitudes to religious freedom in early modern Europe.

We do not rule out changing culture and values as drivers of the origins of religious and political liberalism. Rather, accounts of changes in ideas and values *complement* our argument. One point of complementarity is that institutions interacted with, and helped to shape, cultural attitudes. Reliance on identity rules meant that it was otherwise disadvantaged minorities who engaged most intensely with the market. Many individuals therefore disdained moneylending and trade all the more because of its association with Jews for instance. Evidence for this is provided by Grosfled, Rodnyansky, and Zhuravskaya (2013), who find that the treatment of Jews in Eastern Europe has generated a persistent anti-market culture. To show that this relation is causal they exploit the boundary of the Pale of Settlement – where Jews were confined in Tzarist Russia. Current inhabitants of the Pale are less likely to vote for market liberal parties, less supportive of democracy, and less likely to be engaged in entrepreneurship, but have higher levels of trust. To explain these findings, they suggest that where Jews and non-Jews lived side-by-side in the Pale, non-Jews developed bonding trust based on hostility to the market dominant Jewish minority. The institutions governing Jewish settlement not only confined Jews to specific occupations but also produced a culture among non-Jews that was characterized by hostility toward others and antipathy toward markets and trade. Individuals within the Pale today show greater support for communism and more hostility to the market compared to individuals in otherwise identical areas just outside of it.

16.2.3 New Ideas

Intellectuals are naturally attracted to the claim that ideas are the driving force of history. The argument that the idea of religious liberty eventually won over and persuaded elites is implicit in many accounts (Bainton, 1951; Zagorin, 2003). Numerous historians have documented the rise of the idea of religious liberty in Western Europe in the wake of the Reformation.[17] While the idea of religious toleration was neither uniquely European nor new to the post-Reformation period, these authors argue that the experience of the Reformation gave rise to a particularly rich debate out of which the concept of religious freedom emerged.

Social and cultural historians have recognized that the emphasis on the power of ideas in the traditional literature needs to be tempered and complemented by an appreciation of the context in which ideas develop and are understood. Our argument is in keeping with historians such as Kaplan (2007) and Christman (2015), who argue that the conventional accounts of the rise of toleration overstate the extent to which elites and rulers were influenced by advocates of toleration.

Ideas certainly matter. The question is *when* do ideas matter. Liberal ideas were necessary, but not sufficient for the rise of religious freedom. In the absence of liberal ideas, higher capacity states would likely have had less need to impose religious homogeneity on heterogeneous populations or rely on religion for political legitimacy. However, without the development of liberal ideas, such states would have been less likely to develop a commitment to religious liberalism in the way that states in nineteenth-century Europe did.

Contrary to an older historical literature that associated religious toleration with the emergence of Protestantism, the Reformation itself did not generate a widespread or influential intellectual movement for greater religious toleration. Diarmaid MacCulloch points out that only one sixteenth century English writer considered the possibility of religious toleration – Thomas More in his *Utopia* – yet "Utopia was precisely that – nowhere – and More's persecuting practice while he held political power made it clear that he thought that the best place for religious freedom was nowhere" (MacCulloch, 2016, 119).

As discussed in Chapter 7, Michael Servetus was executed for heresy in Geneva at the behest of Calvin. In protest (though without naming Servetus) Sebastian Castellio wrote *Concerning Heretics and Whether They Should Be Persecuted, and How They Should Be Treated*. In *Concerning Heretics*, Castellio argued that religion can never justify killing and that Servetus's execution was essentially murder. Instead, he proposed a separation of religion from politics. Castellio's attacks on Calvin attracted considerable attention in the Protestant world, but the larger message he sought to convey was not absorbed. No other major thinker followed him in advocating for religious freedom in the sixteenth century.[18] Nor were his writings politically influential. Every European ruler during this period remained ideologically committed to religious uniformity (even though practical reasons meant that they had to tolerate religious heterodoxy).

Even in the seventeenth century, advocates of religious freedom remained on the fringes of respectable political discourse. This was true for Spinoza and Bayle at the end of the seventeenth century.[19] Into the eighteenth century authors did not freely and publicly advocate for religious freedom. They wrote anonymously or under pseudonyms.[20] And they wrote esoterically, often disguising the more subversive implications of their thought.[21] Religious skeptics such as Fra Paolo Sarpi disguised their disbelief with conventional pieties and did not openly call for religious freedom.[22] Locke, who is celebrated as an advocate of religious toleration, argued publicly that religious toleration could be withdrawn from Catholics and atheists. It is debated whether this was a sincere reflection of his beliefs or merely a position he adopted in order to stay on the right side of religious and secular authorities. Regardless, the fact that he took this position shows how far a belief in unconditional religious freedom was from mainstream political debate at the end of the seventeenth century.

After 1700, advocates for toleration like Voltaire became influential as advisors to absolutist rulers such as Frederick the Great of Prussia. What changed was not the ideas themselves – Voltaire wrote with more wit and humor than Castellio but his arguments were not fundamentally different or more convincing – but the political and economic context. The political equilibrium was very different in England after 1689 and in Prussia in the 1740s than it had been in sixteenth-century Geneva.

We have sought to account for this change in political equilibria. Changing beliefs mattered but so did changing material and political conditions. Neither a change in the scale and scope of political organizations – state capacity, for short – nor a change in ideology or values on their own were sufficient to generate the transition to liberal modernity. The main contribution of this book is outlining how and why this change in political equilibria took place.

This is not to claim that ideas and intellectual history are irrelevant. Rather, we argue that the conventional emphasis on the ideas of thinkers such as Locke and Voltaire is incomplete. Their discourse thus has to be situated in the context of political debates of their time and in the incentives that rulers and policymakers faced.[23] Our argument complements those who claim ideas about toleration were important because we show how the incentives faced by political elites changed in such a way so as to make them more receptive to intellectual arguments for toleration.

16.3 Implications of Our Argument for Today

What does our argument imply about the prospects for liberalism and religious freedom today?

Religious freedom is enshrined in the laws and constitutions of most developed countries. Of course, limitations on this freedom still exist – it is harder to establish a mosque than a church in many parts of the United States, for example. There is an established state church in the United

Kingdom and in France; it is forbidden for Muslim women to cover their head with the hijab.[24] Despite these restrictions, however, it is still accurate to describe the Western world as religiously liberal.

The comparative religious freedom enjoyed in today's developed countries is the product of a long historical process that began in Western Europe in the sixteenth century. In other parts of the world it is a recent and fragile transplant. Religious freedom is contested in the Middle East, but also to a lesser extent in Africa, Russia, China, and Southeast Asia. Our argument suggests that we should find genuine religious freedom and the coexistence of many different religious groups in modern states that have well developed fiscal and legal capacity and market economies. Weak states, on the other hand, will be characterized either by religious homogeneity or if they do have a variety of religions, all religions bar the dominant one, will at best experience conditional toleration.

Contemporary evidence supports our argument. Figure 16.1 shows the extent of religious regulation across countries between 1990 and 2008.[25] Regulation of religion includes whether or not there are restrictions on religious observance, bans on religious clothing, limits on conversation or proselytizing targeted against specific minorities, limits on abortion and on the registration of religions, or the existence of religious classes in public schools. Limits on religious freedom are greatest in the Middle East, Russia, South America, and China. These societies do not possess developed liberal states; they range from illiberal autocracies to weak states that struggle to rule effectively.

Religious liberty emerged historically in places with relatively strong states as a response to the challenges of governing using identity rules when confronted with a diverse citizenry. While it is extremely difficult to measure fiscal and legal capacity across every country in the world, we can proxy for state capacity using the amount of tax revenues collected.[26] We find a strong negative correlation between government regulation of religion and state capacity (Figure 16.2).[27]

The simple averages in Figure 16.2 do not establish a causal relationship. There may be a third factor, related to both state capacity and government regulation of religion, driving the relationship. For example, perhaps countries with a more educated population demand more tolerance and are also willing to pay more in taxes for public goods (such as education).

Is there evidence for our theoretical mechanisms driving the relationship between regulation of religion and state capacity? Figures 16.3 and 16.4 show the relationship between religious fractionalization – the probability that any two randomly chosen individuals in a country are from a different religion – and government regulation of religion, after controlling for the influences of income, literacy rates, and rule of law.[28] Figures 16.3 and

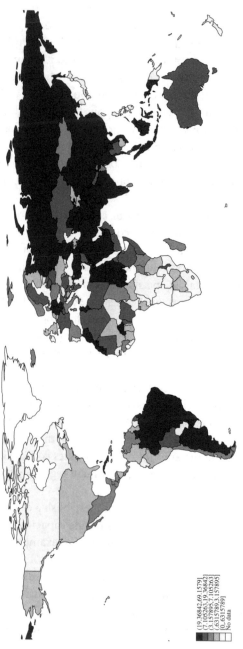

[19.36842,69.1579]
[7.105263,19.36842]
[3.157895,7.105263]
[.6315789,3.157895]
[0,.6315789]
No data

Figure 16.1 Religious regulation, 1990–2008. Higher scores indicate higher levels of regulation. Data: Akbaba and Fox (2011).

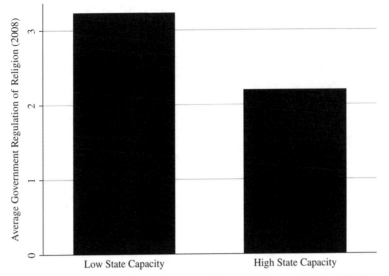

Figure 16.2 Religious regulation, 1990–2008 and state fiscal capacity. Data: Akbaba and Fox (2011).

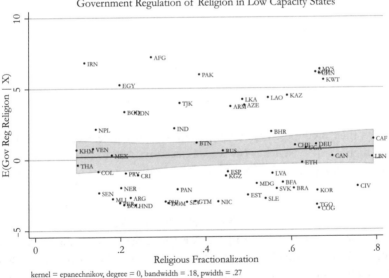

Figure 16.3 Religious fractionalization and government regulation of religion in low-capacity states.

16.4 suggest that in low-capacity countries there is no relationship between religious fractionalization and government regulation of religion. But in countries with high state capacity, as religious fractionalization increases, the government is less likely to regulate religion. Governments with low

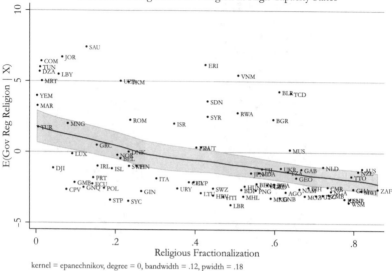

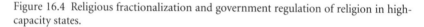

Figure 16.4 Religious fractionalization and government regulation of religion in high-capacity states.

capacity can use identity rules to regulate religion in all sorts of different ways and not feel pressure to adopt more general rules. By contrast, in the high-capacity states, it becomes costly to impose regulations on religion if you have a highly heterogeneous population. As such, it is the countries in the lower right-hand corner of Figure 16.4 where religious liberty is greatest.

On their own these data do not establish that the development of modern high-capacity states is (or was) a necessary step to achieving religious liberty. Perhaps people from minority religious groups migrate to states with high degrees of religious liberty, rather than the causality running the other direction. But this is why we have investigated how the history of state centralization and religious liberty actually unfolded in Western Europe.

In the short term, the prospects for minorities in weak states are troubling. To see why, it is useful to return to the distinction we have made between intolerance toward minorities and their persecution. In weak states, such as Iraq or Nigeria today, it is possible for multiple religions to coexist, as they have for many years, without persecutions occurring on a constant basis. These groups simply live in different areas, and often under different laws. However, in such a situation there is no religious freedom. Separation ensures a lack of persecution, but it also inhibits intergroup trade, political participation, and the free exchange of ideas. In such societies, long periods of peaceful coexistence can suddenly break down and result in intergroup violence and ethnic cleansing, as has happened in much of the Middle East in recent years. This separation is possible within weak states, but by their nature, high-capacity states are forced to confront religious heterogeneity head on rather than letting groups exist in separate legal and fiscal spheres. Thus, in the absence of investments in state capacity, one lesson from the European experience is that institutions supporting religious freedom will either fail to emerge, or be unstable when they do, in the developing world.

If a developing country is able to build capacity, the implications of our argument are more optimistic. While the state is a potential source of oppression and persecution, our argument suggests that a state strong enough to enforce general rules has historically been a precondition for the emergence of a liberal society – a society in which individuals are free to pursue their private interests. The rise of such a state is by no means sufficient: intellectual developments and the rise of commercial society are also vital. But as our argument has shown, ideas alone are not enough and the key to the rise of liberal society has been change at the level of political institutions.

Notes

1. See Altran (2002) and Bellah (2011). Also see Iyigun (2015) for a recent analysis of the rise of monotheism.

2. For more detailed and nuanced discussions of the problems raised by this issues see Kukathas (2003) and Levy (2015).

3. This period was also brief. It looms large in the historical memory because of the martyrologies of John Foxe and others, and because in the popular imagination the religious killings of the mid-sixteenth century merge with the horrors of the Thirty Years' War of the seventeenth century under the broad label of religious wars.

4. In modern scholarship it is closely linked to the theory of liberal peace, which we do not discuss here (see Oneal and Russett, 1999). The term *doux commerce* does not appear in Montesquieu's writings, a point made to us by Hank Clark. See Terjanian (2013).

5. Adam Smith argued that "Society may subsist among different men, as among different merchants, from a sense of its utility, without any mutual love or affection; and though no man in it should owe any obligation, or be bound in gratitude to any other, it may still be upheld by a mercenary exchange of good offices according to an agreed valuation" (Smith, 1759, Chapter III) is no doubt, in part, an allusion to Pierre Bayle's claim that society could exist among atheists – something other advocates of religious toleration in the late seventeenth century like John Locke denied.

6. This emphasis on identity is relatively novel in economics but it has been explored by Akerlof and Kranton (2000) and more recently by Carvalho, Koyama, and Sacks (2017) and Carvalho and Koyama (2018).

7. Jha's argument implies that financial instruments can play a key role in generating peace between conflicting ethnic and religious groups. Specifically, when the

ethnic identity is correlated with economic endowments the probability of peaceful interactions between different groups depends on whether these endowments are complements or substitutes. Financial instruments can mediate conflict because they allow individuals to effectively trade endowments and turn potentially conflictual relationships into mutually beneficial ones. Jha and Shayo (2017) found that by allocating Jewish voters in Israel financial assets, they were able to shift individuals toward voting for parties that favored restarting the peace process with the Palestinian authorities.

8. Jedwab, Johnson, and Koyama (2017) found a similar result in their study of the Black Death and Jewish persecution. Cities where there were substitutes for Jewish moneylending were more likely to persecute Jews than cities without such alternatives.

9. Similarly Grosfeld, Sakalli, and Zhuravskaya (2017) found that pogroms in nineteenth-century Russia were more severe in localities where Jews were concentrated among creditors.

10. The "goldsmiths claimed that the 'unholy intrigues, usury, violations, evils schemings and caballing' of the Jews would damage any professional group of the city, such as retailers and craftsmen" (Weber, 2004, 86). For details on Jewish settlement in Florence see Poliakov (1977, 1965), who interprets their eventual admission in 1437 as a means by which the Medici sought to ruin rival banking families while benefiting the poor, who would have greater access to credit.

11. See Norris and Inglehart (2004) and Franck and Iannaccone (2014). It particular, advocates of the secularization thesis overestimated religiosity in the past and this led them to overestimate the extent of the decline in religiosity observed in the twentieth century. In America in 1776, on the eve of Revolution, only 17 percent of the population belonged to a church (Finke and Stark, 2005, 23).

12. This is the subject of a vast recent literature (Armstrong, 2000). For economically informed accounts of this phenomenon see Berman (2000), Iannaccone and Berman (2006), Berman (2009), Binzel and Carvalho (2017), Carvalho and Koyama (2016), and Carvalho et al. (2017).

13. This is the method of constrained maximization employed in all economics textbooks to study the basic consumption problem facing an individual choosing between different goods subject to a budget constraint. And following the lead of Gary Becker, economists have successfully employed this framework to study a range of areas from demography and the economics of the family to the study of crime and the economics of religion. The canonical statement of this approach is Stigler and Becker (1977).

14. D'Acunto, Prokopczuk, and Weber (2018) explore the financial legacy of Jewish persecutions in Germany. They find that households in German counties where more Jewish persecution occurred in the Black Death period and there was more intensive antisemitism in the Nazi period invest less in stocks, have lower savings in bank deposits, and are less likely to get a mortgage today.

15. For a survey of the evidence of the deep persistence of some cultural values, see Bisin and Verdier (2011). Other important papers in this literature include Alesina and Fuchs-Schündeln (2007), Grosfled et al. (2013), and Alesina et al. (2013). See the excellent surveys by Nunn (2012) and Alesina and Giuliano (2015).

16. For example, in the late 1990s the majority of the US population opposed homosexual marriage, as did all mainstream politicians. This consensus held up until the late 2000s but it rapidly unravelled after 2010. In 2001, 57 percent of Americans

were opposed to gay marriage and 35 percent were in favor. By 2014, 52 percent of Americans were in favor of gay marriage (Pew Research 2017).

17. See Jordan (1932, 1936), Lecler (1960), and Kamen (1967).

18. This episode is described by Zagorin (2003).

19. Spinoza's influence on subsequent thinkers was tremendous. But it was an esoteric influence. Israel (2001, 2006) traces the way that the ideas of radical Enlightenment thinkers and particularly Spinoza shaped the toleration debate in early modern Europe even though almost all other writers openly denounced him.

20. Melzer notes: "Decartes's *Discourse on Method*, Spinzoa's *Theological-Political Treatise*, Locke's *Two Treatise of Government*, Hume's *Treatise of Human Nature*, Montesquieu's *Spirit of the Laws* and *Persian Letters*, as well as the major writings of Voltaire, Diderot, and Holbach – all were originally published anonymously" (Melzer, 2014, 249).

21. The classical statement on esoteric writing is Strauss (1952). A definitive survey of the prevalence of esoteric writing until the modern period is Melzer (2014).

22. See Wooton (2002).

23. Our first point is in line with the arguments of those influenced by Quentin Skinner and the Cambridge school. Our second point is a call for more studies of the political economy of European states in the medieval and early modern period.

24. See Barro and McCleary (2005) for details on the existence of state religions across the world and Carvalho (2013) for an analysis of bans on the wearing of headscarves.

25. These data are drawn from the Religion and State database (Akbaba and Fox, 2011).

26. This is what we did, for example, in Chapter 11. This is also consistent with similar studies adopting a cross-country approach [See, e.g., Besley and Persson (2011)].

27. State capacity here is defined in terms of tax revenues collected as a percentage of GDP. If a country collects more than the average in the sample, then we define it as a high-capacity state. If it collects less than the sample average, it is a low-capacity state.

28. We construct the figures as follows. We regress government regulation of religion on measures of GDP per capita (from the UN), adult literacy rates (from the CIA), and rule of law (from the World Bank). We then generate the residuals from this regression. We do the same using religious fractionalization as the dependent variable. Then we plot the two generated residuals in the figures.

Bibliography

Aberth, John (2010, 2000). *From the Brink of the Apocalypse: Confronting Famine, War, Plague, and Death in the Later Middle Ages*. Routledge, London.

Abramitzky, Ran (2018). *The Mystery of the Kibbutz*. Princeton University Press, Princeton, NJ.

Abramson, Scott (2017). 'The economic origins of the territorial state', *International Organization*. **71**(1), 97–130.

Abulafia, David (1998). *Frederick II: A Medieval Emperor*. Oxford University Press, Oxford.

Abulafia, David (2011). *The Great Sea*. Allan Lane, London.

Acemoglu, Daron, Davide Cantoni, Simon Johnson, and James A. Robinson (2011). 'The consequences of radical reform: The French Revolution', *American Economic Review*. **101**(7), 3286–3307.

Acemoglu, Daron, Tarek A. Hassan, and James A. Robinson (2011). 'Social structure and development: A legacy of the Holocaust in Russia', *The Quarterly Journal of Economics*. **126**(2), 895–946.

Acemoglu, Daron, Simon Johnson, and James Robinson (2005). 'The rise of Europe: Atlantic trade, institutional change, and economic growth', *American Economic Review*. **95**(3), 546–579.

Acemoglu, Daron, and James A. Robinson (2012). *Why Nations Fail*. Crown Business, New York.

Acemoglu, Daron, and James A. Robinson (2017). The emergence of weak, despotic and inclusive states. Working Paper 23657. National Bureau of Economic Research, Cambridge, MA.

Acemoglu, Daron, and James A. Robinson (2019). The Narrow Corridor to Liberty: The Red Queen and the Struggle of State against Society. Penguin, New York.

Adams, Geoffrey (1991). *The Huguenots and French Opinion, 1685–1787: The Enlightenment Debate on Toleration*. Wilfrid Laurier University Press, Toronto.

Adler, H. G. (1960). *The Jews in Germany*. University of Notre Dame Press, Notre Dame, Indiana.

Agobard of Lyons (2001). 'Medieval sourcebook: On hail and thunder'. Translated by W. J. Lewis from the Latin text in pp. 3–15 of Agobardi Lugdunensis Opera Omnia, edited by L. Van Acker. Turnholt: Brepols, 1981 (Corpus Christianorum. Continuatio Mediaevalis, 52); Biblical quotations are translated following the Douai translation of the Vulgate with adjustments as necessary.
https://sourcebooks.fordham.edu/source/Agobard-OnHailandThunder.asp

Akbaba, Yasemin, and Jonathan Fox (2011). 'The religion and state-minorities dataset', *Journal of Peace Research.* **48**(6), 807–816.

Akerlof, George A., and Rachel E. Kranton (2000). 'Economics and identity', *Quarterly Journal of Economics.* **115**(3), 715–753.

Alesina, Alberto, and Nicola Fuchs-Schündeln (2007). 'Goodbye Lenin (or not?): The effect of communism on people', *American Economic Review.* **97**(4), 1507–1528.

Alesina, Alberto, and Paola Giuliano (2015). 'Culture and institutions', *Journal of Economic Literature.* **53**(4), 898–944.

Alesina, Alberto, Paola Giuliano, and Nathan Nunn (2013). 'On the origins of gender roles: Women and the plough', *The Quarterly Journal of Economics.* **128**(2), 469–530.

Allen, Douglas W. (2011). *The Institutional Revolution.* Chicago University Press, Chicago.

Altran, Scott (2002). *In Gods We Trust: The Evolutionary Landscape of Religion.* Oxford University Press, Oxford.

Álvarez Nogal, Carlos, and Leanrdro Prados De La Escosura (2007). 'The decline of Spain (1500 1850): Conjectural estimates', *European Review of Economic History.* **11**(03), 319–366.

Álvarez Nogal, Carlos, and Leanrdro Prados De La Escosura (2013). 'The rise and fall of Spain (1270–1850)', *The Economic History Review.* **66**(1), 1–37.

Ames, Christine Caldwell (2015). *Medieval Heresies: Christianity, Judaism, and Islam.* Cambridge University Press, Cambridge.

Anderson, Benedict (1983). *Imagined Communities: Reflections on the Origin and Spread of Nationalism.* Verso, London.

Anderson, Gary M. (1988). 'Mr. Smith and the preachers: The economics of religion in the wealth of nations', *Journal of Political Economy.* **96**(5), 1066–1088.

Anderson, Perry (1974*a*). *Lineages of the Absolutist State.* Verso, London.

Anderson, Perry (1974*b*). *Passages from Antiquity to Feudalism.* Verso, London.

Anderson, R. Warren, Noel D. Johnson, and Mark Koyama (2017). 'Jewish persecutions and weather shocks 1100–1800', *Economic Journal.* **127**(602), 924–958.

Anderson, R. Warren (2013). 'Portuguese inquisitorial sentencing trends', *Homo Oeconomicus.* **1**, 37–59.

Angrist, Joshua D., and Jörn-Steffen Pischke (2010). 'The credibility revolution in empirical economics: How better research design is taking the con out of econometrics', *Journal of Economic Perspectives.* **24**(2), 3–30.

Anonymous (1957). *The Song of Roland.* Peguin Books, New York. Translated by Dorothy L. Sayers.

Arbatli, Cemal Eren, and Gunes Gokmen (2016). Minorities, human capital and long-run development: Persistence of Armenian and Greek influence in Turkey. CESifo Working Paper Series No. 6268.

Arendt, Hannah (1951). *The Origins of Totalitarianism.* Houghton Mifflin Harcourt, New York.

Armstrong, Karen (2000). *The Battle for God.* Alfred A. Knopf, New York.

Arnold, Benjamin (1991). *Princes and Territories in Medieval Germany.* Cambridge University Press, Cambridge.

Arnold, Benjamin (2000). 'Emperor Frederick II (1194–1250 and the political particularism of the German princes', *Journal of Medieval History.* **26**(3), 239–252.

Arnold, John H. (2001). *Inquisition and Power: Catharism and the Confessing Subject in Medieval Languedoc.* University of Pennsylvania Press, Philadelphia.

Arnold, Thomas (2001). *The Renaissance at War.* Cassell, London.

Arruóada, Benito (2016). 'How Rome enabled impersonal markets', *Explorations in Economic History*. **61**(2), 68–84.

Ashworth, William J. (2003). *Customs and Excise: Trade, Production, and Consumption in England, 1640–1845*. Oxford University Press, Oxford.

Assis, Yom Tov (1997). *The Golden Age of Aragonese Jewry*. The Littman Library of Jewish Civilization, London.

Athey, Susan, and Guido W. Imbens (2017). 'The state of applied econometrics: Causality and policy evaluation', *Journal of Economic Perspectives*. **31**(2), 3–32.

Atran, Scott, and Joseph Henrich (2010). 'The evolution of religion: How cognitive by-products, adaptive learning heuristics, ritual displays, and group competition generate deep commitments to prosocial religions', *Biological Theory*. **5**, 1–13.

Augustine (2003). *The City of God*. New York, Penguin.

Auriol, Emmanuelle, and Jean-Philippe Platteau (2017). 'Religious co-option in autocracy: A theory inspired by history', *Journal of Development Economics*. **127**, 395 –412.

Avneri, Zvi (1968). *Germania Judaica, Bd. 2: Von 1238 bis zur Mitte des 14 Jahrhunderts*. JCB Mohr, Tübingen.

Bach, H. I. (1984). *The German Jew: A synthesis of Judaism and Western Civilization, 1730–1930*. Oxford University Press, Oxford.

Bachrach, Bernard S. (1977). *Early Medieval Jewish Policy in Western Europe*. University of Minnesota Press, Minneapolis.

Bainton, Roland H. (1941). 'The struggle for religious liberty', *Church History*. **10**(2), 95–124.

Bainton, Roland H. (1951). *The Travail of Religious Liberty*. Harper & Brothers New York.

Bairoch, Paul (1988). *Cities and Economic Development, from the Dawn of History to the Present*. University of Chicago Press, Chicago. Translated by Christopher Braider.

Bairoch, Paul (1990). The impact of crop yields, agricultural productivity, and transport costs on urban growth between 1800 and 1910. In A.van der Woude, A.Hayami and J.de Vries, eds, *Urbanization in History*. Oxford University Press, Oxford, pp. 134–151.

Baldwin, John W. (1970). *Masters, Princes and Merchants*. Vol. 1, Princeton University Press, Princeton, NJ.

Baldwin, John W. (1986). *The Government of Philip Augustus: Foundations of French Royal Power in the Middle Ages*. University of California Press, Berkeley, Los Angeles, London.

Balla, Eliana, and Noel D. Johnson (2009). 'Fiscal crisis and institutional change in the Ottoman Empire and France', *The Journal of Economic History*. **69**(3), 809–845.

Bang, Peter (2008). *The Roman Bazaar*. Cambridge University Press, Cambridge.

Barber, Malcolm (1981*a*). 'Lepers, Jews and Moslems: The plot to overthrow Christendom in 1321', *History*. **66**(216), 1–17.

Barber, Malcolm (1981*b*). 'The Pastoureaux of 1320', *The Journal of Ecclesiastical History*. **32**(2), 144–166.

Barber, Malcolm (2000). *The Cathars*. Longman, Harlow.

Barnes, Timothy D. (1981). *Constantine and Eusebius*. Harvard University Press, Cambridge, MA.

Baron, Salo W. (1947). *Modern Nationalism and Religion*. Books for Libraries Press, Freeport, New York.

Baron, Salo W. (1965). *A Social and Religious History of the Jews*. Vol. IX: Under Church and Empire, Columbia University Press, New York.

Baron, Salo W. (1967). *A Social and Religious History of the Jews*, Vol. XII: Economic Catalyst, Columbia University Press, New York.

Barro, Robert J., and Rachel M. McCleary (2005). 'Which countries have state religions?', *The Quarterly Journal of Economics*. **120**(4), pp. 1331–1370.

Bateman, Victoria N. (2011). 'The evolution of markets in early modern Europe, 1350–1800: a study of wheat prices', *The Economic History Review*. **64**(2), 447–471.

Bates, M Searle (1945). *Religious Liberty: An Inquiry*. International Missionary Council, New York.

Bayes, Daniel H. (2004). A tradition of state dominance. In J.Kindopp and C. L.Hamrin, eds, 'God and Caesar in China', Brookings Institution, Washington, DC, pp. 25–39.

Beales, Derek (1990). Social forces and enlightened policies. In H. M.Scott, ed., 'Enlightened Absolutism', Macmillan Education Limited, Basingstoke, Hampshire, pp. 37–53.

Beales, Hugh Lancelot (1928). *The Industrial Revolution 1750–1850: An Introductory Essay*. Frank Cass & Co. Ltd, London.

Becker, Gary S. (1971). *The Economics of Discrimination*. University of Chicago Press, London.

Becker, Sascha O., Erik Hornung, and Ludger Woessmann (2011). 'Education and catch-up in the industrial revolution', *American Economic Journal: Macroeconomics*. **3**(3), 92–126.

Becker, Sascha O., and Ludger Woessmann (2009). 'Was Weber wrong? a human capital theory of Protestant economic history', *The Quarterly Journal of Economics*. **124**(2), 531–596.

Becker, Sascha O., and Luigi Pascali (2018). Religion, division of labor and conflict: Anti-Semiticsm in German regions over 600 years, American Economic Review, in press.

Becker, Sascha O., Steven Pfaff, and Jared Rubin (2016). 'Causes and consequences of the Protestant Reformation', *Explorations in Economic History*. **62**, 1 –25.

Behringer, Wolfgang (1995). 'Weather, hunger and fear: Origins of the European Witch Hunts in Climate, Society and Mentality', *German History*. **13**(1), 1–27.

Behringer, Wolfgang (1997). *Witchcrat Persecutions in Bavaria*. Cambridge University Press, Cambridge. Translated by J.C. Grayson and David Lederer.

Behringer, Wolfgang (2004). *Witches and Witch-Hunts*. Polity Press, Cambridge.

Beik, William (1985). *Absolutism and Society in Seventeenth-Century France*. Cambridge University Press, Cambridge.

Bein, Alex (1990). *The Jewish Question: Biography of a World Problem*. Herzel Press, London and Toronto. Translated by Harry Zohn.

Beiner, Ronald (1993). 'Machiavelli, Hobbes, and Rousseau on civil religion', *The Review of Politics*. **55**(4), 617–638.

Bekar, Cliff T., and Clyde G. Reed (2013). 'Land markets and inequality: Evidence from medieval England', *European Review of Economic History*. **17**(3), 294–317.

Bell, Dean Phillip (2008). *Jews in the Early Modern World*. Rowman & Littlefield, Lanham, MD.

Bellah, Robert N. (2011). *Religion in Human Evolution*. Harvard University Press, Cambridge, MA.

Belloc, Marianna, Francesco Drago, and Roberto Galbiati (2016). 'Earthquakes, religion, and transition to self-government in Italian cities', *Quarterly Journal of Economics*. **131**(4), 1875–1926.

Benabou, Roland, David Ticchi, and Andrea Vindigni (2015a). Forbidden fruits: The political economy of science, religion, and growth. Working Paper 21105. National Bureau of Economic Research, Cambridge, MA.

Benabou, Roland, Davide Ticchi, and Andrea Vindigni (2015b). Religion and innovation. American Economic Review, Papers and Proceedings, 105(5), 346–351.

Benbassa, Esther (1999). *The Jews of France*. Princeton University Press, Princeton, NJ. Translated by M.B. DeBevoise.

Benedict, Philip (1996). *Un roi, une loi, deux dois*: Parameters for the history of Catholic-Reformed co-existence in France, 1555–1685. In O. P.Grell and B.Scribner, eds, *'Tolerance and Intolerance in the European Reformation'*. Cambridge University Press, Cambridge, pp. 65–93.

Benedict, Philip (2001). *The Faith and Fortunes of France's Huguenots: 1600–1685*, Ashgate Publishing, Aldershot.

Benedictow, Ole J. (2005). *The Black Death 1346–1353: The Complete History*. The Boydell Press, Woodbridge.

Berkovitz, Jay A. (1989). *The Shaping of Jewish Identity in Nineteenth-Century France*. Wayne State University Press, Detroit.

Berman, Eli (2000). 'Sect, subsidy, and sacrifice: An economist's view of Ultra-Orthodox Jews', *The Quarterly Journal of Economics*. **115**(3), 905–953.

Berman, Eli (2009). *Radical, Religious, and Violent*, MIT Press, Cambridge, MA.

Berman, Harold J. (1983). *Law and Revolution: The Formation of the Western Legal Tradition*. Harvard University Press, Cambridge, Massachuestts.

Bernard, L. L. (1956). 'Foucault, Louvois, and the revocation of the Edict of Nantes', *Church History*. **25**(1), 27–40.

Bernhofen, Daniel, Markus Eberhardt, Jianan Li, and Stephen Morgan (2016). Assessing market (dis)integration in early modern China and Europe, Discussion Papers 2015–12, University of Nottingham, GEP.

Besley, Timothy, and Torsten Persson (2011). *Pillars of Prosperity*. Princeton University Press, Princeton, NJ.

Bever, Edward (2008). *The Realities of Witchcraft and Popular Magic in Early Modern Europe*. Palgrave MacMillan, London.

Bever, Edward (2009). 'Witchcraft prosecutions and the decline of magic', *Journal of Interdisciplinary History*. **40**(2), 263–293.

Bikhchandani, Sushil, David Hirshleifer, and Ivo Welch (1992). 'A theory of fads, fashion, custom, and cultural change as informational cascades', *Journal of Political Economy*. **100**(5), 992–1026.

Binzel, Christine, and Jean-Paul Carvalho (2017). 'Education, social mobility and religious movements: The Islamic revival in Egypt', *The Economic Journal*. **127**, 2553–2580.

Bisin, Alberto, and Thierry Verdier (2011). The economics of cultural transmission and socialization. In J.Benhabib, A.Bisin and M. O.Jackson, eds, *'Handbook of Social Economics'*. Vol. 1A, Elsevier, The Netherlands, North-Holland, pp. 339–414.

Bisson, Thomas (2009). *The Crisis of the Twelfth Century: Power, Lordship, and the Origins of European Government*. Princeton University Press, Princeton, NJ.

Black, Jeremy (2004). *Kings, Nobles and Commoners: States and Societies in Early Modern Europe*. I.B. Tauris & Co Ltd, London.

Blanning, T. C. W. (1970). *Joseph II and Enlightened Despotism*. Long Group Limited, London.

Blaydes, Lisa (2017). 'State building in the Middle East', *Annual Review of Political Science*. **20**, 487–504.

Blaydes, Lisa, and Christopher Paik (2016). 'The impact of Holy Land crusades on state formation: War mobilization, trade integration, and political development in medieval Europe', *International Organization*. **70**(3), 551–586.

Blaydes, Lisa, and Eric Chaney (2013), 'The feudal revolution and Europe's rise: Political divergence of the Christian and Muslim worlds before 1500 CE', *American Political Science Review*. **107**(1), 16–34.

Bloch, Marc (1961). *Feudal Society*. Vol. 1, University of Chicago Press, Chicago. Translated by L.A. Mayon.

Bloch, Marc (1964). *Feudal Society*. Vol. 2, University of Chicago Press, Chicago. Translated by L.A. Mayon.

Bloom, Herbert I. (1936). *The Economic Activities of the Jews of Amsterdam in the Seventeenth and Eighteenth Centuries*. Kennikat Press, Port Washington, NY.

Blum, Jerome (1978). *The End of the Old Order in Rural Europe*. Princeton University Press, Princeton, NJ.

Boccaccio, Giovanni (2005, 1371). *The Decameron*. Dodo Press, London. Translated by J.M. Rigg.

Bockstette, Valerie, Areendam Chanda, and Louis Putterman (2002). 'States and markets: The advantage of an early start', *Journal of Economic Growth*. **7**(4), 347–369.

Boettke, Peter J., and Rosolino A. Candela (2017). 'The liberty of progress: Increasing returns, institutions, and entrepreneurship', *Social Philosophy and Policy*. **34**(2), 136–163.

Bogart, Dan, and Gary Richardson (2009). 'Making property productive: Reorganizing rights to real and equitable estates in Britain, 1660–1830', *European Review of Economic History*. **13**(1), 3–30.

Bogart, Daniel, and Gary Richardson (2011). 'Property rights and Parliament in industrializing Britain', *Journal of Law & Economics*. **54**(2), 241 – 274.

Boguet, Henry (1929). *An Examen of Witches*. Kessinger Publishing, London. Translated by E.A. Ashwin and edited by Montague Summers.

Bois, Guy (1976, 2009). *Crisis of Feudalism*. Cambridge University Press, Cambridge.

Bonney, Richard, ed. (1995). *The Rise of the Fiscal State in Europe c.1200–1815*. Clarendon Press, OUP, Oxford.

Bonney, Richard, ed. (1999). *Economic Systems and State Finance*. Oxford University Press, Oxford.

Bonney, Richard and Margaret Bonney (2011). European state finance database. http://esfdb.websites.bta.com/Database.aspx

Bosher, J. F. (1964). *The Single Duty Project: A Study of the Movement for a French Customs Union in the Eighteenth Century*. University of London Press, London.

Bosker, Maarten, Eltjo Buringh, and Jan Luiten van Zanden (2013). 'From Baghdad to London: unravelling urban development in Europe and the Arab world 800–1800', *Review of Economics and Statistics*. **95**(4), 1418–1437.

Bossy, John (1985). *Christianity in the West, 1400–1700*. Oxford University Press, Oxford.

Bostridge, Ian (1996). Witchcraft repealed. In J.Barry, M.Hester and G.Roberts, eds, 'Witchcraft in Early Modern Europe', Cambridge University Press, Cambridge, pp. 309–334.

Bosworth, C.E. (1982). The concept of *Dhimma* in early Islam. In B.Braude and B.Lewis, eds, '*Christians and Jews in the Ottoman Empire*'. Vol. I, Holmes & Meier, New York, pp. 37–55.

Botticini, Maristella (1997). 'New evidence on Jews in Tuscany, CA. 1310–1435: The "friends & family" connection again', *Zakhor. Rivista di Storia degli Ebrei d'Italia.* **1**, 77–93.

Botticini, Maristella, and Zvi Eckstein (2005). 'Jewish occupational selection: Education, restrictions, or minorities', *Journal of Economic History.* **65**, 922–948.

Botticini, Maristella, and Zvi Eckstein (2012). *The Chosen Few,* Princeton University Press, Princeton, NJ.

Boxer, C.R. (1951). *The Christian Century in Japan.* University of California Press, Berkeley.

Braddick, Michael J. (1996). *Nerves of State: Taxation and the Financing of the English State, 1558–1714.* Manchester University Press, Manchester.

Brand, Paul (2003). The Jewish community of England in the records of English royal government. In P.Skinner, ed., '*The Jews in Medieval Britain : Historical, Literary, and Archaeological Perspectives'.* Boydell and Brewer, New York, pp. 73–85.

Brann, Ross (2002). *Power in the Portrayal: Representations of Jews and Muslims in Eleventh and Twelfth-Century Spain.* Princeton University Press, Princeton, NJ.

Braude, Benjamin (1982). Foundation myths of the Millet system. In B.Bruade and B.Lewis, eds, *Christians and Jews in the Ottoman Empire.* Vol. I, Holmes & Meier, New York, pp. 69–89.

Braude, Benjamin, and Bernard Lewis (1982). Introduction. In B.Bruade and B.Lewis, eds, *Christians and Jews in the Ottoman Empire.* Vol. I, Holmes & Meier, New York, pp. 1–37.

Braudel, Fernand (1972, 1949). *The Mediterranean, and the Mediterranean World in the Age of Phillip II.* Vol. II, University of California Press, Berkeley. Translated by Siân Reynolds.

Braudel, Fernand (1979, 1982). *The Wheels of Commerce.* Phoenix Press, London.

Brenner, Robert (1976). 'Agrarian class strucure and economic development in pre-industrial Europe', *Past & Present.* **70**(1), 30–75.

Brenner, Robert (1993). *Merchants and Revolution.* Princeton University Press, Princeton, NJ.

Brewer, John (1988). *The Sinews of Power.* Harvard University Press, Cambridge, MA.

Briggs, Chris (2006). Credit in the later medieval village: The example of Willingham, Cambridgeshire, 1377–1458. Presented at the Economic History Society Conference 2006.

Briggs, Chris (2008). 'Seigniorial control of villagers' litigation beyond the manor in later medieval England', *Historical Research.* **81**(213), 399–422.

Briggs, Chris, and Mark Koyama (2014). Medieval microcredit. unpublished manuscript.

Briggs, Robin (1996). *Witches and Neigbours.* Penguin Books, London.

Broadberry, Stephen, Bruce M. S. Campbell, Alexander Klein, Mark Overton, and Bas van Leeuwen (2011). British economic growth, 1270–1870: An output-based approach. London School of Economics working paper.

Brook, Timothy (1988). 'Censorship in eighteenth-century China: A view from the book trade', *Canadian Journal of History.* **22**, 177–196.

Brook, Timothy (2005). *The Chinese State in Ming Society.* Routledge, London.

Brown, Peter (2012). *Book cover Through the Eye of a Needle: Wealth, the Fall of Rome, and the Making of Christianity in the West, 350–550* AD. Princeton University Press, Princeton, NJ.

Brown, Peter (2013). *The Rise of Western Christendom.* The tenth anniversary revised edition edn, John Wiley & Sons, Malden, MA.

Brown, Reva Berman, and Sean McCartney (2005). 'The exchequer of the Jews revisited: The operation and effect of the Saccarium Judeorum', *The Medieval History Journal*. **8**, 303–321.

Buchanan, James M. (1975). *The Limits of Liberty*. Liberty Fund, Indianapolis.

Burkman, Thomas W. (1974). 'The Urakami Incidents and the Struggle for Religious Toleration in Early Meiji Japan', *Japanese Journal of Religious Studies*. **1**(2/3), 143–216.

Cahnman, Werner J. (1974). 'Pariahs, strangers and Court-Jews: A conceptual clarification', *Sociological Analysis*. **35**(3), 155–166.

Calendar of the Patent Rolls, preserved in the Public Record Office, Henry III AD. 1247–1258, ed. (1908). Her Majesty's Stationery Office, London.

Cam, Helen (1962). *Law-Finders and Law-Makers in Medieval England*. Merlin Press, London.

Cameron, Euan (1986). *The Reformation of Heretics: The Waldenses of the Alps, 1480–1580*. Clareden Press, Oxford.

Campbell, Bruce M.S. (2010). 'Nature as historical protagonist', *Economic History Review*. **63**(2), 281–314.

Campbell, Bruce M.S. (2016). *The Great Transition: Climate, Disease and Society in the Late-Medieval World*. Cambridge University Press, Cambridge.

Cantoni, Davide (2015). 'The economic effects of the Protestant Reformation: Testing the Weber hypothesis in the German lands', *Journal of the European Economic Association*. **13**(4), 561–598.

Carr, E.H. (1961). *The Struggle for Mastery in Europe 1848–1918*. Oxford University Press, Oxford.

Carugati, Federica, Gillian K Hadfield and Barry Weingast (2015). 'Building legal order in ancient Athens', *Journal of Legal Analysis*. **7**(2), 291–324.

Carvalho, Jean-Paul (2013). 'Veiling', *The Quarterly Journal of Economics*. **128**(1), 337–370.

Carvalho, Jean-Paul, and Mark Koyama (2016). 'Jewish emancipation and schism: Economic development and religious change', *Journal of Comparative Economics*. **44**(3), 29–39.

Carvalho, Jean-Paul, and Mark Koyama (2018). Resisting education. Working Paper.

Carvalho, Jean-Paul, Mark Koyama, and Michael Sacks (2017). 'Education, identity and community: Lessons from Jewish emancipation', *Public Choice*. **171**(1), 119–143.

Casanova, José (1994). *Public Religions in the Modern World*. University of Chicago Press, Chicago.

Cesarani, David (1999). British Jews. In R.Liedtke and S.Wendehorst, eds, *The Emancipation of Catholics, Jews, and Protestants*. Manchester University Press, Manchester, pp. 34–56.

Chadwick, Owen (1975). *The Secularization of the European Mind in the Nineteenth Century*. Cambridge University Press, Cambridge.

Chadwick, Owen (1990). *The Penguin History of the Chruch: The Reformation*. Penguin, London.

Chaney, Eric (2013). 'Revolt on the Nile: Economic shocks, religion and political power', *Econometrica*. **81**(5), 2033–2053.

Chaney, Eric (2016). Religion and the rise and fall of Islamic science. Working Paper. Department of Economics, Harvard University. Cambridge, MA.

Chaney, Eric, and Richard Hornbeck (2016). 'Economic growth in the Malthusian era: Evidence from the 1609 Spanish expulsion of the Moriscos', *Economic Journal*. **126**(594), 1404–1440.

Chazan, Robert (1973–1974). 'Anti–usury efforts in thirteenth century Narbonne and the Jewish response', *Proceedings of the American Academy for Jewish Research.* **41**, 45–67.

Chazan, Robert (1997). *Medieval Sterotypes and Modern Antisemitism.* University of California Press, Berklely, U.S.A.

Chazan, Robert (2010). *Reassessing Jewish Life in Medieval Europe.* Cambridge University Press, Cambridge.

Childs, John (2001). *Warfare in the Seventeenth Century.* Cassell, London.

Childs, W.R. (1991). 'my brother': Edward II, John of Powerdham and the chronicles, 1318. In I.Wood, G. A.Loud and J.Taylor, eds, *Church and Chronicle in the Middle Ages: Essays Presented to John Taylor.* Hambledon, London, pp. 149–163.

Chilosi, David, Tommy E. Murphy, Roman Studer, and A. Coükun Tunçer (2013). 'Europe's many integrations: Geography and grain markets, 1620–1913', *Explorations in Economic History.* **50**(1), 46–68.

Christakos, George, Richardo A. Olea, Marc L. Serre, Hwa-Lung Yu, and Lin-Lin Wang (2005). *Interdisciplinary Public Health Reasoning and Epidemic Modelling: The Case of Black Death.* Springer, Berlin.

Christman, Victoria (2015). *Pragmatic Toleration: The Politics of Religious Heterodoxy in Early Reformation Antwerp 1515–1555.* University of Rochester Press, Rochester NY.

Church, William F. (1969). *The Impact of Absolutism in France: National Experience Under Richelieu, Mazarin, and Louis XIV.* John Wiley & Sons, New York.

Church, William F. (1972). *Richelieu and Reason of State.* Princeton University Press, Princeton, NJ.

Cinnirella, Francesco, and Jochen Streb (2017). Religious toleration as engine of innovation, 6797, CESifo Working Papers.

Cipolla, Carol M. (1976). *Before the Industrial Revolution.* Methuen and Co, London.

Clapp, Edwin J. (1907). *The Navigable Rhine.* Houghton Murray Company, Boston.

Clark, Gregory (1996). 'The political foundations of modern economic growth, 1540–1800', *Journal of Interdisciplinary History.* **26**, 563–588.

Clark, Gregory (2005). 'The condition of the working class in England, 1209–2004', *Journal of Political Economy.* **113**(6), 1307–1340.

Classen, CP (1972). *Anabaptism; a Social History, 1525–1618: Switzerland, Austria, Moravia, South and Central Germany.* Cornell University Press, Ithaca, NY.

Coffey, John (2000). *Persecution and Toleration in Protestant England, 1558–1689.* Longman, London.

Cohen, Mark (1994). *Under Crescent and Cross.* Princeton University Press, Princeton, NJ.

Cohen, Norman (1957). *The Pursuit of the Millenium, Revolutionary Millenarians and Mystical Anarchists of the Middle Ages.* Pimilco, London.

Cohn, Norman (1975). *Europe's Inner Demons.* Pimlico, London.

Cohn, Samuel K. (2007). 'The Black Death and the burning of Jews', *Past & Present.* **196**(1), 3–36.

Collins, James B. (1988). *Fiscal Limits of Absolutism.* University of California Press, Berkeley, Los Angeles.

Collins, James B. (1994). *Classes, Estates, and Order in Early Modern Brittany.* Cambridge University Press, Cambridge.

Collins, James B. (1999). State Building in Early-Modern Europe: The Case of France State Building in Early-Modern Europe: The Case of France. In V.Lieberman, ed.,

Beyond Binary Histories: Re-imagining Eurasia to c.1830. University of Michigan Press, Ann Arbor, pp. 159–190.

Collins, Paul (2013). *The Birth of the West*. Public Affairs, New York.

Colvin, Christopher L. (2017). 'Banking on a religious divide: Accounting for the success of the Netherlands' Raiffeisen Cooperatives in the crisis of the 1920s', *The Journal of Economic History*. **77**(3), 866–919.

Coşgel, Metin M., and Thomas J. Miceli (2009). 'State and religion', *Journal of Comparative Economics*. **37**(3), 402–416.

Coşgel, Metin M., Thomas J. Miceli, and Jared Rubin (2012). 'The political economy of mass printing: Legitimacy and technological change in the Ottoman empire', *Journal of Comparative Economics*. **40**(3), 357–371.

Cosmides, Leda, and John Tooby (1992). Cognitive adaptions for social exchange. In Jerome H. Barkow, Leda Cosmides, and John Tooby (eds.). 'Adapted Mind', Oxford University Press, Oxford, pp. 163–228.

Cottret, Bernard (2003). Religious or secular? the Edict of Nantes, reformation and state formation in late sixteenth century France. In R.Whelan and C.Baxter, eds, *The Edict of Nantes and Its Implications in France, Britain, and Ireland*. Four Courts Press, Dublin, pp. 107–127.

Cox, Gary W (2011). 'War, moral hazard, and ministerial responsibility: England after the Glorious Revolution', *The Journal of Economic History*. **71**(01), 133–161.

Cox, Gary W. (2015). 'Marketing sovereign promises: The English model', *The Journal of Economic History*. **75**(1), 190–218.

Cox, Gary W. (2016). *Marketing Sovereign Promises: Monopoly Brokerage and the Growth of the English State*. Cambridge University Press, Cambridge.

Cramer, Alice Carver (1940). 'The Jewish Exchequer, an inquiry into its fiscal function', *The American Historical Review*. **45**(2), 327–337.

Czarnecki, James G. (1978). 'The significance of Judas in Giotto's Arena Chapel frescos', *The Early Renaissance*. **5**, 35–47.

D'Acunto, Francesco, Marcel Prokopczuk, and Michael Weber. Distrust in finance lingers: Jewish persecution and households' investments. (2018). Historical anti-semitism, ethnic specialization, and financial development. Review of Economic Studies, in press.

Davies, J.D. Griffith (1935). *King Henry IV*. Arthur Barker Limited, London.

Davies, Norman (1981). *God's Playground: A History of Poland*. Vol. 1, Clarendon Press, Oxford.

Davies, Rees (2003). 'The medieval state: The tyranny of a concept?', *Journal of Historical Sociology*. **16**(2), 280–300.

Davis, R.G., and J.H. Deaton (1981). *The English Parliament in the Middle Ages*. Manchester University Press, Oxford.

de Jouvenel, Betrand (1948). *On Power, the Natural History of Its Growth*. Liberty Fund, Indianapolis. Translated by J.F. Huntington.

de Lara, Yadira Gonzalez, Avner Greif, and Saumitra Jha (2008). 'The administrative foundations of self-enforcing constitutions', *American Economic Review*. **98**(2), 105–109.

De Long, J. Bradford, and Andrei Shleifer (1993). 'Princes and merchants: European city growth before the Industrial Revolution', *Journal of Law & Economics*. **36**(2), 671–702.

de Roover, Raymond (1967). 'The scholastics, usury, and foreign exchange', *The Business History Review*. **41**, 257–271.

de Vries, Jan (1976). *Economy of Europe in an Age of Crisis*. Cambridge University Press, Cambridge.

Deane, Jennifer Kolpacoff (2011). *A History of Medieval Heresy and Inquisition*. Rowman & Littlefield Lanham, MD.

Derbes, Anne, and Mark Sandona (2004), Reading the Arena Chapel. In A.Derbes and M.Sandona, eds, *The Cambridge Companion to Giotto*. Cambridge University Press, Cambridge, pp. 197–212.

Diaz-Cayeros, Alberto, and Saumitra Jha (2017). Can contract failures foster ethnic assimilation? evidence from Cochineal in Mexico. Stanford Working Paper.

Dicey, A.V. (1908). *Introduction to the Study of the Law of the Constitution*. MacMillan and Co. Limited, London.

Dickson, P.G.M. (1993, 1967). *The Financial Revolution in England*. Gregg Revivals, Aldershot.

Diefendorf, Jeffry M. (1980). *Business and Politics in the Rhineland, 1789–1834*. Princeton University Press, Princeton, NJ.

Dienfendorf, Barbara B. (1998). The failure of peace before Nantes. In R. L.Goodbar, ed., *The Edict of Nantes: Five Essays and A New Translation*. The National Huguenot Society, Bloomington, MN, pp. 1–11.

Dincecco, Mark (2009). 'Fiscal centralization, limited government, and public revenues in Europe, 1650–1913', *Journal of Economic History*. **69**(1), 48–103.

Dincecco, Mark (2010). 'Fragmented authority from ancien régime to modernity: A quantitative analysis', *Journal of Institutional Economics*. **6**(03), 305–328.

Dincecco, Mark, and Massimiliano Gaetano Onorato (2016). 'Military conflict and the rise of urban Europe', *Journal of Economic Growth*. **21**(259–82).

Dincecco, Mark, and Massimiliano Gaetano Onorato (2017). *From Warfare to Welfare*. Cambridge University Press, Cambridge.

Dittmar, Jeremiah E. (2011). 'Information technology and economic change: The impact of the printing press', *The Quarterly Journal of Economics*. **126**(3), 1133–1172.

Dobson, Barrie (2003). The medieval York Jewry reconsidered. In P.Skinner, ed., 'The Jews in Medieval Britain: Historical, Literary, and Archaeological Perspectives', Boydell and Brewer, New York, pp. 145–156.

Doepke, Matthias, and Fabrizio Zilibotti (2008). 'Occupational choice and the spirit of capitalism', *The Quarterly Journal of Economics*. **123**(2), 747–793.

Donaldson, David, and Richard Hornbeck (2016). 'Railroads and American economic growth: A "market access" approach', *Quarterly Journal of Economics*. **131**(2), 799–858.

Douglas, Mary (1991). 'Witchcraft and leprosy: Two strategies of exclusion', *Man*. **26**(4), 723–736.

Drake, H.A. (2002). *Constantine and the Bishops: The Politics of Intolerance*. Johns Hopkins University Press, Baltimore.

Drechlichman, Mauricio, and Hans-Joachim Voth (2008). Institutions and the resource curve in early modern spain. In E.Helpman, ed., 'Institutions and Economic Performance', Harvard University Press, Cambridge, MA.

Drelichman, Mauricio (2005). 'All that glitters: Precious metals, rent seeking and the decline of Spain', *European Review of Economic History*. **9**(03), 313–336.

Drelichman, Mauricio (2009). 'License to till: The privileges of the Spanish Mesta as a case of second-best institutions', *Explorations in Economic History*. **46**(2), 220–240.

Drelichman, Mauricio, and Hans-Joachim Voth (2010). 'The sustainable debts of Phillip II: A reconstruction of Castile's fiscal position, 1566–1696', *The Journal of Economic History*. **70**(4), 813–822.

Drelichman, Mauricio, and Hans-Joachim Voth (2011). 'Serial defaults, serial profits: Returns to sovereign lending in Habsburg Spain, 1566–1600', *Explorations in Economic History*. **48**(1), 1–19.

Drelichman, Mauricio, and Hans-Joachim Voth (2014). *Lending to the Borrower from Hell*. Princeton University Press, Princeton, NJ.

Duby, Georges (1973). *The Early Growth of the European Economy*. Weidenfeld and Nicolson, London. Translated by Howard B. Clarke.

Dunbabin, Jean (1985). *France in the Making, 853–1180*. Oxford University Press, Oxford.

Dupâquier, Jacques (1988). *Histoire de la population Française*. Vol. 4 volumes, Presses Universitaires de France.

Dyer, Christopher (2005). *An Age of Transition? Economy and Society in England in the Later Middle Ages*. Clarendon Press, Oxford.

Edwards, John (2011). *Mary I: England's Catholic Queen*. Yale University Press, New Haven, CT.

Eire, Carlos (2016). *Reformations*. Yale University Press, New Haven, CT.

Eisenbach, Artur (1991). *The Emancipation of the Jews in Poland, 1780–1870*. Basil Blackwell, Oxford. Translated by Janina Dorosz.

Eistenstadt, S. N. (2009). Introduction. In L. H.Wakeman, ed., *Telling Chinese History: A Selection of Essays by Frederick E. Wakeman Jr.*. University of California Press, Berkeley, pp. ix–xix.

Ekelund, Robert B., and Robert D. Tollison (1981). *Mercantilism as a Rent-Seeking Society*. Texas A & M University Press, College Station, TX.

Ekelund, Robert B., and Robert D. Tollison (2011). *The Economic Origins of Roman Christianity*. Chicago University Press, Chicago.

Ekelund, Robert B., Robert F. Hebert, and Robert D. Tollison (2002). 'An economic analysis of the Protestant Reformation', *Journal of Political Economy*. **110**(3), 646–671.

Ekelund, Robert B., Robert Hebert, and Robert D. Tollison (1989). 'An economic model of the medieval Church: Usury as a form of rent seeking', *Journal of Law and Economic Organization*. **5**(2), 307–331.

Ekelund, Robert B., Robert Hebert, and Robert Tollison (2006). *The Marketplace of Christianity*. MIT Press, Cambridge, MA.

Ekelund, Robert B., Robert Hebert, Robert Tollison, Gary Anderson, and Audrey Davidson (1996). *Sacred Trust: The Medieval Church as an Economic Firm*. Oxford University Press, Oxford.

Ellenson, David (1994). *Between Tradition and Culture*. Scholars Press, Atlanta, GA.

Elliott, John H. (1961). 'The Decline of Spain', *Past & Present*. **20**(1), 52–75.

Elliott, John H. (1992). 'A Europe of composition monarchies', *Past & Present*. **137**, 48–71.

Elon, Amos (2002). *The Pity of It All*. Metropolitan Books, New York.

Elton, G.R. (1953). *The Tudor Revolution in Goverment*. Cambridge University Press, Cambridge.

Elukin, Jonathan (2007). *Living Together, Living Apart*. Princeton University Press, Princeton, NJ.

Emery, Ricard W. (1959). *The Jews of Perpignan*. Columbia University Press, New York.

Encrevé, André (1999). French protestants. In R.Liedtke and S.Wendehorst, eds, *The Emancipation of Catholics, Jews, and Protestants*. Manchester University Press, Manchester, pp. 56–82.

Encyclopedia Judaica (2007). 2nd edn, Macmillan Reference. Edited by Michael Berenbaum and Fred Skolnik.

Epstein, S. R. (2000). *Freedom and Growth, the Rise of States and Markets in Europe, 1300–1700*. Routledge, London.

Epstein, S. R. (2001). Introduction: Town and Country in Europe, 1300–1800. In S. R.Epstein, ed., 'Town and Country in Europe, 1300–1800', Routledge, London, pp. 1–30.

Evans, Peter, Dietrich Rueschemeyer, and Theda Skocpol, eds (1985). *Bringing the State Back In*. Cambridge University Press, Cambridge.

Evans, Robert H.W. (1991). Joseph II and Nationality in the Habsburg Lands. In H.Scott, ed., 'Enlightened Absolutism: Reform and Reformers in Later Eighteenth-Century Europe', Houndmills, UK, pp. 209–219.

Fairman, H. W. (1958). The kingship rituals of Egypt. In S.Hooke, ed., 'Myth, Ritual, and Kingship', Clarendon Press, Oxford, pp. 74–104.

Feldman, Noah (2005). *Divided by God*. Farrar, Straus and Giroux, New York.

Félix, Joël, and Frank Tallett (2009). The French experience, 1661–1815. In C.Storrs, ed., *Fiscal Military State in Eighteenth-Century Europe*. Ashgate, Abingdon, Oxfordshire, pp. 147–166.

Felsenstein, Frank (1999). *Anti-Semitic Stereotypes: A Paradigm of Otherness in English Popular Culture, 1660–1830*. John Hopkins University Press, Baltimore, MD.

Ferguson, Niall, ed. (1999). *Virtual History: Alternatives aand Counterfactuals*. Papermac, London.

Ferguson, Niall (1998). *The House of Rothschild: Money's prophets, 1798–1848*. Penguin, London.

Fernández-Morera, Darío (2016). *The Myth of the Andalusian Paradise*. ISI Books, Wilmington, DE.

Finer, Shmuel, and Natalie Naimark-Goldberg (2011). *Cultural Revolution in Berlin: Jews in the Age of Enlightenment*. The Bodleian Library, Oxford.

Finke, Roger, and Rodney Stark (2005). *The Churching of America, 1776–2005*. Rutgers University Press, New Brunswick, NJ.

Finley, Theresa, and Mark Koyama (2018). Plague, Politics, and Pogroms: The Black Death, Fragmented States, and the Persecution of Jews in the Holy Roman Empire. Journal of Law and Economics, **61**(2), 253–277.

Finley, Theresa S, Raphaël Franck, and Noel D Johnson (2017). 'The effects of land redistribution: Evidence from the French Revolution', *GMU Working Paper in Economics No. 17–29*.

Fischer, Gunther, Harrij van Nelthuizen, Mahendra Shah, and Freddy Nachtergaele (2002). *Global Agro-Ecological Assessment for Agriculture in the 21st Century: Methodology and Results*. Food and Agriculture Organization of the United Nations, Rome.

Fisher, David Hackett (1989). *Albion's Seed: Four British Folkways in America*. Oxford University Press, Oxford.

Fleming, Robin (1985). 'Monastic lands and England's defence in the Viking age', *The English Historical Review*. **100**(395), 247–265.

Fleming, Robin (1993). 'Rural elites and urban communities in Late-Saxon England', *Past & Present*. **141**(1), 3–37.

Foa, Anna (2000). *The Jews of Europe after the Black Death*. University of California Press, Berkeley.

Fortune, Stephen Alexander (1984). *Merchants and Jews: The Struggle for British West Indian Commerce, 1650–1750*. University Press of Florida, Gainesville.

Foucault, Michel (2012). *Discipline & Punish: The Birth of the Prison*. Vintage, Knopf Doubleday Publishing Group.

Franck, Raphaël and Laurence R. Iannaccone (2014). 'Religious decline in the 20th century West: testing alternative explanations', *Public Choice*. **59**, 385–414.

Franck, Raphaël, and Noel D Johnson (2016). 'Can public policies lower religiosity? Evidence from school choice in France, 1878–1902', *The Economic History Review*. **69**(3), 915–944.

Friedländer, Saul (1997). *Nazi Germany and the Jews*. The Years of Persecution, 1933–1939, Vol. I. Harper Collins, New York.

Friedländer, Saul (2008). *Nazi Germany and the Jews. 1939–1945: The Years of Extermination*. Vol. II, Harper Perennial, New York.

Fukuyama, Francis (2011). *The Origins of Political Order*. Profile Books, London.

Fuller, Lon L. (1969). *The Morality of Law*. Yale University Press, New Haven, CT.

Fusaro, Maria (2015). *Political Economies of Empire in Early Modern Mediterranean*. Cambridge University Press, Cambridge.

Fynn-Paul, Jeffrey (2009). 'Empire, monotheism and slavery in the greater Mediterranean region from antiquity to the early modern era', *Past & Present*. (205), 3–40.

Ganshof, F.L. (1951). *Feudalism*. Longman, London. Translated by Philip Grierson.

Garrioch, David (2014). *The Huguenots of Paris and the Coming of Religious Freedom. 1685–1789*. Cambridge University Press, Cambridge.

Gaskill, Malcolm (1996). Witchcraft in early modern Kent: Stereotypes and the background to accusations. In J.Barry, M.Hester and G.Roberts, eds, 'Witchcraft in Early Modern Europe', Cambridge University Press, Cambridge, pp. 237–257.

Gaus, Gerald F. (1983). *The Modern Liberal Theory of Man*. St. Martin's Press, London.

Gellner, Ernst (1983). *Nations and Nationalism*. 2nd (2008) edn, Cornell University Press, Ithaca, NY.

Geloso, Vincent (2015). 'Toleration of Catholics in Quebec and British Public Finances, 1760 to 1775', *Essays in Economic and Business History*. **33**, 51–81.

Gennaioli, Nicola, and Hans-Joachim Voth (2015). 'State capacity and military conflict', *Review of Economic Studies*. **82**(4), 1409–1448.

Gernet, Jacques (1972). *A History of Chinese Civilization*. Translated by J.R. Foster. ed. Cambridge University Press, Cambridge.

Gershman, Boris (2016). 'Witchcraft beliefs and the erosion of social capital: Evidence from Sub-Saharan Africa and beyond', *Journal of Development Economics*. **120**, 182–208.

Gill, Anthony (2008). *The Political Origins of Religious Liberty*. Cambridge University Press, Cambridge.

Gilmour, Ian (1992). *Riot, Risings and Revolution*. Pimilco, London.

Given, James B. (1989). 'The inquistors of Languedoc and the medieval technology of power', *The American Historical Review*. **94**(2), 336–359.

Given, James B. (1990). *State and Society in Medieval Europe*. Cornell University Press, Ithaca, NY.

Goff, Jacques Le (1979). The usurer and purgatory. In The Dawn of Modern Banking, Yale University Press, New Haven, CT. pp. 25–53.

Goff, Jacques Le (2009). *Saint Louis*. University of Notre Dame Press, Notre Dame, Indiana. Translated by Gareth Evan Gollrad.

Goffart, Walter (1989). *Rome's Fall and After*. A&C Black, London.

Golb, Norman (1998). *The Jews in Medieval Normandy*. Cambridge University Press, Cambridge.

Goldfarb, Michael (2009). *Emancipation*. Simon & Schuster, New York.

Goldhagen, Daniel (2013). *The Devil That Never Dies*. Little Brown and Company, New York.

Goldsmith, James Lowth (2003). *Lordship in France, 500–1500*. Peter Lang, New York.

Goldstein, Alice (1984). 'Urbanization in Baden, Germany: Focus on the Jews, 1825–1925', *Social Science History*. **8**(1), 43–66.

Goldstone, Jack A. (1991). *Revolution and Rebellion in the Early Modern World*. University of California Press, Berkeley.

Goldstone, Jack A. (2000). 'The rise of the west-or not? A revision to socio-economic history', *Sociological Theory*. **18**(2), 175–194.

Goldstone, Jack A. (2002). 'Efflorescences and economic growth in world history: Rethinking the "rise of the west" and the Industrial Revolution', *Journal of World History*. **13**(2), 323–389.

Graetz, Michael (1996). *The Jews in Nineteenth-Century France*. Stanford University Press, Stanford, CA.

Grafe, Regina. (2012). *Distant Tyranny: Markets, Power, and Backwardness in Spain, 1650–1800*. Princeton Economic History of the Western World, Princeton University Press, Princeton, NJ.

Grafe, Regina, and Maria Alejandra Irigoin (2006). 'The Spanish Empire and its legacy: Fiscal redistribution and political conflict in colonial and post-colonial Spanish America', *Journal of Global History*. **1**, 241–267.

Graham, Gordon (2016). Adam Smith and religion. In R. P.Hanley, ed., *Adam Smith: His Life, Thought, and Legacy*. Princeton University Press, Princeton, NJ.

Graham-Leigh, Elaine (2005). *The Southern French Nobility and the Albigensian Crusade*. The Boydell Press, Woodbridge.

Graupe, Heinz Moshe (1978). *The Rise of Modern Judaism: An intellectual history of German Jewry 1650–1942*. Robert E. Kreiger Publishing, New York. Translated by John Robinson.

Gray, Marion W. (1986). 'Prussia in transition: Society and politics under the Stein reform ministry of 1808', *Transactions of the American Philosophical Society*. **76**(1), 1–175.

Green, Toby (2007). *Inquisition: The Reign of Fear*. Thomas Dunne Books, New York.

Greenberg, Louis (1976). *The Jews in Russia: The Struggle Schocken for Emancipation*. Schooken Books, New York.

Greenfeld, Liah (2006). *Nationalism and the Mind: Essays on Modern Culture*. Oneworld Publications, Braintree, MA.

Greengrass, Mark (1987). *The French Reformation*. Basil Blackwell, Oxford.

Greengrass, Mark (2014). *Christendom Destroyed: Europe 1517–1648*. Oxford University Press, Oxford.

Gregory, Annabel (1991). 'Witchcraft, politics and "good neighbourhood" in early seventeenth-century Rye', *Past & Present*. **133**(1), 31–66.

Gregory, Brad S. (2012). *The Unintended Reformation*. Belknap Press of Harvard University Press, Cambridge, MA.

Greif, Avner (2006*a*). 'History lessons: The birth of impersonal exchange: The community responsibility system and impartial justice', *Journal of Economic Perspectives.* **20**(2), 221–236.

Greif, Avner (2006*b*). *Institutions and the Path to the Modern Economy.* Cambridge University Press, Cambridge.

Greif, Avner (2007). The impact of administrative power on political and economic developments. In E.Helpman, ed., 'Institutions and Growth', Harvard University Press, Cambridge, MA.

Greif, Avner, and David D. Laitin (2004). 'A theory of endogenous institutional change', *American Political Science Review.* **98**(4), 633–652.

Greif, Avner, and Jared Rubin (2018). Political Legitimacy and the Institutional Foundations of Constitutional Government: The Case of England. Manuscript.

Grim, Brian J., and Roger Finke (2011), *The Price of Freedom Denied.* Cambridge University Press, Cambridge.

Grosfeld, Irena, Seyhun Orcan Sakalli, and Ekaterina Zhuravskaya (2017). Middleman minorities and ethnic violence: Anti-Jewish pogroms in the Russian Empire. No. 12154 CEPR Discussion Papers.

Grosfled, Irena, Alexander Rodnyansky, and Ekaterina Zhuravskaya (2013). 'Persistent anti-market culture: A legacy of the Pale of Settlement after the Holocaust', *American Economic Journal: Economic Policy.* **5**(3), 189–226.

Grosjean, Pauline (2014). 'A history of violence: The culture of honor and homicide in the US south', *Journal of the European Economic Association.* **12**(5), 1285–1316.

Guenée, Bernard (1985). *State and Rulers in Later Medieval Europe.* Basil Blackwell, Oxford. Translated by Juliet Vale.

Guiot, Joel, and Christopher Corona (2010). 'Growing season temperature in Europe and climate forcings over the past 1400 years', *PLoS One.* **5**(4), 1–15.

Guiso, L., P. Sapienza, and L. Zingales (2006). 'Does culture affect economic outcomes?', *The Journal of Economic Perspectives.* **20**(2), 23–48.

Haddock, David D., and Lynne Kiesling (2002). 'The Black Death and property rights', *The Journal of Legal Studies.* **31**(S2), S545–S587.

Hadfield, Gillian K., and Barry R. Weingast (2012). 'What is law? a coordination model of the characteristics of legal order', *Journal of Legal Analysis.* **4**(1), 1–44.

Hall, Felicity (2003). *Reformation in Britain and Ireland.* Oxford University Press, Oxford.

Hamilton, Alexander, James Madison, and John Jay (1788, 2004). *The Federalist.* Barnes & Noble Books, New York.

Hamilton, Bernard (1999). The Albigensian crusade and heresy. In D.Abulafia, ed., *New Cambridge Medieval History.* Vol. 5, Cambridge University Press, Cambridge, pp. 164–182.

Hamscher, Albert N. (1976). *The Parlement of Paris After the Fronde, 1653–1673.* University of Pittsburgh Press, Pittsburgh.

Hamscher, Albert N. (2012). *The Royal Financial Administration and the Prosecution of Crime in France, 1670–1789.* University of Delaware Press, Newark.

Han, Yu-Shan (1947). 'The role of the historian in China', *Pacific Historical Review.* **16**(2), 134–143.

Hanawalt, Barbara A. (1984). 'Keepers of the light: Late medieval English parish guilds', *Journal of Medieval and Renaissance Studies.* **14**(1), 21–37.

Harling, Philip, and Peter Mandler (1993). 'From "fiscal-military" state to laissez-faire state, 1760–1850', *The Journal of British Studies.* **32**(1), 44–70.

Harper, Kyle (2017). *The Fate of Rome*. Princeton University Press, Princeton, NJ.

Harris, W. V. (2006). 'A revisionist view of Roman money', *Journal of Roman Studies*. **96**, 1–24.

Hartwell, Ronald Max (1981). 'Taxation in England during the Industrial Revolution', *Cato Journal*. **1**(1), 129–153.

Hayek, F.A. (1960). *The Constitution of Liberty*. Routledge, London.

Hayek, F.A. (1973). *Law, Legislation, and Liberty*. Vol. V: Rules and Order, University of Chicago Press, Chicago.

Hayek, F.A. (1976). *Law, Legislation, and Liberty:* Vol. II, *The Mirage of Social Justice*. University of Chicago Press, Chicago.

Hayek, F.A. (1982). *Law, Legislation and Liberty*. Vol. II: The Political Order of a Free People. University of Chicago Press, Chicago.

Hayes, Peter (2017). *Why? Explaining the Holocaust*. W.W. Norton & Company, New York.

Heather, Peter (2006). *The Fall of the Roman Empire: A New History of Rome and the Barbarians*. Oxford University Press, Oxford.

Heather, Peter (2009). *Empires and Barbarians: Migration, Development, and the Birth of Europe*. Macmillan, London.

Heather, Peter (2014). *The Restoration of Rome: Barbarian Popes and Imperial Pretenders*. Oxford University Press, Oxford.

Heckscher, Eli F. (1955). *Mercantilism*. Vol. I, George Allen & Unwin London. Translated by E.F. Soderlund.

Hejeebu, Santhi, and Deirdre N. McCloskey (2004). 'The reproving of Karl Polanyi', *Critical Review*. **13**(3/4), 285–314.

Heldrin, Leander, James A. Robinson, and Sebastian Vollmer (2015). Monks, gents and industrialization: The long-run impact of the English dissolution of the monasteries. Working Paper 21450. National Bureau of Economic Research, Cambridge, MA.

Henningsen, Gustav (1980). *The Witches' Advocate*. University of Nevada Press, Reno, Nevada.

Herdt, Jennifer A. (1997). *Religion and Faction in Hume's Moral Philosophy*. Cambridge University Press, Cambridge.

Herlihy, David (1961). 'Church property on the European continent, 701–1200', *Speculum*. **36**(1), 81–105.

Hill, Christopher (1956). *Economic Problems of the Church: From Archbishop Whitgift to the Long Parliament*. Oxford University Press, Oxford.

Hill, Christopher (1964). *Society and Puritanism in Pre-Revolutionary England*. Martin Secker and Warburg Limited, Manchester.

Hill, Christopher (2002). *The Century of Revolution, 1603–1714*. Routledge, London.

Hirschman, Albert O. (1977). *The Passions and the Interests: Political Arguments for Capitalism Before Its Triumph*. Princeton University Press, Princeton, NJ.

Hoffman, Philip T., and Jean-Laurent Rosenthal (1997). The political economy of warfare and taxation in early modern Europe. In J. V.Nye and J.Drobak, eds, The *Frontiers of the New Institutional Economics*. Academic Press, San Diego, CA, pp. 31–55.

Hoffman, Philip T. (2011). 'Prices, the military revolution, and western Europe's comparative advantage in violence', *Economic History Review*. **64**(1), 39–59.

Hoffman, Philip T. (2012). 'Why Was It Europeans Who Conquered the World?' *The Journal of Economic History*. **72**(3), 601–633.

Hoffman, Philip T. (2015a). 'What do states do? Politics and economic history', *The Journal of Economic History*. **75**, 303–332.

Hoffman, Philip T. (2015*b*). *Why Did Europe Conquer the World?*. Princeton University Press, Princeton, NJ.

Holdsworth, W.S. (1903). *A History of English Law*. Vol. VIII, Metheuen and Co. Limited, London.

Holt, Mack P. (1998). The memory of all things past: Provisions of the Edict of Nantes (1598). In R. L.Goodbar, ed., 'The Edict of Nantes: Five Essays and A New Translation', The National Huguenot Society, Bloomington, MN. pp. 27–39.

Holt, Mack P. (2005). *The French Wars of Religion, 1562–1629*. Cambridge University Press, Cambridge.

Hornung, Erik (2014). 'Immigration and the Diffusion of Technology: The Huguenot Diaspora in Prussia', *American Economic Review*. **104**(1), 84–122.

Horrox, Rosmery, ed. (1994). *The Black Death*. Manchester University Press, Manchester.

Howes, Anton (2017). The Spread of Improvement: Why Innovation Accelerated in Britain 1547–1851. Manuscript.

Howland, Douglas (2001). 'Translating liberty in nineteenth-century Japan', *Journal of the History of Ideas*. **62**(1), 161–181.

Hoyt, Robert S. (1950). *The Royal Demsene in English Constitutional History: 1066–1272*. Cornell University Press, Ithaca, NY.

Huang, Pei (1974). *Autocracy at Work: A study of the Yung-cheng period, 1723–1735*. Indiana University Press, Bloomington.

Huff, Toby (1993). *The Rise of Early Modern Science*. Cambridge University Press, Cambridge.

Hume, David (1748). *An Enquiry Concerning Human Understanding*. Harvard Classics, Cambridge, MA.

Hume, David (1983, 1778). *The History of England from the Invasion of Julius Caesar to the Revolution of 1688*. Vol. 4, Liberty Fund, Indianapolis, IN.

Huntington, S. P. (1968). *Political Order in Changing Societies*. Yale University Press, New Haven, CT.

Hutton, Ronald (1996). *The Stations of the Sun*. Oxford University Press, Oxford.

Hyde, J.K. (1966). *Padua in the Age of Dante*. Manchester University Press, Manchester.

Hyslop, Beatrice (1934). *French Nationalism in 1789 According to the General Cahiers*. Cambridge University Press, Cambridge.

Iannaccone, Laurence, R., and Eli Berman (2006). 'Religious extremism: The good, the bad, and the deadly', *Public Choice*. **128**(1), 109–129.

Iannaccone, Laurence R. (1992). 'Sacrifice and stigma: Reducing free-riding in cults, communes, and other collectives', *Journal of Political Economy*. **100**(2), 271–291.

Iannaccone, Laurence R. (1995). 'Voodoo economics? Reviewing the rational choice approach to religion', *Journal for the Scientific Study of Religion*. **34**(1), 76–88.

Iannaccone, Laurence R. (1998). 'Introduction to the economics of religion', *Journal of Economic Literature*. **36**(3), 1465–1495.

Iannaccone, Laurence R, Roger Finke, and Rodney Stark (1997). 'Deregulating religion: The economics of church and state', *Economic Inquiry*. **35**(2), 350–364.

Iogna-Prat, Dominique (2002). *Order and Exlusion*. Cornell University Press, Ithaca, NY. Translated by Graham Robert Edwards.

Irwin, Douglas A. (1989). 'Political economy and Peel's repeal of the corn laws', *Economics and Politics*. **1**(1), 41–59.

Irwin, Douglas A. (1993). 'Free trade and protection in nineteenth-century Britain and France revisited: A comment on Nye', *The Journal of Economic History*. **53**(1), 146–152.

Irwin, Douglas A. (1996). *Against the Tide: An Intellectual History of Free Trade*. Princeton University Press Princeton, NJ.

Israel, Jonathan (1985). *European Jewry in the Age of Mercantilism, 1550–1750*. Oxford University Press, Oxford.

Israel, Jonathan (2001). *Radical Enlightenment: Philosophy and the Making of Modernity, 1650–1750*. Oxford University Press, Oxford.

Israel, Jonathan (2005). Diasporas Jewish and Non-Jewish in the world maritime empires. In I. B.McCabe, G.Harlaftis and I. P.Minoglou, eds, Diaspora Entrepreneurial Networks: Four Centuries of History, Berg, New York, pp. 3–27.

Israel, Jonathan (2006). *Enlightenment Contested: Philosophy, Modernity, and the Emancipation of Man 1670–1752*. Oxford University Press, Oxford.

Israel, Jonathan I. (1983). 'Central European Jewry during the Thirty Years' War', *Central European History*. **16**(1), 3–30.

Iyer, Syria (2016). 'The new economics of religion', *Journal of Economic Literature*. **54**(2), 395–441.

Iyigun, Murat (2008). 'Luther and Suleyman', *The Quarterly Journal of Economics*. **123**(4), 1465–1494.

Iyigun, Murat (2015). *War, Peace, and Prosperity in the Name of God*. University of Chicago Press, Chicago.

Jacob, Margaret C. (2006). *Strangers Nowhere in the World*. University of Pennsylvania Press, Philadelphia.

Jacobs, Joseph (1898). 'Aaron of Lincoln', *The Jewish Quarterly Review*. **10**(4), 629–648.

Jarvis, A., H.I. Reuter, A. Nelson, and E. Guevara (2008). Hole-filled SRTM for the globe version 4, available from the CGIAR-CSI SRTM 90m Database (http://srtm.csi.cgiar.org), Technical report, NASA.

Jebwab, Remi, Noel D. Johnson, and Mark Koyama (2016). Bones, bacteria and break points: The heterogeneous spatial effects of the Black Death and long-run growth. Working Paper.

Jedwab, Remi, Noel D. Johnson, and Mark Koyama (2017). Negative shocks and mass persecutions: Evidence from the Black Death. No. 77720. University Library of Munich, Germany.

Jenkinson, Hilary (1927). A moneylender's bonds of the twelfth century. In H.Davis, ed., In Essays in History, Presented to Reginald Lane Poole, Oxford University Press, Oxford, pp. 190–210.

Jenson, Gary (2007). *The Path of the Devil*. & Littlefield Rowman Lanham, MD.

Jersch-Wenzel, Stefi (1997). Legal status and emancipation. In M. A.Meyer, ed., *German-Jewish History in Modern Times*. Vol. 2, Columbia University Press, New York, pp. 5–49.

Jha, Saumitra (2013). 'Trade, complementaries and religious tolerance: Evidence from India', *American Journal of Political Science*. **107**(4), 806–832.

Jha, Saumitra (2015). 'Financial asset holdings and political attitudes: Evidence from revolutionary England', *Quarterly Journal of Economics*. **130**(3), 1485–1545.

Jha, Saumitra (2018). 'Trading for peace', *Economic Policy*. 33(95), 485–526.

Jha, Saumitra, and Moses Shayo (2017). Valuing peace: The effects of financial market exposure on votes and political attitudes, Technical report, Stanford University Graduate School of Business Research Paper No. 16–7.

Johnson, Eric (1999). *Nazi Terror: Gestap, Jews, and Ordinary Germans*. Basic Books, New York.

Johnson, Noel D. (2006). 'Banking on the king: The evolution of the royal revenue farms in old regime France', *The Journal of Economic History*. **66**(4), 963–991.

Johnson, Noel D. (2015). Taxes, national identity, and nation building: Evidence from France. GMU Working Paper in Economics No. 15.33.

Johnson, Noel D., and Mark Koyama (2013). 'Legal centralization and the birth of the secular state'. *Journal of Comparative Economics*. **41**(4), 959–978.

Johnson, Noel D., and Mark Koyama (2014*a*). 'Tax farming and the origins of state capacity in England and France', *Explorations in Economic History*. **51**(1), 1–20.

Johnson, Noel D., and Mark Koyama (2014*b*). 'Taxes, lawyers, and the decline of witch trials in France', *Journal of Law and Economics*. **57**, 77–112.

Johnson, Noel D., and Mark Koyama (2017). 'Jewish communities and city growth in preindustrial Europe', *Journal of Development Economics*. **127**(1), 119–143.

Jongman, Willem M. (2015). Reconstructing the Roman economy. In L.Neal and J. G.Williamson, eds, *The Cambridge History of Capitalism*. Cambridge University Press, Cambridge, pp. 75–100.

Jordan, William Chester (1986). 'Christian excommunication of the Jews in the Middle Ages: A restatement of the issues', *Jewish History*. **1**(1), 31–38.

Jordan, William Chester (1989). *The French Monarchy and the Jews: From Philip Augustus to the Last Capetians*. University of Pennsylvania Press, Philadelphia.

Jordan, William Chester (1998). 'Jews, regalian rights, and the constitution in Medieval France', *AJS Review*. **23**, 1–16.

Jordan, W.K. (1932). *The Development of Religious Toleration in England*. Vol. I, Cambridge University Press, Cambridge.

Jordan, W.K. (1936). *The Development of Religious Toleration in England*. Vol. II, Cambridge University Press, Cambridge.

Kamen, Henry (1967). *The Rise of Toleration*. World University Library, New York.

Kamen, Henry (1971). *The Iron Century, Social Change in Europe 1550–1660*. Weidenfeld and Nicolson, London.

Kamen, Henry (1978). 'The decline of Spain: A historical myth?', *Past & Present*. **81**, 24–50.

Kamen, Henry (1985). *Inquisition and Society in Spain in the Sixteenth and Seventeenth Centuries*. Indiana University Press, Bloomington.

Kamen, Henry (1988). 'The Mediterranean and the expulsion of Spanish Jews in 1492', *Past & Present*. **119**, 30–55.

Kaplan, Benjamin (2007). *Divided by Faith*. Harvard University Press, Cambridge, MA.

Karaman, Kivanc, and Şevket Pamuk (2013). 'Different paths to the modern state in Europe: The interaction between warfare, economic structure and political regime', *American Political Science Review*. **107**(3), 603–626.

Katz, David S. (1991). The Jews of England and 1688. In P.Grell, J. I.Israel and N.Tyacke, eds, *From Persecution to Toleration: The Glorious Revolution and Religion in England*. Oxford University Press, Oxford.

Katz, David S. (1994). *The Jews in the History of England, 1485–1850*. Clarendon Press, Oxford.

Katz, Jacob (1974). *Out of the Ghetto*. Harvard University Press, Cambridge, MA.

Katz, Jacob (2000). *Tradition and Crisis*. Syracuse University Press, New York. Translated by Bernard Dov Cooperman.

Kaufmann, Thomas (2017). *Luther's Jews*. Oxford University Press, Oxford.

Keller, Wolfgang, and Carol H. Shiue (2014). 'Endogenous formation of free trade agreements: Evidence from the Zollverein's impact on market integration', *The Journal of Economic History*. **74**, 1168–1204.

Kelley, Donald R. (1972). 'Martyrs, Myths, and the massacre: The background of St. Bartholomew', *The American Historical Review*. **77**(5), pp. 1323–1342.

Kelly, Christopher (2004). *Ruling the Later Roman Empire*. Belknap Press, Cambridge, MA.

Kelly, Henry Ansgar (1989). 'Inquisition and the persecution of heresy: Misconceptions and abuses', *Church History*. **58**(4), 439–451.

Kennedy, Paul (1987). *The Rise and Fall of the Great Powers, 1500–1980*. Vintage Books, New York.

Kettering, Sharon (1986). *Patrons, Brokers, and Clients in Seventeenth-Century France*. Oxford University Press, Oxford.

Kieckhefer, Richard (1979). *Repression of Heresy in Medieval Germany*. University of Pennsylvania Press, Philadelphia.

Kieckhefer, Richard (1995). 'The office of inquisition and medieval heresy: The transition from personal to institutional jurisdiction', *The Journal of Ecclesiastical History*. **46**(1), 36–61.

Kirschner, Julius, and Karl F. Morrison, eds (1986). *Readings in Western Civilization: Medieval Europe*. Vol. 4, University of Chicago Press, Chicago.

Kiser, Edgar, and Joachim Schneider (1994). 'Bureaucracy and efficiency: An analysis of taxation in early modern Prussia', *American Sociological Review*. **59**(2), 187–204.

Kiser, Edgar, and Joshua Kane (2001). 'Revolution and state structure: The bureaucratization of tax administration in early modern England and France', *American Journal of Sociology*. **107**(1), 183–223.

Klein, Daniel B. (2014). 'Lost language, lost liberalism'. http://www.lostlanguage.org/

Knecht, R.J. (1982). *Francis I*. Cambridge University Press, Cambridge.

Ko, Chiu Yu, Mark Koyama, and Tuan-Hwee Sng (2018). 'Unified China; Divided Europe', *International Economic Review*. **59**(1), 285–327.

Kober, Adolf (1947). 'Jewish communties in Germany from the age of Enlightenment to their destruction by the Nazis', *Jewish Social Studies*. **9**(3), 195–238.

Koyama, Mark (2010*a*). 'Evading the "taint of usury": The usury prohibition as a barrier to entry', *Explorations in Economic History*. **47**(4), 420–442.

Koyama, Mark (2010*b*). 'The political economy of expulsion: The regulation of Jewish moneylending in medieval England', *Constitutional Political Economy*. **21**(4), 374–406.

Koyama, Mark (2014). 'The law & economics of private prosecutions in Industrial Revolution England', *Public Choice*. **159**(1), 277–298.

Koyama, Mark (2016). 'The long transition from a natural state to a liberal economic order', *International Review of Law and Economics*. **47**, 29–39.

Koyama, Mark, Chiaki Moriguchi, and Tuan-Hwee Sng (2017). Geopolitics and Asia's Little Divergence: State building in China and Japan after 1850. Journal of Economic Behavior & Organization. 155, 178–204.

Kuhn, Philip A. (1990). *Soulstealers: The Chinese Sorcery Scare of 1768*. Harvard University Press, Cambridge.

Kuhn, Philip A. (2002). *Origins of the Modern Chinese State*. Stanford University Press, Stanford, California.

Kukathas, Chandran (2003). *The Liberal Archipelago: A Theory of Diversity and Freedom*. Oxford University Press, Oxford.

Kung, James Kai-sing, and Chicheng Ma (2014). 'Can cultural norms reduce conflicts? Confucianism and peasant rebellions in Qing China', *Journal of Development Economics*. **111**, 132–149.

Kuran, Timur (1989). 'Sparks and prairie fires: A theory of unanticipated political revolution', *Public Choice*. **61**(1), 41–74.

Kuran, Timur (1995). *Private Truths, Public Lies*. Harvard University Press, London, United Kingdom.

Kuran, Timur (1998). Moral overload and its alleviation. In A.Ben-Ner and L.Putterman, eds, *Economics, Values, and Organization*. Cambridge University Press, Cambridge, pp. 231–266. Foreword by Amartya Sen.

Kuran, Timur (2004). 'The economic ascent of the Middle East's religious minorities: The role of Islamic legal pluralism', *Journal of Legal Studies*. **33**, 475–515.

Kuran, Timur (2006). *Islam and Mammon*. Princeton University Press, Princeton, NJ.

Kuran, Timur (2010). *The Long Divergence*. Princeton University Press, Princeton, NJ.

Kuran, Timur (2016). 'Legal roots of authoritarian rule in the Middle East: Civic legacies of the Islamic Waqf', *The American Journal of Comparative Law*. **64**(2), 419–454.

Kuran, Timur (2018). 'Islam and economic performance: Historical and contemporary links', *Journal of Economic Literature*. **56**, 1292–1359.

Kuznets, Simon (1960). Economic structure and life of the Jews. In L.Finkelstein, ed., *The Jews: Their History, Culture, and Religion*. Jewish Publication Society of America, Philadelphia, pp. 1597–1666.

Kuznets, Simon (1966). *Modern Economic Growth*. Yale University Press, New Haven, CT.

Kymlicka, Will (1996). Two modes of pluralism and tolerance. In D.Heyd, ed., *Toleration*. Princeton University Press, Princeton, NJ. pp. 81–1065.

Labrousse, Elizabeth (1998). Reflections on the Edict of Nantes. In R. L.Goodbar, ed., *The Edict of Nantes: Five Essays and A New Translation*. The National Huguenot Society, Bloomington, MN. pp. 33–41.

Ladurie, Emmanuel Le Roy (1977). *The French Peasantry 1450–1660*. Translated by Alan Sheridan. Scolar Press, Aldershot.

Ladurie, Emmanuel Le Roy (1978). *Montaillou*. Scolar Press, London. Translated by Barbara Bray.

Lai, Cheng-Chung, ed. (2000). *Adam Smith Across Nations: Translations and Receptions of the Wealth of Nations*. Clarendon Press, Oxford.

Lambert, Malcolm (1977). *Medieval Heresy*. Blackwell Publishers, Oxford.

Lambert, Malcolm (1998). *The Cathars*. Basil Blackwell, Oxford.

Lamoreaux, Naomi R. (2011). 'The mystery of property rights: A U.S. perspective', *The Journal of Economic History*. **71**(02), 275–306.

Langbein, John H. (1977). *Torture and the Law of Proof*. University of Chicago Press, Chicago.

Langholm, Odd (1992). *Economics in the Medieval Schools: Wealth Exchange, Value, Money, and Usury According to the Paris Theological Tradition 1200–1350*. E.J. Brill, Leiden.

Langmuir, Gavin I. (1990). *Toward a Definition of Antisemitism*. University of California Press, Berkeley.

Lansing, Carol (1998). *Power and Purity*. Oxford University Press, Oxford.

Larner, Christina (1980). Crimen exceptum? The crime of witchcraft in Europe. In V.Gatrell, B.Lenman and G.Parker, eds, *Crime and the Law: The Social History of Crime in Western Europe since 1500*. Europa, London, pp. 49–75.

Larner, Christina (1981). *Enemies of God: The Witch-hunt in Scotland*. Chatto & Windus, London.

Laurin, K., A. F. Shariff, J. Henrich, and A. C. Kay (2012). 'Outsourcing punishment to god: Beliefs in divine control reduce earthly punishment', *Proceedings of the Royal Society B-Biological Science*. **279**, 3272–3281.

Laursen, John Christian (1999). Orientation: Clarifying the conceptual issues. In J. C.Laursen, ed., *Religious Toleration: 'The Variety of Rites' from Cyrus to Defoe*. Macmillan, London, pp. 1–8.

Lea, H.C. (1973). *The Ordeal*. Sources of Medieval History, University of Pennsylvania Press.

Lea, Henry Charles (1907). *A History of the Inquisition of Spain*. Vol. III, Macmillan, London.

Leather, Charles G., and J. Patrick Raines (1992). 'Adam Smith on competitive religious markets', *History of Political Economy*. **24**(2), 499–513.

Lecler, Joseph (1955). *Toleration and the Reformation*. Vol. I, Association Press, New York.

Lecler, Joseph (1960). *Toleration and the Reformation*. Vol. II, Association Press, New York.

Leeson, Peter T., and Jacob W. Russ (2018). 'Witch trials', *The Economic Journal*. **128**, 2066–2105.

Lehmann, Hartmut (1995). The Jewish minority and the Christian majority in early modern central Europe. In R. P.-C.Hsia and H.Lehmann, eds, *In and Out of the Ghetto: Jewish-Gentile Relations in Late Medieval and Early Modern Germany*. Cambridge University Press, Cambridge, pp. 305–311.

Leibniz, Gottfried Wilhelm (1972). Two letters to Bossuet concerning the re-unification of Christendom. In P.Riley, ed., Leibniz: Political Writings, Cambridge University Press, Cambridge, pp. 188–191.

Lerner, Robert E. (1965). 'The uses of heterodoxy: The French monarchy and unbelief in the thirteenth century', *French Historical Studies*. **4**(2), 189–202.

Levack, Brian P. (1996). State-building and witch hunting in early modern Europe. In J.Barry, M.Hester and G.Roberts, eds, *Witchcraft in Early Modern Europe*. Cambridge University Press, Cambridge, pp. 96–118.

Levack, Brian P. (1999). The decline and end of witchcraft prosecutions. In B.Ankarloo and S.Clark, eds, Witchcraft and Magic in Europe, the eighteenth and nineteenth centuries, Unversity of Pennsylvania Press, Philadelphia, pp. 1–94.

Levack, Brian P. (2006). *The Witch-Hunt in Early Modern Europe*. 3rd edn, Person, Harlow.

Levack, Brian P. (2008). *Witch-Hunting in Scotland*. Routledge, London.

Levenson, Alan T. (2012). *The Wiley-Blackwell History of Jews and Judaism*. Wiley-Blackwell, London.

Levy, David M (2002). *How the Dismal Science Got Its Name: Classical Economics and the Ur-Text of Racial Politics*. University of Michigan Press, Ann Arbor, MI.

Levy, Jacob (2015). *Rationalism, Pluralism, and Freedom*. Oxford University Press, Oxford.

Lewis, Bernard (1986). *Semites and Anti-Semites*. George Weidenfeld and Nicholson Ltd, London.

Lewis, Carenza (2016). 'Disaster recovery: new archaeological evidence for the long-term impact of the "calamitous" fourteenth century', *Antiquity*. **90**, 777–797.

Lipman, V. D. (1967). *The Jews of Medieval Norwich*. Jewish Historical Society of England, London. Edited by A.M. Habermann of Norwich.

Lipset, Seymour Martin (1963). *Political Man: The Social Bases of Politics*. Anchor Books, New York.

Lopez, Robert S. (1971). *The Commercial Revolution of the Middle Ages, 950–1350*. Prentice Hall, Englewood Cliifs, NJ.

Low, Alfred F. (1979). *Jews in the Eyes of Germans: From the Enlightenment to Imperial Germany*. Institute for the Study of Human Issues, Philadelphia.

Lowenstein, Steven M. (1981). The 1840s and the creation of the German-Jewish religious reform movement. In W. E.Mosse, A.Paucker and R.Rürup, eds, Revolution and Evolution in German-Jewish History, J.C.B Mohr, Tübingen, pp. 255–298.

Luther, Martin (1553). *The Jews and Their Lies*. Christian Nationalist Crusade, Los Angeles.

Lynch, John (1992). *Spain 1516–1598: From Nation State to World Empire*. Blackwell Publishers, Oxford.

Lynn, John A. (1997). *Giant of the Grand Siècle: The French Army, 1610–1715*. Cambridge University Press, Cambridge.

Ma, Debin (2013). 'State capacity and the great divergence: The case of Qing China', *Eurasian Geography and Economics*. **54**(56), 484–498.

Ma, Debin, and Jared Rubin (2017). The paradox of power: Understanding fiscal capacity in imperial China and absolutist regimes. REPEC Working Paper No. 17–02.

Macaulay, Thomas Babington (1967, 1848). *History of England*. Vol. I, Heron Books, London.

MacCulloch, Diarmaid (2003). *Reformation, Europe's House Divided 1490–1700*. Allen Lane, London.

MacCulloch, Diarmaid (2016). *All Things Made New: Writings on the Reformation*. Allen Lane, London.

Macfarlane, Alan (1970). *Witchcraft in Tudor and Stuart England*. Routledge & Kegan Paul, London.

Machin, G. I. T. (1963). 'The Catholic emancipation crisis of 1825', *The English Historical Review*. **78**(308), 458–482.

Machin, Ian (1999). British Catholics. In R.Liedtke and S.Wendehorst, eds, *The Emancipation of Catholics, Jews, and Protestants*. Manchester University Press, Manchester, pp. 11–33.

MacKinnon, James (1962). *Calvin and the Reformation*. Russell & Russell, New York.

Maddicott, J. R. (1994). *Simon De Montefort*. Cambridge University Press, Cambridge.

Madigan, Kevin (2015). *Medieval Christianity: A New History*. Yale University Press, New Haven, CT.

Magnus, Shulamit S. (1997). *Jewish Emancipation in a German City: Cologne, 1798–1871*. Stanford University Press, Stanford, CA.

Mahler, Raphael (1985). *Hasidism and the Jewish Enlightenment*. The Jewish Publication Society of America, Philadelphia. Translated from Yddish by Eugene Orenstein; translated from Hebrew by Aaron Klein and Jenny Machlowitz Klein.

Maimon, Solomon (1954). *The Autobiography of Solomon Maimon*. The East and West Library, London. Translated by J. Clark Murray.

Maine, Henry Sumner (1861). *Ancient Law: Its Connection with the Early History of Society and Its Relation to Modern Ideas*. John Murray, London.

Maloney, Robert P. (1973). 'The teaching of the fathers on usury: An historical study on the development of Christian thinking', *Vigiliae Christianae*. **27**(4), 241–265.

Mandeville, Bernard (1924, 1714). *The Fable of the Bees: Or Private Vices, Publick Benefits*. Liberty Fund, Indianapolis.

Mandrou, Robert (1979). *Possession et sorcellerie au xviiê siècle: Textes inédits*. Fayard.

Mann, Michael (1986). *The Sources of Social Power*. Vol. I, Cambridge University Press, Cambridge.

Markish, Shimon (1986). *Erasmus and the Jews*. University of Chicago Press, Chicago.

Marshall, John (2006). *John Locke, Toleration and Early Enlightenment Culture*. Cambridge University Press, Cambridge.

Marshall, Peter (2016). *Heretics and Believers: A History of the English Reformation*. Yale University Press, New Haven, CT.

Masschaele, James (1993). 'Transport costs in medieval England', *The Economic History Review*. **46**(2), 266–279.

Matar, Nabil I. (1993). 'John Locke and the Jews', *The Journal of Ecclesiastical History*. **44**, 45–62.

Mathias, Peter, and Patrick O'Brien (1976). 'Taxation in Britain and France, 1715–1810: A comparison of the social and economic incidence of taxes collected for the central governments', *Journal of European Economic History*. **5**(3), 601–50.

McCloskey, Deirdre N. (2006). *The Bourgeois Virtues, Ethics of an Age of Commerce*. University of Chicago Press, Chicago.

McCloskey, Deirdre N. (2010). *Bourgeois Dignity: Why Economics Can't Explain the Modern World*. University of Chicago Press, Chicago.

McCloskey, Deirdre N. (2016). *Bourgeois Equality*. University of Chicago Press, Chicago.

McCloskey, Donald N., and John Nash (1984). 'Corn at interest: The extent and cost of grain storage in Medieval England', *The American Economic Review*. **74**, 174–187.

McCormick, Michael (2001). *Origins of the European Economy*. Cambridge University Press, Cambridge.

McFarlane, K.B. (1972). *Lancastrian Kings and Lollard Knights*. Oxford at the Clarendon Press, Oxford.

McGarvie, Mark Douglas (2005). *One Nation Under Law: America's Early National Struggles to Separate Church and State*. Northern Illinois University Press, DeKalb, IL.

McGrath, Patrick (1967). *Papists and Puritans Under Elizabeth I*. Blandord Press, London.

McKechnie, William Sharp (1905). *Magna Carta: A Commentary on the Great Charter of King John*. James Maclehose and Sons, Glawsgow.

McNeil, William H. (1974). *Plagues and Peoples*. Basil Blackwell, Oxford.

Mearscheimer, John J. (2001). *The Tragedy of Great Power Politics*. W. W. Norton & Company, New York.

Melitz, Jacques (1971). 'Some further reassessment of the scholastic doctrine of usury', *Kyklos*. **24**(3), 473–492.

Melzer, Arthur (2014). *Philosophy Between the Lines: The Lost Art of Esoteric Writing*. University of Chicago Press, Chicago.

Menache, Sophia (1985). 'Faith, myth, and politics: The sterotype of the Jews and their expulsion from England and France', *The Jewish Quarterly Review*. **75**, 351–374.

Menache, Sophia (1997). 'Mathew Paris's attitudes toward Anglo–Jewry', *Journal of Medieval History*. **23**, 139–162.

Menocal, Maria Rosa (2002). *The Ornament of the World: How Muslims, Jews, and Christians Created a Culture of Tolerance in Medieval Spain*. Back Bay Books / Little, Brown and Company, New York.

Mentzer, Raymond A., Jr. (1984). 'Heresy proceedings in Languedoc, 1500–1560', *Transactions of the American Philosophical Society*. **74**(5), pp. 1–183.

Merrick, Jeffrey W. (1990). *The Desacralization of the French Monarchy in the Eighteenth Century*. Louisiana State University Press, Baton Rouge.

Merrill, Thomas (2015). *Hume and the Politics of Enlightenment*. Cambridge University Press, Cambridge.

Meyer, Michael A. (1988). *Response to Modernity: A History of the Reform Movement in Judaism*. Oxford University Press, Oxford.

Meyer, Michael A., ed. (1997). *German-Jewish History in Modern Times*. Vol. 2, Columbia University Press, New York.

Michalopoulos, Stelios, Alireza Naghavi, and Giovanni Prarolo (2016). 'Islam, inequality and pre-industrial comparative development', *Journal of Development Economics*. **120**(C), 86–98.

Michalopoulos, Stelios, Alireza Naghavi, and Giovanni Prarolo (2017). 'Trade and geography in the origins and spread of Islam', *Economic Journal*. doi: 10.1111/ecoj.12557.

Midelfort, Eric (1972). *Witch Hunting in Southwestern Germany*. Stanford University Press, Stanford, CA.

Milgram, Stanley (1963). 'Behavioral study of obedience', *The Journal of Abnormal and Social Psychology*. **67**(4), 371–378.

Mill, John Stuart (1859, 1989). *On Liberty*. Cambridge University Press, Cambridge.

Miller, Maureen C. (2005). *Power and the Holy in the Age of the Investiture Conflict: A Brief History with Documents*. Bedford Cultural Editions Series, Bedford/St. Martin's.

Mintzker, Yair (2017). *The Many Deaths of Jew Süss*. Princeton University Press, Princeton, NJ.

Mitchell, Sydney Knox (1951). *Taxation in Medieval England*. Yale University Press, New Haven, CT.

Mokyr, Joel (2002). *The Gift of Athena: Historical Origins of the Knowledge Economy*. Princeton University Press, Princeton, NJ.

Mokyr, Joel (2009). *The Enlightened Economy*. Yale University Press, New Haven, CT.

Mokyr, Joel (2016). *Culture of Growth*. Princeton University Press, Princeton, NJ.

Mokyr, Joel, and John V. C. Nye (2007), 'Distribution coalitions, the Industrial Revolution, and the origins of economics growth in Britain', *Southern Economic Journal*. **74**(1), 50–70.

Momigliano, Arnaldo (1980). 'A note on Max Weber's definition of Judaism as a pariah-religion', *History and Theory*. **19**(3), 313–318.

Monter, E. William (2002). Witch trials in continental Europe, 1560–1660. In B.Ankarloo, S.Clark and E. W.Monter, eds, *Witchcraft and Magic in Europe, the Period of the Witch Trials*. The Athlone Press, London, pp. 3–52.

Monter, William (1990). *Frontiers of Heresy: The Spanish Inquisition from the Basque Lands to Sicily*. Cambridge University Press, Cambridge.

Monter, William (1999). *Judging the French Reformation*. Harvard University Press, Cambridge, MA.

Montesquieu, Charles de (1748, 1989). *The Spirit of the Laws*. Cambridge University Press, Cambridge. Translated by Anne M. Cohler, Basia C. Miller, and Harold S. Stone.

Moore, Barrington (1966). *Social Origins of Dictatorship and Democracy*. Beacon Press, Boston, MA.

Moore, Barrington (2000). *Moral Purity and Persecution in History*. Princeton University Press, Princeton, NJ.

Moore, Michael Edward (2011). *A Sacred Kingdom: Bishops and the Rise of Frankish Kingship, 300–850*. The Catholic University of America Press, Washington, DC.

Moore, R.I. (1999). The Birth of Europe as a Eurasian phenomenon. In V.Lieberman, ed., *Beyond Binary Histories: Re-imagining Eurasia to c.1830*. University of Michigan Press, Ann Arbor, pp. 139–158.

Moore, Robert I. (1987). *The Formation of a Persecuting Society: Power and Deviance in Western Europe, 950–1250*. Basil Blackwell, Oxford.

Moore, Robert I. (1992). 'Anti-Semitism and the Birth of Europe', *Christianity and Judaism*. pp. 33–57.

Moore, Robert I. (2008). 'The war against heresy in medieval Europe', *Historical Research*. **81**(212), 189–210.

Moore, Robert I. (2012). *The War on Heresy*. Profile Books, London.

Moote, A. Lloyd (1971). *The Revolt of the Judges*. Princeton University Press, Princeton, NJ.

Morck, Randall, and Bernard Yeung (2011). 'Economics, history, and causation', *Business History Review*. **85**(1), 39–63.

More, Alexander F., Nicole E. Spaulding, Pascal Bohleber, et al. (2017). 'Next-generation ice core technology reveals true minimum natural levels of lead (Pb) in the atmosphere: Insights from the Black Death', *GeoHealth*. **1**(4), 211–219.

Morgan, Edmund S. (1963). *Visible Saints: The History of a Puritan Idea*. Cornell University Press, Ithaca, NY.

Morris, Colin (1989). *The Papal Monarchy : the Western Church from 1050 to 1250*. Clarendon Press, Oxford.

Mortimer, Ian (2008). *The Fears of Henry IV*. Vintage Books, London.

Moser, Petra, Alessandra Voena, and Fabian Waldinger (2014). 'German Jewish Émigrés and US invention', *American Economic Review*. **104**(10), 3222–3255.

Mousnier, Roland (1979). *The Institutions of France Under the Absolute Monarchy, 1598–1789: Society and the State*. University of Chicago Press, Chicago.

Mundill, Robin R. (1998). *England's Jewish Solution: Experiment and Expulsion, 1262–1290*. Cambridge University Press, Cambridge.

Mundill, Robin R. (2010). *The King's Jews: Money, Massacre and Exodus in Medieval England*. Continuum, London.

Murray, Charles (2003). *Human Accomplishment*. Perennial, New York.

Nahon, Gérard (1975). 'Pour une géographie administrative des Juifs dans la France de Saint Louis', *Revue Historique*. **254**(2 (516)), pp. 305–343.

Nederman, Cary J. (2000). *Worlds of Difference: European Discourses of Toleration c. 1100–c.1500*. Pennsylvania State University Press, University Park, Pennsylvania.

Nelson, Benjamin (1969, 1949). *The Idea of Usury*. University of Chicago Press, London.

Netanyahu, Benzion (1995). *The Origins of the Inquisition in Fifteenth Century Spain*. Random House, New York.

Nexon, Daniel H. (2009). *The Struggle for Power in Early Modern Europe*. Princeton University Press, Princeton, NJ.

Nicholas, David (2003). *Urban Europe, 1100–1700*. Palgrave MacMillian, London.

Nicholls, David (1988). 'The theatre of martyrdom in the French Reformation', *Past & Present*. (121), pp. 49–73.

Nietzsche, Friedrich (1999, 1911). *Thus Spoke Zarathustra*. Dover Publications, Mineola, NY.

Nirenberg, David (1996). *Communities of Violence*. Princeton University Press, Princeton, NJ.

Nirenberg, David (2013). *Anti-Judaism: The Western Tradition.* W.W. Norton & Company, New York.

Nohl, Johannes (1924). *The Black Death: A Chronicle of the Plague.* George Allen & Unwin. Translated by C.H. Clarke.

Noonan, John T. (1957). *The Scholastic Analysis of Usury.* Harvard University Press, Cambridge, MA.

Norenzayan, Ara (2013). *Big Gods: How Religion Transformed Cooperation and Conflict.* Princeton University Press, Princeton, NJ.

Norenzayan, Ara, Azim F. Shariff, Will M. Gervais, Aiyana K. Willard, Rita A. McNamara, Edward Slingerland, and Joseph Henrich (2016). 'The cultural evolution of prosocial religions', *Behavioral and Brain Sciences.* **39**, 1–65.

Norris, Pippa, and Ronald Inglehart (2004). *Sacred and Secular: Religion and Politics Worldwide.* 2nd edn, 2011. Cambridge University Press, Cambridge.

North, Douglass C. (1981). *Structure and Change in Economic History.* W. W. Norton, New York.

North, Douglass C. (1990). *Institutions, Institutional Change, and Economic Performance.* Cambridge University Press, Cambridge.

North, Douglass C., and Barry Weingast (1989). 'Constitutions and commitment: The evolution of institutions governing public choice in seventeenth century England', *Journal of Economic History.* **49**, 803–832.

North, Douglass C., John Joseph Wallis, and Barry R. Weingast (2009). *Violence and Social Orders: A Conceptual Framework for Interpreting Recorded Human History.* Cambridge University Press, Cambridge.

Noymer, Andrew (2007). 'Contesting the cause and severity of the Black Death: A review essay', *Population and Development Review.* **33**(3), 616–627.

Nunn, Nathan (2012). 'Culture and the historical process', *Economic History of Developing Regions.* **27**(1), 108–126.

Nunn, Nathan, and Diego Puga (2012). 'Ruggedness: The blessing of bad geography in Africa', *The Review of Economics and Statistics.* **94**(1), 20–36.

Nussli, Christos (2011). http://www.euratlas.com/about.html.

Nye, John V. C. (2007). *War, Wine, and Taxes: The Political Economy of Anglo-French Trade, 1689–1900.* Princeton University Press, Princeton, NJ.

Oakeshott, Michael (2006). *Lectures in the History of Political Thought.* edited by Terry Nardin and Luke O'sullivan, Imprint Academic, Exeter.

Oberman, Heiko A. (1981). *The Roots of Anti-Semitism.* Fortress Press, PA. Translated by James I. Porter.

O'Brien, Charles H. (1969). 'Ideas of religious toleration at the time of Joseph II. A study of the Enlightenment among Catholics in Austria', *Transactions of the American Philosophical Society.* **59**(7), 1–80.

O'Brien, Patrick K. (1988). 'The political economy of British taxation, 1660–1815', *The Economic History Review.* **41**(1), 1–32.

O'Brien, Patrick K. (2001). Fiscal exceptionalism: Great Britain and its European Rivals from Civil War to Triumph at Trafalgar and Waterloo. London School of Economics Working Paper.

O'Brien, Patrick K. (2011). 'The nature and historical evolution of an exceptional fiscal state and its possible significance for the precocious commercialization and industrialization of the British economy from Cromwell to Nelson', *The Economic History Review.* 408–446.

Ocibal, J. (1976). Louis XIV and the Edict of Nantes. In R.Hatton, ed., *Louis XIV and Absolutism*. London, pp. 154–176.

Ogilvie, Sheilagh (1996). The beginnings of industrialization. In S.Ogilvie, ed., *Germany: A New Social and Economic History*. Vol. II: 1630–1800', Edward Arnold, pp. 263–308.

Ogilvie, Sheilagh (2003). *A Bitter Living: Women, Markets, and Social Capital in Early Modern Germany*. Oxford University Press, Oxford.

Ogilvie, Sheilagh (2014). 'The Economics of Guilds', *Journal of Economic Perspectives*. **28**(4), 169–192.

Oldenbourg, Zoe (1961). *Massacre at Montségur*. Phoenix Press, London.

Oneal, John R., and Bruce Russett (1999). 'Assessing the liberal peace with alternative specifications: Trade still reduces conflict', *Journal of Peace Research*. **36**(4), 423–442.

O'Rourke, K. H., and J. G. Williamson (1999). *Globalization and History: The Evolution of a Nineteenth-Century Economy*. MIT Press, Cambridge, MA.

Osborne, John W. (1984). 'William Cobbett's anti-Semitism', *The Historian*. **47**(1), 86–92.

Oster, Emily (2004). 'Witchcraft, weather and economic growth in Renaissance Europe', *Journal of Economic Perspectives*. **18**(1), 215–228.

Pangle, Thomas (2010). *The Theological Basis of Liberal Modernity in Montesquieu's Spirit of the Laws*. University of Chicago Press, Chicago.

Paris, Matthew (1852). *English History, from the Year 1235 to 1272*. Vol. I, Henry G Bohn, London.

Parker, Charles H. (1993). 'French Calvinists as the children of Israel: An Old Testament self-consciousness in Jean Crespin's Histoire des Martyrs before the wars of religion', *The Sixteenth Century Journal*. **24**(2), pp. 227–248.

Parker, Geoffrey (1976). 'The "military revolution," 1560–1660–a myth?' *The Journal of Modern History*. **48**(2), 195–214.

Parker, Geoffrey (1984). *The Thirty Years War*. Routledge & Kegan Paul, London.

Parker, Geoffrey (1988). *The Military Revolution: Military Innovation and the Rise of the West, 1500–1800*. Cambridge University Press, Cambridge.

Parker, Geoffrey (1998). *The Grand Strategy of Philip II*. Yale University Press, New Haven, CT.

Parker, Geoffrey (2013). *Global Crises: War, Climate Change and Catastrophe in the Seventeenth Century*. Yale University Press, New Haven, CT.

Parker, Geoffrey (2014). *Imprudent King: A New Life of Philip II*. Yale University Press, New Haven.

Parker, T. M. (1968). The Papacy, Catholic Reform, and Christian Missions. In R.Wernham, ed., *The New Cambridge Modern History*. Vol. III: *The Counter-Reformation and Price Revolution 1559–1610*. Cambridge University Press, Cambridge, pp. 44–71.

Parkes, James (1976). *The Jew in the Medieval Community*. Sepher-Hermon Press, Brooklyn, NY.

Parry, Marc (2016). 'Shackles and dollars: Historians and economists clash over slavery', *The Chronicle of Higher Education*.
http://www.chronicle.com/article/ShacklesDollars/238598

Pegg, Mark Gregory (2001). *The Corruption of Angels*. Princeton University Press, Princeton, NJ.

Pegg, Mark Gregory (2008). *A Most Holy War*. Oxford University Press, Oxford.

Pérez, Joseph (2006). *The Spanish Inquisition: A History*. Yale University Press, New Haven, CT.

Pérez, Joseph (2007). *History of a Tragedy: The Expulsion of the Jews from Spain*. University of Illinois Press, Urbana and Chicago. Translated by Lysa Hochroth with an introduction by Helen Nader.

Peter of les Vaux-de Cernay (1998). *The History of the Albigensian Crusade*. The Boydell Press, Woodbridge, Suffolk. Translated by W.A. and M.D. Sibly.

Peters, Edward (1985). *Torture*. University of Pennsylvania Press, Philadelphia.

Pincus, Steve (2009). *1688 The First Modern Revolution*. Yale University Press, New Haven, CT.

Pincus, Steve C. A., and James A. Robinson (2014). *Institutions, Property Rights, and Economic Growth: The Legacy of Douglass North*. Cambridge University Press, New York, In What really happened during the Glorious Revolution?

Pinker, Steven (2011). *The Better Angels of Our Nature: Why Violence has Declined*. Viking, London.

Platt, Stephen R. (2012). *Autumn in the Heavenly Kingdom*. Alfred A. Knopf, New York.

Platteau, Jean-Philippe (2000). *Institutions, Social Norms, and Economic Development*. Harwood Academic Publishers, Amsterdam.

Platteau, Jean-Philippe (2017). *Islam Instrumentalized*. Cambridge University Press, Cambridge.

Plaut, W. Gunther, ed. (1963). *The Rise of Reform Judaism*. World Union For Progressive Judaism, New York.

Ploeckl, Florian (2013). 'The internal impact of a customs union; Baden and the Zollverein', *Explorations in Economic History*. **50**(3), 387–404.

Poliakov, Lèon (1955). *The History of Anti-Semitism*. Vol. 1, University of Pennsylvania Press, Philadelphia. Translated by Richard Howard.

Poliakov, Lèon (1977, 1965). *Jewish Bankers and the Holy See*. Routledge & Kegan Paul, London. Translated by Miriam Kochan.

Pollack, A.F., and F.W. Maitland (1895). *The History of England Law, Before the Time of Edward I*. Vol. 1, Cambridge University Press, Cambridge.

Popper, Karl (1945). *The Open Society and Its Enemies*. Routledge, London.

Posner, Richard A. (1980). 'A theory of primitive society, with special reference to law', *Journal of Law and Economics*. **23**, 1–53.

Postan, M. M., ed. (1966). *The Cambridge Economic History of Europe*, Vol. I: *The Agrarian Life of the Middle Ages*. 2nd edn, Cambridge University Press, Cambridge.

Potter, David, ed. (1997). *The French Wars of Religion: Selected Documents*. Macmillan, London.

Potter, Mark (2000). 'Good offices: Intermediation by corporate bodies in early modern French public finance', *The Journal of Economic History*. **60**(3), 599–626.

Potter, Mark (2003). 'War finance and absolutist state development in early modern Europe: An examination of French venality in the seventeenth century', *The Journal of Early Modern History*. **7**(1–2), 120–147.

Pulzer, Peter (1992). *Jews and the German State*. Blackwell, Oxford.

Purzycki, Benjamin Grant, Coren Apicella, Quentin D. Atkinson, et al. (2016). 'Moralistic gods, supernatural punishment and the expansion of human sociality', *Nature*. **530**(7590), 327–330.

Quaife, G.R. (1987). *Godly Zeal and Furious Rage*. Routledge, London.

Raistrick, Arthur (1968). *Quakers in Science and Industry*. David & Charles Limited, Newton Abbot.

Rasmussen, Dennis C. (2017). *The Infidel and the Professor*. Princeton University Press, Princeton, NJ.

Rawlings, Helen (2006). *The Spanish Inquisition*. Blackwell Publishing, Oxford.

Rawls, John (1971). *A Theory of Justice*. Basic Books, New York.

Rawls, John (1993). *Political Liberalism*. Columbia University Press, New York.

Ray, Jonathan (2005). 'Beyond tolerance and persecution: Reassessing our approach to medieval "convivencia"', *Jewish Social Studies*. **11**(2), 1–18.

Ray, Jonathan (2011). Whose Golden Age? Some Thoughts on Jewish-Christian Relations in Medieval Iberia. In 'Studies in Christian-Jewish Relations', Vol. 6, pp. 1–11. Center for Christian-Jewish Learning at Boston College.

Reynonds, Susan (1994). *Fiefs and Vassals*. Oxford University Press, Oxford.

Richardson, Gary (2005). 'Craft guilds and Christianity in late-medieval England: A rational choice analysis', *Rationality and Society*. **17**, 139–189.

Richardson, Gary, and Michael McBride (2009). 'Religion, longevity, and cooperation: The case of the craft guild', *Journal of Economic Behavior and Organization*. **71**(2), 172–186.

Richarz, Monika (1975). 'Jewish social mobility in Germany during the time of emancipation (1790–1871)', *Leo Baeck Institute Yearbook*. **20**(1), 69–77.

Ridley, Matt (2010). *The Rational Optimist*. Harper, New York.

Rist, Rebecca (2016). *Popes and Jews: 1095–1291*. Oxford University Press, Oxford.

Rivkin, Ellis (1971). *The Shaping of Jewish History: A Radical New Interpretation*. Charles Scribner's Sons, New York.

Rodrik, Dani (2015). *Economics Rules: The Rights and Wrongs of The Dismal Science*. W. W. Norton New York.

Roelker, Nancy Lyman (1996). *One King, One Faith*. University of California Press, Berkeley.

Root, Hilton (1989). 'Tying the king's hands: Credible commitments and royal fiscal policy during the old regime', *Rationality and Society*. **1**(2), 240–259.

Root, Hilton L. (1987). *Peasants and King in Burgundy: Agrarian Foundations of French Absolutism*. University of California Press, Berkeley.

Roper, Lyndal (2004). *Witch Craze*. Yale University Press, New Haven, CT.

Rose, Paul Lawrence (1990). *Revolutionary Antisemitism in Germany From Kant to Wagner*. Princeton University Press, Princeton, NJ.

Rosevere, Henry (1991). *The Financial Revolution 1660–1760*. Longman, London.

Ross, Alan S. C. (1956). 'The assize of bread', *The Economic History Review*. **9**(2), 332–342.

Roth, Cecil (1950). 'Genoese Jews in the Thirteenth Century', *Speculum*. **25**(2), 190–197.

Roth, Cecil (1961). 'The economic history of the Jews', *The Economic History Review*. **14**, 131–135.

Rothschild, Emma (2001). *Economic Sentiments, Adam Smith, Condorcet, and the Enlightenment*. Harvard University Press, Cambridge, MA.

Rough, Robert H. (1980). 'Enrico Scrovegni, the *Cavalieri Gaudenti* and the Arena Chapel in Padua', *The Art Bulletin*. **62**, 24–35.

Roux, Pierre (1916). *Les fermes d'impôts sous l'ancien régime*. Rousseau et cie, Paris, France.

Rowe, William T. (2009). *China's Last Empire*. Belknap Press of Harvard University Press, Cambridge, MA.

Rubin, Jared (2009). 'Social insurance, commitment, and the origin of law: Interest bans in early Christianity', *Journal of Law and Economics*. **52**(4), 761–786.

Rubin, Jared (2010). 'Bills of exchange, interest bans, and impersonal exchange in Islam and Christianity', *Explorations in Economic History*. **47**(2), 213–227.

Rubin, Jared (2014). 'Printing and Protestants: An empirical test of the role of printing in the Reformation', *The Review of Economics and Statistics*. **96**(2), 270–286.

Rubin, Jared (2017). *Rulers, Religion, and Riches: Why the West Got Rich and the Middle East Did Not*. Cambridge University Press, Cambridge.

Rubin, Miri (1987). *Charity and Community in Medieval Cambridge*. Cambridge University Press, Cambridge.

Rubin, Miri (2004). *Gentile Tales: The Narrative Assault on Late Medieval Jews*. University of Pennsylvania Press, Philadelphia.

Ruffini, Francesco (1912). *Religious Liberty*. Williams & Norgate, New York. Translated by J. Parker Heyes.

Ruffle, Bradley J. and Richard Sosis (2006). 'Cooperation and the in-group-out-group bias: A field test on Israeli kibbutz members and city residents', *Journal of Economic Behavior & Organization*. **60**(2), 147–163.

Runciman, Steven (1970). *The Orthodox Churches and the Secular State*. Oxford University Press, Oxford.

Rürup, Reinhard (1969). 'Jewish emancipation and Bourgeois society', *Leo Baeck Institute Yearbook*. **14**(1), 67–91.

Russell, Conrad (1971). *The Crisis of Parliaments of English History 1509–1660*. Oxford University Press, Oxford.

Rustow, Marina (2008). *Heresy and the Politics of Community: The Jews of the Fatimid Caliphate*. Cornell University Press, Ithaca, NY.

Ryan, Alan (2012). *The Making of Modern Liberalism*. Princeton University Press, Princeton, NJ.

Sabl, Andrew (2009). 'The last artificial virtue: Hume on toleration and its lessons', *Political Theory*. **37**(4), 511–538.

Sahle, Esther (2017). 'Quakers, coercion, and pre-modern growth: Why Friends' formal institutions for contract enforcement did not matter for early modern trade expansion', *The Economic History Review*. **71**(2), 418–436.

Saleh, Mohamed (2015). 'The reluctant transformation: State industrialization, religion, and human capital in nineteenth-century Egypt', *Journal of Economic History*. **75**(1), 65–94.

Saleh, Mohamed (2018). 'On the road to heaven: Taxation, conversions, and the Coptic-Muslim socioeconomic gap in medieval Egypt', *Journal of Economic History*. **78**(2), 394–434.

Saleh, Mohamed, and Jean Tirole (2018). Taxing unwanted populations: Fiscal policy and conversions in early Islam. Working Paper. Toulouse School of Economics.

Salmon, J.H.M. (1975). *Society in Crisis: France in the Sixteenth Century*. Ernest Benn Limited, London.

Sargent, A.J. (1968). *The Economic Policy of Colbert*. Burt Franklin, New York.

Scales, Len (2005). Late medieval Germany: An under-stated nation?. In L.Scales and O.Zimmer, eds, 'Power and the Nation in European History', Cambridge University Press, Cambridge, pp. 166–191.

Scanlon, T. M. (1996). The difficulty of tolerance. In D.Heyd, ed., 'Toleration', Princeton University Press, Princeton, NJ, pp. 226–241.

Schechter, Frank I. (1913). 'The rightlessness of Mediaeval English Jewry', *The Jewish Quarterly Review*. **4**(2), 121–151.

Scheidel, Walter (2009). From the 'Great Convergence' to the 'First Great Divergence': Roman and Qin-Han state formation and its aftermath. In W.Scheidel, ed., *Rome and China: Comparative Perspectives on Ancient World Empires*. Oxford University Press, Oxford, pp. 11–23.

Schlegel, Ursula (1998, 1955). On the picture program of the Arena Chapel. In A.Ladis, ed., *Giotto and the World of Early Italian Art*. Garland Publishing, New York.

Schumpeter, Joseph A. (1942). *Capitalism, Socialism, and Democracy*. Harper Perennial Modern Classics, New York.

Scott, H. M. (1990). Reform in the Habsburg monarchy. In H. M.Scott, ed., *Enlightened Absolutism*. Macmillan Education Limited, Basingstoke, Hampshire, pp. 145–189.

Scott, James C. (1999). *Seeing Like a State: How Certain Schemes to Improve the Human Condition Have Failed*. The Institution for Social and Policy Studies Series, Yale University Press, New Haven, CT.

Scott, James C. (2009). *The Art of Not Being Governed: An Anarchist History of Upland Southeast Asia*. Yale University Press, New Haven, CT.

Scott, Jonathan (2003). "Good Night Amsterdam". Sir George Downing and Anglo-Dutch statebuilding', *The English Historical Review*. **118**(476), 334–356.

Scoville, W. C. (1960). *The Persecution of Huguenots and French economic development, 1680–1720*. University of California Press, Berkeley.

Scribner, Bob (1996). Preconditions of tolerance and intolerance in sixteenth-century Germany. In O. P.Grell and B.Scribner, eds, *Tolerance and Intolerance in the European Reformation*. Cambridge University Press, Cambridge, pp. 32–47.

Sehat, David (2011). *The Myth of American Religious Freedom*. Oxford University Press, Oxford.

Shariff, A., A. Norenzayan and J. Henrich (2009). *The Birth of High Gods: How the Cultural Evolution of Supernatural Policing Agents Influenced the Emergence of Complex, Cooperative Human Societies, Paving the Way for Civilization*. Lawrence Erlbaum Associates Mahwah, NJ, pp. 119–136.

Shariff, Azim F., and Ara Norenzayan (2007). 'God is watching you', *Psychological Science*. **18**(9), 803–809.

Sharpe, James (1996). *Instruments of Darkness*. Hamish Hamilton London.

Shatzmiller, Joseph (1990). *Shylock Reconsidered: Jews, Moneylending, and Medieval Society*. University of California Press, Berkeley.

Shatzmiller, Joseph (2013). *Cultural Exchange: Jews, Christians, and the Art in the Medieval Marketplace*. Princeton University Press, Princeton, NJ.

Shaw, Brent D. (2011). *Sacred Violence*. Cambridge University Press, Cambridge.

Shaw, W.A. (1896). *The History of Currency, 1252 to 1894*. 2nd edn, Burt Franklin, New York.

Shepardson, Nikki (2007). *Burning Zeal: The Rhetoric of Martyrdom and the Protestant Community in Reformation in Reformation France, 1520–1570*. Lehigh University Press, Bethlehem, PA.

Shepkaru, Shmuel (2012). 'The preaching of the First Crusade and the persecutions of the Jews', *Medieval Encounters*. **18**(1), 93–135.

Shiue, Carol H., and Wolfgang Keller (2007). 'Markets in China and Europe on the eve of the Industrial Revolution', *American Economic Review*. **97**(4), 1189–1216.

Skinner, Quentin (2009). 'A genealogy of the modern state', *Proceedings of the British Academy*. **162**, 325–370.

Slavin, Philip (2012). 'The Great Bovine Pestilence and its economic and environmental consequences in England and Wales, 1318–50', *The Economic History Review.* **65**(4), 1239–1266.

Slingerland, Edward, Joseph Henrich, and Ara Norenzayan (2013). The evolution of prosocial religions. In P. J.Richerson and M. H.Christiansen, eds, *Cultural Evolution: Society, Technology. Language and Religion.* MIT Press, Cambridge, MA.

Smith, Adam (1759). *The Theory of Moral Sentiments.* UP, Cambridge.

Smith, Adam (1776). *An Inquiry into the Nature and Causes of the Wealth of Nations.* Clarendon Press, Oxford.

Smith, Daniel J. (2014). 'Heterogeneity and exchange: Safe-conducts in medieval Spain', *The Review of Austrian Economics.* **27**(2), 183–197.

Snyder, Timothy (2015). *Black Earth: The Holocaust As History and Warning.* Tim Duggan Books, New York.

Soifer, Maya (2009). 'Beyond convivencia: Critical reflections on the historiography of interfaith relations in Christian Spain', *Journal of Medieval Iberian Studies.* **1**(1), 19–35.

Solt, Leo F. (1990). *Church and State in Early Modern England, 1509–1640.* Oxford University Press, Oxford.

Soman, Alfred (1989). 'Decriminalizing witchcraft: Does the French experience furnish a European model?' *Criminal Justice History.* **10**, 1–22.

Soman, Alfred (1992). *Sorcellerie et justice criminelle: Le Parlement de Paris: 16e-18e siècles.* Variorum, Hampshire.

Sorkin, David (1987). 'The genesis of the ideology of emancipation: 1806–1840', *Leo Baeck Institute Yearbook.* **32**(1), 11–40.

Sosis, Richard, and Bradley J. Ruffle (2003). 'Religious ritual and cooperation: Testing for a relationship on Israeli religious and secular kibbutzim', *Current Anthropology.* **44**(5), 713–722.

Southern, Richard (1970). *Western Society and the Church in the Middle Ages.* Penguin, New York.

Sowerby, Scott (2013). *Making Toleration: The Repealers and the Glorious Revolution.* Harvard University Press, Cambridge, MA.

Spaulding, Robert Mark (2011). 'Revolutionary France and the transformation of the Rhine', *Central European History.* **44**, 203–226.

Spitzer, Yannay (2015a). Pogroms, networks, and migration: The Jewish migration from the Russian Empire to the United States 1881–1914. Working Paper. Hebrew University of Jerusalem.

Spizer, Yannay (2015b). Pale in comparison: The economic ecology of Jews as a rural service minority. Working Paper. Hebrew University of Jerusalem.

Spohnholz, Jesse (2011). *The Tactics of Toleration: A Refugee Community in the Age of Religious Wars.* University of Delaware Press, Newark, DE.

Stacey, Robert C. (1985). 'Royal taxation and the social structure of medieval Anglo-Jewry: The tallages of 1239–1242', *Hebrew Union College Annual.* **56**, 175–249.

Stacey, Robert C. (1997). 'Parliamentary negotiation and the expulsion of the Jews from England', *Thirteenth Century England.* **VI**, 77–103.

Stacey, Robert C. (2000). Antisemitism and the medieval English state. In J. R.Maddicott and D. M.Palliser, eds, *The Medieval State: Essays Presented to James Campbell.* Hambledon Press, London, pp. 163–177.

Stampfer, Shaul (2003). 'What actually happened to the Jews of Ukraine in 1648?' *Jewish History.* **17**(2), 207–227.

Stark, Rodney (1996). *The Rise of Christianity: How the Obscure, Marginal Jesus Movement Became the Dominant Religious Force in the Western World in a Few Centuries.* Princeton University Press, Princeton, NJ.

Stark, Rodney (1999). 'Micro foundations of religion: A revised theory', *Sociological Theory.* **17**(3), 264–289.

Stark, Rodney (2001). 'Gods, rituals, and the moral order', *Journal for the Scientific Study of Religion.* **40**(4), 619–636.

Stark, Rodney (2004). *For the Glory of God: How Monotheism Led to Reformations, Science, Witch-Hunts, and the End of Slavery.* Princeton University Press, Princeton, NJ.

Stasavage, David (2002). 'Credible commitment in early modern Europe: North and Weingast revisited', *Journal of Law, Economics, and Organization.* **18**(1), 155–86.

Stein, S. (1956). 'Usury and the medieval English church courts', *Journal of Semitic Studies.* **1, 2,** 141–162.

Steinberg, Stephen (1965). 'Reform Judaism: The origin and evolution of a 'church movement'', *Journal for the Scientific Study of Religion.* **5**(1), 117–129.

Stephenson, Paul (2009). *Constantine: Unconqurered Emperor, Christian Victor.* Quercus, London.

Stigler, George J., and Gary S. Becker (1977). 'De Gustibus Non Est Disputandum', *American Economic Review.* **67**(2), 76–90.

Stone, Harry (1959). 'Dickens and the Jews', *Victorian Studies.* **2**(3), 223–253.

Stone, Valerie E., Leda Cosmides, John Tooby, Neal Kroll, and Robert T. Knight (2002). 'Selective impairment of reasoning about social exchange in a patient with bilateral limbic system damage', *Proceedings of the National Academy of Sciences of the USA.* **99**(17), 11531–11536.

Stow, Kenneth R. (1981). 'Papal and Royal Attitudes toward Jewish Lending in the Thirteenth Century', *AJS Review.* **6**, 161–184.

Stow, Kenneth R. (1992). *Alienated Minority: The Jews of Medieval Latin Europe.* Harvard University Press, Cambridge, MA.

Strauss, Leo (1952). *Persecution and the Art of Writing.* The Free Press, Glencoe, IL.

Strayer, Joseph (1940, 1971c). The Laicization of French and English society in the thirteenth century. In J. F.Benton and T. N.Bisson, eds, Medieval Statecraft and the Perspectives of History, Princeton University Press, Princeton, NJ, pp. 251–265.

Strayer, Joseph (1963, 1971b). The historical experience of nation-building in Europe. In J. F.Benton and T. N.Bisson, eds, Medieval Statecraft and the Perspectives of History, Princeton University Press, Princeton, pp. 341–348.

Strayer, Joseph (1965). Feudalism in western Europe. In R.Coulborn, ed., *The Idea of Feudalism.* Archon Books, Hamden, CT, pp. 15–26.

Strayer, Joseph (1969, 1971a). France: The holy land, the choosen people and the most Christian king. In J. F.Benton and T. N.Bisson, eds, 'Medieval Statecraft and the Perspectives of History', Princeton University Press, Princeton, NJ, pp. 300–314.

Strayer, Joseph (1970). *On the Medieval Origins of the Modern State.* Princeton University Press, Princeton, NJ.

Streit, Kevin T. (1993). 'The expansion of the English Jewish community in the reign of King Stephen', *Albion: A Quarterly Journal Concerned with British Studies.* **25**(2), 177–192.

Strohm, Paul (1998). *England's Empty Throne: Usurpation and the Language of Legitimacy, 1399–1422.* Yale University Press, New Haven, CT.

Sumpton, Jonathan (1999). *The Hundred Years War II: Trial by Fire.* University of Pennsylvania Press, Philadelphia.

Sutcliffe, Adam (2000). 'Can a Jew be a Philosophe? Isaac de Pinot, Voltaire, and Jewish participation in the Enlightenment', *Jewish Social Studies*. **6**(3), 31–51.

Sutherland, N.M. (1980). *The Huguenot Struggle for Recognition*. Yale University Press, New Haven, CT.

Sutherland, N.M. (1984). Persecution and toleration in reformation Europe. In W.Sheils, ed., *Persecution and Toleration*. Basil Blackwell, Oxford, pp. 153–162.

Swanson, Heather (1999). *Medieval British Towns*. Macmillan, Basingstoke.

Symmachus, Quintus Aurelius (1896). *The memorial of Symmachus, prefect of the city*. From Letter of St. Ambrose, based on H. De Romestin, trans. in Library of Nicene and Post Nicene Fathers, 2nd Series, Vol. X (New York: 1896), 414–422. https://sourcebooks.fordham.edu/halsall/source/ambrose-sym.asp

Tabellini, Guido (2008). 'Presidential address institutions and culture', *Journal of the European Economic Association*. **6**(2–3), 255–294.

Tacitus, Publius Cornelius (1931). *The Annals of Tacitus*. Vol. III, Loeb Classical Library, Cambridge MA. Translated by J. Jackson.

Taitz, Emily (1994). *The Jews of Medieval France: The Community of Champagne*. Greenwood Press, Westport, CT.

Tawney, R.H. (1926). *Religion and the Rise of Capitalism*. Verso, London.

Taylor, Charles (2007). *A Secular Age*. Belknap Press of Harvard University Press, Cambridge MA.

Tazbir, Janusz (1973). *A State without Stakes*. The Kościuzko Foundaton Twayne Publishers, Panstowowy Instytut Wydawiczy.

Temin, Peter, and Hans-Joachim Voth (2005). 'Credit rationing and crowding out during the industrial revolution: Evidence from Hoare's Bank, 1702–1862', *Explorations in Economic History*. **42**(3), 325–348.

Terjanian, Anoush Fraser (2013). *Commerce and Its Discontents in Eighteenth-Century French Political Thought*. Cambridge University Press, Cambridge.

Teter, Magda (2006). *Jews and Heretics in Catholic Poland*. Cambridge University Press, Cambridge.

Theilmann, John, and Frances Cate (2007). 'A plague of plagues: The problem of plague diagnosis in medieval England', *The Journal of Interdisciplinary History*. **37**(3), 371–393.

Thomas, Keith (1971). *Religion and the Decline of Magic*. Penguin Books, London.

Tilly, Charles (1990). *Coercion, Capital, and European States, AD 990–1990*. Blackwell, Oxford.

Toch, Michael (1997). 'The formation of a diaspora: The settlement of Jews in the medieval German Reich', *Aschkenas*. **7**, 55–78.

Tocqueville, Alexis de (1998). *The Old Regime and the Revolution*. Vol. 1, University of Chicago Press, Chicago.

Tomasi, John (2012). *Free Market Fairness*. Princeton University Press, Princeton, NJ.

Tracy, James D. (1999). *Europe's Reformation, 1450–1650*. Rowman & Littlefield Publishers, Oxford.

Trivellato, Francesca (2009). *The Familiarity of Strangers*. Yale University Press, New Haven, CT.

Trout, Andrew (1978). *Jean-Baptiste Colbert*. Twayne Publishers, Boston.

Tuetey, Alexandre (1886). *La sorcellerie dans le pays de Montbèliard au XVIIe siècle*. Dôle.

Tullock, Gordon (1967). 'The welfare costs of tariffs, monopolies, and theft', *Western Economics Journal*. pp. 224–232.

Ullman, Walter (1961). *Principles of Government and Politics in the Middle Ages*. Methuen and Co. Limited, London.

van Dam, Raymond (2007). *The Roman Revolution of Constantine*. Cambridge University Press, Cambridge.

van Eijinatten, Joris (2003). *Liberty and Concord in the United Provinces*. Brill, Lieden.

van Etten, Jacob (2017). 'R package gdistance: Distances and routes on geographical grids', *Journal of Statistical Software*. **76**(13), 1–21.

van Nimwegen, Olaf (2006). *The Dutch Army and the Military Revolutions, 1599–1688*. The Boydell Press, Woodbridge. Translated by Andrew May.

van Zanden, Jan Luiten (2009). *The Long Road to the Industrial Revolution. The European Economy in a Global Perspective, 1000–1800*. Brill, Leiden.

Vaubel, Roland (2017). 'The making of state religion: Political economy and historical evidence', *Critical Research on Religion*. **5**(1), 9–33.

Ventura, Jaume, and Hans-Joachim Voth (2015). Debt into growth: How sovereign debt accelerated the first industrial revolution. University of Zurich, Department of Economics Working Paper 194.

Versluis, Arthur. (2006.). *The New Inquisitions: Heretic-Hunting and the intellectual origins of modern totalitarianism*. Oxford University Press, New York.

Vidal-Robert, Jordi (2013). War and inquisition: Repression in early modern Spain. Working Paper, Department of Economics, University of Warwick.

Vidal-Robert, Jordi (2014). Long-run effects of the Spanish Inquisition, CAGE Online Working Paper Series, Competitive Advantage in the Global Economy (CAGE) 192.

Vital, David (1999). *A People Apart: The Jews in Europe 1789–1939*. Oxford University Press, Oxford.

Voigtländer, Nico, and Hans-Joachim Voth (2012). 'Persecution perpetuated: The medieval origins of anti-Semitic violence in Nazi Germany', *Quarterly Journal of Economics*. **127**(3), 1–54.

Voigtländer, Nico, and Hans-Joachim Voth (2013a). 'Married to intolerance: Attitudes toward intermarriage in Germany, 1900–2006', *American Economic Review*. **103**(3), 79–85.

Voigtländer, Nico, and Hans-Joachim Voth (2013b). 'The three horsemen of riches: Plague, war, and urbanization in early modern Europe', *Review of Economic Studies*. **80**, 774–811.

Volckart, Oliver (2000a). 'The open constitution and its enemies: Competition, rent seeking, and the rise of the modern state', *Journal of Economic Behavior & Organization*. **42**(1), 1–17.

Volckart, Oliver (2000b). 'State buildng by bargaining for monopoly rents', *Kyklos*. **53**(3), 265–291.

Volckart, Oliver (2002). 'No Utopia: Government without territorial monopoly in medieval central Europe', *Journal of Institutional and Theoretical Economics (JITE)*. **158**(2), 325–343.

Volckart, Oliver (2004). 'The economics of feuding in late medieval Germany', *Explorations in Economic History*. **41**(3), 282–299.

Voltaire, François-Marie Arouet (1964). *Philosophical Letters*. Prentice-Hall, Englewood Cliffs, NJ.

Vries, Peter (2015). *State, Economy, and the Great Divergence: Great Britain and China, 1680s–1850s*. Bloomsbury, London.

Wailly, Natalis de (1857). 'Mémoire sur les variations de la livre tournois, depuis le règne de saint Louis jusqu'a 1 '{etablissement de la monnaie decimate', *Mémoires de l'Academie des Inscriptions et Belles-Lettre*. **21**(11), 398–401.

Waite, Gary K. (2009). *Eradicating the Devil's Minions: Anabaptists and Witches in Reformation Europe, 1535–1600 H*. University of Toronto Press, Toronto.

Wakeman, Frederic (1998). 'Boundaries of the public sphere in Ming and Qing China', *Daedalus*. pp. 167–189.

Walbank, F. W. (1978). *Awful Revolution: The Decline of the Roman Empire in the West*. University of Liverpool Press, Liverpool.

Waldinger, Fabian (2010). 'Quality matters: The expulsion of professors and the consequences for PhD student outcomes in Nazi Germany', *Journal of Political Economy*. **118**(4), 787–831.

Waldinger, Fabian (2012). 'Peer effects in science: Evidence from the dismissal of scientists in Nazi Germany', *Review of Economic Studies*. **79**(2), 838–861.

Wallis, John Joseph (2018). Leviathan Denied: Rules, Organizations, Governments, and Social Dynamics. Manuscript.

Walsham, Alexandra (1993). *Church Papists: Catholicism, Conformity and Confessional Polemic in Early Modern England*. The Boydell Press, Woodbridge, Suffolk.

Waltz, Kenneth N. (1979). *Theory of International Politics*. Waveland Press, Long Grove, IL.

Walzer, Michael (1997). *On Toleration*. Yale University Press, New Haven, CT.

Ward-Perkins, Bryan (2005). *The Fall of Rome, and the End of Civilization*. Oxford University Press, Oxford.

Weber, Eugen (1976). *Peasants into Frenchmen: The Modernization of Rural France 1870–1914*. Stanford University Press, Stanford, CA.

Weber, Klaus (2004). 'Were Merchants More Tolerant? "Godless Patrons of the Jews" and the Decline of the Sephardi Community in Late Seventeenth-Century Hamburg', *Jewish Culture and History*. **7**(1–2), 77–92.

Weber, Max (1927). *General Economic History*. Greenberg New York. Translated by Frank H. Knight.

Weber, Max (1930). *The Protestant Ethic and the Spirit of Capitalism*. Allen and Unwin, London, U.K.

Weber, Max (1968). *Economy and Society*. Bedminster Press, New York.

Weigley, Russell F. (1991). *The Age of Battles: The Quest for Decisive Warfare from Breitenfeld to Waterloo*. Pimlico London.

Werth, Nicholas (1997). The state against its people: Violence, repression, and terror in the Soviet Union, *in* S.Courtois, N.Werth, J.-L.Panné, A.Paczkowski, K.Bartošek and J.-L.Margolin, eds, 'The Black Book of Communism'.

Whaley, Joachim (1985). *Religious Toleration and Social Change in Hamburg 1529–1819*. Cambridge University Press, Cambridge.

Whaley, Joachim (2012). *Germany and the Holy Roman Empire 1493–1806*. Vol. 1, Oxford University Press, Oxford.

Whelan, Frederick G. (1990). 'Church establishments, liberty & competition in religion', *Polity*. **23**(2), 155–185.

Wickham, Chris (2009). *The Inheritance of Rome*. Viking, New York.

Wickham, Chris (2016). *Medieval Europe*. Yale University Press, New Haven, CT.

Wickham, Christopher (2005). *Framing the Middle Ages*. Oxford University Press, Oxford.

Williams, Gerhild Scholz (1995). *Defining Dominion: The Discorses of Magic and Witchcraft in Early Modern France and Germany*. The University of Michigan Press, Ann Arbor.

Williamson, Jeffrey G. (1984). 'Why was British growth so slow during the Industrial Revolution?' *The Journal of Economic History*. **44**(3), pp. 687–712.

Wilson, Christie Sample (2011). *Beyond Belief: Surviving the Revocation of the Edict of Nantes in France*. Lehigh University Press, Bethlehem.

Wilson, Peter (2009). Prussia as a fiscal-military state, 1640–1806, *in* C.Storrs, ed., 'Fiscal Military State in Eighteenth-Century Europe', Ashgate, Abingdon, Oxfordshire, pp. 95–124.

Wilson, Peter H. (2009). *The Thirty Years War: Europe's Tragedy*. Harvard University Press, Cambridge, MA.

Wistrich, Robert S. (1990). *The Jews of Vienna in the Age of Franz Joseph*. Oxford University Press, Oxford.

Wolf, Kenneth Baxter (2009). 'Convivencia in medieval Spain: A brief history of an idea', *Religion Compass*. **3**(1), 72–85.

Wolfe, Michael (1998). The Edict of Nantes: French origins and European impacts. In R. L.Goodbar, ed., 'The Edict of Nantes: Five Essays and a New Translation', The National Huguenot Society, Bloomington, MN. pp. 11–19.

Wooton, David (2002). *Paolo Sarpi: Between Renaissance and Enlightenment*. Cambridge University Press, Cambridge.

Wooton, David (2015). *The Invention of Science*. Allan Lane, London.

Xue, Melanie Meng (2017). High-value work and the rise of women: The cotton revolution and gender equality in China. SSRN Working Paper No. 2389218.

Xue, Melanie Meng, and Mark Koyama (2017). Autocratic Rule and Social Capital: Evidence from Imperial China. No. 84249. University Library of Munich, Germany.

Yanagizawa-Drott, David (2014). 'Propaganda and conflict: Evidence from the Rwandan genocide', *The Quarterly Journal of Economics*. **129**(4), 1947–1994.

Zagorin, Perez (2003). *How the Idea of Religious Toleration Came to the West*. Princeton University Press, Princeton, NJ.

Zamoyski, Adam (2015). *Phantom Terror: Political Paranoia and the Creation of the Modern State, 1789–1848*. Basic Books, New York.

Ziegler, Philip (1969). *The Black Death*. Collins, London.

Index